D1000031

WITHDRAWN

THE ESSENCE OF
STIGLER

THE ESSENCE OF
S·T·I·G·L·E·R

EDITED BY

KURT R. LEUBE
THOMAS GALE MOORE

FOREWORD BY W. GLENN CAMPBELL

HOOVER INSTITUTION PRESS

STANFORD UNIVERSITY, STANFORD, CALIFORNIA

CALVIN T. RYAN LIBRARY
KEARNEY STATE COLLEGE
KEARNEY, NEBRASKA

The Hoover Institution on War, Revolution and Peace, founded at
Stanford University in 1919 by the late President Herbert Hoover,
is an interdisciplinary research center for advanced study on
domestic and international affairs in the twentieth century. The
views expressed in its publications are entirely those of the
authors and do not necessarily reflect the views of the staff,
officers, or Board of Overseers of the Hoover Institution.

Hoover Press Publication 346

Copyright 1986 by the Board of Trustees of the
  Leland Stanford Junior University

All rights reserved. No part of this publication may be reproduced,
stored in a retrieval system, or transmitted in any form or by any
means, electronic, mechanical, photocopying, recording, or otherwise, without written permission of the publisher.

First printing, 1986

Manufactured in the United States of America

90 89 88 87 86   9 8 7 6 5 4 3 2 1

Library of Congress Cataloging in Publication Data

Stigler, George Joseph, 1911–
  The essence of Stigler.

  (Hoover Press publication ; 346)
  1. Stigler, George Joseph, 1911–   . 2. Economics.
I. Leube, Kurt R. II. Moore, Thomas Gale. III. Title.
HB119.S75A25 1986   330.1   86-20110
ISBN 0-8179-8461-5
ISBN 0-8179-8462-3 (pbk.)

WE DEDICATE THIS VOLUME
IN GRATEFUL APPRECIATION TO
PROFESSOR GEORGE J. STIGLER
—MENTOR, TEACHER, AND INTELLECTUAL—
ON THE OCCASION OF HIS 75TH BIRTHDAY.

CONTENTS

PART THREE: STIGLER'S CONTRIBUTIONS TO INDUSTRIAL ORGANIZATION

PART FOUR: STIGLER'S CONTRIBUTIONS TO THE HISTORY OF ECONOMIC THOUGHT

PART FIVE: THE WIT OF GEORGE J. STIGLER

FOREWORD

This volume is being published to honor the seventy-fifth birthday of one of the most distinguished economic theorists and scholars of our century. George J. Stigler's colleagues in the economics profession elected him president of the American Economic Association twenty years ago, making him one of the youngest men ever to hold this prestigious post. But it was not until 1982 that he received the full measure of recognition that was due him. When I heard that he had been awarded the Nobel Prize in Economics, I am sure I was not the only one who thought simultaneously: "Of course" and "Long overdue."

I first encountered George Stigler's writings forty years ago when I was teaching economics at Harvard University. I was impressed then, as I am to this day, both by his penetrating analysis of complex theoretical issues and by his ability to present his ideas lucidly, often with sardonic wit. If every economist took the trouble to write as well as he does, economics would not be saddled with the label "the dismal science" that Thomas Robert Malthus gave it more than a century and a half ago.

In that intervening period, no one has done less than George Stigler to make economics dismal, nor more to make it a science. He is fiercely impatient with all forms of a priori theorizing and concepts that have no empirical groundings in reality. He is truly a scientist—an empiricist—eager to put all theories to the test. His special genius has been to conceive and design rigorous empirical tests that either would verify or invalidate some influential theory. To take but one example, he challenged the widely held idea that government regulation of economic activity is beneficial to consumers. Such "truths" have not been able to survive his critical scrutiny. Due to his writings—and his influence on his students—belief in the beneficial effects of economic regulation is no longer a reigning dogma among economists. Instead, a rising generation of young economists view the benefits of regulation with skepticism and irreverence.

When future writers look back on the past decade to the massive wave of deregulation that is sweeping the American economy, they will recognize George Stigler's profound impact on economic theory and public policy. Before he arrived on the scene, it would have been inconceivable to find articles being written or published "In Defense of Regulation." Now such articles are increasingly common, but their authors—the die-hard defenders of regulation—are an embattled and dwindling minority in the economics profession. Like Copernicus, Stigler toppled a reigning theory and changed the way a whole area of human inquiry is perceived.

The Essence of Stigler is a skillful distillation of George Stigler's prolific genius. We are grateful to Kurt R. Leube and Thomas Gale Moore for jointly making the selections and editing this book, and to Dr. Moore for finding time, amid his duties as a member of President Reagan's Council of Economic Advisers, to write an illuminating introduction to this volume.

I am especially proud that Professor Stigler has been closely associated with the Hoover Institution for fifteen years. He has been a visiting scholar several times, and has served since 1972 as the chairman of the advisory committee of our Domestic Studies Program. In that capacity, he has screened and evaluated hundreds of applications from young scholars eager to come to the Institution for a year to work in the field of economic analysis and public policy. He has been uncommonly generous in giving these younger economists the full benefits of his critical powers. On behalf of all my colleagues, I send him birthday greetings, coupled with the hope that his long and active association with us has many more years to run.

W. GLENN CAMPBELL
Director, Hoover Institution

ACKNOWLEDGMENTS

The Hoover Institution is publishing this book to celebrate George J. Stigler's seventy-fifth birthday. The idea stems from a discussion between the editors in early summer 1985. It is very difficult to select the essence of such an extensive oeuvre. Although many worthwhile pieces have been omitted due to limitations of space, the editors are pleased that their choices received George Stigler's full approval. We wish to thank him for his cooperation in this endeavor.

Without the assistance of the Hoover Institution and Director W. Glenn Campbell, Principal Associate Director John Cogan, and Senior Research Fellow Robert Hessen, this book would never have been produced.

Our thanks are also due to the fine Hoover Institution Press staff and to Audrey Carlson and Glen Pullen for their diligent help throughout the whole production process.

George J. Stigler: A Biographical Introduction

◆ Kurt R. Leube ◆

I

George J. Stigler was born on January 17, 1911, in Renton, Washington, a suburb of Seattle. As the only child of Joseph and Elizabeth Stigler, who separately emigrated to the United States from Central Europe at the end of the nineteenth century, he grew up in a relatively relaxed environment.

Stigler attended schools in Seattle and graduated from the University of Washington with a B.B.A. in 1931. "Due to a lack of proper guidance," his undergraduate training was primarily in applied business courses and political science. He went on to receive an M.B.A. from Northwestern University in Chicago the following year. There his exposure to the stimulating economist Coleman Woodbury increased Stigler's interest in economics and scholarship as a career. In 1933 he enrolled at the University of Chicago.

The department of economics at Chicago, illuminated by such great scholars of classical liberalism as Frank H. Knight, Henry Simons, and Jacob Viner and favored with a brilliant coterie of graduate students (including Kenneth Boulding and Sune Carlson), had a major impact on Stigler. His lifelong friendship with two fellow students, Milton Friedman and W. Allen Wallis (who, together with Stigler, were later to be called the "three musketeers" of the modern Chicago tradition), developed at the university in the 1950s. The vibrant intellectual atmosphere among these teachers and students had a strong and lasting influence on Stigler.

Stigler's thesis on the history of economic thought, for which he received his Ph.D. in 1938, was written under the dominating intellectual force of Frank H. Knight. Though Stigler once joked that he could never bring himself to read through it because it would prove too embarrassing, his dissertation was successfully published as his first book in 1940.[1]

II

Stigler began his teaching career in 1936 at Iowa State College, in Ames, under the chairmanship of T. W. Shultz. In December of the same year he married Margaret L. Mack, who had been a fellow student at Chicago. They had three sons: Stephen, a statistician; David, a lawyer; and Joseph, a social worker. Margaret Stigler died in the summer of 1970.

Stigler's first major article appeared in 1937 in the *Journal of Political Economy*. "The Economics of Carl Menger" was on the subjective Austrian School, whose methodological individualism differs from Stigler's own empirical and positive approach. After two years at Iowa State College, Stigler was invited by Frederic Garver to join Francis Boddy and Arthur Marget at the University of Minnesota, an offer he accepted in 1938. The war, however, led to a general retrenchment of academic life, and in 1942 Stigler took a leave of absence from Minnesota to work at the National Bureau of Economic Research (NBER) in New York. Some of the quantitative studies he produced there on output, employment, and productivity trends in the American economy were later published, and through his exposure to such figures as Arthur Burns, Geoffrey Moore, and his old friend Milton Friedman, Stigler became convinced of the importance of empirical evidence in appraising economic theories.[2]

Though he was to remain a member of the research staff until 1976, Stigler left the NBER to become a member of the Statistical Research Group at Columbia University. There, under the directorship of W. Allen Wallis, he worked with Friedman and Harold Hotelling on the statistical analysis of military problems. In 1945, near the end of the war, Stigler returned to Minnesota, where he was soon joined by Friedman. Later that year he published "The Cost of Subsistence," an early work on linear programming.

Although by 1938 Stigler had already begun working and publishing extensively in microeconomic theory, it was not until after the war that his pioneering empirical work on price theory culminated in the publication of *Price Theory* (1946).[3] Also published in 1946 was *Roofs or Ceilings?*, written with Friedman, in which Stigler convincingly argued that rent controls on housing had the inevitable effect of distorting rental markets, thereby eventually leading to a misallocation of space. This slender book enraged liberals when it appeared and has since become must reading for economists. In his trail-blazing essay "The Economics of Minimum Wage Legislation" (1946), Stigler went on to analyze the harmful effects of minimum wages on resource allocation, aggregate demand, family income, and poverty.[4]

The reunion with Friedman in Minnesota did not last long, for Stigler accepted an offer from Brown University in 1946, and Friedman went to Chicago that same year to join the Chicago school.

III

After only one year as a full professor at Brown, Stigler went on to Columbia, where he was to spend the next eleven years teaching theory, industrial organization, and the history of economic thought. His new colleagues included A. F. Burns, A. Hart, and Ragnar Nurske.

In 1947 two of Stigler's monographs that had originated during his stint at the NBER, *Domestic Servants in the United States* and *Trends in Output and Employment*, were published.[5] It was in the latter that Stigler performed the first total factor productivity measure, in which he related output to an index of all inputs.

That same year Stigler accepted the invitation of F. A. von Hayek to join a group of free market–oriented scholars from all over the world at a meeting near Vevey, Switzerland. From this small circle of like-minded but rather isolated thinkers, brought together to discuss the relevant ways and means of defending a free society, the exclusive Mont Pelerin Society emerged. As one of its founding fathers, Stigler was later to serve as its president from 1976 to 1978. It was at this first meeting of the Society that he met Aaron Director, with whom he formed a close friendship. Director strongly influenced Stigler's ideas on industrial organization and public regulation; many years later (in 1970), Stigler presented one of Director's ideas in his essay "Director's Law of Public Income Redistribution."

In 1948 Stigler was invited to lecture at the London School of Economics. During the late 1940s and early 1950s, he published several studies on industrial organization, revised *Price Theory*, and published his essay "The Division of Labor is Limited by the Extent of the Market" (1951), in which he demonstrated that the division of labor is a fundamental principle of economic organization.[6]

In 1955 Stigler was awarded a Guggenheim Fellowship and spent some five months in Geneva, Switzerland. He subsequently published his important essay "Perfect Competition, Historically Contemplated" (1957) and his careful study "Bernard Shaw, Sidney Webb, and the Theory of Fabian Socialism" (1959) (both included in this volume). It was during the 1950s that Stigler developed the "survivor technique," a method of determining the efficient and optimum sizes of enterprises in an industry. This culminated in his renowned essay on "The Economies of Scale" (1958). Though this controversial paper was written at the NBER, it was not ultimately published in the NBER's series.

IV

Stigler returned to the University of Chicago's department of economics in 1958 as Charles R. Walgreen Distinguished Service Professor. In so doing, he joined the new Chicago school at its stage of high prosperity. With its emphasis on monetarism and reduced government and its distinct free-market approach, the Chicago school was to deeply influence economics and politics and to remain Stigler's intellectual home for the rest of his life.

That same year Stigler published his powerful (though somewhat neglected) essay "The Goals of Economic Policy" (1958), and his profound mistrust of government policies led him to question the value of many governmentally imposed regulatory laws. Some of his articles from the late 1950s already indicated his growing interest in the study of public regulation.[7]

In the early 1960s, Stigler embarked upon detailed studies of the economic effects of regulations, beginning with his path-breaking essay "What Can Regulators Regulate?" (1960), written with Claire Friedland. In this empirical study, Stigler and Friedland examined the electrical rates charged by regulated and unregulated utilities, and they concluded that regulation had no meaningful effect on prices. Several other empirical studies of public regulatory policies followed and shed light on the far-reaching and unintended side effects of regulatory policies.[8]

These empirical studies of the forces that gave rise to public regulation contributed to new areas of economic research. This new approach became known as the public choice school, represented by such figures as James Buchanan and Gordon Tullock. Stigler's economic analysis of the costs and benefits of public regulation to the various parties involved was in sharp contrast to the approach in the political sciences. For political scientists, any regulation represented the legislative response to a public demand for the protection of the so-called public interest. But, as Stigler demonstrated in his work on regulation, the theory of "public interest" did a poor job of explaining why society adopts these policies. His own public choice theory, on the other hand, was an analysis suggesting that the behavior of government bureaucrats was dictated by self-interest. Thus regulators did not always serve the "public interest"—instead, they sometimes served the very interests they were ostensibly trying to regulate.

In 1963 Stigler published *The Intellectual and the Marketplace*, a highly successful collection of short pieces that includes his brilliant essay of the same title. Unfortunately, only a few of these witty and sharply cut jewels could be reprinted in this volume.

In 1964, as elected president of the American Economic Association, Stigler delivered his programmatic address "The Economist and the State," in which he refined his philosophical and theoretical arguments on the protection of the individual from the state. A year later, he published *Essays in the History of Economics*, a collection covering his writings on the subject from the 1940s into the 1960s and again revealing Stigler as a master of the history of ideas.

V

In 1966, twenty years after its publication, a greatly revised third edition of Stigler's *The Theory of Price* appeared (his successful text is still used today in graduate schools nationwide). The same year another contribution to the problem of regulation, "The Economic Effects of the Antitrust Laws" (1966), was published. Five years and several essays later it was followed by "The Theory of Economic Regulation" (1971). All these studies became very influential. Stigler's many contributions to the field of industrial organization in the 1950s and 1960s culminated with the publication of *The Organization of Industry* in 1968.

During the 1960s and 1970s Stigler served on several public committees. He chaired the Federal Price Statistics Review Committee in 1960 and the presidential Task Force on Competition and Productivity in 1970. His close connection to the Hoover Institution on War, Revolution and Peace at Stanford University, where he serves as both Visiting Scholar and chairman of the advisory committee for the Domestic Studies Program, dates back for several years. In 1974 Stigler became an editor of *The Journal of Political Economy*, and in 1977, director of the Center for the Study of the Economy and the State at the University of Chicago.

In 1975, Stigler dedicated his collection of essays on regulation, *The Citizen and the State*, to his close friend and colleague, Aaron Director. When F. A. von Hayek turned 80 in 1979, Stigler contributed to his former colleague's festschrift an essay tracing the roots of government's great expansion throughout the Western world during the past hundred years.[9]

Stigler's deep concern with liberty and the protection of the individual from the state led to his treatment of "Economics or Ethics" in 1981, delivered as one of the Tanner Lectures on Human Values at Harvard University. The first part of these lectures gave rise to his latest book, *The Economist as Preacher* (1982), a collection of essays on the question of intellectual influence.

Much to his own surprise, Stigler was awarded the Nobel Prize in Economic Sciences in the fall of 1982 for "his seminal studies of industrial structures, functioning of markets and causes and effects of public regulation." The prize was one more victory for the Chicago school of economics, further increasing its influence and prestige. Stigler's Nobel lecture, "The Process and Progress of Economics" (1982), was an important methodological essay in which he applied his theory of information to the market for new ideas in economic science.

Stigler's most important contributions to economics have been in the area of information theory. His empirical work in antitrust areas convinced him of the existence of different prices for near-homogeneous goods, resulting in his conclusion that it is the "expensiveness of knowledge" that sustains price differences. His theory of search for the lowest price by a buyer, or the highest by the seller, led him to conclude that knowledge loses quality over time—that we can expect frequently purchased goods to vary less in price than infrequently purchased goods of the same value. For Stigler, price dispersion is a manifestation of the "measure of ignorance in the market." His extensive studies on the existence of price dispersion under different economic conditions at a given time led to his famous essay, "The Economics of Information" (1961), in which he applied his theory to different fields. In contrast to traditional theory, which assumed that consumers and firms were perfectly informed about the marketplace, Stigler argued that information was like any commodity, difficult and expensive to collect. Individuals would obtain only as much information as they thought would be sufficient. Stigler showed they were essential features of the market and could not be cured by government intervention.

Stigler's theoretical work on information and regulation has explained carefully observed phenomena. His current work is in a related area—the problem of information in political life—and is a study of what a society would be like if it had all the information necessary for an intelligent vote.

George J. Stigler is truly "one of the outstanding economists of the world." His pioneering contributions to economics have opened doors to new and undeveloped areas of research. His work in the history of economic thought has profoundly influenced contemporary economic research. Throughout his career he has been a highly influential, popular (if demanding) teacher, widely reputed for his disarming wit and fine sense of humor. Just one example might suffice: Stigler named his boat *Treatise*, so that when asked what he is doing in his spare time he could answer, "working on my treatise."

NOTES

1. George J. Stigler, *Production and Distribution Theories* (New York: Macmillan, 1940).

2. Stigler, *Domestic Servants in the United States* (New York: NBER, 1947), *Trends in Output and Employment* (New York: NBER, 1947), *Employment and Compensation in Education* (New York: NBER, 1950).

3. Stigler, "Social Welfare and Differential Prices," *Journal of Political Economy* (August 1938), "Production and Distribution in the Short Run," *Journal of Political Economy* (June 1939), "Notes on the Theory of Duopoly," *Journal of Political Economy* (August 1940).

4. Stigler, "The Economics of Minimum Wage Legislation," *American Economic Review* (June 1946).

5. See note 2.

6. Stigler, "The Division of Labor Is Limited by the Extent of the Market," *Journal of Political Economy* (June 1951).

7. Stigler, "Mergers and Preventive Anti-Trust Policy," *Pennsylvania Law Review* (November 1955), "The Tenable Range of Functions of Local Government" in Joint Economic Committee, *Federal Expenditure Policy for Economic Growth and Stability* (Washington, D.C.: November 1957), "Prometheus Incorporated: Conformity or Coercion?" in R. Spiller, ed., *Social Control in a Free Society*, Benjamin Franklin Lectures (Philadelphia: University of Philadelphia Press, 1960).

8. Stigler, "Public Regulation of the Securities Markets," *Journal of Business* (April 1964).

9. Stigler, "Why Have the Socialists Been Winning?" *Ordo* 30 (1969) [Festschrift for F. A. von Hayek].

10. Stigler, "Economics or Ethics?" in *The Tanner Lectures on Human Values*, vol. 2 (Salt Lake City: University of Utah Press, 1981).

Introduction

◆ Thomas Gale Moore ◆

George Stigler is rumored to have said, when asked to give a reference on his colleague and friend Milton Friedman, "He was one of the century's greatest economists in a poor century." Although many might question whether this is really a poor century for economists, most would agree that George Joseph Stigler should be listed among the greats of the century. To quote Stigler directly, from a lecture honoring Henry Simons, "The real tribute to a scholar is the continued life of his intellectual work." Stigler's works are among the most cited in economic literature, ample proof of their continuing vitality. This compilation brings together twenty-three of his greatest pieces.

Stigler's contributions have ranged over virtually all of microeconomics, the history of economic thought, and political economy. The essays reprinted in this volume are only a small sample of his prodigious output. From the publication of his doctoral thesis in 1940 to the present, he has written not only extensively but with wit and clarity, characteristics not common among economists.

George Stigler has always been the quiescent academic, the scholar's scholar, an individual driven by curiosity about the world around him. He has carefully eschewed advocacy; in fact, he believes that "preaching," as he terms it, is vain. Government carries out policies that may appear to be stupid or wrong, but the policies exist because some influential group benefits. Therefore, the purpose of economics is not to preach, nor to build elaborate theoretical models of hypothetical economies, but rather to study the world around us in order to better understand its workings. Most of Stigler's work outside the history of economic thought has been in this vein.

One of his earliest works, "The Economics of Minimum Wage Legislation," was a pathfinding examination of the impact of legislated wage minimums on employment. He analyzed the distorting effect of the minimum wage on allocation of resources; its negligible effect on aggregate employment; and the absence of a relationship between changing relative wages and the diminishing of poverty. Subsequently other scholars empirically confirmed these theoretical conclusions.

It was perhaps his interest in the history of economic thought that led Stigler to turn his attention next to Adam Smith's famous theorem that the division of labor is limited by the extent of the market. This proposition sets up a dilemma: either a firm, by specializing, should be able to monopolize the market, or the theorem is false. Actually, Stigler showed that although this may be true for many functions, there will always be some functions with diminishing returns that limit the size of firms.

Stigler's essay "The Economies of Scale" set forth a new approach to estimating the optimal size or sizes of firms. In this work, he showed that engineering estimates of optimal size are almost always misleading. However, if the size distribution of firms is measured at two or more times, then the size that survives or grows is optimal, while sizes that shrink are clearly failing a market test.

Stigler's curiosity about the world around him led him to ask why markets function the way they do. Why do we see, in most markets, not one single price, but many prices? Why don't markets clear instantaneously? Why is there unemployment? From these questions came his analysis of "The Economics of Information," which in turn spawned a whole new literature in economics. In this essay Stigler showed that information is costly, resulting in a rational consumer or producer who cannot and will not attempt to secure perfect information. Search is carried out to the point where the marginal expected gain is equal to the marginal cost of additional search. Thus it does not pay for individuals with high value of time to conduct much search, but for those whose time is cheap, additional exploration of opportunities is warranted.

In "Free Riders and Collective Action: An Appendix to Theories of Economic Regulation" Stigler demonstrated that the simple proposition, "staying out of a coalition is free," is incorrect and should be reformulated as the "cheap rider." It is "rational" for firms to join in collective activity in many cases. There are a variety of factors that lead to collective bodies. For example, an association can provide valuable services and, with some of the rents collected, can also provide public goods to its members. If the number of firms is small, the proportion that join collective activity will be high; if small firms do not make the entire range of output of the larger enterprises, they feel constrained to join collective action to assure their interests are not ignored.

Though Stigler generally avoided preaching, in "The Intellectual and the Marketplace" he explored and defended the market system. He argued that "intellectuals" should appreciate the competitive system, since the values of intellectuals are based on the competition of ideas. He acknowledged the antipathy of intellectuals for greed, but chided them for some hypocrisy. Their condemnation of tastes in the marketplace is often pure snobbery. Part of the mistrust of the marketplace rises from a failure to understand that one man's gain in business is not another's loss; rather, there is a net gain for all. Intellectuals also dislike the marketplace because the resulting distribution of income is insufficiently egalitarian. Stigler showed that incomes have not become more unequal, nor has the role of inherited wealth been a dominant factor in distribution of income. The most significant effect on the distribution of income is created by the inheritance of intelligence, energy, and general ability.

"The Goals of Economic Policy" preceded "The Intellectual and the Marketplace" by five years, yet it also dealt with attitudes of intellectuals. Though acknowledging the usual goals of economic policy—maximum output, growth of the economy, and minimum inequality of income—Stigler suggests that the overriding goal should be individual liberty. Although this latter goal often seems in conflict with inequality of income, in actuality it is the only goal that separates our economic policy from that of the Marxists.

Stigler vigorously took the economics profession to task for failing to test or adequately justify its advocacy of public policies. In "The Economist and the State," drawing on his vast knowledge of the history of economic thought, Stigler documented how the classical economists opposed government actions, providing neither empirical foundation nor good theoretical justification for their position. In recent decades modern economists have taken the opposite view and recommended government action, again with nothing more substantial than assertions and quotations. Even though economics has been an empirical science since the early nineteenth century, Stigler accurately predicted that the revolution was just beginning, and future government actions would be subject to empirical investigations.

In "Economic Competition and Political Competition" Stigler compared the marketplace with voting and political parties. He argued that local communities compete with other communities for residents in terms of services provided and taxes charged. He also concluded that the Hotelling form of competition between parties can actually be satisfied by a single political party that meets the demand of the median voter. He argues that it is wrong to view the outcome of elections as all-or-nothing results. Rather, a party that secures

49 percent of the vote has a major impact on policy, not much less than the one with 51 percent. This suggests that political parties have strong incentives to maximize votes. It also implies that there is somewhat greater gain from voting than is normally assumed, since even voting for a loser provides some influence over the ultimate outcome.

Stigler's Nobel memorial lecture, "The Process and Progress of Economics," dealt with the amalgamation of new ideas into the profession. Often valuable new ideas fail to be adopted the first time they are advanced. At some later time, however, the same proposition will be put forward and widely accepted. Part of the explanation lies in the profession's readiness for the new concept, which cannot be too radical. As Stigler stated, "nature does not move in jumps." To illustrate, he observed how quickly economists adopted his proposed application of theory to information, even though Cournot had previously explained oligopoly theory in terms of the information one competitor has about another. Stigler's formulation, however, was widely accepted and an extensive literature has since developed on the subject.

On the other hand, Stigler's important work on "The Theory of Economic Regulation" was more grudgingly accepted, probably because the theory was less congenial to many economists and was hence followed by less work. Nevertheless, since economists have no better explanation for the existence of regulation, his formulation has become the perceived wisdom.

Two years after Stigler's seminal work on the economics of information, he applied the same approach to oligopoly theory. In "A Theory of Oligopoly" Stigler explored the problems oligopolists face in establishing and enforcing collusion. His basic premise was that there are no truly homogeneous important markets where both buyers and sellers are indifferent between suppliers and customers. Moreover, whenever there are heterogeneous markets, profit maximization requires differential pricing. To be truly effective, collusion can take the form of either merging or employing a joint sales agent. Both involve significant costs, and are barred by law in the United States. Therefore, firms must agree on price and enforce the agreement.

Enforcement involves the detection of cheating. Cheating will pay when a seller discounts to a large customer. However, the higher probability of detection when giving discounts to numerous small firms makes it less likely that the oligopolist will cheat in their favor. Stigler discusses how the entry of new customers, as well as the willingness and frequency with which customers shift suppliers, will affect the probability of detecting cheating. He concludes that (1) the gain in sales from any one rival by secret price cutting is not sensitive to the number of rivals; (2) the incentive to secret price cutting falls as the number of customers per seller increases; (3) the incentive to secret price cutting rises as the probability of repeat purchases falls.

In 1967, Stigler published "The Dominant Firm and the Inverted Umbrella," which offers one of the best explanations for a common type of cartel behavior. It gives an excellent explanation for the behavior of Saudi Arabia and the oil cartel, even though this piece was written well before there was any significant OPEC.

Stigler's insistence on the importance of testing government policies was the basis for his paper on "The Economic Effects of the Antitrust Laws." He criticized the approach taken by most economists, which is to assume the answer. He then compared interlocking directorates within Great Britain, which has no antitrust law, with those of the United States, and found a negligible number of interlocking directorates within the United Kingdom. In comparing a sample of seven industries, Stigler found that in five of the industries concentration was higher in Great Britain. However, because the market is much smaller in the United Kingdom, higher concentrations are to be expected. Stigler also found a decline in horizontal mergers after the passage of the antimerger amendment in 1950. He concluded that antitrust cases brought against efficient types of collusion are more likely to be successful than those that are less efficient, which tend to conduct innocuous trade-association–type activities.

A theme running through much of Stigler's research is his refusal to regard intentions as the same as results. Much of his own work in regulation, and the work he has stimulated for others, has been the study of the results of a given government rule. Government prohibition of a certain action does not necessarily mean anything changes, for the action might not have been taken even if it had been legal (or an action might continue despite the prohibition). From this unique perspective has grown a vast amount of literature on the impact of government regulations. Stigler's study "What Can Regulators Regulate: The Case of Electricity" is one of the best (and was certainly the first) in this area. In this paper he examined the impact of state regulation on electric utility prices and failed to find that regulation helped consumers or harmed producers.

His continued research in this field has revealed that regulations fail in their ostensible purpose, to protect the public. Rather, they confer benefits on others. This revelation stimulated Stigler to explore the field of political economy. What are the factors that determine which industries will seek regulations or protection and under what conditions? Which industries will be successful in securing government aid, and what form will that aid take? His study of "The Theory of Economic Regulation" explained how various interest groups could use political processes to seek rents.

George Stigler's 1983 Nobel essay was in part a return to some ideas he put forward in 1955 in "The Nature and Role of Originality in Scientific Progress." Through this earlier work he demonstrated that in most cases there is a long intellectual history behind a new idea before the originator advances the proposition, which takes some persuasion to convince the profession to actually accept. Stigler points to a number of areas in which John Stuart Mill originated ideas, yet, because he failed to sell them, received little credit. Not only must an idea be sold before becoming known as significant and original work, it must also be correct and lead to new insights that other scholars can expand and elaborate upon.

Much of Stigler's work is based on both his knowledge and analysis of the history of economic thought. Consequently, many of his papers can be classified both in the history of economic thought and in basic price theory. His 1957 paper "Perfect Competition, Historically Contemplated" reflects well this dual nature of his work. Starting with Adam Smith, Stigler traced the concept of competition from the idea of rivalry to a more mathematical and rigorous definition in the works of F. Y. Edgeworth. Finally, under Frank Knight, the concept of competition received such a rigorous formulation that it became clear that, as far as the real world was concerned, competition did not exist. Recognizing the importance the normative role of the concept of perfect competition has played, Stigler suggested using a narrower concept called "market competition" to describe the absence of monopoly power in a market.

In "Bernard Shaw, Sidney Webb, and the Theory of Fabian Socialism" Stigler analyzed the economics of the Fabians. Their criticism of capitalism rested on Henry George's assertions about rent. By analogy they extended the critique to include interest and capital and thus condemned capitalism. With this indictment, they faulted the income distribution that resulted from capitalism. Stigler showed that their extension of rent theory to interest is invalid, and in some well-chosen words and examples, punctured the discussion of the inequities of an unequal distribution of income:

> Dr. John Upright, the young physician, devoted every energy of his being to the curing of the illnesses of his patients. No hours were too long, no demand on his skill or sympathies too great, if a man or child could be helped. He received $2,000 net each year, until he died at the age of 41 from overwork. Dr. Henry Leisure, on the contrary, insisted that even patients with broken legs be brought to his office only on Tuesdays, Thursdays, and Fridays, between 12:30 and 3:30 P.M. He preferred to take three patients simultaneously, so he could advise while playing bridge, at which he cheated. He received $2,000 net each year, until he retired at the age of 84.

Stigler's Tanner lectures, presented at Harvard in 1980, were entitled "Economics or Ethics?" This three-part series consisted of "The Economist as Preacher," "The Ethics of Competition: The Friendly Economists," and "The Ethics of Competition: The Unfriendly Critics." In these essays Stigler returned to some of the themes in "The Intellectual and the Marketplace" and

"The Economist and the State." In the first Tanner lecture he argued that economists have done very little preaching. There is an occasional word in the works of Adam Smith that connotes a moral judgment, but most economists' output has taken the form of an explanation of how the economic system works. In fact, Stigler cites Frank Knight's remark that "anything which is inevitable is ideal," an epigram that suggests the futility of preaching.

When economists have preached, their goal has been the attainment of economic efficiency. As Stigler stated, "An economist is a person who, reading of the confinement of Edmond Dantes in a small cell, laments his lost alternative product." However, Stigler is not adverse to preaching to his own profession, admonishing them to worry less about political action being mistaken and to concentrate more on explaining the political process.

A second goal espoused by many economists is equity. Smith thought that income distribution should be determined by the market, but there has been a gradual shift over the last two hundred years toward the notion of egalitarianism. This particular ethic, however, did not originate with economists; rather, it came into the profession from the ethos of the time. Stigler concluded that when they do assume the role of preachers, economists are successful only if they preach what the public wants to hear.

In the second Tanner lecture Stigler discussed the issue of economists' ethical values. He found that the two strongest values held are a belief in the capability of the market to distribute resources efficiently and a belief in the desirability of marginal productivity as a norm for compensation. Though economists may get their ethical system from the times, Stigler shows that they differ from noneconomists in one important aspect: they perceive markets as ethical in the sense that the exchanges are voluntary.

In the concluding Tanner lecture Stigler took on the critics of competition. He argued that critics of capitalism invent abuses, denounce some virtues as abuses, exaggerate shortcomings, and are blind to difficulties of alternative economic systems. Intellectuals have been hostile to the market system for thousands of years. They perceive materialism as hostile to their ethical values and believe their own self-interest is best served in expansion of the government's economic role. Stigler emphasized that the intellectual's opposition to the free market is based on self-interest: "Man is eternally a utility-maximizer, in his home, in his office—be it public or private—in his church, in his scientific work, in short, everywhere."

In "Why Have the Socialists Been Winning?" Stigler argues that the growth of government in the Western world is not a mistake; rather, it is the result of powerful political groups using the state to further their own interests. Stigler does not offer good solutions to this tendency; he rules out sacrificing democracy, limiting the vote to certain groups, or requiring supermajorities to pass legislation.

The last four essays in this volume contain delightful examples of George Stigler's brilliant wit, which flows throughout his works. "The Alarming Cost of Model Changes: A Case Study" is a satire of an earlier article, "The Costs of Automobile Model Changes Since 1949." In this latter piece, three well-known economists calculated the cost of model changes and argued that the public would have saved greatly had there been no change. Stigler counters by observing that vast savings would have accrued had there been no new books published since 1900. Since there is nothing new under the sun, great savings would have been possible had there been no new newspapers. As Stigler quipped, "most new knowledge is false; and the news got around in Athens."

In "A Certain Galbraith in an Uncertain Age" Stigler cut to ribbons Galbraith's BBC series. In the main Stigler confined his criticism to the book that was based on the series, although neither was a great success.

"Stigler's Law of Demand and Supply Elasticities" proposed that "all demand curves are inelastic and all supply curves are inelastic, too." Stigler gave an empirical demonstration of the validity of this law by quoting academics, businessmen, and government officials. He then argued that theory demonstrates the truth of these propositions. Since all products are only a small portion of the expense of other products then, following the Marshall proof, the third condition of inelastic demand is that only a small part of the expenses of production of the commodity should consist of the price of that factor. Moreover, expectations of higher prices keep people buying in the face of higher prices. Stigler goes on to give an irrefutable mathematical "proof."

In the final essay, the delightful "A Sketch of the History of Truth in Teaching," Stigler argued that since government was now requiring that advertising be "truthful" and manufactured products be safe, the same standards should be applied to teaching. In this marvelous work, Stigler tells of a mythical Harvard Business School graduate who sued his alma mater and teacher for imparting false information. Although Harvard won initially on appeal, the judge remarked: "It seems paradoxical beyond endurance to rule that a manufacturer of shampoos may not endanger a student's scalp but a premier educational institution is free to stuff his skull with nonsense." In this fantasy, though Harvard ultimately prevailed, the government moved to establish the Federal Bureau of Academic Reading, Writing, and Research to license scholarly activities.

No summary of Stigler's writings can give an adequate account of his scholarly brilliance and his unique contribution to economic literature. To understand the full depth of his intellect and scholarship, one must read and reread his works. Fortunately, not only is this necessary, it is a pleasure. His writings intermingle humor with great insight to a degree seldom found in economic thought. Stigler has authored many other worthwhile works that are not reproduced here. It is our hope that this particular collection will encourage readers to seek out his many other writings as well.

STIGLER'S
CONTRIBUTIONS
TO ECONOMICS

◆

◆ PART ◆ ONE ◆

THE ECONOMICS OF
MINIMUM WAGE LEGISLATION

• 1 •

The minimum wage provisions of the Fair Labor Standards Act of 1938 have been repealed by inflation. Many voices are now taking up the cry for a higher minimum, say, of 60 to 75 cents per hour.

Economists have not been very outspoken on this type of legislation. It is my fundamental thesis that they can and should be outspoken, and singularly agreed. The popular objective of minimum wage legislation—the elimination of extreme poverty—is not seriously debatable. The important questions are rather: (1) does such legislation diminish poverty? (2) are there efficient alternatives? The answers are, if I am not mistaken, unusually definite for questions of economic policy. If this is so, these answers should be given.

Some readers will probably know my answers already ("no" and "yes," respectively); it is distressing how often one can guess the answer given to an economic question merely by knowing who asks it. But my personal answers are unimportant; the arguments on which they rest, which are important, will be presented under four heads:

1. Effects of a legal minimum wage on the allocation of resources.

2. Effects on aggregate employment.

From the *American Economic Review* 36, no. 3 (June 1946). Permission to reprint courtesy of the American Economic Association.

3. Effects on family income.

4. Alternative policies to combat poverty.

I. The Allocation of Resources

The effects of minimum wages may in principle differ between industries in which employers do and do not have control over the wage rates they pay for labor of given skill and application. The two possibilities will be discussed in turn.

Competitive Wage Determination

Each worker receives the value of his marginal product under competition. If a minimum wage is effective, it must therefore have one of two effects: first, workers whose services are worth less than the minimum wage are discharged (and thus forced into unregulated fields of employment, or into unemployment or retirement from the labor force); or, second, the productivity of low-efficiency workers is increased.

The former result, discharge of less efficient workers, will be larger the more the value of their services falls short of the legal minimum, the more elastic the demand for the product, and the greater the possibility of substituting other productive services (including efficient labor) for the inefficient workers' services. The discharged workers will, at best, move to unregulated jobs where they will secure lower returns. Unless inefficient workers' productivity rises, therefore, the minimum wage reduces aggregate output, perhaps raises the earnings of those previously a trifle below the minimum; and reduces the earnings of those substantially below the minimum. These are undoubtedly the main allocational effects of a minimum wage in a competitive industry.

The second and offsetting result, the increase of labor productivity, might come about in one of two ways: the laborers may work harder; or the entrepreneurs may use different production techniques. The threat of unemployment may force the inefficient laborers to work harder (the inducement of higher earnings had previously been available, and failed), but this is not very probable. These workers were already driven by the sharp spurs of poverty, and for many the intensity of effort must be increased beyond hope (up to 50 or more percent) to avoid discharge.

The introduction of new techniques by the entrepreneurs is the more common source of increased labor productivity. Here again there are two possibilities.

First, techniques which were previously unprofitable are now rendered

TABLE 1.1

EMPLOYMENT, AVERAGE ANNUAL EARNINGS OF FULL-TIME WAGE EARNERS,
AND PERCENTAGE WAGES FORM OF VALUE-ADDED,
IN LOW-WAGE MANUFACTURING INDUSTRIES, 1939

Industry	Employment	Average Earnings	Wages as Percent of Value-Added
Men's and boys' furnishings	166,945	$632	52.2
Canned and preserved foods	134,471	660	28.0
Cigars	50,897	673	42.0
Cotton manufactures	409,317	715	51.1
Fertilizer	18,744	730	24.0
Wood containers	45,070	735	47.2
Women's accessories	58,952	740	41.3
Misc. fabricated textiles	49,242	746	36.2
Misc. apparel	38,288	769	45.5
Rayon and silk manufactures	119,821	779	54.4
Animal and vegetable oils	21,678	781	25.1
Costume jewelry, etc.	25,256	782	43.5
Sawmills, etc.	265,185	810	52.0
Leather products	280,411	847	50.9
All Manufacturing		1,153	36.8

SOURCE: Census of Manufactures, 1939.

profitable by the increased cost of labor. Costs of production rise because of the minimum wage, but they rise by less than they would if other resources could not be substituted for the labor. Employment will fall for two reasons: output falls; and a given output is secured with less labor. Commonly the new techniques require different (and hence superior) labor, so many inefficient workers are discharged. This process is only a spelling-out of the main competitive effect.

Second, entrepreneurs may be shocked out of lethargy to adopt techniques which were previously profitable or to discover new techniques. This "shock" theory is at present lacking in empirical evidence but not in popularity.

There are several reasons for believing that the "shock" theory is particularly inappropriate to the industries paying low wages. All of the large manufacturing industry categories which in 1939 paid relatively low wages (measured by the payroll of wage earners divided by their average number) are listed in Table 1.1. A study of this table suggests two generalizations: (1) the low-wage industries are competitive, and (2) the ratio of wages to total-processing-cost-

TABLE 1.2

HYPOTHETICAL DATA ILLUSTRATING EMPLOYER WAGE DETERMINATION

Number of Workers	Wage Rate	Marginal Cost of a Worker	Value of the Marginal Product[a]
10	$12		$36
20	14	$16	34
30	16	20	32
40	18	24	30
50	20	28	28
60	22	32	26
70	24	36	24

[a] Or marginal value product, if this is less.

plus-profit is higher than in high-wage industries. The competitive nature of these industries argues that the entrepreneurs are not easygoing traditionalists: vigorous competition in national markets does not attract or tolerate such men. The relatively high labor costs reveal that inducements to wage-economy are already strong. These considerations both work strongly against the shock theory in low-wage manufacturing industries in 1939.[1] Since these industries were on the whole much less affected by the war than other manufacturing industries, they will probably be present in the postwar list of low-wage industries. The low-wage industries in trade and services display the same characteristics and support the same adverse conclusion with respect to the shock theory.[2]

Employer Wage Determination

If an employer has a significant degree of control over the wage rate he pays for a given quality of labor, a skillfully set minimum wage may increase his employment and wage rate and, because the wage is brought closer to the value of the marginal product, at the same time increase aggregate output. The effect may be elucidated with the hypothetical data in Table 1.2. If the entrepreneur is left alone, he will set a wage of $20 and employ 50 men; a minimum wage of $24 will increase employment to 70 men.

This arithmetic is quite valid, but it is not very relevant to the question of a national minimum wage. The minimum wage which achieves these desirable ends has several requisites:

1. It must be chosen correctly: too high a wage (over $28 in our example) will decrease employment. The accounting records describe, very imperfectly, existing employment and wages; the optimum minimum wage can be set only if the demand and supply schedules are known over a considerable range. At present there is no tolerably accurate method of deriving these schedules, and one is entitled to doubt that a legislative mandate is all that is necessary to bring forth such a method.
2. The optimum wage varies with occupation (and, within an occupation, with the quality of worker).
3. The optimum wage varies among firms (and plants).
4. The optimum wage varies, often rapidly, through time.

A uniform national minimum wage, infrequently changed, is wholly unsuited to these diversities of conditions.[3]

We may sum up: the legal minimum wage will reduce aggregate output, and it will decrease the earnings of workers who had previously been receiving materially less than the minimum.

II. Aggregate Employment

Although no precise estimate of the effects of a minimum wage upon aggregate employment is possible, we may nevertheless form some notion of the direction of these effects. The higher the minimum wage, the greater will be the number of covered workers who are discharged. The current proposals would probably affect a twentieth to a tenth of all covered workers, so possibly several hundred thousand workers would be discharged. Whatever the number (which no one knows), the direct unemployment is substantial and certain; and it fairly establishes the presumption that the net effects of the minimum wage on aggregate employment are adverse.

This presumption is strengthened by the existing state of aggregate money demand. There is no prospective inadequacy of money demand in the next year or two—indeed, the danger is that it is excessive. If the minimum wage were to increase the relative share of wage earners and, hence, the propensity to consume—which requires the uncertain assumption that the demand for inefficient labor is inelastic—the increment of consumer demand will be unnecessary, and perhaps unwelcome.[4] (Conversely, the direct unemployment resulting from the wage law would diminish faster in a period of high employment.)

It is sufficient for the present argument that no large increase in employment will be induced by the legislation. Actually, there is a presumption that a minimum wage will have adverse effects upon aggregate employment.

III. Wage Rates and Family Income

The manipulation of individual prices is neither an efficient nor an equitable device for changing the distribution of personal income. This is a well-known dictum that has received much documentation in analyses of our agricultural programs. The relevance of the dictum to minimum wage legislation is easily demonstrated.

One cannot expect a close relationship between the level of hourly wage rates and the amount of family income. Yet family income and needs are the fundamental factors in the problem of poverty. The major sources of discrepancy may be catalogued.

First, the hourly rates are effective only for those who receive them, and it was shown in Section I that the least productive workers are forced into uncovered occupations or into unemployment.

Second, hourly earnings and annual earnings are not closely related. The seasonality of the industry, the extent of overtime, the amount of absenteeism, and the shift of workers among industries, are obvious examples of factors which reduce the correlation between hourly earnings and annual earnings.

Third, family earnings are the sum of earnings of all workers in the family, and the dispersion of number of workers is considerable. The summary in Table 1.3 for low income wage-earner families in Minnesota in 1939, shows that in the $250–$500 income class one-twentieth of the families had more than one earner and in the higher income classes the fraction rose to one-eighth.

Fourth, although wages are, of course, the chief component of the income of low-wage families, they are by no means the only component. It is indicated in Table 1.4 that a tenth of the wage-earner families had cash investment

TABLE 1.3

PERCENTAGE DISTRIBUTION OF WAGE-EARNER FAMILIES
BY NUMBER OF EARNERS: MINNESOTA, 1939

Family Income	One Earner	Two Earners	Three Earners	Four or more Earners
$250– 500	94.5	4.6	.7	.2
500– 750	92.4	7.1	.3	.2
750–1000	86.7	10.7	1.5	1.1
1000–1250	88.5	10.4	1.1	.1

SOURCE: *Minnesota Incomes, 1938–39*, vol. II (St. Paul: Minnesota Resources Commission, 1942), p. 152.

TABLE 1.4

COMPOSITION OF INCOME OF WAGE-EARNER FAMILIES: MINNESOTA, 1939

Income Class	Total	Wages and Salaries	INCOME Entrepreneurial Income	Room and Board	INVESTMENT INCOME Cash	Total
1. Percentage of Families Receiving Income						
$250– 500		99.9	26.5	1.3	12.3	28.2
500– 750		100.0	25.2	1.7	10.1	24.2
750–1000		100.0	21.4	2.7	9.4	31.2
1000–1250		100.0	18.4	3.0	10.4	22.8
2. Average Amount						
250– 500	$ 387	$ 308		–$ 9	$64	
500– 750	631	560		62	82	
750–1000	865	766		53	82	
1000–1250	1124	1032		91	96	

SOURCE: *Minnesota Incomes, 1938–39*, vol. I (St. Paul: Minnesota Resources Commission, 1942), p. 42; vol. II, p. 200.

income, a quarter had entrepreneurial income, and a quarter owned their homes.

All of these steps lead us only to family income; the leap must still be made to family needs. It is argued in the next section that family composition is the best criterion of need, and whether this be accepted or not, it is clearly an important criterion. The great variation in family size among wage-earner families is strongly emphasized by the illustrative data in Table 1.5; an income adequate for one size is either too large or too small for at least half the families in that income class.

The connection between hourly wages and the standard of living of the family is thus remote and fuzzy. Unless the minimum wage varies with the amount of employment, number of earners, nonwage income, family size, and many other factors, it will be an inept device for combatting poverty even for those who succeed in retaining employment. And if the minimum wages varies with all of these factors, it will be an insane device.

IV. THE PROBLEM OF POVERTY

Minimum wage legislation commonly has two stated objectives: the reduction of employer control of wages, and the abolition of poverty. The former and

TABLE 1.5

PERCENTAGE DISTRIBUTION OF WAGE-EARNER FAMILIES BY NUMBER
OF PERSONS: CHICAGO AND ATLANTA, 1936

	NUMBER OF PERSONS IN FAMILY			
Income Class	2	3 or 4	5 or 6	7 or more
1. Chicago				
$ 0– 250	39.6	43.6	14.9	2.0
250– 500	35.3	45.8	17.6	1.3
500– 750	31.8	53.7	13.0	1.6
750–1000	29.0	56.5	12.4	2.1
2. Atlanta				
0– 250	30.	55.	15.	0.
250– 500	20.1	48.1	16.5	5.3
500– 750	22.6	46.9	24.4	6.2
750–1000	21.6	48.1	23.5	6.7

SOURCES: *Family Income in Chicago, 1935–36* (Bur. of Lab. Stat., bull. no. 642 [Washington: Supt. Docs., 194]), vol. I, p. 117; *Family Income in the Southeastern Region* (Bur. of Lab. Stat., bull. no. 647 [Washington: Supt. Docs., 194]), vol. I, p. 148.

much lesser purpose may better be achieved by removing the condition of labor immobility which gives rise to employer control. Labor immobility would be reduced substantially by public provision of comprehensive information on employment conditions in various areas and industries. The immobility would be further reduced by supplying vocational training and loans to cover moving costs. But employer wage control is not the important problem; let us turn to the elimination of poverty.

Incomes of the poor cannot be increased without impairing incentives. Skillful policies will, for a given increase in the incomes of the poor, impair incentives less than clumsy policies. But the more completely poverty is eliminated, given the level of intelligence with which this is done, the greater will be the impairment of incentives. This is a price we must pay, just as impairment of incentives is a price we have willingly paid to reduce the inequality of income by progressive income and estate taxes. Society must determine, through its legislators, what minimum income (or addition to income) should be guaranteed to each family. We shall assume that this difficult decision has been made.

One principle is fundamental in the amelioration of poverty: those who are equally in need should be helped equally. If this principle is to be achieved, there must be an objective criterion of need; equality can never be achieved when many cases are judged (by many people) "on their merits." We are driven almost inexorably to family size and composition as this criterion of need. It is obviously imperfect; the sickly require more medical care than the healthy.[5] But it is vastly easier to accord special treatment to certain families for a few items like medical care than to accord special treatment to every family for the sum of all items of expenditure.

It is a corollary of this position that assistance should not be based upon occupation. The poor farmer, the poor shopkeeper, and the poor miner are on an equal footing. There may be administrative justification (although I doubt it) for treating the farmer separately from the urban dweller, but there is no defense in equity for helping the one and neglecting the other. To render the assistance by manipulating prices is in any case objectionable: we help the rich farmer more than the poor, and give widely differing amounts of help to the poor farmer from year to year.

The principle of equity thus involves the granting of assistance to the poor with regard to their need (measured by family composition) but without regard to their occupation. There is a possible choice between grants in kind and in money. The latter commends itself strongly: it gives full play to the enormous variety of tastes and it is administratively much simpler. Yet it raises a problem which will be noticed shortly.

Even if these general observations be accepted, the structure of administration is of grave importance, and I do not pretend to have explored this field. There is great attractiveness in the proposal that we extend the personal income tax to the lowest income brackets with negative rates in these brackets. Such a scheme could achieve equality of treatment with what appears to be a (large) minimum of administrative machinery. If the negative rates are appropriately graduated, we may still retain some measure of incentive for a family to increase its income. We should no doubt encounter many perplexing difficulties in carrying out this plan, but they are problems which could not be avoided, even though they might be ignored, by a less direct attack on poverty.

One final point: we seek to abolish poverty in good part because it leads to undernourishment. In this connection, dietary appraisals show that in any income class, no matter how low, a portion of the families secure adequate diets, and in any income class, as high as the studies go, a portion do not. The proportion of ill-fed, to be sure, declines substantially as income rises, but it does not disappear. We cannot possibly afford to abolish malnutrition, or mal-housing, or mal-education, only by increasing incomes.

Either of two inferences may be drawn. The program of increasing income must be supplemented by a program of education—in diet, in housing, in education. Or the assistance to the poor should be given in kind, expertly chosen. The latter approach is administratively very complex, but quicker and in direct expenditure vastly more economical. These factors affect our choice, but a thought should be given also to the two societies to which they lead.

Notes

1. The current extensive and confident uses made of labor productivity indexes seem to me inappropriate to their ambiguity and inaccuracy. For those who are less skeptical, I may add that for the period 1929 to 1937, output per worker can be approximated for nine of the industries in Table 1.1 (using data from S. Fabricant's *Employment in Manufacturing, 1899–1939* [New York, Nat. Bur. of Econ. Research, 1942]). In six of the nine industries the increase in labor productivity equalled or exceeded that of all manufacturing.

2. We should perhaps also notice that, even if the shock theory were of general applicability, the maintenance or increase of employment would require also that (1) demand be elastic, and (2) low-efficiency workers continue to be used with the improved techniques.

3. One can go much farther: even administratively established minima, varying with firm and time, would be impossibly difficult to devise and revise, and their effects on private investment would be extremely adverse.

4. This line of argument implies that a minimum wage is more likely to have beneficial effects in depression (if the demand for the relevant labor is inelastic), but it does not imply that the beneficial effects are likely.

5. One could argue that rural families should receive less help, to offset the lower prices at which food and housing are procured. The group is of sufficient size and perhaps sufficiently identifiable to justify separate treatment. But there are grounds other than political expediency for rejecting this proposal.

THE DIVISION OF LABOR
IS LIMITED BY THE
EXTENT OF THE MARKET

· 2 ·

Economists have long labored with the rate of operation of firm and industry, but they have generally treated as a (technological?) datum the problem of what the firm does—what governs its range of activities or functions. It is the central thesis of this paper that the theorem of Adam Smith which has been appropriated as a title is the core of a theory of the functions of firm and industry, and a good deal more besides. I shall (1) make some brief historical remarks on the theorem, (2) sketch a theory of the functions of a firm, (3) apply this theory to vertical integration, and (4) suggest broader applications of the theorem.

I. HISTORICAL INTRODUCTION

When Adam Smith advanced his famous theorem that the division of labor is limited by the extent of the market, he created at least a superficial dilemma. If this proposition is generally applicable, should there not be monopolies in most industries? So long as the further division of labor (by which we may understand the further specialization of labor and machines) offers lower costs for larger outputs, entrepreneurs will gain by combining or expanding and

From the *Journal of Political Economy* 59, no. 3 (June 1951). Copyright 1951 by the University of Chicago.

driving out rivals. And here was the dilemma: either the division of labor is limited by the extent of the market, and, characteristically, industries are monopolized; or industries are characteristically competitive, and the theorem is false or of little significance. Neither alternative is inviting. There were and are plenty of important competitive industries; yet Smith's argument that Highlanders would be more efficient if each did not have to do his own baking and brewing also seems convincing and capable of wide generalization.

In the pleasant century that followed on the *Wealth of Nations*, this conflict was temporarily resolved in favor of Smith's theorem by the simple expedient of ignoring the conditions for stable competitive equilibrium. Ricardo, Senior, and J. S. Mill—and their less famous confreres—announced the principle of increasing returns in manufacturing—for Senior it was even an axiom. The exclusion of agriculture was based on the empirical judgment, not that further division of labor was impossible, but that it was a weaker tendency than that of diminishing returns from more intensive cultivation of a relatively fixed supply of land.

This was hardly a satisfactory solution, and, when Marshall came to reformulate classical economics into a comprehensive and internally consistent system, the dilemma could no longer be ignored. He refused to give up either increasing returns or competition, and he created three theories (of course, not only for this purpose) which insured their compatibility. First, and perhaps most important, he developed the concept of external economies—economies outside the reach of the firm and dependent upon the size of the industry, the region, the economy, or even the whole economic world. Second, he emphasized the mortality of able entrepreneurs and the improbability that a single business would be managed superlatively for any length of time. Third, he argued that each firm might have a partial monopoly—a separate, elastic demand curve for its product—so that, with expansion of its output, the price would usually fall faster than average costs would.

For a time this reconciliation of competition and increasing returns served its purpose, but, as the center of price theory moved toward the firm, Smith's theorem fell into the background. External economies were a rather nebulous category relative to anything so concrete and definite as economists for a time believed the costs of a firm to be. It was pointed out by Professor Knight, moreover, that economies external to one industry may (and perhaps must) be internal to another. The industries in which the economies are internal will tend to monopoly; and, incidentally, it is no longer a foregone conclusion that such economies will be shared with the buyers. Since external economies seemed a refractory material for the popular analytical techniques, they were increasingly neglected.

Marshall's theory of business mortality was also increasingly neglected, with even less explicit consideration. It was not an approach that harmonized well with the economics of a stationary economy, and again the theory was very inconvenient to incorporate into cost and demand curves (especially if one will not use the concept of a representative firm). If the economies of scale within the firm were as strong as Marshall pictured them, moreover, it was not clear that continuously high-quality entrepreneurship was necessary to achieve monopoly. And could the giant firm not grow quickly by merger as well as hesitantly by internal expansion?

Marshall's third theory, of the falling demand curve for the individual firm, lost popularity for a generation because it was incompatible with perfect competition rigorously defined, and this became increasingly the standard model of analysis. And, paradoxically, when the falling demand curve was rediscovered and popularized in the 1930s by the proponents of imperfect and monopolistic competition, they used it not to examine the broad movements of industries and of economies but to focus price theory on the physiology and pathology of the firm.

In 1928, to retrace a step, the neglect of increasing returns had gone so far that Allyn Young felt the need to restore perspective by an emphatic endorsement of the fundamental importance of Smith's theorem: "That theorem, I have always thought, is one of the most illuminating and fruitful generalizations which can be found anywhere in the whole literature of economics."[1] His position seemed persuasive, but he did not resolve the technical difficulties of incorporating the extent of the market into competitive price theory. Indeed, he openly avoided this problem, asserting that the firm and perhaps also the industry were too small to serve as units of analysis in this area. And so, although Young's and Marshall's and Smith's position is often given lip service to this day, the tributes are tokens of veneration, not evidences of active partnership with the theory of the firm and the competitive industry.

II. The Functions of a Firm

The firm is usually viewed as purchasing a series of inputs, from which it obtains one or more salable products, the quantities of which are related to the quantities of the inputs by a production function. For our purpose it is better to view the firm as engaging in a series of distinct operations: purchasing and storing materials; transforming materials into semifinished products and semifinished products into finished products; storing and selling the outputs; extending credit to buyers; and so on. That is, we partition the firm not among the markets in which it buys inputs but among the functions or processes which constitute the scope of its activity.

The costs of these individual functions will be related by technology. The cost of one function may depend upon whether the preceding function took

16 ♦ ECONOMICS

FIGURE 2.1

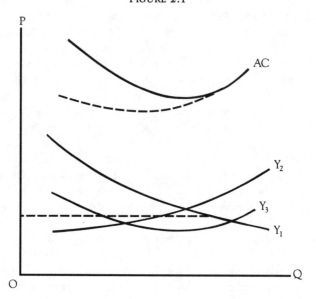

place immediately before or in the immediate vicinity, as when hot ingots are processed with a saving of heat. Or the interrelationships among processes may be remote, as when the entrepreneur must neglect production in order to supervise marketing.

Let us ignore for a moment these interrelationships of costs of various functions in order to achieve a simple geometrical picture of the firm's costs of production. If the cost of each function depends only on the rate of output of that function, we may draw a unique cost curve for it. Furthermore, if there is a constant proportion between the rate of output of each function and the rate of output of the final product (as when every 100 pounds of cement is bagged), we may draw the cost curves of all functions on one graph, and the (vertical) sum of these costs of various functions will be the conventional average-cost curve of the firm.

We should expect to find many different patterns of average costs of functions: some falling continuously (Y_1); some rising continuously (Y_2); some conventionally U-shaped (Y_3) (see Figure 2.1). It is not impossible, of course, that the average cost of some operations first rises and then falls.

Now consider Smith's theorem. Certain processes are subject to increasing returns; why does the firm not exploit them further and in the process become a monopoly? Because there are other functions subject to diminishing returns, and these are, on balance, at least so costly that average cost of the final product does not diminish with output. Then why does the firm not abandon the functions subject to increasing returns, allowing another firm (and industry) to specialize in them to take full advantage of increasing returns? At a given time these functions may be too small to support a specialized firm or firms. The sales of the product may be too small to support a specialized merchant; the output of a byproduct may be too small to support a specialized fabricator; the demand for market information may be too small to support a trade journal. The firm must then perform these functions for itself.

But, with the expansion of the industry, the magnitude of the function subject to increasing returns may become sufficient to permit a firm to specialize in performing it. The firms will then abandon the Process (Y_1), and a new firm will take it over. This new firm will be a monopoly, but it will be confronted by elastic demands: it cannot charge a price for the process higher than the average cost of the process to the firms which are abandoning it. With the continued expansion of the industry, the number of firms supplying process Y_1 will increase, so that the new industry becomes competitive and the new industry may, in turn, abandon parts of process Y_1 to a new set of specialists.

The abandonment of function Y_1 by the original industry will alter each firm's cost curves: the curve Y_1 will be replaced by a horizontal line (ignoring quantity discounts) at a level lower than Y_1 in the effective region. The cost curve of the product (drawn with broken lines in Figure 2.1) will be lower, and, on present assumptions, the output at which average costs are a minimum (if only one such output exists) becomes smaller.

Certain functions are also subject to increasing cost: why not abandon or at least restrict the scale of operation of these functions? The foregoing discussion is also applicable here, with one change. When the industry grows, the original firms need not wholly abandon the increasing-cost processes. Part of the required amount of the process (say, engine castings for automobiles) may be made within the firm without high average (or marginal) costs, and the remainder purchased from subsidiary industries.

In order to give a simple geometrical illustration, we have made two assumptions. The first is that the rate of output of the process and the rate of output of the final product are strictly proportional. This will be approximately true of some functions (such as making parts of a single final product), but it will also be untrue of other functions (such as advertising the product). If we drop the assumption, the substance of our argument will not be affected, but our geometrical picture becomes more complicated.[2]

Our second assumption, that the costs of the functions are independent, is more important. Actually, many processes will be rival: the greater the rate of output of one process, the higher the cost of a given rate of output of the other process or processes. Sometimes the rivalry will be technological (as in many multiple-product firms), but almost always it will also be managerial: the wider the range of functions the firm undertakes, the greater the tasks of coordination. Other processes will be complementary: the greater the rate of output of one process, the lower the cost of a given rate of output of the other processes. A most curious example of complementarity is the circular flow of materials within a plant; thus, in the course of making steel, steel plants supply a large part of their requirements for scrap.

If, on balance, the functions are rival, then usually the firm will increase its rate of output of the final product when it abandons a function; and I think that this is generally the case. For example, in the famous study of the Lancashire textile industry by Chapman and Ashton, it was found that firms engaged in both spinning and weaving in 1911 had, on average, 47,634 spindles, while those engaged only in spinning had, on average, 68,055 spindles.[3] But this is not necessary—indeed, they found the converse relationship in number of looms—and the effect of the range of functions on the size of the firm requires much study before we can reach safe generalizations.

III. Vertical Integration

Many economists believe that, with the growth of firms (and industries?), functions are usually taken over from previous independent industries. For example, United States Steel Corporation now mines its ores, operates its own ore-hauling railroads and ships, and, at the other end, fabricates barrels, oil-field equipment, and houses. (The number of economic views based chiefly on half-a-dozen giant corporations would repay morbid study.)

Broadly viewed, Smith's theorem suggests that vertical disintegration is the typical development in growing industries, vertical integration in declining industries.[4] The significance of the theorem can therefore be tested by an appeal to the facts on vertical integration.

Unfortunately, there are no wholly conclusive data on the trend of vertical integration. The only large-scale quantitative information at hand comes from a comparison of the 1919 study by Willard Thorp with the 1937 study by Walter Crowder of central offices (companies with two or more manufacturing establishments). In 1919, 602 manufacturing companies, or 13.0 percent of a moderately complete list of 4,635 companies, had two or more establishments making successive products, that is, the product of one establishment was the raw material of another establishment.[5] In 1937, successive functions were found in 565 companies (or 10.0 percent of a more complete list of 5,625 companies).[6] In 1919, successive functions were found in 34.4 percent of all complex central offices (companies with establishments in two or more industries); in 1937, in only 27.5 percent. Multiplant companies probably grew in relative importance during this period, so it is possible that a larger share of manufacturing output came from vertically integrated firms. But, so far as these multiplant companies are concerned, there seems to have been a tendency away from vertical integration.[7]

If one considers the full life of industries, the dominance of vertical disintegration is surely to be expected. Young industries are often strangers to the established economic system. They require new kinds or qualities of materials and hence make their own; they must overcome technical problems in the use of their products and cannot wait for potential users to overcome them; they must persuade customers to abandon other commodities and find no specialized merchants to undertake this task. These young industries must design their specialized equipment and often manufacture it, and they must undertake to recruit (historically, often to import) skilled labor. When the industry has attained a certain size and prospects, many of these tasks are sufficiently important to be turned over to specialists. It becomes profitable for other firms to supply equipment and raw materials, to undertake the marketing of the product and the utilization of by-products, and even to train skilled labor. And, finally, when the industry begins to decline, these subsidiary, auxiliary, and complementary industries begin also to decline, and eventually the surviving firms must begin to reappropriate functions which are no longer carried on at a sufficient rate to support independent firms.

We may illustrate this general development from the cotton textile machinery industry, much of whose history has recently become available.[8] This industry began as a part of the textile industry: each mill built a machine shop to construct and repair its machines. The subsequent history is one of progressive specialism, horizontal as well as vertical: at various times locomotives, machine tools, the designing of cotton mills, and direct selling were abandoned. When the cotton textile market declined in the 1920s, the machinery firms added new products, such as paper machinery, textile machinery for other fabrics, and wholly novel products, such as oil burners and refrigerators. Indeed, one is impressed that even the longer cyclical fluctuations seem to have affected the extent of specialism in much the same way as have the secular trends.

Of course, this is not the whole story of vertical integration, and it may be useful to sketch some of the other forces at work. The most important of these other forces, I believe, is the failure of the price system (because of monopoly or public regulation) to clear markets at prices within the limits of the marginal cost of the product (to the buyer if he makes it) and its marginal-value product (to the seller if he further fabricates it). This phenomenon was strikingly illustrated by the spate of vertical mergers in the United States during and immediately after World War II, to circumvent public and private price control and allocations. A regulated price of OA was set (Figure 2.2), at which an output of OM was produced. This quantity had a marginal value of OB to

FIGURE 2.2

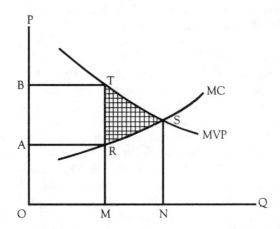

buyers, who were rationed on a nonprice basis. The gain to buyers and sellers combined from a free price of *NS* was the shaded area, *RST*, and vertical integration was the simple way of obtaining this gain. This was the rationale of the integration of radio manufacturers into cabinet manufacture, of steel firms into fabricated products, etc.

Although nonprice rationing provides the most striking examples of this force toward vertical integration, private monopolies normally supply the same incentive. Almost every raw-material cartel has had trouble with customers who wish to integrate backward, in order to negate the cartel prices. Since the cartel members are sharply limited in their output quotas, the discounted future profits of a cartel member need not be high, even with very high prices; so it is profitable for buyers to integrate backward by purchase (as well as by seeking noncartelized supply sources). The Rhenish-Westphalian Coal Cartel, for example, was constantly plagued by this problem:

> While a few of the members of the original syndicate agreement of 1893 had been steel companies which produced a part of their own coal and coke requirements, the steel industry, for the most part, had relied upon fuel purchased in the market. The stiffening of prices coupled with the inelastic terms of sale resulting from the operation of the coal syndicate, now caused the steel companies to seek to free themselves from dependence upon the syndicate.
> . . . [D]efensive measures were adopted by all classes of consumers. Some of the large industrial consumers . . . acquired their own mines individually or in groups. Among these were such important companies as the Vereinigte Stahlwerke, Rhenische Stahlwerk-Admiral, Badische Anilin- und Soda-

fabrik, Norddeutsche Lloyd, Friedrich Krupp, and a number of others representing the electric, gas, railway equipment, rubber and other industries. Also some cities such as Cologne and Frankfurt were among them.[9]

Monopoly is a devious thing, and it leads to vertical integration for other reasons also. A firm cannot practice price discrimination in the stages in which it does not operate; only by fabricating cable could the Aluminum Company of America sell cable at less than the ingot price in competition with copper, while maintaining a higher price on less competitive products.[10] Again, it is possible that vertical integration increases the difficulty of entry by new firms, by increasing the capital and knowledge necessary to conduct several types of operation rather than depend on rivals for supplies or markets.

These remarks are not intended to constitute a theory of vertical integration. There is doubt, indeed, that we want a theory of vertical integration except as part of a theory of the functions of a firm. As soon as one tries to classify the variegated details of production, one finds how artificial and arbitrary "vertical" relationships are. Whether one wishes to treat vertical relationships separately or as part of a general theory, however, Smith's theorem promises to be a central part of the explanation.

IV. WIDER IMPLICATIONS

If Smith's theorem is less than a complete theory of the division of functions among industries, it is also something more than this: it sheds light on several aspects of the structure and workings of economies. A few of the implications of the principle of increasing specialization will be discussed very tentatively.

One expects to find some relationship between the functional structure of an industry and its geographical structure—after all, reductions of transportation costs are a major way of increasing the extent of the market. (A reminder is hardly necessary that we are dealing with highly interdependent forces and that unilateral causation is implicitly assumed for simplicity and emphasis.) Localization is one method of increasing the economic size of an industry and achieving the gains of specialization. The auxiliary and complementary industries that must operate in intimate cooperation can seldom do so efficiently at a distance. I venture that, within a market area, geographical dispersion is a luxury that can be afforded by industries only after they have grown large (so that even the smaller production centers can reap the major gains of specialization) and that it must be sacrificed for geographical concentration, once the industry begins to shrink in size.

Closely related to this is the influence of localization upon the size of plant. The individual plants can specialize in smaller ranges of products and functions in highly localized industries (the size of the industry in some sense being held constant). In the United States geographically concentrated industries usually have fairly small plants.[11] There is also some evidence that the plants of an industry are smaller in the larger production centers. For example, in 1937 the average shoe factory in industrial areas had 137 employees, in other areas, 314 employees.[12] The dominance of medium-sized plants in highly localized industries has also been found in England.[13]

During the nineteenth century it was often said that England had the advantage of an "early start"; and this ambiguous statement had an element of truth which Smith's theorem more clearly expresses. As the largest economy in the world, it could carry specialism further than any other country, especially those "general" specialties (like railroads, shipping, banking, etc.) which are not closely attached to any one industry. England's advantage was a big start, as well as an early one.

Those too numerous people who believe that transactions between firms are expensive and those within firms are free will do well to study the organization of England during this period of eminence. In Birmingham, the center of the metal trades, specialism was carried out to an almost unbelievable extent. Consider the small-arms industry in 1860, when Birmingham was still the leading production center of the world:

Of the 5800 people engaged in this manufacture within the borough's boundaries in 1861 the majority worked within a small district round St Mary's Church. . . . The reason for the high degree of localization is not difficult to discover. The manufacture of guns, as of jewellery, was carried on by a large number of makers who specialized on particular processes, and this method of organization involved the frequent transport of parts from one workshop to another.

The master gun-maker—the entrepreneur—seldom possessed a factory or workshop. . . . Usually he owned merely a warehouse in the gun quarter, and his function was to acquire semi-finished parts and to give those out to specialized craftsmen, who undertook assembly and finishing of the gun. He purchased materials from the barrel-makers, lock-makers, sight-stampers, trigger-makers, ramrod-formers, gun-furniture makers, and, if he were engaged in the military branch, from bayonet-forgers. All of these were independent manufacturers executing the orders of several master gun-makers. . . . Once the parts had been purchased from the "material-makers," as they were called, the next task was to hand them out to a long succession of "setters-up," each of whom performed a specific operation in connection with the assembly and finishing of the gun. To name only a few, there were those who prepared the front sight and lump end of the barrels; the jiggers, who attended to the breech end; the stockers, who let in the barrel and lock and shaped the stock; the barrel-strippers, who prepared the gun for rifling and proof; the hardeners, polishers, borers and riflers, engravers, browners, and finally the lock-freers, who adjusted the working parts.[14]

At present there is widespread imitation of American production methods abroad, and "backward" countries are presumably being supplied with our latest machines and methods. By a now overly familiar argument, we shall often be a seriously inappropriate model for industrialization on a small scale. Our processes will be too specialized to be economical on this basis. The vast network of auxiliary industries which we can take for granted here will not be available in small economies. Their educational institutions will be unable to supply narrowly specialized personnel; they will lack the specialists who can improve raw materials and products. At best, the small economies that imitate us can follow our methods of doing things this year, not our methods of changing things next year; therefore, they will be very rigid. This position has been stated well by one observant citizen of a backward economy, Benjamin Franklin:

> Manufactures, where they are in perfection, are carried on by a multiplicity of hands, each of which is expert only in his own part, no one of them a master of the whole; and if by any means spirited away to a foreign country, he is lost without his fellows. Then it is a matter of extremest difficulty to persuade a complete set of workmen, skilled in all parts of a manufactory, to leave their country together and settle in a foreign land. Some of the idle and drunken may be enticed away, but these only disappoint their employers, and serve to discourage the undertaking. If by royal munificence, and an expense that the profits of the trade alone would not bear, a complete set of good and skilful hands are collected and carried over, they find so much of the system imperfect, so many things wanting to carry on the trade to advantage, so many difficulties to overcome, and the knot of hands so easily broken by death, dissatisfaction, and desertion, that they and their employers are discouraged altogether, and the project vanishes into smoke.[15]

The division of labor is not a quaint practice of eighteenth-century pin factories; it is a fundamental principle of economic organization.

NOTES

1. "Increasing Returns and Economic Progress," *Economic Journal* 38 (1928); 529.

2. We can either draw separate cost curves for the various functions or combine them on one chart, with the scales of the functions chosen so that the optimum amount of each function is shown for the given rate of final output.

3. S. J. Chapman and T. S. Ashton, "The Sizes of Businesses, Mainly in the Textile Industries," *Journal of the Royal Statistical Society* 77 (1914): 538.

4. This is not a wholly rigorous implication, however. With the growth of industries, specialism of firms may take the form of dealing with a narrower range of products as well as performing fewer functions on the same range of products.

5. W. Thorp, *The Integration of Industrial Operation* (Washington: 1924), p. 238. I have omitted railroad repair shops and also the 301 companies having establishments which made successive products, because mining establishments were included.

6. W. F. Crowder, *The Integration of Manufacturing Operations* ("T.N.E.C. Monographs," no. 27 [Washington: 1941]), p. 197.

7. The ratio of "value-added" to value of product is a crude index of the extent of vertical integration *within* establishments. It is interesting to note that in the seventeen industries in which this ratio was highest in 1939 in manufacturing, the average number of wage-earners was 16,540. In the seventeen industries in which the ratio was lowest, the average number of wage-earners was 44,449. Thus the vertically integrated establishments were in smaller industries than the vertically disintegrated establishments (see National Resources Planning Board, *Industrial Location and National Resources* [Washington: 1943], p. 270).

8. G. S. Gibb, *The Saco-Lowell Shops* (Cambridge: Harvard University Press, 1950); T. R. Navin, *The Whitin Machine Works Since 1831* (Cambridge: Harvard University Press, 1950).

9. A. H. Stockder, *Regulating an Industry* (New York; 1932), pp. 8, 11, and 36.

10. D. H. Wallace, *Market Control in the Aluminum Industry* (Cambridge: Harvard University Press, 1937), pp. 218–19, 380.

11. National Resources Planning Board, op. cit., pp. 250 ff.

12. Ibid., p. 257.

13 P. S. Florence, *Investment, Location, and Size of Plant* (Cambridge: 1948).

14. G. C. Allen, *The Industrial Development of Birmingham and the Black Country, 1860–1927* (London: 1929), pp. 56–57, 116–17. Commenting on a later period, Allen says: "On the whole, it can be said that specialization was most apparent in the engineering industries in which output was rapidly expanding; while the policy of broadening the basis [product line] was found, mainly, either in the very large concerns, or in industries in which the decline of the older markets had forced manufacturers to turn part of their productive capacity to serve new demands" (ibid., pp. 335–36). The later history of the gun trade, in which American innovations in production techniques were revolutionary, suggests that the organization in Birmingham was defective in its provision for technical experimentation.

15. "The Interest of Great Britain in America," cited by V. S. Clark, *History of Manufactures in the United States* (New York: 1949), I, p. 152. Clark adds: "In these words Franklin was but reciting the history of the most important colonial attempts to establish a new industry or to enlarge an old one with which he was personally familiar."

THE ECONOMIES
OF SCALE*

· 3 ·

The theory of the economies of scale is the theory of the relationship between the scale of use of a properly chosen combination of all productive services and the rate of output of the enterprise. In its broadest formulation this theory is a crucial element of the economic theory of social organization, for it underlies every question of market organization and the role (and locus) of governmental control over economic life. Let one ask himself how an economy would be organized if every economic activity were prohibitively inefficient upon alternately a small scale and a large scale, and the answer will convince him that here lies a basic element of the theory of economic organization.

The theory has limped along for a century, collecting large pieces of good reasoning and small chunks of empirical evidence but never achieving scientific prosperity. A large cause of its poverty is that the central concept of the theory—the firm of optimum size—has eluded confident measurement. We have been dangerously close to denying Lincoln, for all economists have been ignorant of the optimum size of firm in almost every industry all of the time, and this ignorance has been an insurmountable barrier between us and the understanding of the forces which govern optimum size. It is almost as if one

From the *Journal of Law and Economics* 1 (October 1958). Copyright 1958 by the University of Chicago.

* This paper was prepared at the National Bureau of Economic Research. I must thank Nestor Terleckyj for performing most of the statistical work.

were trying to measure the nutritive values of goods without knowing whether the consumers who ate them continued to live.

The central thesis of this paper is that the determination of the optimum size is not difficult if one formalizes the logic that sensible men have always employed to judge efficient size. This technique, which I am old-fashioned enough to call the survivor technique, reveals the optimum size in terms of private costs—that is, in terms of the environment in which the enterprise finds itself. After discussing the technique, we turn to the question of how the forces governing optimum size may be isolated.

I. THE SURVIVOR PRINCIPLE

The optimum size (or range of sizes) of enterprises in an industry is now ascertained empirically by one of three methods. The first is that of direct comparison of actual costs of firms of different sizes; the second is the comparison of rates of return on investment; and the third is the calculation of probable costs of enterprises of different sizes in the light of technological information. All three methods are practically objectionable in demanding data which are usually unobtainable and seldom up-to-date. But this cannot be the root of their difficulties, for there is up-to-date information on many economic concepts which are complex and even basically incapable of precise measurement (such as income). The plain fact is that we have not demanded the data because we have been unable to specify what we wanted.

The comparisons of both actual costs and rates of return are strongly influenced by the valuations which are put on productive services, so that an enterprise which over- or undervalues important productive services, will under- or overstate its efficiency. Historical cost valuations of resources, which are most commonly available, are in principle irrelevant under changed conditions. Valuations based upon expected earnings yield no information on the efficiency of an enterprise—in the limiting case where all resources are so valued, all firms would be of equal efficiency judged by either average costs or rates of return. The ascertainment on any scale of the maximum value of each resource in alternative uses is a task which only the unsophisticated would assume and only the omniscient would discharge. The host of valuation problems are accentuated by the variable role of the capital markets in effecting revaluations and the variable attitudes of the accountants toward the revaluations.[1]

The technological studies of costs of different sizes of plant encounter equally formidable obstacles. These studies are compounded of some fairly precise (although not necessarily very relevant) technical information and some crude guesses on nontechnological aspects such as marketing costs,

transportation rate changes, labor relations, etc.—that is, much of the problem is solved only in the unhappy sense of being delegated to a technologist.
Even ideal results, moreover, do not tell us the optimum size of firm in industry
A in 1958, but rather the optimum size of new plants in the industry, on the
assumption that the industry starts *de novo* or that only a small increment of
investment is being made.

The survivor technique avoids both the problems of valuation of resources
and the hypothetical nature of the technological studies. Its fundamental
postulate is that the competition of different sizes of firms sifts out the more
efficient enterprises. In the words of Mill, who long ago proposed the
technique:

> Whether or not the advantages obtained by operating on a large-scale
> preponderate in any particular case over the more watchful attention, and
> greater regard to minor gains and losses usually found in small establish-
> ments, can be ascertained, in a state of free competition, by an unfailing
> test. . . . Wherever there are large and small establishments in the same
> business, that one of the two which in existing circumstances carries on the
> production at the greater advantage will be able to undersell the other.[2]

Mill was wrong only in suggesting that the technique was inapplicable under
oligopoly, for even under oligopoly the drive of maximum profits will lead to
the disappearance of relatively inefficient sizes of firms.

The survivor technique proceeds to solve the problem of determining the
optimum firm size as follows: classify the firms in an industry by size, and
calculate the share of industry output coming from each class over time. If the
share of a given class falls, it is relatively inefficient, and in general is more
inefficient the more rapidly the share falls.

An efficient size of firm, on this argument, is one that meets any and all
problems the entrepreneur actually faces: strained labor relations, rapid innovation, government regulation, unstable foreign markets, and what not. This
is, of course, the decisive meaning of efficiency from the viewpoint of the
enterprise. Of course, social efficiency may be a very different thing: the most
efficient firm size may arise from possession of monopoly power, undesirable
labor practices, discriminatory legislation, etc. The survivor technique is not
directly applicable to the determination of the socially optimum size of
enterprise, and we do not enter into this question. The socially optimum firm
is fundamentally an ethical concept, and we question neither its importance
nor its elusiveness.

Not only is the survivor technique more direct and simpler than the
alternative techniques for the determination of the optimum size of firm, it is
also more authoritative. Suppose that the cost, rate of return, and tech-

nological studies all find that in a given industry the optimum size of firm is one which produces 500 to 600 units per day, and that costs per unit are much higher if one goes far outside this range. Suppose also that most of the firms in the industry are three times as large, and that those firms which are in the 500 to 600-unit class are rapidly failing or growing to a larger size. Would we believe that the optimum size was 500 to 600 units? Clearly not: an optimum size that cannot survive in rivalry with other sizes is a contradiction, and some error, we would all say, has been made in the traditional studies. Implicitly all judgments on economies of scale have always been based directly upon, or at least verified by recourse to, the experience of survivorship.

This is not to say that the findings of the survivor technique are unequivocal. Entrepreneurs may make mistakes in their choice of firm size, and we must seek to eliminate the effects of such errors either by invoking large numbers of firms so errors tend to cancel or by utilizing time periods such that errors are revealed and corrected. Or the optimum size may be changing because of changes in factor prices or technology, so that perhaps the optimum size rises in one period and falls in another. This problem too calls for a close examination of the time periods which should be employed. We face these problems in our statistical work below.

We must also recognize that a single optimum size of firm will exist in an industry only if all firms have (access to) identical resources. Since various firms employ different kinds or qualities of resources, there will tend to develop a frequency distribution of optimum firm sizes. The survivor technique may allow us to estimate this distribution; in the application below we restrict ourselves to the range of optimum sizes.

The measure of the optimum size is only a first step toward the construction of a theory of economies of scale with substantive content, but it is the indispensable first step. We turn in later sections of this paper to the examination of the methods by which hypotheses concerning the determinants of optimum size may be tested.

II. Illustrative Survivorship Measures

The survivor principle is very general in scope and very flexible in application, and these advantages can best be brought out by making concrete applications of the principle to individual industries. These applications will also serve to display a number of problems of data and interpretation which are encountered in the use of the survivor technique. We begin with the American steel industry.

In order that survivorship of firms of a given size be evidence of comparative efficiency, these firms must compete with firms of other sizes—all of

TABLE 3.1
DISTRIBUTION OF OUTPUT OF STEEL INGOT CAPACITY
BY RELATIVE SIZE OF COMPANY

Company Size (percent of industry total)	1930	1938	1951
1. Percent of Industry Capacity			
Under ½	7.16	6.11	4.65
½ to 1	5.94	5.08	5.37
1 to 2½	13.17	8.30	9.07
2½ to 5	10.64	16.59	22.21
5 to 10	11.18	14.03	8.12
10 to 25	13.24	13.99	16.10
25 and over	38.67	35.91	34.50
2. Number of Companies			
Under ½	39	29	22
½ to 1	9	7	7
1 to 2½	9	6	6
2½ to 5	3	4	5
5 to 10	2	2	1
10 to 25	1	1	1
25 and over	1	1	1

SOURCES: *Directory of Iron and Steel Works of the United States and Canada*, 1930, 1938; *Iron Age*, January 3, 1952.

the firms must sell in a common market. We have therefore restricted the analysis to firms making steel ingots by open-hearth or Bessemer processes.[3] Size has perforce been measured by capacity, for production is not reported by individual companies, and capacity is expressed as a percentage of the industry total to eliminate the influence of the secular growth of industry and company size.[4] The geographical extent of the market is especially difficult to determine in steel, for the shifting geographical pattern of consumption has created a linkage between the various regional markets. We treat the market as national, which exaggerates its extent, but probably does less violence to the facts than a sharp regional classification of firms. The basic data are given in Table 3.1.

Over two decades covered by Table 3.1 (and, for that matter, over the last half century) there has been a persistent and fairly rapid decline in the share of the industry's capacity in firms with less than half a percent of the total, so that we may infer that this size of firm is subject to substantial diseconomies of scale.[5] The firms with .5 to 2.5 percent of industry capacity showed a moderate decline, and hence were subject to smaller diseconomies of scale. The one firm with more than one-fourth of industry capacity declined moderately, so it too had diseconomies of scale. The intervening sizes, from 2.5 to 25 percent of industry capacity, grew or held their share so they constituted the range of optimum size.

The more rapid the rate at which a firm loses its share of the industry's output (or, here, capacity), the higher is its private cost of production relative to the cost of production of firms of the most efficient size.[6] This interpretation should not be reversed, however, to infer that the size class whose share is growing more rapidly is more efficient than other classes whose shares are growing more slowly; the difference can merely represent differences in the quantities of various qualities of resources.[7] In the light of these considerations we translate the data of Table 3.1 into a long run average cost curve for the production of steel ingots and display this curve in Figure 3.1. Over a wide range of outputs there is no evidence of net economies or diseconomies of scale.

Although the survivor test yields an estimate of the shape of the long run cost curve, it does not allow an estimate of how much higher than the minimum are the costs of the firm sizes whose shares of industry output are declining. Costs are higher the more rapid the rate at which the firm size loses its share of industry output, but the rate at which a firm size loses a share of industry output will also vary with numerous other factors. This rate of loss of output will be larger, the less durable and specialized the productive resources of the firm, for then exit from the industry is easier. The rate of loss will also be larger, the more nearly perfect the capital and labor markets, so that resources can be obtained to grow quickly to more efficient size. The rate of loss will be smaller, given the degree of inefficiency, the more profitable the industry is, for then the rate of return of all sizes of firms is larger relative to other industries.

By a simple extension of this argument, we may also estimate the most efficient size of *plant* in the steel ingot industry during the same period (Table 3.2). We again find that the smallest plants have a tendency to decline relative to the industry, and indeed this is implied by the company data. There is no systematic tendency toward decline in shares held by plants between .75 percent and 10 percent of the industry size. We may therefore infer that the tendency of very small plants and companies to decline relative to the industry is due to the diseconomy of a small plant, and the tendency of the largest company (U.S. Steel) to decline has been due to diseconomies of multiplant operation beyond a certain scale.

An equally important and interesting industry, passenger automobiles, uncovers different problems. Here we can use production data instead of capacity, and have no compunctions in treating the market as national in scope. The basic data for the individual firms are given in Table 3.3.

FIGURE 3.1

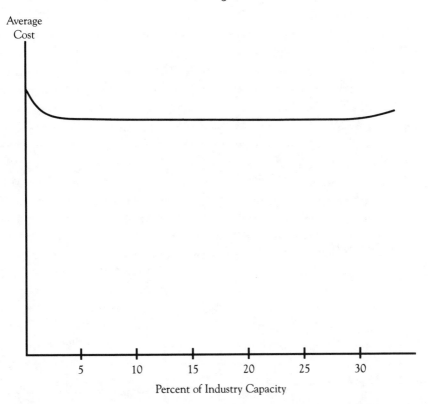

A striking feature of the automobile industry is the small number of firms, and this poses a statistical problem we have glossed over in our discussion of steel: what confidence can be attached to changes in the share of industry output coming from a firm size when that size contains very few firms? For the automobile industry (unlike steel) we possess annual data, and can therefore take into account the steadiness of direction or magnitude of changes in share of various firm sizes, and to this extent increase our confidence in the estimates. We may also extend the period which is surveyed, although at the risk of combining periods with different sizes of optimum firms. Aside from recourse to related data (the survivorship pattern of the industry in other countries, for example), there is no other method of reducing the uncertainty of findings for small number industries.

The survivorship record in automobiles (summarized in Table 3.4) is more complicated than that for steel. In the immediate prewar years there was

TABLE 3.2

DISTRIBUTION OF OUTPUT OF STEEL INGOT CAPACITY

Plant Size (percent of industry total)	1930	1938	1951
1. Percent of Industry Capacity			
Under ¼	3.74	3.81	3.25
¼ to ½	6.39	5.81	7.20
½ to ¾	6.39	4.18	3.82
¾ to 1	9.42	12.29	10.93
1 to 1¾	21.78	15.56	20.67
1¾ to 2½	13.13	16.73	17.01
2½ to 3¾	23.49	17.18	8.10
3¾ to 5	8.82	12.07	12.46
5 to 10	6.82	12.37	16.56
2. Number of Plants			
Under ¼	40	29	23
¼ to ½	20	16	18
½ to ¾	11	7	6
¾ to 1	11	14	12
1 to 1¾	18	13	15
1¾ to 2½	6	8	8
2½ to 3¾	8	6	3
3¾ to 5	2	3	3
5 to 10	1	2	3

SOURCE: Same as Table 3.1.

already a tendency for the largest company to produce a rising share and for the 2.5 to 5 percent class to produce a sharply declining share; the smallest and next to largest sizes showed no clear tendency. In a longer span of time, however, the smallest companies reveal a fairly consistently declining share.[8] In the immediate postwar period, the 2.5 to 5 percent size class was strongly favored by the larger companies' need to practice price control in a sensitive political atmosphere, and the same phenomenon reappeared less strongly in the first two years after the outbreak of Korean hostilities. From this record we would infer that there have been diseconomies of large size, at least for the largest size of firm, in inflationary periods with private or public price control, but substantial economies of large scale at other times. The long-run, average-cost curve is saucer-shaped in inflationary times, but shows no tendency to rise at the largest outputs in other times.

TABLE 3.3

PERCENTAGES OF PASSENGER AUTOMOBILES PRODUCED IN UNITED STATES
BY VARIOUS COMPANIES, 1936–1941 AND 1946–1955

Year	General Motors	Chrys-ler	Ford	Hudson	Nash	Kaiser	Willys Over-land	Packard	Stude-baker	Other
1936	42.9	23.6	22.6	3.3	1.5	—	0.7	2.2	2.4	0.8
1937	40.9	24.2	22.6	2.7	2.2	—	2.0	2.8	2.1	0.5
1938	43.9	23.8	22.3	2.5	1.6	—	0.8	2.5	2.3	0.3
1939	43.0	22.7	21.8	2.8	2.3	—	0.9	2.6	3.7	0.3
1940	45.9	25.1	19.0	2.3	1.7	—	0.7	2.1	3.1	0.1
1941	48.3	23.3	18.3	2.1	2.1	—	0.8	1.8	3.2	0.1
1946	38.4	25.0	21.2	4.2	4.6	0.6	0.3	1.9	3.6	0.2
1947	40.4	21.7	21.3	2.8	3.2	4.1	0.9	1.6	3.5	0.5
1948	40.1	21.2	19.1	3.6	3.1	4.6	0.8	2.5	4.2	0.7
1949	43.0	21.9	21.0	2.8	2.8	1.2	0.6	2.0	4.5	0.2
1950	45.7	18.0	23.3	2.1	2.8	2.2	0.6	1.1	4.0	0.1
1951	42.2	23.1	21.8	1.8	3.0	1.9	0.5	1.4	4.2	0.1
1952	41.5	22.0	23.2	1.8	3.5	1.7	1.1	1.4	3.7	—
1953	45.7	20.3	25.2	1.2	2.2	1.0		1.3	3.0	—
1954	52.2	13.1	30.6	1.7		0.3		0.5	1.6	—
1955	50.2	17.2	28.2	2.0		0.1		2.3		—

SOURCE: *Hard's Automotive Yearbook*, 1951, 1955, 1956.

The automobile example suggests the method by which we determine whether changing technology, factor prices, or consumer demands lead to a change in the optimum firm size. We infer an underlying stability in the optimum size in those periods in which the survivorship trends are stable. Indeed it is hard to conceive of an alternative test; one can judge the economic importance, in contrast to technological originality, of an innovation only by the impact it has upon the size distribution of firms.

Before we leave these applications of the survivorship technique we should indicate its flexibility in dealing with other problems which seem inappropriate to our particular examples. For example, a Marshallian may object that firms must begin small and grow to optimum size through time, so that the size structure of the industry in a given period will reflect this historical life pattern as well as the optimum size influences. In an industry such as retail trade this interpretation would be quite plausible. It can be met by studying the survivor experience of firm sizes in the light of the age or rate of growth of the firms.

TABLE 3.4

PERCENTAGE OF PASSENGER AUTOMOBILES PRODUCED BY
VARIOUS COMPANY SIZES

| Year | COMPANY SIZE (AS PERCENT OF INDUSTRY) | | | | NUMBER OF COMPANIES | |
	Over 35 percent	10–35 percent	2½–5 percent	Under 2½ percent	2½–5 percent	Under 2½ percent
1936	42.9	46.2	3.3	7.6	1	5[a]
1937	40.9	46.8	5.5	6.8	2	4[a]
1938	43.9	46.1	5.0	5.0	2	4[a]
1939	43.0	44.4	9.1	3.5	3	4[a]
1940	45.9	44.1	3.1	6.9	1	6[a]
1941	48.4	41.6	3.2	6.8	1	5
1946	38.4	46.2	12.4	3.0	3	4
1947	40.4	43.0	13.6	3.0	4	3
1948	40.1	40.3	18.0	1.5	5	2
1949	43.0	42.9	10.0	4.0	3	4
1950	45.7	41.3	6.8	6.1	2	5
1951	42.2	44.9	7.2	5.7	2	5
1952	41.5	45.2	7.2	6.1	2	5
1953	45.6	45.5	3.0	5.8	1	4
1954	52.2	43.7	0	4.1	0	4
1955	50.2	45.4	0	4.4	0	3

SOURCE: Table 3.3
[a] Or more.

Again, one may argue that firms of different sizes have different comparative advantages at different stages of the business cycle. Such a hypothesis could be dealt with by comparing average survivorship patterns in given cycle stages with those calculated for full cycles.

Let us now turn to the methods by which one may test hypotheses on the determinants of optimum size.

III. INTERINDUSTRY ANALYSES OF THE DETERMINANTS OF OPTIMUM SIZE

Once the optimum firm size has been ascertained for a variety of industries, the relationship between size and other variables can be explored. This is in fact the customary procedure for economists to employ, and the present investigation differs, aside from the method of determining optimum size, only in being more systematic than most such investigations. For example, numerous economists have asserted that advertising is a force making for large firms, and they usually illustrate this relationship by the cigarette industry. Will the relationship still hold when it is tested against a list of industries which has not been chosen to illustrate it? This is essentially the type of inquiry we make here.

Although the survivor method makes lesser demands of data than other methods to determine optimum firm size, it has equally exacting requirements of information on any other variable whose influence is to be studied. In the subsequent investigation of some 48 ("three-digit") manufacturing industries, whose optimum firm size is calculated from data in *Statistics of Income*, we have therefore been compelled to exclude some variables for lack of data and to measure others in a most imperfect manner. The industries we study, and the measures we contrive, are given in Table 3.5; we describe their derivation below.

1. *Size of firm*. The optimum size of firm in each industry is determined by comparing the percentage of the industry's assets possessed by firms in each asset class in 1948 and 1951.[9] Those classes in which the share of the industry's assets was stable or rising were identified, and the average assets of the firms within these sizes was calculated.[10] The range of optimum sizes is also given in Table 3.5. An industry was excluded if it had a very large noncorporate sector (for which we could not measure firm size) or gave strong evidence of heterogeneity by having two widely separated optimum sizes (as, for example, in "aircraft and parts").

2. *Advertising expenditures*. We have already remarked that extensive advertising is often mentioned as an explanation for the growth of large firms, especially in consumer goods industries such as cigarettes, liquor, and cosmetics. The argument supporting this view can take one of three directions. First, national advertising may be viewed as more efficient than local advertising, in terms of sales per dollar of advertising at a given price. Second, long continued advertising may have a cumulative impact. Finally, and closely related to the preceding point, the joint advertising of a series of related products may be more efficient than advertising them individually. We measure the variable by the ratio of advertising expenditures to sales, both taken from *Statistics of Income*.

3. *Technology and research*. A host of explanations of firm size are related to technological characteristics and research. Complicated production processes may require large companies, or at least large plants. The economies of research are held to be substantial; the outcome of individual projects is uncertain, so small programs are more risky; a balanced research team may be fairly large; and much capital may be

TABLE 3.5

BASIC DATA ON FORTY-EIGHT MANUFACTURING INDUSTRIES

Industry	Optimum Company Size (in thousand dollars of total assets) (1948–51)	Optimum Range Class Limits (in thousand dollars) From	To	Average Establishment Size (in thousand dollars of value-added) (1947)	Number of Chemists and Engineers per 100 Employed (1950)	Advertising Expenditure as percent of Gross Sales (1950)
Motor vehicles, incl. bodies and truck trailers	$827,828	$100,000	open	$ 3,715	1.5879	0.4395
Petroleum refining	765,716	100,000	open	3,420	6.9171	0.4562
Blast furnaces, steel works and rolling mills	525,485	100,000	open	8,310	2.0956	0.1321
Dairy products	446,483	100,000	open	110	0.7865	1.5221
Distilled, rectified and blended liquors	248,424	100,000	open	2,090	0.9041	1.3674
Pulp, paper, and paperboard	203,794	100,000	open	1,645	1.4927	0.3357
Paints, varnishes, lacquers, etc.	175,404	100,000	open	394	6.0431	1.3539
Railroad equipment, incl. locomotives and streetcars	150,217	100,000	open	3,407	2.7171	0.3611
Tires and tubes	141,600	10,000	open	11,406	2.0974a	0.9453
Grain mill products excl. cereals preparations	128,363	100,000	open	210	1.0344	1.2492
Drugs and medicines	123,662	100,000	open	552	6.2599	8.3858
Smelting, refining, rolling, drawing and alloying of nonferrous metals	100,398	10,000	open	1,658	2.9845b	0.4088
Office and store machines	65,914	10,000	open	1,411	2.5860	1.5812
Bakery products	58,960	50,000	100,000	192	0.2359	2.1335
Yarn and thread	44,375	10,000	open	687	0.4461	0.3238
Carpets and other floor coverings	37,337	10,000	100,000	1,119	1.2391	1.7295
Broadwoven fabrics (wool)	31,265	10,000	open	1,211	0.4461	0.3400
Watches, clocks, and clock work operated devices	31,025	10,000	50,000	705	1.2027c	5.3238
Cement	29,554	10,000	100,000	1,600	2.1277	0.2726
Malt liquors and malt	28,922	10,000	open	1,750	0.9041	4.7962
Agricultural machinery and tractors	28,291	1,000	open	684	2.1816	0.8956

Industry						
Structural clay products	24,001	10,000	100,000	253	1.6292	0.4552
Newspapers	23,428	10,000	100,000	168	0.1348[d]	0.1948
Knit goods	17,918	10,000	100,000	273	0.1244	0.8522
Confectionary	13,524	5,000	50,000	335	0.5950	2.6281
Commercial printing including lithographing	11,939	5,000	50,000	97	0.1348[d]	0.6474
Furniture—household, office, public building, and professional	11,378	5,000	50,000	209	0.3990[e]	0.9152
Men's clothing	10,077	5,000	50,000	247	0.0456[f]	0.8795
Dyeing and finishing textiles, excl. knit goods	9,625	5,000	50,000	545	1.1223	0.3472
Canning fruit, vegetables and seafood	6,536	1,000	open	240	0.9144	1.8462
Broadwoven fabrics (cotton)	5,847	50	open	2,595	0.4461[g]	0.2822
Footwear, excl. rubber	4,359	1,000	100,000	524	0.1474	1.1619
Paperbags, and paperboard containers and boxes	4,127	1,000	100,000	428	0.6939	0.1854
Cigars	3,753	250	50,000	174	0.2274[h]	2.3188
Meat products	2,665	500	100,000	322	0.5983	0.4264
Nonferrous foundries	2,365	500	50,000	172	2.9845[a]	0.2793
Fur goods	1,966	1,000	5,000	55	0.0456[f]	0.4119
Partitions, shelving, lockers, etc.	1,545	500	50,000	121	0.3990[e]	0.8678
Narrow fabrics and other small wares	1,382	500	5,000	226	0.4461[g]	0.3212
Wines	1,304	500	5,000	227	0.9041[i]	3.5854
Women's clothing	1,304	500	50,000	150	0.0456[f]	0.9150
Books	1,137	50	50,000	399	0.1348[d]	2.8796
Periodicals	1,117	250	10,000	307	0.1348[d]	0.5245
Leather—tanning, curing and finishing	764	0	10,000	720	0.8140	0.1813
Concrete, gypsum and plaster products	762	250	10,000	53	2.1277[c]	0.6855
Window and door screens, shades and venetian blinds	667	100	10,000	110	0.3990[e]	1.0581
Non-alcoholic beverages	546	100	50,000	75	0.9041[i]	4.0740
Millinery	468	250	5,000	108	0.0456[f]	0.4438

[a] Rubber products.
[b] Primary nonferrous.
[c] Cement, and concrete, gypsum, and plaster products.
[d] Printing, publishing and allied industries.
[e] Furniture and fixtures.
[f] Apparel and accessories.
[g] Yarn, thread, and fabric mills.
[h] Tobacco manufactures.
[i] Beverage industries.

required to bring a new process to a commercial stage and to wait for a return upon the outlay.

At present there is no direct measure available for either the importance of research or the intricacy of technology.[11] We use an index, chemists and engineers as a ratio to all employees, that may reflect both influences, but probably very imperfectly. When it becomes possible to make a division of these personnel between research and routine operation, a division which would be very valuable for other purposes also, the interpretation of an index of technical personnel will be less ambiguous.

4. *Plant size.* Plant size normally sets a minimum to company size, and therefore exerts an obvious influence on the differences among industries in company size. We are compelled to resort to a measure of plant size—value added per establishment in 1947—which is not directly comparable to company size because the 1947 Census of Manufactures did not report corporate establishments at the requisite level of detail.[12]

Preliminary analysis revealed that there is no significant relationship between firm size and advertising expenditures, so this variable was omitted from the statistical calculations. The average ratio of advertising expenditures to sales was 1.97 percent in consumer goods industries and 0.57 percent in producer goods industries, but in neither group was there a significant relationship between the ratio and firm size.[13]

A regression analysis confirms the impression one gets from Table 3.5 that the other variables we examine are positively related to optimum firm size:

$$X_1 = -5.092 + 34.6X_2 + 42.7X_3,$$
$$(10.8) \quad (12.2)$$

where X_1 is firm size, in millions of dollars of assets,

X_2 is plant size, in millions of dollars of value added,

X_3 is engineers and chemists per 100 employees.

The standard errors of the regression coefficients are given below the coefficients.[14]

An examination of Table 3.5 suggests that the correlation would be higher if the data were somewhat more precise. The size of plant is unduly low in motor vehicles, because of the inclusion of suppliers of parts. Moreover, the plant sizes have not been estimated by the survivor technique. Technological personnel are exaggerated in nonferrous foundries because we are compelled to use the ratio for a broader class, and the same is true of concrete products. The relatively small size of company in footwear, as compared to plant size, is at least partially due to the fact that the machinery was usually leased, and hence not included in assets. Industries which are "out of line" have not been omitted, however, for similar considerations may have caused other industries to be "in line." Yet the general impression is that the correlation would rise substantially with improved measurements of the variables.

The range of optimum sizes is generally wide, although the width is exaggerated, and our measurements impaired, because the largest asset class (over $100 million) embraces numerous firms of very different sizes—growth and inflation are outmoding the size classes used in *Statistics of Income*. In ten industries only this largest size has had a rising share of industry assets, and in another nine industries it is included in the range of sizes with rising shares. When the upper limit of optimum sizes is known, the range of optimum sizes is typically three or four times the average size of the firms in these sizes.

The results of this exploratory interindustry study are at least suggestive— not only in their specific content but also in pointing out a line of attack on the economies of scale that escapes that confession of failure, the case method. The chief qualifications that attach to the findings are due to the imperfections of the data: the industry categories are rather wide; and the measure of technical personnel is seriously ambiguous. At least one finding—a wide range of optimum firm sizes in each industry—is so general as to deserve to be taken as the standard model in the theory of production.

IV. INTRAINDUSTRY ANALYSIS OF THE DETERMINANTS OF OPTIMUM SIZE

One may also examine the varying fates of individual firms within an industry in the search for explanations of optimum size. If, for example, firms moving to optimum size were vertically integrated and those moving to or remaining in nonoptimum size were not so integrated, we could infer that vertical integration was a requisite of the optimum firm in the industry. This approach has the advantage over the interindustry approach of not requiring the assumption that a determinant such as advertising or integration works similarly in all industries.

The intraindustry analysis, however, has a heavy disadvantage; it can be applied only to those variables for which we can obtain information on each firm and in industries with numerous firms hardly any interesting variables survive this requirement. Because we could examine so few influences, and because the results were so consistently negative, we shall be very brief in describing our results in the industry—petroleum refining—in which this approach was tried.

The basic survivor experience for companies and plants in petroleum refining is given in Tables 3.6 and 3.7, for the postwar period 1947–1954. In each case only operating plants are included, and asphalt plants and companies are excluded. Capacities are measured in terms of crude oil; as in the case of steel plants, actual outputs cannot be obtained for all companies.[15]

There is a family resemblance between the data for petroleum and steel companies: in each case there has been a substantial reduction in the share of

TABLE 3.6

DISTRIBUTION OF PETROLEUM REFINING CAPACITY
BY RELATIVE SIZE OF COMPANY

Company Size (percent of industry capacity)	1947	1950	1954
1. Percent of Industry Capacity			
Under 0.1	5.30	4.57	3.89
0.1 to 0.2	4.86	3.57	3.00
0.2 to 0.3	2.67	2.16	2.74
0.3 to 0.4	2.95	2.92	1.65
0.4 to 0.5	2.20	0	.89
0.5 to 0.75	3.04	4.66	5.05
0.75 to 1.00	.94	0	1.58
1.0 to 2.5	11.70	12.17	10.53
2.5 to 5	9.57	16.70	14.26
5 to 10	45.11	42.15	45.69
10 to 15	11.65	11.06	10.72
2. Number of Companies			
Under 0.1	130	108	92
0.1 to 0.2	34	24	22
0.2 to 0.3	11	9	11
0.3 to 0.4	8	8	5
0.4 to 0.5	5	0	2
0.5 to 0.75	5	8	8
0.75 to 1.00	1	0	2
1.0 to 2.5	6	7	6
2.5 to 5.0	3	5	5
5.0 to 10.0	7	6	7
10.0 to 15.0	1	1	1
Total	211	176	161

SOURCE: Bureau of Mines, Petroleum Refineries, including Cracking Plants in the United States, January 1, 1947, January 1, 1950, January 1, 1954, Information Circulars 7455 (March 1948), 7578 (August 1950), and 7963 (July 1954).

TABLE 3.7

DISTRIBUTION OF PETROLEUM REFINING CAPACITY BY RELATIVE SIZE OF PLANT

Plant Size	1947	1950	1954
1. Percent of Industry Capacity			
Under 0.1	8.22	7.39	6.06
0.1 to 0.2	9.06	7.60	7.13
0.2 to 0.3	6.86	4.95	3.95
0.3 to 0.4	5.45	4.99	7.28
0.4 to 0.5	4.53	6.56	4.06
0.5 to 0.75	9.95	10.47	11.82
0.75 to 1.0	5.35	7.07	8.33
1.0 to 1.5	12.11	10.36	13.38
1.5 to 2.5	17.39	23.64	22.45
2.5 to 4.0	21.08	16.96	15.54
2. Number of Plants			
Under 0.1	184	158	138
0.1 to 0.2	64	53	51
0.2 to 0.3	27	19	16
0.3 to 0.4	15	14	21
0.4 to 0.5	10	15	9
0.5 to 0.75	17	16	19
0.75 to 1.0	6	8	10
1.0 to 1.5	10	8	11
1.5 to 2.5	9	12	12
2.5 to 4.0	7	5	5
Total	349	308	292

SOURCE: Same as Table 3.6.

the largest company. In the petroleum refining industry, the size range from one-half of 1 percent to 10 percent has contained all the size classes which have stable or rising shares of industry capacity.

The plant survivor data suggest that the disappearance of the smaller companies has been due to the relative inefficiency of the smaller plants, for all plant size classes with less than one-half of 1 percent of the industry's capacity have also declined substantially. The sizes between one-half of 1 percent and 2.5 percent of industry capacity have all grown relatively, and the top plant size has declined moderately, so that the growth of company sizes beyond 2.5 percent of industry capacity has presumably been due to the economies of multiple plant operation.

It has been claimed that backward integration into crude oil pipe lines was

TABLE 3.8

INDUSTRY SHARES OF PETROLEUM REFINING COMPANIES WITH
AND WITHOUT CRUDE PIPE LINES IN 1950

Company Size (average of 1947, 1950, and 1954 percentage of industry capacity)	COMPANIES WITH PIPE LINES			COMPANIES WITHOUT PIPE LINES		
	Number 1950	Share 1947	Share 1954	Number 1950	Share 1947	Share 1954
Under 0.1	25	1.40	1.12	60	2.87	2.18
0.1 to 0.2	17	2.19	2.50	5	0.77	0.77
0.2 to 0.3	6	1.48	1.63	2	0.34	0.50
0.3 to 0.4	5	1.90	1.63	0	—	—
0.4 to 0.5	1	0.40	0.55	2	0.54	1.22
0.5 to 0.75	7	3.59	4.72	1	0.38	0.61
0.75 to 1.0	0	—	—	0	—	—
1.0 to 2.5	7	11.54	13.10	0	—	—
2.5 to 5.0	4	11.11	11.69	0	—	—
5.0 to 10.00	7	45.11	45.69	0	—	—
10.0 to 15.0	1	11.65	10.72	0	—	—
Not in existence all years	16	2.30	0.05	79	2.43	1.33
Total	96	92.67	93.40	149	7.33	6.60

SOURCE: *International Petroleum Register.*

necessary to successful operation of a petroleum refinery. We tabulate some of the material bearing on this hypothesis in Table 3.8. There does not appear to be any large difference between the changes in market shares of firms with and without pipe lines. Since all firms with more than 0.75 percent of industry refining capacity have some pipe lines, a comparison (not reproduced here) was made between changes in their market shares and crude pipe line mileage per 1,000 barrels of daily refining capacity. There was no relationship between the two variables.[16]

The intraindustry analysis has its chief role, one may conjecture, in providing a systematic framework for the analysis of the data commonly employed in industry studies. A complete analysis of the plausible determinants of firm size requires such extensive information on the individual firms in the industry as to make this an unattractive method of attack on the general theory.

V. Conclusion

The survivor technique for determining the range of optimum sizes of a firm seems well adapted to lift the theory of economies of scale to a higher level of substantive content. Although it is prey to the usual frustrations of inadequate information, the determination of optimum sizes avoids the enormously difficult problem of valuing resources properly that is encountered by alternative methods.

Perhaps the most striking finding in our exploratory studies is that there is customarily a fairly wide range of optimum sizes—the long-run marginal and average-cost curves of the firm are customarily horizontal over a long range of sizes. This finding could be corroborated, I suspect, by a related investigation: if there were a unique optimum size in an industry, increases in demand would normally be met primarily by near proportional increases in the number of firms, but it appears that much of the increase is usually met by expansion of the existing firms.

The survivor method can be used to test the numerous hypotheses on the factors determining the size of firm which abound in the literature. Our exploratory study suggests that advertising expenditures have no general tendency to lead to large firms, and another experiment (which is not reported above) indicates that fixed capital-sales ratios are also unrelated to the size of firms. The size of plant proves to be an important variable, as is to be expected, and the survivor method should be employed to determine the factors governing plant size. A rather ambiguous variable, the relative share of engineers and chemists in the labor force, also proves to be fairly important, and further data and work is necessary to disentangle research and routine technical operations. The determination of optimum size permits the investigator to examine any possible determinants which his imagination nominates and his data illuminate.

Notes

1. These problems are discussed by Milton Friedman in *Business Concentration and Price Policy*, pp. 230 ff. (1955).

2. *Principles of Political Economy*, p. 134 (Ashley ed.). Marshall states the same argument in Darwinian language: "For as a general rule the law of substitution—which is nothing more than a special and limited application of the law of survival of the fittest—tends to make one method of industrial organization supplant another when it

offers a direct and immediate service at a lower price." *Principles of Economics*, p. 597 (8th ed., 1920).

3. Crucible steel, which is made by smaller companies on average, is viewed as a separate, but closely related, industry.

4. Capacity is least objectionable as a measure of firm size in an industry where production is continuous round the clock and the upward trend of output confers relevance on capacity. Both steel and our later example of petroleum refining meet these conditions.

5. In 1930 the firm with .5 percent of the industry capacity had a capacity of 364,000 net tons; in 1951, 485,000 net tons. Of course, we could have employed absolute firm size classes, but they are less appropriate to many uses.

6. How shall we assess the efficiency of a size of firm which merely holds its share of industry output or capacity? Although more subtle interpretations are possible, it seems simplest to view this size class as one whose trend of industry share is imperfectly estimated from the data, and that with fuller data (i.e., for more firms or a longer period), all firm sizes would display rising or falling industry shares.

7. For example, one firm size within the optimum range may utilize superior salesmen, another firm size inferior salesmen (at suitably lower rates of pay), and the relative numbers of the two types will influence the relative growth in the industry shares of the two sizes.

8. See Federal Trade Commission, *Report on Motor Vehicle Industry*, p. 29 (1939).

9. These particular dates were dictated by the data; there were large changes in industry classification in 1948, and no minor industry data were tabulated for 1952. A better, but more laborious, determination of optimum size could have been made if the data for intervening years were utilized.

10. A rough allowance for sampling fluctuations was made by comparing three-asset class moving averages.

11. In earlier experiments with two-digit manufacturing industries, capital-sales ratios were found to be uncorrelated with optimum firm size.

12. But even if plants were measured by assets there would be some incomparability arising out of the fact that many large firms operate in many industries but are classified according to their dominant activity.

13. The respective rank correlation coefficients were $-.187$ and $-.059$.

14. The correlation coefficients are:

$$r_{12} - .460 \qquad r_{12.3} - .400$$
$$r_{13} - .471 \qquad r_{13.2} - .413$$
$$r_{23} - .252 \qquad r_{23.1} - .046$$

15. One percent of industry capacity was 52,508 barrels per day in 1947, and 76,811 barrels in 1954. Tentative calculations for regional markets indicate that the results are not greatly affected by using a national base.

16. A corresponding investigation was made for research laboratories, which are reported in the *Directory of Research Laboratories* of the National Research Council. That the results showed no relationship between firm size and size of laboratories is not surprising, for the work of the research laboratories would influence only the firm's long-term growth.

THE ECONOMICS
OF INFORMATION[1]

· 4 ·

One should hardly have to tell academicians that information is a valuable resource: knowledge *is* power. And yet it occupies a slum dwelling in the town of economics. Mostly it is ignored: the best technology is assumed to be known; the relationship of commodities to consumer preferences is a datum. And one of the information-producing industries, advertising, is treated with a hostility that economists normally reserve for tariffs or monopolists.

There are a great many problems in economics for which this neglect of ignorance is no doubt permissible or even desirable. But there are some for which this is not true, and I hope to show that some important aspects of economic organization take on a new meaning when they are considered from the viewpoint of the search for information. In the present paper I shall attempt to analyze systematically one important problem of information—the ascertainment of market price.

I. THE NATURE OF SEARCH

Prices change with varying frequency in all markets, and, unless a market is completely centralized, no one will know all the prices which various sellers (or

From the *Journal of Political Economy* 69, no. 3 (June 1961). Copyright 1961 by the University of Chicago.

TABLE 4.1

ASKING PRICES FOR TWO COMMODITIES

A. CHEVROLETS, CHICAGO, FEBRUARY 1959[a]		B. ANTHRACITE COAL, DELIVERED (WASHINGTON, D.C.), APRIL, 1953[b]	
Price (dollars)	No. of Dealers	Price per Ton (dollars)	No. of Bids
2,350–2,400	4	15.00–15.50	2
2,400–2,450	11	15.50–16.00	2
2,450–2,500	8	16.00–16.50	2
2,500–2,550	4	16.50–17.00	3
		17.00–18.00	1
		18.00–19.00	4

[a] Allen F. Jung, "Price Variations Among Automobile Dealers in Metropolitan Chicago," *Journal of Business* 33 (January, 1960): 31–42.
[b] Supplied by John Flueck.

buyers) quote at any given time. A buyer (or seller) who wishes to ascertain the most favorable price must canvass various sellers (or buyers)—a phenomenon I shall term "search."

The amount of dispersion of asking prices of sellers is a problem to be discussed later, but it is important to emphasize immediately the fact that dispersion is ubiquitous even for homogeneous goods. Two examples of asking prices, of consumer and producer goods respectively, are displayed in Table 4.1. The automobile prices (for an identical model) were those quoted with an average amount of "higgling": their average was $2,436, their range from $2,350 to $2,515, and their standard deviation $42. The prices for anthracite coal were bids for federal government purchases and had a mean of $16.90 per ton, a range from $15.46 to $18.92, and a standard deviation of $1.15. In both cases the range of prices was significant on almost any criterion.

Price dispersion is a manifestation—and, indeed, it is the measure—of ignorance in the market. Dispersion is a biased measure of ignorance because there is never absolute homogeneity in the commodity if we include the terms of sale within the concept of the commodity. Thus, some automobile dealers might perform more service, or carry a larger range of varieties in stock, and a portion of the observed dispersion is presumably attributable to such differences. But it would be metaphysical, and fruitless, to assert that all dispersion is due to heterogeneity.

At any time, then, there will be a frequency distribution of the prices quoted by sellers. Any buyer seeking the commodity would pay whatever price is asked by the seller whom he happened to canvass, if he were content to buy

TABLE 4.2
DISTRIBUTION OF HYPOTHETICAL MINIMUM PRICES
BY NUMBERS OF BIDS CANVASSED

No. of Prices Canvassed	PROBABILITY OF MINIMUM PRICE OF		Expected Minimum Price
	$2.00	$3.00	
1	.5	.5	$2.50
2	.75	.25	2.25
3	.875	.125	2.125
4	.9375	.0625	2.0625
∞	1.0	0	2.00

from the first seller. But, if the dispersion of price quotations of sellers is at all large (relative to the cost of search), it will pay, on average, to canvass several sellers. Consider the following primitive example: let sellers be equally divided between asking prices of $2 and $3. Then the distribution of minimum prices, as search is lengthened, is shown in Table 4.2. The buyer who canvasses two sellers instead of one has an expected saving of 25 cents per unit, etc.

The frequency distributions of asking (and offering) prices have not been studied sufficiently to support any hypothesis as to their nature. Asking prices are probably skewed to the right, as a rule, because the seller of reproducible goods will have some minimum but no maximum limit on the price he can accept. If the distribution of asking prices is normal, the distributions of minimum prices encountered in searches of one, two, and three sellers will be those displayed in Figure 4.1. If the distribution is rectangular, the corresponding distributions would be those shown in Panel B. The latter assumption does not receive strong support from the evidence, but it will be used for a time because of its algebraic simplicity.

In fact, if sellers' asking prices (p) are uniformly distributed between zero and one, it can be shown that:[2] (1) the distribution of minimum prices with n searches is

$$n(1-p)^{n-1},$$ (1)

(2) the average minimum price is

$$\frac{1}{n+1},$$

and (3) the variance of the average minimum price is

$$\frac{n}{(n+1)^2(n+2)}.$$

FIGURE 4.1

DISTRIBUTION OF MINIMUM PRICES WITH VARYING AMOUNTS OF SEARCH

A. Normal Distribution

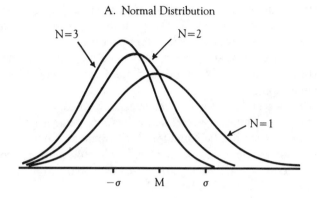

B. Uniform Distribution

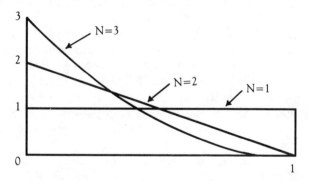

Whatever the precise distribution of prices, it is certain that increased search will yield diminishing returns as measured by the expected reduction in the minimum asking price. This is obviously true of the rectangular distribution, with an expected minimum price of $1/(n+1)$ with n searches, and also of the normal distributions.[3] In fact, if a distribution of asking prices did not display this property, it would be an unstable distribution for reasons that will soon be apparent.[4]

For any buyer the expected savings from an additional unit of search will be approximately the quantity (q) he wishes to purchase times the expected reduction in price as a result of the search,[5] or

$$q \left| \frac{\partial P_{min}}{\partial_n} \right| . \qquad (2)$$

The expected saving from given search will be greater, the greater the dispersion of prices. The saving will also obviously be greater, the greater the expenditure on the commodity. Let us defer for a time the problem of the time period to which the expenditure refers, and hence the amount of expenditure, by considering the purchase of an indivisible, infrequently purchased good— say, a used automobile.

The cost of search, for a consumer, may be taken as approximately proportional to the number of (identified) sellers approached, for the chief cost is time. This cost need not be equal for all consumers, of course: aside from differences in tastes, time will be more valuable to a person with a larger income. If the cost of search is equated to its expected marginal return, the optimum amount of search will be found.[6]

Of course, the sellers can also engage in search and, in the case of unique items, will occasionally do so in the literal fashion that buyers do. In this— empirically unimportant—case, the optimum amount of search will be such that the marginal cost of search equals the expected increase in receipts, strictly parallel to the analysis for buyers.

With unique goods the efficiency of personal search for either buyers or sellers is extremely low, because the identity of potential sellers is not known— the cost of search must be divided by the fraction of potential buyers (or sellers) in the population which is being searched. If I plan to sell a used car and engage in personal search, less than one family in a random selection of one hundred families is a potential buyer of even a popular model within the next month. As a result, the cost of search is increased more than one hundredfold per price quotation.

The costs of search are so great under these conditions that there is powerful inducement to localize transactions as a device for identifying potential buyers and sellers. The medieval markets commonly increased their efficiency in this respect by prohibiting the purchase or sale of the designated commodities within a given radius of the market or on nonmarket days. The market tolls that were frequently levied on sellers (even in the absence of effective restrictions on nonmarket transactions) were clear evidence of the value of access to the localized markets.

Advertising is, of course, the obvious modern method of identifying buyers and sellers: the *classified* advertisements in particular form a meeting place for potential buyers and sellers. The identification of buyers and sellers reduces drastically the cost of search. But advertising has its own limitations: advertising itself is an expense, and one essentially independent of the value of the item advertised. The advertising of goods which have few potential buyers relative to the circulation of the advertising medium is especially expensive. We shall temporarily put advertising aside and consider an alternative.

The alternative solution is the development of specialized traders whose chief service, indeed, is implicitly to provide a meeting place for potential buyers and sellers. A used-car dealer, turning over a thousand cars a year, and presumably encountering three or five thousand each of buying and selling bids, provides a substantial centralization of trading activity. Let us consider these dealer markets, which we shall assume to be competitive in the sense of there being many independent dealers.

Each dealer faces a distribution of (for example) buyers' bids and can vary his selling prices with a corresponding effect upon purchases. Even in the markets for divisible (and hence nonunique) goods there will be some scope for higgling (discrimination) in each individual transaction: the buyer has a maximum price given by the lowest price he encounters among the dealers he has searched (or plans to search), but no minimum price. But let us put this range of indeterminacy aside, perhaps by assuming that the dealer finds discrimination too expensive,[7] and inquire how the demand curve facing a dealer is determined.

Each dealer sets a selling price, p, and makes sales to all buyers for whom this is the minimum price. With a uniform distribution of asking prices by dealers, the number of buyers of a total of N_b possible buyers who will purchase from him is

$$N_i = KN_b n(1-p)^{n-1}, \tag{3}$$

where K is a constant.[8] The number of buyers from a dealer increases as his price is reduced, and at an increasing rate.[9] Moreover, with the uniform distribution of asking prices, the number of buyers increases with increased search if the price is below the reciprocal of the amount of search.[10] We should generally expect the high-price sellers to be small-volume sellers.

The stability of any distribution of asking prices of dealers will depend upon the costs of dealers. If there are constant returns to scale, the condition of equal rates of return dictates that the difference between a dealer's buying and selling prices be a constant. This condition cannot in general be met: any dealer can buy low, and sell high, provided he is content with a small volume of transactions, and he will then be earning more than costs (including a competitive rate of return). No other dealer can eliminate this noncompetitive rate of profit, although by making the same price bids he can share the volume of business, or by asking lower prices he can increase the rewards to search and hence increase the amount of search.

With economies of scale, the competition of dealers will eliminate the profitability of quoting very high selling and very low buying prices and will render impossible some of the extreme price bids. On this score, the greater the decrease in average cost with volume, the smaller will be the dispersion of prices.[11] Many distributions of prices will be inconsistent with any possible cost conditions of dealers,[12] and it is not evident that strict equalities of rates of return for dealers are generally possible.

If economies of scale in dealing lead to a smaller dispersion of asking prices than do constant costs of dealing, similarly greater amounts of search will lead to a smaller dispersion of observed selling prices by reducing the number of purchasers who will pay high prices. Let us consider more closely the determinants of search.

Determinants of Search

The equation defining optimum search is unambiguous only if a unique purchase is being made—a house, a particular used book, and so on. If purchases are repetitive, the volume of purchases based upon the search must be considered.

If the correlation of asking prices of dealers in successive time periods is perfect (and positive!), the initial search is the only one that need be undertaken. In this case the expected savings of search will be the present value of the discounted savings on all future purchases, the future savings extending over the life of the buyer or seller (whichever is shorter).[13] On the other hand, if asking prices are uncorrelated in successive time periods, the savings from search will pertain only to that period,[14] and search in each period is independent of previous experience. If the correlation of successive prices is positive, customer search will be larger in the initial period than in subsequent periods.[15]

The correlation of successive asking prices of sellers is usually positive in the handful of cases I have examined. The rank correlation of anthracite price bids (Table 4.1) in 1953 with those in 1954 was .68 for eight bidders; that for Chevrolet dealers in Chicago February and August of 1959 was .33 for twenty-nine dealers—but, on the other hand, it was zero for Ford dealers for the same dates. Most observed correlations will, of course, be positive because of stable differences in the products or services, but our analysis is restricted to conditions of homogeneity.

As a rule, positive correlations should exist with homogeneous products. The amount of search will vary among individuals because of differences in their expenditures on a commodity or differences in cost of search. A seller who wishes to obtain the continued patronage of those buyers who value the gains of search more highly or have lower costs of search must see to it that he is quoting relatively low prices. In fact, good will may be defined as continued patronage by customers without continued search (that is, no more than occasional verification).

A positive correlation of successive asking prices justifies the widely held view that inexperienced buyers (tourists) pay higher prices in a market than do experienced buyers.[16] The former have no accumulated knowledge of asking prices, and even with an optimum amount of search they will pay higher prices on average. Since the variance of the expected minimum price decreases with additional search, the prices paid by inexperienced buyers will also have a larger variance.

If a buyer enters a wholly new market, he will have no idea of the dispersion of prices and hence no idea of the rational amount of search he should make. In such cases the dispersion will presumably be estimated by some sort of sequential process, and this approach would open up a set of problems I must leave for others to explore. But, in general, one approaches a market with some general knowledge of the amount of dispersion, for dispersion itself is a function of the average amount of search, and this in turn is a function of the nature of the commodity:

1. The larger the fraction of the buyer's expenditures on the commodity, the greater the savings from search and hence the greater the amount of search.

2. The larger the fraction of repetitive (experienced) buyers in the market, the greater the effective amount of search (with positive correlation of successive prices).

3. The larger the fraction of repetitive sellers, the higher the correlation between successive prices, and hence, by condition (2), the larger the amount of accumulated search.[17]

4. The cost of search will be larger, the larger the geographical size of the market.

An increase in the number of buyers has an uncertain effect upon the dispersion of asking prices. The sheer increase in numbers will lead to an increase in the number of dealers and, *ceteris paribus*, to a larger range of asking prices. But, quite aside from advertising, the phenomenon of pooling information will increase. Information is pooled when two buyers compare prices: if each buyer canvasses s sellers, by combining they effectively canvass 2s sellers, duplications aside.[18] Consumers compare prices of some commodities (for example, liquor) much more often than of others (for example, chewing gum)—in fact, pooling can be looked upon as a cheaper (and less reliable) form of search.

Sources of Dispersion

One source of dispersion is simply the cost to dealers of ascertaining rivals' asking prices, but even if this cost were zero the dispersion of prices would not vanish. The more important limitation is provided by buyers' search, and, if the conditions and participants in the market were fixed in perpetuity, prices would immediately approach uniformity. Only those differences could persist which did not remunerate additional search. The condition for optimum search would be (with perfect correlation of successive prices):

$$q\left|\frac{\partial p}{\partial n}\right| = i \times \text{marginal cost of search,}$$

where i is the interest rate. If an additional search costs one dollar, and the interest rate is 5 percent, the expected reduction in price with one more search would at equilibrium be equal to $0.05/q$—a quantity which would often be smaller than the smallest unit of currency. But, indivisibilities aside, it would normally be unprofitable for buyers or sellers to eliminate all dispersion.

The maintenance of appreciable dispersion of prices arises chiefly out of the fact that knowledge becomes obsolete. The conditions of supply and demand, and therefore the distribution of asking prices, change over time. There is no method by which buyers or sellers can ascertain the new average price in the market appropriate to the new conditions except by search. Sellers cannot maintain perfect correlation of successive prices, even if they wish to do so, because of the costs of search. Buyers accordingly cannot make the amount of investment in search that perfect correlation of prices would justify. The greater the instability of supply and/or demand conditions, therefore, the greater the dispersion of prices will be.

In addition, there is a component of ignorance due to the changing identity of buyers and sellers. There is a flow of new buyers and sellers in every market, and they are at least initially uninformed on prices and by their presence make the information of experienced buyers and sellers somewhat obsolete.

The amount of dispersion will also vary with one other characteristic which is of special interest: the size (in terms of both dollars and number of traders) of the market. As the market grows in these dimensions, there will appear a set of firms which specialize in collecting and selling information. They may take the form of trade journals or specialized brokers. Since the cost of collection of information is (approximately) independent of its use (although the cost of dissemination is not), there is a strong tendency toward monopoly in the provision of information: in general, there will be a "standard" source for trade information.

II. Advertising

Advertising is, among other things, a method of providing potential buyers with knowledge of the identity of sellers. It is clearly an immensely powerful instrument for the elimination of ignorance—comparable in force to the use of the book instead of the oral discourse to communicate knowledge. A small five-dollar advertisement in a metropolitan newspaper reaches (in the sense of being read) perhaps twenty-five thousand readers, or fifty readers per penny, and, even if only a tiny fraction are potential buyers (or sellers), the economy they achieve in search, as compared with uninstructed solicitation, may be overwhelming.

Let us begin with advertisements designed only to identify sellers; the identification of buyers will not be treated explicitly, and the advertising of price will be discussed later. The identification of sellers is necessary because the identity of sellers changes over time, but much more because of the turnover of buyers. In every consumer market there will be a stream of new buyers (resulting from immigration or the attainment of financial maturity) requiring knowledge of sellers, and, in addition, it will be necessary to refresh the knowledge of infrequent buyers.

Suppose, what is no doubt too simple, that a given advertisement of size a will inform c percent of the potential buyers in a given period, so $c=g(a)$.[19] This contact function will presumably show diminishing returns, at least beyond a certain size of advertisement. A certain fraction, b, of potential customers will be "born" (and "die") in a stable population, where "death" includes not only departure from the market but forgetting the seller. The value of b will obviously vary with the nature of the commodity; for example, it will be larger for commodities which are seldom purchased (like a house). In a first period of advertising (at a given rate) the number of potential customers reached will be cN, if N is the total number of potential customers. In the second period cN $(1-b)$ of these potential customers will still be informed, cbN new potential customers will be informed, and

$$c[(1-b)n-cN(1-b)]$$

old potential customers will be reached for the first time, or a total of

$$cN[1+(1-b)(1-c)].$$

This generalizes, for k periods, to

$$cN[1+(1-b)(1-c)+\ldots+(1-b)^{k-1}(1-c)^{k-1}],$$

and, if k is large, this approaches

$$\frac{cN}{1-(1-c)(1-b)}=\lambda N. \tag{4}$$

The proportion (λ) of potential buyers informed of the advertiser's identity thus depends upon c and b.

If each of r sellers advertises the same amount, λ is the probability that any one seller will inform any buyer. The distribution of N potential buyers by the number of contacts achieved by r sellers is given by the binomial distribution:

$$N(\lambda+[1-\lambda])^r,$$

with, for example,

$$\frac{Nr!}{m!(r-m)!}\lambda^m(1-\lambda)^{r-m}$$

buyers being informed of exactly m sellers' identities. The number of sellers known to a buyer ranges from zero to r, with an average of $r\lambda$ sellers and a variance of $r\lambda(1-\lambda)$.[20]

The amount of relevant information in the market, even in this simple model, is not easy to summarize in a single measure—a difficulty common to frequency distributions. If all buyers wished to search s sellers, all buyers knowing less than s sellers would have inadequate information, and all who knew more than s sellers would have redundant information, although the redundant information would not be worthless.[21] Since the value of information is the amount by which it reduces the expected cost to the buyer of his purchases, if these expected reductions are $\Delta C_1, \Delta C_2, \ldots$, for searches of 1, 2,..., the value of the information to buyers is approximately

$$\sum_{m=1}^{r}\frac{r!}{m!(r-m)!}\lambda^m(1-\lambda)^{r-m}\Delta C_m.$$

The information possessed by buyers, however, is not simply a matter of chance; those buyers who spend more on the commodity, or who search more for a given expenditure, will also search more for advertisements. The buyers with more information will, on average, make more extensive searches, so the value of information will be greater than this last formula indicates.

We may pause to discuss the fact that advertising in, say, a newspaper is normally "paid" for by the seller. On our analysis, the advertising is valuable to the buyer, and he would be willing to pay more for a paper with advertisements than for one without. The difficulty with having the sellers insert advertisements "free" and having the buyer pay for them directly is that it would be difficult to ration space on this basis: the seller would have an incentive to supply an amount of information (or information of a type) the buyer did not wish, and, since numerous advertisements are supplied jointly, the buyer could not register clearly his preferences regarding advertising. (Catalogues, however, are often sold to buyers.) Charging the seller for the advertisements creates an incentive for him to supply to the buyer only the information which is desired.

It is commonly complained that advertising is jointly supplied with the commodity in the sense that the buyer must pay for both even though he wishes only the latter. The alternative of selling the advertising separately from the commodity, however, would require that the advertising of various sellers (of various commodities) would be supplied jointly: the economies of disseminating information in a general-purpose periodical are so great that some form of jointness is inescapable. But the common complaint is much exaggerated: the buyer who wishes can search out the seller who advertises little (but, of course, enough to be discoverable), and the latter can sell at prices lower by the savings on advertising.

These remarks seem most appropriate to newspaper advertisements of the "classified" variety; what of the spectacular television show or the weekly comedian? We are not equipped to discuss advertising in general because the problem of quality has been (and will continue to be) evaded by the assumption of homogeneous goods. Even within our narrower framework, however, the use of entertainment to attract buyers to information is a comprehensible phenomenon. The assimilation of information is not an easy or pleasant task for most people, and they may well be willing to pay more for the information when supplied in an enjoyable form. In principle, this complementary demand for information and entertainment is exactly analogous to the complementary demand of consumers for commodities and delivery service or air-conditioned stores. One might find a paradox in the simultaneous complaints of some peole that advertising is too elaborate and school *houses* too shoddy.

A monopolist will advertise (and price the product) so as to maximize his profits,

$$\pi = Npq\lambda - \phi(N\lambda q) - ap_a,$$

where $p = f(q)$ is the demand curve of the individual buyer, $\phi(Nq\lambda)$ is production costs other than advertising, and ap_a is advertising expenditures. The maximum profit conditions are

$$\frac{\partial \pi}{\partial q}=N\lambda\left(p+q\frac{\partial p}{\partial q}\right)-\phi'N\lambda=0 \tag{5}$$

and

$$\frac{\partial \pi}{\partial a}=Npq\frac{\partial \lambda}{\partial a}-\phi'Nq\frac{\partial \lambda}{\partial a}-p_a=0. \tag{6}$$

Equation (5) states the usual marginal cost–marginal revenue equality, and equation (6) states the equality of (price–marginal cost) with the marginal cost $[p_a/Nq(\partial\lambda/\partial a)]$ of advertising.[22]

With the Cournot spring (where production costs $\phi=0$) the monopolist advertises up to the point where price equals the marginal cost of informing a buyer: the monopolist will not (cannot) exploit ignorance as he exploits desire. The monopolist will advertise more, the higher the "death" rate (b), unless it is very high relative to the "contact" rate (c).[23] The monopolistic situation does not invite comparison with competition because an essential feature—the value of search in the face of price dispersion—is absent.

A highly simplified analysis of advertising by the competitive firm is presented in the Appendix. On the assumption that all firms are identical and that all buyers have identical demand curves and search equal amounts, we obtain the maximum-profit equation:

$$\text{Production cost}=p\left(1+\frac{1}{\eta_{qp}+\eta_{Kp}}\right), \tag{7}$$

where η_{qp} is the elasticity of a buyer's demand curve and η_{Kp} is the elasticity of the fraction of buyers purchasing from the seller with respect to his price. The latter elasticity will be of the order of magnitude of the number of searches made by a buyer. With a uniform distribution of asking prices, increased search will lead to increased advertising by low-price sellers and reduced advertising by high-price sellers. The amount of advertising by a firm decreases as the number of firms increases.

Price advertising has a decisive influence on the dispersion of prices. Search now becomes extremely economical, and the question arises why, in the absence of differences in quality of products, the dispersion does not vanish. And the answer is simply that, if prices are advertised by a large portion of the sellers, the price differences diminish sharply. That they do not wholly vanish (in a given market) is due simply to the fact that no combination of advertising media reaches all potential buyers within the available time.

Assuming, as we do, that all sellers are equally convenient in location, must we say that some buyers are perverse in not reading the advertisements? Obviously not, for the cost of keeping currently informed about all articles which an individual purchases would be prohibitive. A typical household probably buys several hundred different items a month, and, if, on average, their prices change (in some outlets) only once a month, the number of advertisements (by at least several sellers) which must be read is forbiddingly large.

The seller's problem is even greater: he may sell two thousand items (a modest number for a grocery or hardware store), and to advertise each on the occasion of a price change—and frequently enough thereafter to remind buyers of his price—would be impossibly expensive. To keep the buyers in a market informed on the current prices of all items of consumption would involve perhaps a thousandfold increase of newspaper advertising.

From the manufacturer's viewpoint, uncertainty concerning his price is clearly disadvantageous. The cost of search is a cost of purchase, and consumption will therefore be smaller, the greater the dispersion of prices and the greater the optimum amount of search. This is presumably one reason (but, I conjecture, a very minor one) why uniform prices are set by sellers of nationally advertised brands: if they have eliminated price variation, they have reduced the cost of commodity (including search) to the buyer, even if the dealers' margins average somewhat more than they otherwise would.

The effect of advertising prices, then, is equivalent to that of the introduction of a very large amount of search by a large portion of the potential buyers. It follows from our discussion in Section I that the dispersion of asking prices will be much reduced. Since advertising of prices will be devoted to products for which the marginal value of search is high, it will tend to reduce dispersion most in commodities with large aggregate expenditures.

III. Conclusions

The identification of sellers and the discovery of their prices are only one sample of the vast role of the search for information in economic life. Similar problems exist in the detection of profitable fields for investment and in the worker's choice of industry, location, and job. The search for knowledge on the quality of goods, which has been studiously avoided in this paper, is perhaps no more important but, certainly, analytically more difficult. Quality has not yet been successfully specified by economics, and this elusiveness extends to all problems in which it enters.

Some forms of economic organization may be explicable chiefly as devices for eliminating uncertainties in quality. The department store, as Milton Friedman has suggested to me, may be viewed as an institution which searches for the superior qualities of goods and guarantees that they are good quality. "Reputation" is a word which denotes the persistence of quality, and reputation commands a price (or exacts a penalty) because it economizes on search. When economists deplore the reliance of the consumer on reputation—although they choose the articles they read (and their colleagues) in good part on this basis—they implicitly assume that the consumer has a large laboratory, ready to deliver current information quickly and gratuitously.

Ignorance is like subzero weather: by a sufficient expenditure its effects upon people can be kept within tolerable or even comfortable bounds, but it would be wholly uneconomic entirely to eliminate all its effects. And, just as an analysis of man's shelter and apparel would be somewhat incomplete if cold weather is ignored, so also our understanding of economic life will be incomplete if we do not systematically take account of the cold winds of ignorance.

APPENDIX

Under competition, the amount of advertising by any one seller (i) can be determined as follows. Each buyer will engage in an amount s of search, which is determined by the factors discussed above. (Sec. I). He will on average know

$$(r-1)\lambda+\lambda_i$$

sellers, where λ_i is defined by equation (4) for seller i. Hence,

$$\frac{\lambda_i}{(r-1)\lambda+\lambda_i}$$

percent of buyers who know seller i will canvass him on one search, and

$$\left(1-\frac{\lambda_i}{(r-1)\lambda+\lambda_i}\right)^s$$

percent of the buyers who know i will not canvass him in s searches,

$$s \le (r-1)\lambda+\lambda_i.$$

Therefore, of the buyers who know i, the proportion who will canvass him at least once is[24]

$$1-\left(1-\frac{\lambda_i}{(r-1)\lambda+\lambda_i}\right)^s.$$

If we approximate

$$\frac{\lambda_i}{(r-1)\lambda+\lambda_i}$$

by

$$\frac{\lambda_i}{r\lambda}$$

and take only the first two terms of the binomial expansion, this becomes

$$\frac{s\lambda_i}{r\lambda}.$$

The receipts of any seller then become the product of (1) the number of buyers canvassing him,

$$\frac{s\lambda_i}{r\lambda}\lambda_i N=T_i,$$

(2) the fraction K of those canvassing him who buy from him, where K depends upon his relative price (and the amount of search and the number of rivals), and (3) sales to each customer, pq. If $\phi(T_iKq)$ is production costs and αp_a advertising costs, profits are

$$\pi=T_iKpq-\phi(T_iKq)-\alpha p_a.$$

The conditions for maximum profits are

$$\frac{\partial\pi}{\partial p}=T_i\left(K\frac{\partial pq}{\partial p}+pq\frac{\partial K}{\partial p}\right)-T_i\phi'\left(K\frac{\partial q}{\partial p}+q\frac{\partial K}{\partial p}\right)=0 \qquad (8)$$

and

$$\frac{\partial \pi}{\partial a} = Kpq\frac{\partial T_i}{\partial a} - \phi'Kq\frac{\partial T_i}{\partial a} - p_a = 0. \tag{9}$$

The former equation can be rewritten in elasticities as

$$\phi' = p\left(1 + \frac{1}{\eta_{qp} + \eta_{Kp}}\right) \tag{8a}$$

Price exceeds marginal cost, not simply by $(-p/\eta_{qp})$ as with monopoly, but by the smaller amount

$$\frac{-p}{\eta_{qp} + \eta_{Kp}},$$

where η_{Kp} will generally be of the order of magnitude of the number of searches made by a buyer.[25] Equation (2) states the equality of the marginal revenue of advertising with its marginal cost. By differentiating equation (2) with respect to s and taking ϕ' as constant, it can be shown that increased search by buyers will lead to increased advertising by low-price sellers and reduced advertising by high-price sellers (with a uniform distribution of prices).[26]

By the same method it may be shown that the amount of advertising by the firm will decrease as the number of rivals increases.[27] The aggregate amount of advertising by the industry may either increase or decrease with an increase in the number of firms, s, depending on the relationship between λ and α.

NOTES

1. I have benefited from comments of Gary Becker, Milton Friedman, Zvi Griliches, Harry Johnson, Robert Solow, and Lester Telser.

2. If $F(p)$ is the cumulative-frequency function of p, the probability that the minimum of n observations will be greater than p is

$$[1 - F(p)]^n = \left[\int^1 dx\right]^n.$$

3. The expected minimum prices with a normal distribution of mean M and standard deviation σ are

	Expected
Search	Minimum Price
1	M
2	M− .564σ
3	M− .846σ
4	M−1.029σ
5	M−1.163σ
6	M−1.267σ
7	M−1.352σ
8	M−1.423σ
9	M−1.485σ
10	M−1.539σ

4. Robert Solow has pointed out that the expected value of the minimum of a random sample of n observations,

$$E(n)=n\int_0^\infty p(1-F)^{n-1}F'dp,$$

is a decreasing function of n, and

$$[E(n+2)-E(n+1)]-[E(n+1)-E(n)]$$

is positive so the minimum decreases at a decreasing rate. The proofs involve the fact that the density function for the rth observation from the maximum in a sample of n is

$$n\binom{n-1}{r-1}F^{n-r}(1-F)^{r-1}F'dp.$$

5. The precise savings will be (1) the reduction in price times the quantity which would be purchased at the higher price—the expression in the text—*plus* (2) the average saving on the additional purchases induced by the lower price. I neglect this quantity, which will generally be of a smaller order of magnitude.

6. Buyers often pool their knowledge and thus reduce the effective cost of search; a few remarks are made on this method below.

7. This is the typical state of affairs in retailing except for consumer durable goods.

8. Since $n(1-p)^{n-1}$ is a density function, we must multiply it by a dp which represents the range of prices between adjacent price quotations. In addition, if two or more sellers quote an identical price, they will share the sales, so $K=dp/r$, where r is the number of firms quoting price p.

9. For

$$\frac{\partial N_i}{\partial p}=-\frac{(n-1)N_i}{(1-p)}<0,$$

and

$$\frac{\partial^2 N_i}{\partial p^2} = \frac{(n-1)(n-2)N_i}{(1-p)^2} > 0$$

if $n > 2$.

10. Let

$$\log N_i = \log K + \log N_b + \log n + (n-1) \log (1-p).$$

Then

$$\frac{1}{N_i}\frac{\partial N_i}{\partial n} = \frac{1}{n} + \log (1-p) = \frac{1}{n} - p,$$

approximately.

11. This argument assumes that dealers will discover unusually profitable bids, given the buyers' search, which is, of course, only partly true: there is also a problem of dealers' search with respect to prices.

12. With the rectangular distribution of asking prices, if each buyer purchases the same number of units, the elasticity of demand falls continuously with price, so that, if average cost equaled price at every rate of sales (with one seller at each price), marginal costs would have to be negative at large outputs. But, of course, the number of sellers can be less at lower prices.

13. Let the expected minimum price be $p_1 = f(n)_1$ in period 1 (with $f' < 0$) and let the expected minimum price in period 2, with r a measure of the correlation between sellers' successive prices, be

$$p_2 = \left(\frac{p_1}{f(n_2)}\right)^r f(n_2).$$

If the cost of search is λ per unit, total expenditures for a fixed quantity of purchases (Q) per unit of time are, neglecting interest,

$$E = Q(p_1 + p_2) + \lambda(n_1 + n_2).$$

Expenditures are a minimum when

$$\frac{\partial E}{\partial n_1} = Qf'(n_1) + Qr[f(n_1)]^{r-1} \times [f(n_2)]^{1-r}f'(n_1) + \lambda = 0$$

and

$$\frac{\partial E}{\partial n_2}=(1-r)Q[f(n_1)]^r\times[f(n_2)]^{-r}f'(n_2)+\lambda=0.$$

If $r=1$, $n_2=0$, and n_1 is determined by $Qf'(n_1)=-\lambda/2$, the cost of search is effectively halved.

14. See n. 13; if $r=0$, $n_1=n_2$.

15. Let $f(n)=e^{-n}$. Then, in the notation of our previous footnotes,

$$n_1-n_2=\frac{2r}{1-r},$$

approximately.

16. For that matter, a negative correlation would have the same effects.

17. If the number of sellers (s) and the asking-price distributions are the same in two periods, but k are new sellers, the average period-one buyer will have lost proportion k/s of his period-one search.

18. Duplications will occur more often than random processes would suggest, because pooling is more likely between buyers of similar location, tastes, and so on.

19. The effectiveness of the advertisement is also a function of the skill with which it is done and of the fraction of potential buyers who read the medium, but such elaborations are put aside.

20. This approach has both similarities and contrasts to that published by S. A. Ozga, "Imperfect Markets through Lack of Knowledge," *Quarterly Journal of Economics* 74 (February, 1960): 29–52.

21. The larger the number of sellers known, the larger is the range of prices among the sellers and the lower the expected minimum price after s searches. But this effect will normally be small.

22. The marginal revenue from advertising expenditure,

$$\frac{Npq}{p_a}\frac{\partial\lambda}{\partial a},$$

equals the absolute value of the elasticity of demand by equations (5) and (6); see R. Dorfman and P. O. Steiner, "Optimal Advertising and Optimal Quality," *American Economic Review* 44 (1954): 826.

23. Differentiating equation (6) with respect to b, we find that $\partial a/\partial b$ is positive or negative according as

$$b\lessgtr\frac{c}{1-c}.$$

If $c\geq\frac{1}{2}$, the derivative must be positive.

24. The formula errs slightly in allowing the multiple canvass of one seller by a buyer.

25. In the case of the uniform distribution, η_{Kp} is

$$\frac{-(s-1)p}{1-p}.$$

26. The derivative $\partial a/\partial s$ has the sign of $(1+\eta_{Ka})$, and this elasticity equals

$$1+s \log [1-p]$$

with a uniform distribution of prices.

27. By differentiation of equation (2) with respect to r one gets

$$r\frac{\partial a}{\partial r}\left\{\lambda_i\frac{\partial^2\lambda_i}{\partial a^2}+\left(\frac{\partial\lambda_i}{\partial a}\right)^2\right\}=\lambda_i\frac{\partial\lambda_i}{\partial a}\left(1-\frac{r}{K}\frac{\partial K}{\partial r}\right).$$

The term in brackets on the left side is negative by the stability condition; the right side is positive.

Free Riders and Collective Action: An Appendix to Theories of Economic Regulation

· 5 ·

The free rider problem is restated more precisely as the cheap rider problem. It is argued that if one takes account of the frequent or typical asymmetry in the interests of different enterprises in an industry, the individual incentives of many enterprises to participate in joint ventures are substantial.

I. Introduction

The free rider proposition asserts that in a wide range of situations, individuals will fail to participate in collectively profitable activities in the absence of coercion or individually appropriable inducements. The proposition does not specify the circumstances favorable to collective action, and hence does not explain why there are innumerable operating and presumably not wholly ineffective collective bodies—literally thousands of trade associations, for example. The present essay seeks to improve upon this situation.

II. The Proposition

The free rider proposition is easily illustrated. Let the gain to an individual (firm) be equal to G if a collective activity is undertaken. For example, G is the

From the *Bell Journal of Economics and Management Science* 5, no. 2 (August 1974). Permission to reprint courtesy of the *Rand Journal of Economics*.

firm's gain from the tariff which could be obtained by an effective industry lobby. The cost of the collective action is C, and there are n identically sized firms. By hypothesis, the joint action is collectively profitable, so $nG > C$. The individual will refrain from joining the collective action if n is of some appreciable size, on the assumption that the viability of the action does not depend upon his participation. If enough individuals take this position—and at this level of discourse all are symmetrical in position—the collective action will not be taken.

Even at this level of simplicity, it should be apparent that rides, like lunches, cannot be wholly free.[1] If firm i does not join the collective action, it incurs two costs:

1. The probability that the collective action is undertaken will be reduced, so the expected gain is reduced.

2. Even if a sufficient number of the remaining individuals join the collective action, they will not pursue the collective action on so large a scale as if firm i joined: alternatively put, if k firms join and each contributes c_k dollars, if i also joins, the total contribution—$(k+1)c_{k+1}$—will surely rise.

Even with these costs, i may abstain from the collective action, but his "ride" will be cheap, not free.

There is no critical number of individuals for which this argument fails—or holds. Even with $n=2$, there may be a cheap rider—one of two airlines using a field may erect the sleeve to show wind direction. With n large, whatever that may be, it is commonly believed that the proposition is inexorable.

III. The By-product Theory

Moore proposed a possible solution to the problem of reconciling the proposition with the existence of numerous collective bodies:

> If an occupation has an association which furnishes certain services to its members which cannot be purchased at a competitive price elsewhere, then the association is in the position of a monopolist: it faces a downward sloping demand curve. The services it furnishes may be journals, meetings, a certificate of membership, information about new developments, advertisements, and so forth. . . . To the extent that the association faces a downward sloping demand curve, it can act as a monopolist to raise funds for lobbying.[2]

This position was presented by Olson in a more elaborate form in *The Logic of Collective Action*,[3] but also without any attempt at empirical testing.

The by-product theory invites an obvious objection: why should the association be able to charge more than the cost of the services which are appropriable as private goods? If an association seeks to add a charge for collective goods, a rival association which undertook no collective actions could undersell it—and there are no barriers to entry into trade associations. Even if the services, such as the collection of information, have great economies of scale and are "natural monopolies," the argument is not affected: a rival association can still bid away the members of the group with a lower price.[4]

IV. THE SMALL NUMBER SOLUTION

When the number of individuals in the group is small, the probability that each individual will join the group is increased. The factors we have already cited for believing that outsiders do not get a *free* ride are applicable here. First, the probability of collective action depends more strongly on each firm's participation; and second, the scale of operation of the collective action will be appreciably smaller if fewer individuals join. Olson has labelled this small number theory a "special interest" theory of group action.[5]

The arithmetical rules of participation may be formulated as follows:

π_p = the probability of collective action if i joins,
π_{np} = the probability of collective action if i abstains,
$G_i(m, e)$ = the expected gain to i if collective action is taken,
m = the number of individuals joining the coalition, and
$e(m)$ = the expenditures per individual who joins.

Then individual i should join if

$$\pi_p\{G(m, e) - e(m)\} > \pi_{np} G(m-1, e+\Delta e)$$

and, as a Taylor series approximation,

$$G(m-1, e+\Delta e) = G(m, e) - G_m(m, e) + \Delta e G_e(m, e)$$

so

$$(\pi_p - \pi_{np})G(m, e) - \pi_p e(m) - \pi_{np}\{\Delta e G_e(m, e) - G_m(m, e)\} > 0.$$

The expected net gain for i from participation is thus:

FIGURE 5.1

PLAUSIBLE FORMS OF VARIOUS FUNCTIONS

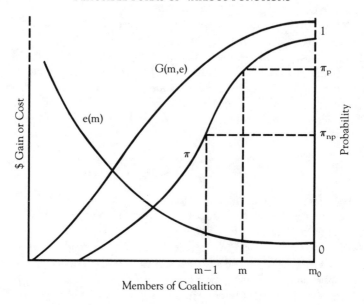

Members of Coalition

1. The increase in the probability of the formation of the coalition times the gain to i if it is formed. The latter term will increase with m; the former probably decreases as m increases.

2. Minus the expected cost of contributions to the coalition. Since π_p increases with m, and e probably decreases with m (diminishing returns to coalition expenditures), the net effect of changes in m is again uncertain.

3. Minus the effect on i's gain of the smaller size of the coalition if i does not join,[6] times π_{np}.

Plausible forms of the various functions are displayed in Figure 5.1, where m_0 is the total number of possible members of the coalition. The smaller m_0, the steeper the probability curve (π), the more rapid the fall in $e(m)$, and the greater the rate of rise of $G(m, e)$—all for a given m. Or so the folklore wisdom has it.

The small number solution has a wider scope than a literal count of numbers would suggest. The size distribution of individuals is highly skewed when these individuals have a size dimension (sales of firm, property of family). The large individuals in a group may therefore properly view themselves as members of a small number industry if their aggregate share of the group's resources is large. Consider, for example, cigar manufacturers. The 1963 data report:

4 largest firms	66 percent of value added
next 4 firms	17 percent of value added
next 12 firms	10 percent of value added
next 30 firms	6 percent of value added
next 143 firms	1 percent of value added

One can debate the proper way to convert this array into an equivalent number of equal-sized firms. If one uses the Herfindahl measure of concentration the equivalent number is about seven or eight.[7] Many, many industries fulfill in good measure the small number condition.

V. The Asymmetry Solution

With trivial exception, every industry produces a wide variety of goods or services. The fabrics in textiles or the metals and woods in furniture, the weight and power of automobiles, the composition and mechanical properties of steel—all are found in profuse variety in the products of industry. The smaller firms in an industry seldom make the full range of products: they specialize in a narrower set of products. Hence, if they are not represented in the coalition, they may find that their cheap ride is to a destination they do not favor. The proposed tariff structure may neglect *their* products; the research program may neglect *their* processes; the labor negotiation may ignore *their* special labor mix.

We may fashion a measure of the divergence of interests of the large and small firms. Let:

s_i=the share of sales of commodity i made by the combined large firms,
$1-s_i$=the share of sales made by the combined small firms,
S_i=the total sales of commodity i,
S_L, S_s=the total sales of large and small firms, respectively,
$S_L+S_s=S$, total sales.

The relative importance of sales of commodity i to the large firms is

$$\frac{s_i S_i}{S_L}$$

and the difference between large and small firms in this relative importance is

$$\Delta_i = S_i \left(\frac{s_i}{S_L} - \frac{(1-s_i)}{S_s} \right).$$

If we define the concentration ratio, k, as the share of total sales made by large firms,

$$k = \frac{S_L}{S_L + s_s},$$

and

$$\Delta_i = \frac{S_i}{S} \left(\frac{s_i}{k} - \frac{(1-s_i)}{1-k} \right).$$

Hence we may use, as our measure of the discordance interest between large and small firms,

$$\Delta^2 = \Sigma \frac{S_i^2}{S^2} \left(\frac{s_i}{k} - \frac{(1-s_i)}{(1-k)} \right)^2 = \frac{1}{S^2 k^2 (1-k)^2} \Sigma \, S_i^2 (s_1 - k)^2.$$

Our central explanation for group action is that Δ^2 can usually be made sufficiently large to bring most of the larger firms into the association.

VI. A Sample of Associations

Whatever the theory says, there is no doubt of the existence of thousands of trade associations in the United States. Often several associations appear—so far as titles can be trusted—to represent the same industry, and often association titles contain trade jargon not necessarily comprehensible to the outsider. To obtain at least a model sample of trade association data, we took a random sample of seventy four-digit Census of Manufacturers (1967-basis) industries,[8] for each of which we chose two companies, with large plants for which that industry was important, from the 1966 *Fortune Plant and Product Directory*.[9] We addressed inquiries to each of the two companies (often subdivisions of larger enterprises) for the name of the trade association(s) which represented them in their activities in the given industry (named by us). The association was then requested to send the literature on its activities and also to report its budget, the number of professional employees, the number of company members, and the share of the covered industry that was represented in the association.

A different type of sample would have been obtained if instead we had begun with associations and inquired as to the activities of their members. The difference is suggested by the following tabulation of useful responses to our inquiries:

1. Essential coincidence of association coverage with four- or five-digit industry.   32 associations

2. Association covers a three-digit industry of which our reporter falls in a four- or five-digit class.   11 associations

3. Association covers a two-digit industry of which our reporter falls in a four- or five-digit class.   11 associations

4. Association covers several industries (not all in one two-digit industry) of which our reporter industry is one.   7 associations

5. Association covers other industries, of which most commonly our reporter company is a supplier or a negligible part.   16 associations

This tabulation assumes that the reporter belongs to a clearly defined four- or five-digit industry, and of course by product variety or corporate ownership it may belong to a much wider flung enterprise. The broadest associations, such as the National Association of Electrical Manufacturers, contain subdivisions which deal with more closely defined industries (e.g., wire and cable, appliances, etc.).

A set of regression equations relating association size to industry characteristics is reported in Table 5.1. In our larger sample, both staff and budget of the association are well related to the size of the covered industry, but not to concentration ratios, which our foregoing discussion would lead us to expect. There is, indeed, some hint of a negative correlation of association resources and concentration ratios. Can it be that very large companies undertake many of the activities allocated to associations in less concentrated fields? The number of members seems directly related to association activity, the share of industry coverage much less so. This finding is consistent with expectations of the asymmetry theory.

TABLE 5.1

TRADE ASSOCIATION REGRESSIONS[a]

x_1 = Association Budget, Thousands of Dollars, 1969–1970
x_2 = Association Staff, 1969–1970
x_3 = Number of Members of Association, 1969–1970
x_4 = Value-Added of Matched Industry, Millions of Dollars, 1967
x_5 = 1967 Concentration Ratio, Four-Digit
x_6 = Share of Industry Belonging to Association, Percent, 1969–1970

	N^b	R^2
$x_2 = 10.44 + 0.00616 x_3 + 0.00667 x_4$	60	0.258
(2.71) (3.02)		
$x_2 = 17.40 + 0.00566 x_3 + 0.00699 x_4 - 0.191 x_5$	60	0.277
(2.46) (3.15) (1.22)		
$x_1 = 554.7 + 0.255 x_3 + 0.742 x_4$	60	0.230
(1.22) (3.67)		
$x_1 = 1148 + 0.212 x_3 + 0.769 x_4 - 16.28 x_5$	60	0.247
(1.00) (3.78) (1.14)	42	0.137
$x_2 = 19.37 + 0.0066 x_3 + 0.0039 x_4 + 0.446 x_6$		
(1.45) (0.72) (1.51)		

[a] t Ratios in parentheses.
[b] Number of industries for which data available.

The crucial omission from our sample is any direct knowledge of the role of asymmetry in the economic interests of members.

NOTES

1. I am indebted to Harold Demsetz for the succeeding argument.

2. T. G. Moore, "The Purpose of Licensing," *Journal of Law and Economics* 4, no. 4 (October 1961): 114.

3. See M. Olson, *The Logic of Collective Action* (Cambridge, Mass.: Harvard University Press, 1965), especially ch. 6.

4. See H. Demsetz, "Why Regulate Utilities?," *Journal of Law and Economics* 11, no. 2 (April 1968): 55–66.

5. In Olson, pp. 141 ff.

6. $\Delta G = \Delta e G_e + \Delta m G_m = \Delta e G_e - G_{ni}$.

7. See G. J. Stigler, *The Organization of Industry* (Homewood, Ill.: Richard D. Irwin, 1968), ch. 4.

8. Confining the sample to industries with coverage and specialization ratios over 75 percent, other than "n.e.c." industries.

9. I wish to thank Claire Friedland for performing the statistical work. We actually chose plants producing the largest five-digit product in the selected four-digit industry, so that both census four- and five-digit data would be applicable.

STIGLER'S
CONTRIBUTIONS TO
POLITICAL ECONOMICS

◆ ◆

◆ *PART* ◆ *TWO* ◆

THE INTELLECTUAL
AND THE MARKETPLACE*

· 6 ·

The intellectual has never felt kindly toward the marketplace: to him it has always been a place of vulgar men and base motives. Whether this intellectual be an ancient Greek philosopher, who viewed economic life as an unpleasant necessity that should never be allowed to become obtrusive or dominant, or whether this intellectual be a modern man, who focuses his scorn on gadgets and Madison Avenue, the basic similarity of view has been pronounced.

Now you and I are "intellectuals," as this word is used. I am one automatically because I am a professor, and buy more books than golf clubs. You are intellectuals because you are in general well educated and because you would rather be a United States senator or a Nobel laureate than head of the Mobil Corporation. The question I wish to pose is not whether intellectuals should love the marketplace—even a professor of economics of outrageously conservative tendencies cannot bring himself to say that the chants of five auctioneers rival a Mozart quintet. The questions are rather: what don't intellec-

Reprinted by permission of the publishers from *The Intellectual and the Marketplace*, enlarged edition, by George J. Stigler (Cambridge, Mass.: Harvard University Press). © 1963 by George J. Stigler, © 1984 by the President and Fellows of Harvard College.

* I wrote this to persuade young intellectuals that we should reexamine the traditional hostility toward private enterprise. I suppose I should not be surprised that it has been more successful in reaffirming businessmen in their faith. This is not an undesirable effect, but a lecturer denouncing cannibalism naturally must view the applause of vegetarians as equivocal evidence of his eloquence.

tuals like about the marketplace? And are they sure that their attitudes are socially useful?

Let us begin by noticing that from certain important viewpoints one would have expected intellectuals to be very kindly disposed toward that system of private enterprise which I call the marketplace.

First, if I may introduce a practical consideration, intellectuals by and large have elevated tastes—they like to eat, dress, and live well, and especially to travel. Walton Hamilton once said that our customary salutation, "Good day," was a vestige of an agricultural society where people were asking for good weather, and he expected city dwellers eventually to greet each other with the phrase "Low prices." If Hamilton's theory is correct, intellectuals will eventually adopt the greeting "Fair Fulbright."

Since intellectuals are not inexpensive, no society, until the rise of the modern enterprise system, could afford many intellectuals. As a wild guess, full-time intellectuals numbered 200 in Athens in the extraordinary age of Pericles, or about one for every 1,500 of population; and at most times in later history, intellectuals fell far, far short of this proportion. Today there are at least one million in the United States (taking only a fraction of those who live by pen and tongue into account), or one for each 200 of population. At least four out of every five owe their pleasant lives to the great achievements of the marketplace. Professors are much more beholden to Henry Ford than to the foundation that bears his name and spreads his assets.

Not only have the productive achievements of the marketplace supported a much larger intellectual class, but also the leaders of the marketplace have personally been strong supporters of intellectuals, and in particular those in the academic world. If one asks where, in the Western university world, the freedom of inquiry of professors has been most staunchly defended and energetically promoted, my answer is this: not in the politically controlled universities, whether in the United States or Germany—legislatures are not overpopulated with tolerant men indifferent to popularity; and not in the self-perpetuating faculties, such as Oxford and Cambridge from 1700 to 1850—even intellectuals can become convinced that they have acquired ultimate truth, and that it can be preserved indefinitely by airing it before students once a year. No, inquiry has been most free in the college whose trustees are a group of top-quality leaders of the marketplace, men who, experience shows, are remarkably tolerant of almost everything except a mediocre and complacent faculty. Economics provides many examples: if a professor wishes to denounce aspects of big business, as I have, he will be wise to locate in a school whose trustees are big businessmen, and I have.

But debts are seldom the basis of friendship, and there is a much more powerful reason the intellectual might be sympathetic to the marketplace: the organizing principles of both areas are the same.

An enterprise system is a system of voluntary contract. Neither fraud nor coercion is within the ethics of the market system. Indeed, there is no possibility of coercion in a pure enterprise system because the competition of rivals provides alternatives to every buyer or seller. All real economic systems contain some monopoly, and hence some coercive power for particular individuals; but the amount and the extent of such monopoly power are usually much exaggerated, and in any case monopoly is not an integral part of the logic of the system.

The intellectual world, and I speak chiefly but not exclusively of scholarship, is also a voluntary system. Its central credo is that opinions are to be formed from free discussion on the basis of full disclosure of evidence. Fraud and coercion are equally repugnant to the scholar. Freedom of thought is preserved by the open competition of scholars and ideas. Authority, the equivalent of monopoly power, is the great enemy of freedom of inquiry. Competition in scholarship is in some ways more violent than in business: the law sets limits on the disparagement of a rival's product, unless it is done in a book review in a learned journal.

Just as real markets have some fraud and monopoly, which impair the claims for the marketplace, so the intellectual world has its instances of coercion and deception, with the coercion exercised by claques and fashion. But again these deviants are outside the logic of the system.

Both areas, moreover, are democratic. The intellectual believes that every able and willing young person should get a good education whatever his race or financial background. The market believes that every able and willing person should be permitted to enter an industry or occupation, whatever his race or educational background. There is food for thought in the fact that racial discrimination has diminished earlier, faster, and more quietly in the marketplace than in political life.

The analogies could be pursued much further, although not without danger of alienating all professors and most businessmen. I shall therefore merely mention, in passing, that both fields pay a fair amount of attention to packaging and advertising, and both fields place an absurdly high value on originality. There are also many minor differences, such as that the intellectual has no desire to know the marketplace, whereas the businessman wishes, or at least believes he wishes, to know the world of the intellectual. The basic fact is that the intellectual believes in the free market of ideas and, what is not quite the same thing, in words.

Yet whatever the latent sympathies of the intellectual for the marketplace, the hostilities are overt. The contempt for the "profit motive" which directs economic activity is widespread, and the suspicion of the behavior to which it leads is deep-seated. The charge that American society is materialistic has been recited more often than the Declaration of Independence, and has been translated into more foreign languages.

In one basic respect I believe that criticism by intellectuals is misplaced, and at times even hypocritical. The American economy produces many goods that are vulgar, silly, or meretricious, as judged by standards that I share with many intellectuals. It seems only proper to cite a few examples, if only to show how selective these standards are. I shall not propose the currently most popular item, the large and powerful automobile, because I have observed that it is mostly intellectuals of short stature who criticize such cars. But other examples are at hand. I am dissatisfied with the tastes of the nine-tenths of the population who believe that nonfictional books are to be read only by young people working for their B.A. I am dissatisfied with a population whose love for interesting music is so narrow that every symphony orchestra requires subsidies. I consider it shocking that more Americans have read *The Affluent Society* than *The Wealth of Nations*.

At the risk of appearing reasonable, I wish to qualify this complaint by observing that the tastes of the American public are more elevated than those of any other large society in history. Most societies have been judged by their cultural aristocracies—indeed, in earlier periods the vast majority of the population was not even considered to be a part of the culture of the society, for this vast majority was illiterate, tradition-bound, and lived for the most part brutishly in crude huts. Our society's tastes are judged by those of the vast majority of the population, and this majority today is generous, uncomplacent, and hardworking, with unprecedentedly large numbers engaged in further self-educaton, or in eager patronage of the arts. Our market-supported legitimate theater, which is surely the best in the world, is a suggestive measure of popular tastes.

These qualifications are not intended to withdraw the charge that the public's tastes should be better, and, for that matter, that the intellectual's tastes should be better. It is in fact a basic function of the intellectual to define the standards of good taste more clearly, and to persuade people to approach them more closely. It is proper to denounce vulgarity of taste, and to denounce it more strongly the more popular it is. It is permissible to reject certain desires completely—as we do when by compulsory education laws we reject the desire for illiteracy—although there is a strong presumption against the use of force in the area of tastes.

When I say that the complaints of deficiencies in tastes are misplaced when they are directed to the marketplace, I mean just that. The marketplace responds to the tastes of consumers with goods and services that are salable, whether the tastes are elevated or depraved. It is unfair to criticize the marketplace for fulfilling these desires, when clearly the defects lie in the popular tastes themselves. I consider it a cowardly concession to a false extension of the idea of democracy to make *sub rosa* attacks on public tastes by denouncing the people who serve them. It is like blaming the waiters in restaurants for obesity.

To escape this response, the more sophisticated intellectuals have argued that people are told what to want by the marketplace—that advertising skillfully depraves and distorts popular desires. There is no doubt an element of truth in this response, but it is an element of trifling size. The advertising industry has no sovereign power to bend men's will—we are not children who blindly follow the last announcer's instructions to rush to the store for soap. Moreover, advertising itself is a completely neutral instrument, and lends itself to the dissemination of highly contradictory desires. While the automobile industry tells us not to drink while driving, the bourbon industry tells us not to drive while drinking. The symphony orchestra advertises, and gets much free publicity, in its rivalry with the rock band. Our colleges use every form of advertising, and indeed the typical college catalogue would never stop Diogenes in his search for an honest man.

So I believe that intellectuals would gain in candor and in grace if they preached directly to the public instead of using advertising as a whipping boy. I believe that they would gain also in virtue if they would examine their own tastes more critically: when a good comedian and a production of Hamlet are on rival channels, I wish I could be confident that less than half the professors were laughing.

The main indictment of the intellectual, however, is that the marketplace operates on the principles of self-interest, and in fact, through competition, compels even the philanthropic businessman to become self-serving. Self-interest, often described with such neutral terms as "egotism," "greed," and "dog-eat-dog," is viewed as a crass, antisocial element of man's character, and an economic system that rests upon, and inculcates, this motive achieves little admiration. In fact, a dislike for profit seeking is one of the few specific attitudes shared by the major religions.

I, too, find naked selfishness an unendearing trait, but I have trouble separating it from the more admirable motives related to it. A prudent regard for one's own survival is generally applauded, even if the individual does not say, "I got out of the way of the oncoming train only to spare my Sunday School class pain." The violent endeavors of an athlete to defeat his rivals are much admired, providing the contest is more or less fair, even though the winner is expected not to say, "I'm glad I won—chiefly because I'm vain, but secondarily for the honor of Sheboygan High School."

Even in fields somewhat removed from the athletic arena, the roles of self-interest and what for lack of a better name I shall call "benevolence" are perplexingly interwoven. I have spent my life among college teachers, although admittedly in the most competitive branch of research and publication. In one sense the disinterest of my colleagues is beyond doubt: I have seen silly people—public officials as well as private—try to buy opinions, but I have not seen or even suspected any cases in which any important economist sold his professional convictions. It is also true that many of the best professors could earn more in other callings.

But on the other hand, the motives that drive economists are not completely clear, either. When they strive to solve a scientific problem, is ambition for their own professional status completely overshadowed by love of knowledge? I wonder. When they write an article to demonstrate the fallacies of someone else's work, is their hatred for error never mixed with a tiny bit of glee at the display of their own cleverness? I wonder.

To shift elsewhere, I have never encountered a political candidate who said, "I am running for office because I, with my dear spouse and future administrative assistant, can earn more in politics than elsewhere." Nor do I expect to. But the language of public interest surely covers a good many acres of self-interest.

A major source of the view that the marketplace places special values on self-interest, beyond those more or less evident in all human behavior, is the belief that one man's gain is another's loss, that business, like the so-called friendly poker session, is a zero-sum game. Not so.

On the one hand, it must be recognized that the great source of market gains is the productivity of the participants. Unlike the poker game, the wealth of our society has been doubling even on a per capita basis every twenty-five years, and the doubling has been due to the labors and ingenuity of the men in the marketplace. Of course, there are also incomes achieved by monopoly rather than by efficiency, by fraud rather than by output; but it would be a wholly extravagant estimate that they amount to 10 percent of the income of the marketplace. There is room for improvement here, but there is vastly more room to admire the prodigious production achievements of the marketplace.

On the other hand, I would emphasize that most of the gains from innovation in the marketplace are passed on to the community at large. A new idea may yield handsome profits for a time, but the rapid rush of competition soon drives the price of the product down to a modest level. Ballpoint pens were first marketed at $12.50 to those penmen eager to write underwater (and, judging by my experience, only underwater); they rapidly fell in price and, as you know, are now so cheap that you have no economic excuse if you do not write the Great American Novel. Sears, Roebuck and Company and Montgomery Ward made a good deal of money in the process of improving our rural marketing structure, but I am convinced that they did more for the poor farmers of America than the sum total of the federal agricultural support programs of the last five decades.

It is an interesting illustration of the great influence of the intellectual that the marketplace itself has become apologetic of its pursuit of profit. The captains of industry now list, in a world in which public relations are becoming as important as efficiency, among their major achievements the great number of bowling alleys or college fellowships they have given to their employees. To boast that large profits demonstrate great efficiency in producing existing products and introducing new ones is considered even by them to be too archaic a form of thought for public consumption. The patron saint of economics, Adam Smith, once wrote: "I have never known much good done by those who affected to trade for the public good. It is an affectation, indeed, not very common among merchants, and very few words need be employed in dissuading them from it." I wonder what those very few words were.

To return to intellectuals, their dislike for the profit motive of the market-place no doubt rests in part on a failure to understand its logic and workings. It is a fact painful to record that the level of economic literacy has not risen noticeably in the twentieth century. Indeed, as professional economics becomes more complicated and its practitioners use an increasingly more formidable apparatus, there seems to have been retrogression in the ability of economists to communicate with other intellectuals. Less than a century ago a treatise on economics began with a sentence such as, "Economics is a study of mankind in the ordinary business of life." Today it will often begin, "This unavoidably lengthy treatise is devoted to an examination of an economy in which the second derivatives of the utility function possess a finite number of discontinuities. To keep the problem manageable, I assume that each individual consumes only two goods, and dies after one Robertsonian week. Only elementary mathematical tools such as topology will be employed, incessantly."

But misunderstanding is not the whole explanation: I cannot believe that any amount of economic training would wholly eliminate the instinctive dislike for a system of organizing economic life through the search for profits. It will still appear to many intellectuals that a system in which men were driven by a reasonably selfless devotion to the welfare of other men would be superior to one in which they sought their own preferment. This ethic is deeply embedded in the major religions.

I personally also believe that the good society will be populated by people who place a great value on other people's welfare. This is, however, not the only attribute of the good society; in particular, in the good society a man should be free within the widest possible limits of other men's limitations on his beliefs and actions. This great ethic of individual freedom clashes with that of benevolence, for I can seldom do positive good to another person without limiting him. I can, it is true, simply give him money, but even in this extreme case where I seem to place no bonds on him, he inevitably faces the question of what conduct on his part will lead me to give money to him again. Usually I will find it hard to be content to do so little good—giving money to improve a man's food or housing or health will seem as inefficient as giving him gasoline so that he will drive more often to museums. Hence, when I give money I shall also insist that it be spent on housing, or on medical care for his children, or on growing wheat in the way that I think is socially desirable, or on the collected works of Burke and de Tocqueville, or of Marx and Lenin. A patron tends to be paternalistic—in a nice way, of course. I am not saying that benevolence is bad, but that like everything else it can be carried to excess.

One final question on motives: why are they so important? Am I to admire a man who injures me in an awkward and mistaken attempt to protect me, and to despise a man who to earn a good income performs for me some great and lasting service? Oddly enough, I suspect an answer is that motive makes a difference—that it is less objectionable to be injured by an incompetent benefactor than by a competent villain. But I leave with you the question: are motives as important as effects?

Several charges related to the dominance of self-interest have rounded out the intellectual's indictment of the marketplace. First, the system makes no provision for men whose talents and interests are not oriented to profit-seeking economic activity. Second, there are cumulative tendencies toward increasing inequality of wealth, which—if unchecked—will polarize the society into a great number of poor and a few very rich. Third, the game in the marketplace is unfair in that inheritance of property plays an immensely larger role in success than the efforts of the individuals themselves. I shall comment briefly on each of these assertions.

The first charge is true: the marketplace will not supply income to a man who will not supply something that people want. People have enormously varied desires, but not enough of them wish to hire men to engage in research on ancient languages nor, eighty years ago, did they hire men to study quantum mechanics. The marketplace does not provide an air force or alms for the poor. It does not even supply babies. I conclude that a society needs more than a marketplace.

The second charge, that there are cumulative tendencies to ever-increasing inequality of wealth, is untrue. I would indeed ignore the charge for fear of reprimand from the Society for the Prevention of Cruelty to Straw Men, were it not that this straw man is so popular. In plain historical fact, the inequality in the distribution of income has been diminishing, and the diminution has been due to market forces even more than to governmental efforts. It is also worth noting that a modern market economy has a less unequal income distribution than in either centrally directed or unindustrialized economies.

The third charge, that inheritance of property plays a dominant role in the distribution of income in the marketplace, is an overstatement. Inheritance of property is important, but it will give some perspective to the charge to notice that property income is only one-fifth of national income, and inherited property is less than half of all property; so less than 10 percent of all income is governed by inheritance of property.

No useful purpose would be served by trying to appraise the proper role of inheritance of property in a few passing remarks. We would have to look carefully at the effects of inheritance on incentives; we would have to look at gifts during life, which are almost equivalent to bequests; and we would have to decide whether privately endowed colleges do enough good to offset the inevitable high-living heirs.

But our greatest problem would be that inheritance extends far beyond a safe deposit box full of bonds and stocks. I have told you that you are intelligent; I now add that the chief reason you are intelligent is that your parents are intelligent. Some of you, especially the younger of you, may find this unbelievable: Mark Twain said he was astonished by how much his father had learned during the short time it took Twain himself to age from eighteen to twenty-one. But inheritance of ability is important, probably more important in its effects on the distribution of income than is the inheritance of property. So a full account of the proper role of inheritance would have to extend to ability, and perhaps even to name and reputation, as the senior senator from Massachusetts might agree. The social and legal institutions governing inheritance in our society are surely open to improvement, but we are unlikely to improve them if we are guided by nothing more than our naive egalitarianism.

And now to my final point. Intellectuals are great believers in the human mind and in its ability to conquer an ever larger part of the immense domain of ignorance. But they have not made much use of the mind in reaching their views on the economic organization appropriate to the good society so far as its basic cultural values go. It is clear that the kinds of traits that are fostered in man are influenced by (but, of course, not only by) the way economic life is organized. After all, throughout history men have spent half their waking hours in economic activity.

Important as the moral influences of the marketplace are, they have not been subjected to any real study. The immense proliferation of general education, of scientific progress, and of democracy are all coincidental in time and place with the emergence of the free enterprise system of organizing the marketplace. I believe this coincidence was not accidental: the economic progress of the past three centuries was both cause and effect of this general growth of freedom. The dominant era of the free marketplace was the nineteenth century. I believe, but with less confidence, that the absence of major wars in that century—the only peaceable century in history—was related to this reign of liberty. I believe, again with less confidence, that the contemporary transformation of the British public from a violent and unruly people into

88 ♦ POLITICAL ECONOMICS

a population of almost painful Victorian rectitude was related to this reign of liberty.

These beliefs may be right or wrong, but they are not matters of taste. They are hypotheses concerning the relationship between economic and social organization, and are subject to analytical development and empirical testing. It is time that we did so, high time. Our ruling attitude toward the marketplace has not changed since the time of Plato. Is it not possible that it is time to rethink the question?

THE GOALS OF
ECONOMIC POLICY*

· 7 ·

I prize the privilege of delivering the first of a series of lectures which will
commemorate the work and character of Henry Calvert Simons. My pleasure
is not in the least diminished by the conviction that he would have protested at
the suggestion of such a lecture series—perhaps likening them to the rigid,
weathered structures erected to military heroes, with the lecturers sometimes
bearing a sufficient resemblance to the nervous, edible birds which hover about
them.

And in one sense he would, of course, be wholly right: the real tribute to a
scholar is the continued life of his intellectual work, and no amount of praise
periodically heaped upon dead ideas will warm them to life. The work of
Simons has received this tribute: it continues to be in the center of a main

From the *Journal of Law and Economics* 18, no. 2 (October 1975). Copyright 1975 by the
University of Chicago.

* It is hard to catch George Stigler in an error. But there is one in his article on Henry Calvert
Simons. George J. Stigler, "Henry Calvert Simons," *Journal of Law and Economics* 17, no. 1
(1974). Stigler there states that all the Simons memorial lectures have been published in the
Journal of Law and Economics. This is incorrect. The first Simons lecture, given in 1958, by
George Stigler on "The Goals of Economic Policy," was not printed in the *Journal of Law and
Economics*, which did not then exist, but in the *Journal of Business*. Fortunately it is an error easy
to correct. The editor of the *Journal of Business* has graciously given permission for the first Simons
lecture to be reprinted in this issue of the *Journal of Law and Economics*. It is hardly necessary to
say that the lecture retains its freshness and its power. Age cannot wither nor custom stale George
Stigler's infinite variety.—Ronald H. Coase.

current of political economy which he did so much to create, and today his thought is as relevant and as farsighted as it was in the moment at which it was written. From this viewpoint, the highest compliment one can pay a scholar is to quarrel with him or to go beyond him, and I am absolutely certain that Simons would second my invitation to future lecturers to exercise the privilege more freely than I shall.

But, in another sense, Simons would have had no right to protest the establishment of these lectures, for they honor something that belongs to his friends as much as to him: his character. This wondrously complex man of exalted integrity, brilliantly witty, exquisite of taste, generous toward others and unreasonably demanding of himself—this man we are entitled to honor, and without permission. I interpret my lecture not as a tribute—he deserves much better than he will receive tonight—but as a reminder to the world that we continue to love our friend.

I

I shall speak tonight on the proper goals of economic policy.

Three goals have long dominated economic policy in this country and in the Western world. The first and most ancient goal is the largest possible output of goods and services. Maximum output has evolved, under the impact of social events and economic analysis, into a two-pronged goal: (1) to employ as fully as possible—that is, as fully as the other goals allow—the resources at society's disposal (unnecessary unemployment of men and capital should be eliminated); and (2) to employ these resources as efficiently as possible. Broadly speaking, no resource should be used in one place if it would produce more elsewhere—it should be impossible to reshuffle resources to achieve more of some goods without getting less of others.

The second goal is the growth of the economy. Natural resources should be prospected, capital accumulated, and new products and technologies discovered. These forward-looking activities have for their common end a steady rise over time in the level of income relative to population.

The last primary goal of economic policy is a comparative newcomer, still a vague sentiment when maximum output had been entrenched for centuries. It is the reduction in income inequality. The goal of equality, or at least of much reduced inequality, has become one of the great forces of our times.

These three goals—maximum output, substantial growth, and minimum inequality of income—have provided the justifications for every important innovation in economic policy. Maximum output is the purpose of our free trade within the United States, the combatting of monopoly, and various anti-depression measures. The growth of income is intended to be served by our various conservation measures, much of public education, our public land policy, and the current flirtation of the federal government with basic research. Minimum inequality is the goal of the personal income tax, agricultural policies, public housing subsidies, unemployment insurance, and a host of other policies. Of course I simplify when I identify a policy with only one goal; it is a poor protagonist of an economic policy who fails to argue that it will serve all the goals of economic policy and that it is also wholly in keeping with the Scriptures.

There are, to be sure, a variety of minor goals of policy. The desire to eliminate racial discrimination has led to certain regulations of economic life, and, again, the desire for personal equality of treatment independent of income has led to other regulations, such as prohibitions on personal railway-rate discrimination. But these goals have had only minor and sporadic effect upon economic policy.

One need hardly emphasize the obvious fact that many of the policies we have adopted have ill served any of these goals. The farm program was adopted to help a class of families with low average incomes and possibly to conserve resources, but quite probably it has increased income inequality, at least within agriculture, and it is extremely doubtful that any useful conservation of resources has been achieved. The tariff was presumably designed to increase domestic output, but economists believe it has never been an effective policy to this end. There have also been plain raids on the federal treasury, such as the silver-purchase program, which have only the most tenuous connection with the goals of policy. But every society makes mistakes in achieving its goals; often it misunderstands the efficacy of a given policy in reaching a given goal, and often the announced goals are merely cloaks worn by particular groups seeking particular ends. These aberrations and deceptions do not constitute a contradiction of the primacy of the goals of maximum output, substantial growth, and decreased income inequality.

A question that can be raised with respect to basic goals is whether they are fully attainable. I would say that they should not be. An abstract goal gives direction to economic policy, just as the North Pole gives direction to a compass, and, just as the compass becomes useless at the magnetic North Pole, so the goals of policy lose their value as guides once they are fulfilled. *Specific* goals, such as so many television sets or highway miles or dollars of tax receipts, must usually be realizable, but general goals should not be fully realizable.

Whether one accepts this position or not, I think it is fair to say that at the present time the basic goals are widely believed to be tolerably well fulfilled in the United States.

Consider income inequality. Few people think that the progression in the personal income tax is seriously insufficient, and many think it is excessive. Public sympathy for groups traditionally viewed as disadvantaged, in particular labor unions and farmers, is at low ebb. It would be wrong to say that "underprivileged classes" has been deleted from the lexicon of neoliberalism, but the concern for them has lost urgency and to some degree has been supplanted by concern for the peoples with highly developed desires in undeveloped economies.

The satisfaction with the productive performance of the American economy is even more complete. We feel rich. We believe that on the average we are denied only luxuries over whose absence no one can wax indignant. It is true that the workingman still has only a black-and-white television set and that his car is several years old, but so what? Who really cares whether a farm program, or a river-and-harbor pork barrel, wastes a billion dollars, or less than one day's output of the American economy? Who believes that the rate of growth of income is seriously inadequate or that unemployment of resources in recent years has been grievously large? Even the critics of the thirties have been silenced or turned into flatterers. In as populous a nation as ours there still exist critics of the productive performance of the economic system, but they are in the uncomfortable position of criticizing the form of a golfer who wins all the tournaments.

This sense of prosperity, I am certain, is a temporary thing. The postwar growth of consumer real income, compared with 1932–1945, has been so sudden and so large that we have not been able to build up new desires, but they are gradually emerging. That celebrated axiom of economics, the insatiability of human desires, has survived the much greater increases in real income achieved at earlier times. In another decade or so we shall be complaining, and with sincere pain, of the widespread need to satisfy elementary decencies such as a summer cottage, the electronic range, the wholly air-conditioned house, and the family psychiatrist. But for the moment we are well-off.

Not only should the basic goals of economic policy be unattainable, they should also be part and parcel of the civilization of a society. Ours are not. Our basic goals are the same as the basic goals of the Russians.

The Russians also believe in equality of income. Their fundamental ethical claim, indeed, is that they will remove all income differences not strictly justifiable by social performance and/or need and in particular will not allot any part of income to a class of private owners of the means of production. I would quarrel violently with their belief that private property is not a basic institution of economic progress, but the argument is being settled for many people by the substantial growth of output of the Russian economy. We may also argue that the inequalities of income in Russia are large and not so closely related to social performance as our own inequalities. Important as these questions are in assessing the extent to which a society achieves its goals, they seem to raise arguments over policies rather than over goals.

And the Russians share the goals of maximum output and rapid economic growth. Indeed, every society that is purposive and nontraditional seeks to do efficiently whatever it seeks to do. The differences among societies arise with respect to what output they seek to maximize. In our society the output to be maximized is chosen primarily by the individual consumers; in the Russian economy the output to be maximized is chosen primarily by a central, dictatorial body. Hence the Russian desired output contains more munitions and heavy industrial equipment, as a share of total output, than the American desired output; but this, again, is a difference in content (of immense importance, to be sure) rather than in goal.

Now, I do not wish to imply that a goal loses validity because it is shared by an unfriendly person. It does not seem sensible to abandon Mozart simply because one encounters a boor who also admires his music. And to spurn a goal such as maximum output is to spurn rational behavior.

Nevertheless, the fact that our economic goals are the same as the Russians' is anomalous: one would expect two great powers to have carried into their economic goals some elements of the political philosophies that lead to their antipathy and rivalry. The fact that our goals and the Russian goals are the same has also contributed mightily to the failure of American foreign policy— a policy which has no cutting edge of political philosophy that might attract the leaders of other countries. We offer the same goals, and differ chiefly in promising less with respect to their fulfilment.

The reason I wish to propose a somewhat different set of goals than those we now profess, however, is not to set ourselves apart from Russia, nor is it to capture the intellectual leadership of the neutral world—although these are not negligible hopes. Even if the United States were the only body of land on earth or in space, we should urgently need to give direction and emphasis to our economic policies. It is high time that we set aside the details of managing a comfortable dormitory and concern ourselves with the kind of society we wish to inhabit.

II

The supreme goal of the Western world is the development of the individual: the creation for the individual of a maximum area of personal freedom, and with this a corresponding area of personal responsibility. Our very concept of the humane society is one in which individual man is permitted and incited to make the utmost of himself. The self-reliant, responsible, creative citizen—the "cult of individualism" for every man, if you will—is the very foundation of democracy, of freedom of speech, of every institution that recognizes the dignity of man. I view this goal as an ultimate ethical value; others may wish to reach it through powerful utilitarian arguments.

It is one thing for a value to have verbal sovereignty; it is quite another for it to permeate the social system. Individualism has few enemies in the United States, but its many friends are becoming less fervent, and its influence upon the course of events is shrinking at an alarming rate. One would incur ostracism in our universities if he denied that man should be free to think what he wishes, but increasingly he is looked upon as a quaint survivor of ancient times if he believes that man should be master of his fate, even when he bears the main effects of his own decisions. The faith in the individual has been much impaired by a fairly new doctrine, a very old belief, and the changing structure of society.

The fairly new doctrine is that of environmental determinism, which we owe to men as diverse as Godwin and Marx. On an ever-widening scale it is being argued that social institutions mold the character of man: that the food and housing, family, neighborhood, and education of the child have a decisive influence upon the way he thinks and behaves as a man. No one can doubt, in the light of generations of social research, that this theory contains much truth. Its thrust is evident: interest is inevitably shifted from man's exertions to the social environment, which to a considerable degree determines the nature and direction of these exertions.

The very old belief is that most men are incapable of conducting their affairs wisely. Only in the nineteenth century did this belief temporarily lose its dominance: at the threshold of the period of universal education it was widely believed that the vast majority of the population could be educated to so high a level of rationality that it could be trusted with the control of public affairs as well as the proper conduct of personal affairs.

Now that the great majority of our population receives at least twelve years of formal education, it is no longer possible to expect great results—one must observe them. And, on the whole, I sense a growing disillusionment, although direct documentation of this disillusionment is rather difficult to present because the miracle of education still provides, for too many intellectuals, the anchor of their democratic faith and the emblem of their ethical respectability.

If I may judge by my own discipline, however, the skepticism of the individual is reappearing in explicit form. The consumer, according to professional economic literature, is a complaisant fellow, quick to follow the self-serving mandates of Madison Avenue or of a long-distance call from a stock broker located just beyond the reach of extradition. This consumer is commonly given only the virtue of consistency, and it is not clear whether his choices are treated as well-ordered because his follies are reflexive, symmetrical, and transitive or because, if they were not, his indifference curves would intersect.

I suspect that other disciplines are becoming equally outspoken, but we may document the declining faith in the individual by something almost as strong as words—actions. Most intellectuals are in favor of increasing governmental control over education (compulsory attendance, certification of teachers, control of curriculums and school year, etc.) and of increasing intervention by state and federal governments in local governmental control of education. Yet education is surely the one field in which, if education imparts either wisdom or logical training, one would most confidently expect that increasing authority be reserved to the individual and the small political unit.

The last component of the declining faith in the individual has been the increasing complexity and mutual dependence of social relationships in an urban industrial society. The effects of an individual's behavior upon others become large. A farmer with deplorable sanitary habits may be an affront to humanity; a similar city dweller is an immediate hazard to his neighbors. An eccentric or timid pioneer (if this latter is not a contradiction in terms) bears the main costs of his deficiencies; a similar entrepreneur can throw a thousand blameless men out of work (not very long, however). A man, in short, can be trusted with hostile Indians but not with friendly citizens.

I hope that I have sketched with some plausibility the causes of the decline of faith in the unregulated and unguided individual, for each contains a good deal of validity. Each has also been much exaggerated. No social research has shown that a man's behavior is independent of his will or that in our society his potentialities of achievement are rigidly set by his environment. Our trust in education has been a narrow, academic faith, and we have almost forgotten that there are such things as nonacademic abilities or that the schoolroom is only one, and not the major, center of education for life. And, if our society is growing more complex, it is also offering a variety of opportunities for individual choice quite beyond the dreams of earlier times.

One can nevertheless concede much validity to the main sources of decline of faith in the individual and yet not budge one inch from the goal of individual freedom. That men are not independent of their environments does not mean that they should be denied the opportunity of determining their lives, and their environments, as far as this is possible. That education does not turn most men into scholars does not reduce the value of allowing them to make their own wise and stupid decisions. That the increasing interdependence of men calls for a continuing review of their rights and duties is no reason for assuming either that no opportunities for new freedom arise or that conflicts can be settled only by coercion. We shall wish to revise the particular content of individual freedom and responsibility as our society and as our understanding of our society change, but always there is the problem—the transcendental problem of all liberal societies—of seeking to enlarge the individual's share in conducting his life. Men are not mere social animals, to be governed into prosperity or tranquilized into nonunhappiness.

Let us return to our traditional goals of economic policy. Two of them—

maximum output and substantial growth—are ethically neutral: they could be adopted by a nation of gourmets or ascetics or warriors, by tyrants or by democrats. What ethical content they possess has been introduced, almost surreptitiously, by defining output as that which is desired by free men.

We have placed the main burden of direction of social policy upon the goal of reduced income inequality, and it cannot bear this burden. It represents, indeed, quite fairly one element of the basic value of individualism: humanitarianism, in the form of the desire to eliminate poverty and its concomitants such as malnutrition and untended illness. Much as we may quarrel among ourselves as to the proper way in which to eliminate such ugly things, all of us wish to be rid of them.

For the rest, minimum income inequality has a very dubious congruence with our basic values. One would fear for the individual in a society where a small group of extremely wealthy individuals had the (monopoly) power to exploit others or the (financial) power to subvert the political process. Neither threat is real or potential: we have too many wealthy people to collude and too few to exert a directive influence upon political life. The goal of minimum income inequality has, at best, an adventitious and, at worst, a perverse relationship to individual freedom.

III

The goal of individual freedom does not lead automatically to a cut-and-dried program of economic policies. Continuing research will have to go into the discovery of the meaning of freedom under changing social conditions, and continuing ingenuity of high order will be required to contrive policies which will increase this freedom. It would be much more attractive if I could propose immediately a series of policies which were wholly novel, irritatingly paradoxical, and—after the smoke of battle had cleared—irresistibly persuasive, but in good conscience I cannot.

Precisely because the tradition of individual freedom has been so fundamental to our political philosophy, the most obvious corollaries of it are well known, and these corollaries, like the goal itself, will appear outmoded to many eyes. Yet the implications of the goal are not simply a formalized description of life at some admired date in history; we have never done as much or as well as we could, and today we are doing very poorly.

Consider the policy of competition. This policy has a basic role in striking down limitations to individual freedom and challenging individual capabilities, in better proportioning rewards to efforts. Yet the policy is rapidly losing its popular support and its vitality. On the one hand, there is a growing faith—it is no more than this—that the giant enterprise is the home of progress; on the other hand, the argument that monopoly reduces income has little emotional appeal to a rich nation.

If we place a main value on the individual, however, there is no justification for our complacency. Since the war our antitrust policy has drifted into a spiritless action against the more blatant forms of conspiracy and monopolization. While the federal government has been opening up these back lots to individual freedom, it has quietly been erecting barriers to individual action throughout the prairies of economic life, with its paternalistic small-business programs and the regulation of competitive industries such as agriculture, motor trucking, and housing.

Our programs to assist distressed industries collide directly with the policy of competition, and they seem to me a clear instance of the abandonment of individual freedom not because it is an obstacle to other goals but because freedom is not at the front of policy. Should we, as we almost always do, ease the problems of these industries by restricting output, stockpiling it, fixing prices—each a policy serving to decrease the freedom and responsibility of the individuals who are in these industries or who wish to enter them? We can achieve the same humanitarian purpose by helping individuals to move to more remunerative industries and localities by providing educational facilities, informational services, travel grants, and other policies designed to widen their range of alternatives.

When did we last initiate a large federal program to increase the range of productive activities open to the individual or to enlarge the scope for individual freedom within an area? Recent answers are hard to come by. The question would be just as difficult to answer if we addressed it to the heads of state and local governments, even could we distract them for a moment from such important work as the licensing of scores of trades such as yacht salesman, exacting oaths from wrestlers that they are not subversive, but mostly imploring a higher governmental level to take over their functions.

We now have innumerable policies designed to protect the consumer, including some that protect him against low prices. Obviously, we should help to protect him against those forms of fraud which he does not actively seek out, but should we protect him against unwise behavior? If we prohibit gambling to preserve him from moral weakness or actuarial myopia, should we not also supervise his investment portfolio to keep his uranium holdings down to a prudent level? My complaint against such policies is less that the wisdom of a course of action is usually debatable than that there is nothing admirable about an involuntary saint.

The policies designed to influence the distribution of income call for thorough restudy in the light of the goal of individual freedom. The main objection to a progressive income taxation beyond that implicit in the alleviation of poverty is that it imposes differential penalties on personal efforts that poorly serve the goal of inciting each individual to do his best. Almost the only instrumental defense for such a tax is that large incomes are "unfair." The main possible meaning of this charge is that large incomes are not fully earned. When this is true, and the extent of its truth has received embarrassingly little study, why do we not deal directly with the institutions which give rise to large, systematic, and persistent earnings beyond what the community believes are just?

The inheritance of wealth may be one such institution. The right to unlimited, or at least very large, bequest has customarily been defended in terms of its effects upon the donor, with very little consideration of the possible effects on the donees. It has traditionally been argued that the donor is led to vast exertions and to continued thrift. Yet the need for relatively free bequest to stimulate large efforts is surely debatable: we find that men also make immense exertions in areas such as politics, the arts, and the sciences, where the chief legacy of a highly successful man to his son is an inferiority complex. On the other hand, the large inheritance of wealth probably has the effect of reducing the incentives to the heir to exercise his full capabilities—he has received the gold medal at the beginning of the race. Since there are precious values in the family itself as an institution, we cannot eliminate all gifts (let alone intellectual gifts!) and bequests, but it may be advisable to tax inheritances (including gifts during life, but *not* estates) much more severely than we already do.

These comments on policies are highly tentative, but I hope that they are sufficient to indicate that a thoroughgoing philosophy of individual freedom and responsibility would lead to programs that are neither consistently "radical" nor consistently "conservative" by our present standards. We do not have such a thoroughgoing philosophy at present; we have been content to defend the freedoms of the individual once or twice a year, when the attack on them is unusually direct and brutal, and complacently design our policies in complete neglect of this goal the remainder of the year. No one has a greater responsibility than the university community, which is among the chief beneficiaries of a regime of freedom, for reviving faith in this goal and for developing its implications for economic and, in fact, for all social policy.

The Economist
and the State

· 8 ·

In 1776 our venerable master offered clear and emphatic advice to his countrymen on the proper way to achieve economic prosperity. This advice was of course directed also to his countrymen in the American colonies, although at that very moment we were busily establishing what would now be called a major tax loophole. The main burden of Smith's advice, as you know, was that the conduct of economic affairs is best left to private citizens—that the state will be doing remarkably well if it succeeds in its unavoidable tasks of winning wars, preserving justice, and maintaining the various highways of commerce.

That was almost two centuries ago, and few modern economists would assign anything like so austere a role to the economic responsibilities of the state. The fact that most modern economists are as confident in prescribing a large economic role to the state as Smith was in denying such a role is not necessarily surprising: professional opinions sometimes change after 188 years, and economic and political institutions are of course even less durable.

But, surprising or not, the shifts in the predominant views of a profession on public policy pose a question which I wish to discuss. That question is: on what basis have economists felt themselves equipped to give useful advice on

From the *American Economic Review* 55, no. 1 (March 1965). Permission to reprint courtesy of the American Economic Association.

Presidential address delivered at the Seventy-seventh Annual Meeting of the American Economic Association, Chicago, December 29, 1964.

the proper functions of the state? By what methods did Smith and his disciples show the incapacity of the state in economic affairs? By what methods did later economists who favored state control of railroads, stock exchanges, wage rates and prices, farm output, and a thousand other things, prove that these were better directed or operated by the state? How does an economist acquire as much confidence in the wisdom of a policy of free trade or fiscal stabilization as he has in the law of diminishing returns or the profit-maximizing propensities of entrepreneurs?

The thought behind these questions is simple. Economists generally share the ruling values of their societies, but their professional competence does not consist in translating popular wishes into an awe-inspiring professional language. Their competence consists in understanding how an economic system works under alternative institutional frameworks. If they have anything of their own to contribute to the popular discussion of economic policy, it is some special understanding of the relationship between policies and results of policies.

The basic role of the scientist in public policy, therefore, is that of establishing the costs and benefits of alternative institutional arrangements. Smith had no professional right to advise England on the Navigations Acts unless he had evidence of their effects and the probable effects of their repeal. A modern economist has no professional right to advise the federal government to regulate or deregulate the railroads unless he has evidence of the effects of these policies.

This position, you must notice, is not quite the familiar one that an economist's value judgments have no scientific status—indeed I shall neither dispute nor praise value judgments. The position is rather that if a subject is capable of study, a scholar ought to study it before he advises legislators. Suppose you deplore disease or, conversely, that you greatly admire the much-persecuted germ. My assertion is that however you stand, you should not support proposals to compel or to forbid people to go to a doctor until you find out whether their attendance on a doctor will increase or decrease the incidence of disease. If this particular example strikes you as absurdly pedantic, I offer two responses. First, will your answer be the same whatever the state of medical science in a country? Second, we shall come to harder problems.

My task, then, is to ask in as hardheaded a way as possible what precisely was the evidence economists provided for their policy recommendations, evidence that successfully linked their proposals with the goals they were seeking to achieve. I begin with Adam.

I

Smith bases his proposals for economic policy upon two main positions. Neither basis is presented in a formal and systematic fashion, and there are serious problems in determining exactly why he wishes most economic life to be free of state regulation.

Smith's first basis for his economic policies was his belief in the efficiency of the system of natural liberty. There can be little doubt that this tough-minded Scotsman, this close friend of that cool and clear thinker, David Hume, had a deep attachment to the natural law of the late enlightenment. But Smith did not propose national liberty as a lay religion of political life. Instead he argued, as a matter of demonstrable economic analysis, that the individual in seeking his own betterment will put his resources where they yield the most to him, and that as a rule the resources then yield the most to society. Where the individual does not know, or does not have the power to advance, his own interests, Smith feels remarkably free to have the state intervene.

Thus Smith says that to restrain people from entering voluntary transactions "is a manifest violation of that natural liberty which it is the proper business of law, not to infringe but to support"; yet he continues:

> But those exertions of the natural liberty of a few individuals, which might endanger the security of the whole society, are, and ought to be, restrained by the laws of all governments; of the most free, as well as of the most despotical. The obligation of building party walls, in order to prevent the communication of fire, is a violation of natural liberty, exactly of the same kind with the regulations of the banking trade which are here proposed.[1]

Natural liberty seems to have been little more than a working rule, and Smith proposes numerous departures from the natural liberty because the participants are incompetent or fail to consider external effects of their behavior.[2] He is quite willing to outlaw payment of wages in kind, which he believes will defraud the worker, and to put a limit on interest rates, because high interest rates encourage lenders to entrust their funds to improvident projectors, and to have a complicated tax system to change the uses of land.

The second foundation of Smith's strong preference for private economic activity was that he deeply distrusted the state. This distrust, I must emphasize, was primarily a distrust of the motives rather than of the competence of the state. Smith makes very little of inept governmental conduct—indeed he clearly believes that as far as efficiency is concerned, the joint stock companies, and even more the universities, are worse offenders than the state. His real complaint against the state is that it is the creature of organized, articulate, self-serving groups—above all, the merchants and the manufacturers. The legislature is directed less often by an extended view of the common good than by "the clamorous importunity of partial interests."[3]

Purely as a matter of professional appraisal, I would say that Smith displayed superb craftsmanship in supporting his first argument—that free individuals would use resources efficiently—but was excessively dogmatic in asserting his second argument, which accepted the competence but rejected the disinterest of the governmental machine. He gives no persuasive evidence that the state achieves the goals of its policies, and in particular he asserts rather than proves that the mercantile system had a large effect upon the allocation of British resources. Nor does he demonstrate that the state is normally the captive of "partial interests."

Smith's intellectual heirs did little to strengthen his case for laissez-faire, except by that most irresistible of all the weapons of scholarship, infinite repetition. Yet they could have done so, and in two directions.

Where Smith finds the competitive market incapable of performing a task, they might have corrected him, for he was sometimes wrong. To a degree this was done: Smith's belief that the market set too low a value on investment in agriculture, and too high a value on foreign investment, was properly criticized by McCulloch,[4] and the aberration on usury was of course promptly challenged by Bentham. But for each of Smith's errors that was corrected, several new ones were introduced. J. S. Mill, for example, gravely argued that the competitive market was incapable of providing a reduction in the hours of work even if all the workers wished it—a mistake I am not inclined to excuse simply because so many later economists repeated it.

What I consider to be a more important weakness in Smith's position, however—his undocumented assumption that the state was efficient in achieving mistaken ends[5]—was not only accepted, but emphatically reaffirmed by his followers. James Mill's identification of the evils of government with the undemocratic control of its instruments was an extreme example, but an instructive and influential one. The holder of the power of government would always use it to further his own ends—so argued Mill with an oppressive show of logical rigor. It followed that only a democratically controlled state would seek the good of the entire public:

> The Community cannot have an interest opposite to its interest. To affirm this would be a contradiction in terms. The Community within itself, and with respect to itself, can have no sinister interest... The Community may act wrong from mistake. To suppose that it could from design would be to suppose that human beings can wish their own misery.[6]

Hence a democracy, unlike a monarchy or an aristocracy, would do no unwise thing except in ignorance. And this exception for ignorance was not a serious one:

> There can be no doubt that the middle rank, which gives to science, to art, and to legislation itself, their most distinguished ornaments, and is the chief

source of all that has exalted and refined human nature, is that portion of the Community of which, if the basis of Representation were ever so far extended, the opinion would ultimately decide. Of the people beneath them, a vast majority would be sure to be guided by their advice and example.[7]

Education of the masses, and their instinctive reverence for the wisdom of their middle-class leaders, those ornaments of society, would thus insure that the democratic state would seldom stray far from the public good. The argument meant that at the time the essay was written the American government was a reliable instrument of public welfare and fifty years later England's government would become so.[8]

It would be possible to document at length this proposition that the classical economists objected chiefly to *unwise* governmental intervention in economic life, but I shall give only two instructive examples.

The first example is provided by that fine Irish economist, Mountifort Longfield. Apropos of certain dubious programs to assist the laborer he wrote, "here Political Economy is merely a defensive science, which attempts to prevent the injudicious interference of speculative legislation."[9] This sounds suitably conservative, but let us continue. Years later, as a witness before a Royal Commission on Railways, he complained that his timid fellow directors of the Great Southern and Western Railway underestimated the long-run elasticity of demand for rail service. To produce the necessary courage he proposed that the government appoint a director with unlimited power to vary the rates of each railroad, with the government taking half of any resulting profits and compensating all of any resulting losses.[10] Longfield wanted not laissez-faire but half fare.

The second example is the major controversy provoked by the campaigns for the ten-hour day for women in factories, which reached success in 1847. This was one of the first of the modern English interventions in the contracts of competent adults, and it invited excommunication by the economic divines. This Factory Act was in fact opposed with vigor by two important economists, Torrens and Senior, but explicitly *not* as a violation of natural right. Torrens prefaced his criticism with a passage that reads better than it reasons:

> The principle of non-interference can be applicable to those circumstances only, in which interference would be productive of mischief; in all those cases in which the interference of the central authority in the transactions between man and man is capable of effecting good or averting evil, *laissez faire* is a criminal abandonment of the functions for the performance of which a central authority is established and maintained.[11]

Hence Torrens, and equally Senior,[12] criticized the ten-hour bill because it would lower weekly wages, increase production costs, and reduce employment by impairing the competitive position of the British textile industry abroad.

Both Senior and Torrens died in 1864, so they had adequate time, one would think, to have tested their predictions of the effects of the ten-hour law. It is wholly characteristic of the insulation of discussions of policy from empirical evidence that no such study was undertaken by them, or by anyone else.

James Mill's oldest son, surprisingly enough, put up a stronger case against state control of economic life than his much more conservative father had. John Stuart did not follow his father in accepting the invariable wisdom of the democratic state, possibly because he was writing well after the Reform Act.[13] He rested the case much more on the defense of individual liberty, and fully three of the five reasons he gave for favoring laissez-faire as a practical maxim were variations on the importance of the dignity, independence, self-reliance, and development of the individual.[14]

Although I reckon myself among the most fervent admirers of individualism, even for other people, I must concede that the younger Mill's position was ambiguous. He does not tell us how to determine whether a given public policy frees or inhibits individuals. Suppose I contemplate a program of public housing. If I bribe or force people into such housing, of course I have reduced their area of choice and responsibility. But I have also, I presumably hope, given a generation of children a chance to grow up in quarters that are not grossly unsanitary and inadequate for physical and moral health. Mill does not tell us whether this policy fosters or inhibits individualism—although I strongly suspect that he would have favored public housing, as he did free public education and limitation of hours of work for young people. If an economist is to be a moral philosopher, however—and I have no doubt that we would do this well too—he should develop his philosophy to a level where its implications for policy become a matter of logic rather than a vehicle for expressing personal tastes.[15]

Let us leap on to Marshall who brought up the rear of this tradition as of so many others in English economics. He conceded an expanding potential role to the state, in the control of monopoly, in the housing of the poor, and in the treatment of poverty generally. Yet he persevered in his preference for private enterprise wherever possible. The preference rested heavily on the belief that bureaucratic management would be burdensome and inefficient.[16] Marshall at this point wrote the boldest sentence of his life:

> If Governmental control had supplanted that of private enterprise a hundred years ago [1807], there is good reason to suppose that our methods of manufacture now would be about as effective as they were fifty years ago, instead of being perhaps four or even six times as efficient as they were then.[17]

Yet the "good reason" was never presented, although it was more important to demonstrate this proposition if true than to answer any other question to which Marshall devoted a chapter or a book or even his life. Marshall's other reason for his distrust of government was the fear that Parliament would become the creature of special interests, and in particular of the trade unions[18]—an unknowing but not unknowledgeable reversion to Adam Smith!

So much for a century of laissez-faire. The main school of economic individualism had not produced even a respectable modicum of evidence that the state was incompetent to deal with detailed economic problems of any or all sorts. There was precious little evidence, indeed, that the state was unwise in its economic activities, unless one was prepared to accept as evidence selected corollaries of a general theory. The doctrine of nonintervention was powerful only so long and so far as men wished to obey.

II

There was no day on which economists ceased to commend reductions in the government's role in economic life and began to propose its expansion. The limitation of hours of work for children was supported well before the attack on the corn laws reached its climax. The statutes liberalizing dealings in property in the 1830s followed at a distance the regulation of passenger ships to protect emigrants.

How else could it be? The distinction between ancient police functions admitted by all and new regulatory functions proposed by some was most elusive. The same economist could and did repel the state with one hand and beckon it with the other.[19]

The expansion of public control over economic life which took place in the mid-nineteenth century in England, and a trifle later in the United States, was usually of this sort: a traditional state function was expanded or a new function was adopted which had close analogies to traditional functions. Economic effects were usually incidental to protective effects: the inspection of factories and mines, the sanitation laws for cities, the embryonic educational system, and most of the controls over railroads were of this sort.[20]

One thing did not change at all, however, from the heyday of laissez-faire: no economist deemed it necessary to document his belief that the state could effectively discharge the new duties he proposed to give to it. The previous assertions of governmental incompetence were met only by counter assertion; the previous hopes of wiser uses of governmental powers by a democracy were deemed too prophetic to deserve the discourtesy of historical test. I shall illustrate this persistent neglect of empirical evidence with the writings of two economists who have almost nothing in common except great ability.

The first is Jevons. Governmental operation of an industry was appropriate, Jevons believed, if four conditions were fulfilled: (1) The work must be of an invariable and routine-line nature, so as to be performed according to fixed rules. (2) It must be performed under the public eye, or for the service of individuals, who will immediately detect and expose any failure or laxity. (3) There must be very little capital expenditure, so that each year's revenue and expense account shall represent, with approximate accuracy, the real commercial success of the undertaking. (4) The operations must be of such a kind that their union under one all-extensive government monopoly will lead to great advantage and economy.[21] On what is this garbled description of a municipal water system based? Mature introspection, of course.

Jevons is equally devoted to the a priori method when he discusses public regulation. The "Principles of Industrial Legislation" are illustrated first with the problem posed by a dangerous machine. Neither worker nor employer, Jevons says, generally displays due concern for the dangers that lurk in the unfenced machine.

> But there remains one other mode of solving the question which is as simple as it is effective. The law may command that dangerous machinery shall be fenced, and the executive government may appoint inspectors to go round and prosecute such owners as disobey the law.[22]

Several aspects of Jevons's position are instructive. There is no showing of evidence on the failure of employers and employees to curb dangerous machinery. There is no showing of evidence that direct controls are simple and effective. Direct controls surely were not effective in factories too small to catch the inspector's eyes, and it is a completely open question whether they were effective elsewhere. And finally, Jevons does not conceive of the possible role of the price system in supplementing, if not replacing, direct inspection by a law making employers responsible for accidents.[23]

But let us recall who Jevons was: he was the economist whose supreme genius lay in his demand for empirical determination of theoretical relationships and his immense resourcefulness in making such determinations. This powerful instinct for empirical evidence spilled over into a proposal that wherever possible new policies should first be tried out at the local governmental level: "we cannot," he said, "really plan out social reforms upon theoretical grounds."[24] But, possible or not, he really so planned out his reforms.

We may learn how a theorist coped with the problem by turning to my second economist, Pigou. In *Wealth and Welfare*[25] he recited four reasons for distrusting the ability of legislatures to control monopolies. They were shallow reasons, but what is instructive is that all of them "can be, in great measure, obviated by the recently developed invention of 'Commissioners,' that is to say, bodies of men appointed by governmental authorities for the express purpose of industrial operation or control." Hence the government is now capable of "beneficial intervention in industries, under conditions which would not have justified such intervention in earlier times."[26]

If time were not the most precious thing that one professor can give to another, I would follow in detail Pigou's travels from this inauspicious beginning. We would be instructed by the evidence which he found sufficient to a series of propositions on the state's competence:

> . . . laws directly aimed at "maintaining competition" are practically certain to fail of their purpose.[27]

> . . . in respect of industries, where the quality of the output is of supreme importance and would, in private hands, be in danger of neglect, public operation is desirable.[28]

> . . . the relative inefficiency of public operation, as compared with private operation, is very large in highly speculative undertakings, and dwindles to nothing in respect of those where the speculative element is practically non-existent.[29]

The evidence, you will hardly need be reminded, consisted of a few quotations from books on municipal trading.

Pigou's views of the competence of the state were, like his predecessors' views, a tolerably random selection of the immediately previous views, warmed by hope. He felt that reliance upon such loose general reflections was unavoidable. On the question of whether public or private operation of an industry would be more efficient in production, we are told "at the outset, it must be made clear that attempts to conduct such a comparison by reference to statistics are fore-doomed to failure."[30] How is it made clear? Very simply: by pointing out that it is unlikely that a public and a private enterprise operate under identical conditions of production. This test of the feasibility of statistical research would rule out all such research, and of course Pigou throughout his life accepted this implication.

Let me say that Pigou did not differ from his less illustrious colleagues in the superficiality of his judgments on the economic competence of the state—here he was at least as shrewd and circumspect as they. He differed only in writing more pages of economic analysis of fully professional quality than any other economist of the twentieth century.

Rather than sample other economists, I shall characterize more generally their role in the period of growing state control over economic life. The traditional and inevitable economic functions of the state such as taxation and the control of the monetary system are not considered in the following remarks. These functions pose no question of the desirability of state action and very different questions of the economist's role in policy. On the basis of a highly incomplete canvass of the literature, I propose three generalizations.

First, there was a large and growing range of policy issues which economists essentially ignored. If we examine the English legislation governing shop closing hours, or pure food and drug inspection, or municipal utilities, or railway and truck and ocean transportation, or the legal status of labor unions, or a host of other questions, we shall find that as a rule economists did not write on the issue, or appear before the Royal Commissions, or otherwise participate in the policy formulation. Before 1914 the detachment from contemporary policy was Olympian, thereafter it was mortal but awesome. American economists, perhaps reflecting their Germanic training, were more interested in policy, so one can cite examples like John R. Commons on regulation of public utilities and on workmen's compensation laws, J. B. Clark and a host of others on the trust problem, and so on. Even here, however, many important economic policies were (and are still) ignored, among them pure food laws, wage legislation, fair employment practices acts, the zoning of land uses, and controls over the capital markets.

Second, even when economists took an active and direct interest in a policy issue, they did not make systematic empirical studies to establish the extent and nature of a problem or the probable efficiency of alternative methods of solving the problem.

It is difficult to support allegations about the absence of a given type of scientific work; often the allegation illuminates only the reading habits of its author. I am reasonably confident, however, that the following subjects were not investigated with even modest thoroughness: (1) the effects of regulation on the level and structure of prices or rates of public utilities; (2) the extent to which safety in production processes and purity in products are achieved by a competitive market and by a regulatory body; (3) the cost to the community of preventing failures of financial institutions by the route of suppressing competition compared with the costs by the route of insurance; (4) the effects of price support systems for distressed industries upon the distribution of income, as compared with alternative policies; and (5) the effects of policies designed to preserve competition. This list is short, but I submit that the examples are important enough to give credence to my generalization on the paucity of systematic empirical work on the techniques of economic policy. From 1776 to 1964 the chief instrument of empirical demonstration on the economic competence of the state has been the telling anecdote.

Third, the economist's influence upon the formulation of economic policy has usually been small. It has been small because he lacked special professional knowledge of the comparative competence of the state and of private enterprise. The economist could and did use his economic theory, and it cannot be denied that the economist's economic theory is better than everyone's else economic theory. But for reasons to which I shall immediately turn, economic theory has not been an adequate platform. Lacking real expertise, and lacking also evangelical ardor, the economist has had little influence upon the evolution of economic policy.

III

If economists have lacked a firm empirical basis for their policy views, one might expect that guidance could be derived from their theoretical systems. In fact, to the degree that a theoretical system has been submitted to a variety of empirical tests, it is a source of more reliable knowledge than an empirical uniformity in solitary confinement. The theory allows tests of the relationship incorporated in the theory that are outside the view of the discoverer of the theory, so these tests are more challenging.

The economists' policy views have in fact been much influenced by their theories. The vast preference for free international trade is surely based in good part upon the acceptance of the classical theory of comparative costs. The general presumption against direct regulation of prices by the state is surely attributable in good part to the belief in the optimum properties of a competitive price system. The growth of support among economists for public regulation of economic activities is at least partly due to the development of the theory of disharmonies between private and social costs, and partly also to the increasingly more rigorous standards of optimum economic performance.

If it would be wrong to deny a substantial influence of economic theory on economists' policy views, it would be wronger still to suggest that the policies follow closely and unambiguously from the general theory. Our first example of free trade will suffice to illustrate the looseness of the connection. Smith supported free trade because he believed that tariffs simply diverted resources from more productive to less productive fields, and the absence of an explanation for the rates of exchange between foreign and domestic commodities did not bother him. A century later Sidgwick argued that on theoretical grounds tariffs were often beneficial to a nation, but that "from the difficulty of securing in any actual government sufficient wisdom, strength, and singleness of aim to introduce protection only so far as it is advantageous to the community" the statesman should avoid protective duties.[31] To the extent that theory was guiding Sidgwick, surely it was a theory of government rather than of economics.

There is one primary reason why the theory is not, as a rule, coercive with respect to the policies that a believer in the theory must accept: a theory can usually be made to support diverse policy positions. Theories present general relationships, and which part of a theory is decisive in a particular context is a matter of empirical evidence. Consider the wages-fund doctrine, if I may be permitted to refer to it without its almost inseparable prefix, notorious. This theory asserted that there was a relatively fixed amount to be paid in wages in the short run, and that if one group got higher wages, other groups would get lower wages or be unemployed. It followed that if a particular group of workers formed a union and managed to raise their wages, other workers would bear the burden, and numerous disciples of the wages-fund doctrine accepted this policy view.[32] But John Stuart Mill could argue, quite in the opposite direction, that since most workers would be at a subsistence level, at most the successful union would inflict only short-run harm on other workers, whereas its higher income could be permanent.[33] And obviously it is a quantitative question whether the short-run costs or the permanent benefits were larger.

What is true of the wages-fund theory is true of other theories: an empirical question always insists upon intruding between the formal doctrine and its concrete application. The truly remarkable fact is not that economists accepting the same theory sometimes differ on policy, but that they differ so seldom. The wide consensus at any time comes, I suspect, from a tacit acceptance of the same implicit empirical assumptions by most economists. All classical economists accepted as a fact the belief that wage earners would not save, although they had no evidence on the matter. All modern economists believe they will never encounter Edgeworth's taxation paradox, with no more evidence. All economists at all times accept the universality of negatively sloping demand curves, and they do so without any serious search for contrary empirical evidence.

These empirical consensuses have no doubt usually been correct—one can know a thing without a sophisticated study. Truth was born before modern statistics. Yet generations of economists also believed that over long periods diminishing returns would inevitably triumph over technological advance in agriculture, a view that agricultural history of the last one hundred years has coolly ignored.

A second and lesser source of the loose connection between theory and policy has been the difficulty of translating theory into policy because of practical politics or administration. The economist refrains from drawing a policy conclusion because its implementation would pose large social or administrative costs. Mill dismissed an income tax because of the inquisitorial burdens it would put on taxpayers; one would have thought that he would remember that an earlier inquisition had been welcomed to Spain. For at least one hundred years economists have recommended that a nation proceed to free trade gradually over a five-year period to ease the transition, and the period is usually lengthened if protectionism is on the ascendant. I have often wondered why we deem it necessary to tell a confirmed drunkard not to reduce his drinking too rapidly.

A third, and fortunately a moderately rare, reason for separating theory from policy is flagrant inconsistency, usually stemming from that great source of inconsistency in intelligent men, a warm heart. Marshall proved—rather unconvincingly, I must say—that the doctrine of consumer surplus instructed us to tax necessaries rather than luxuries.[34] The idea was disposed of in a footnote because it disregarded ability to pay. The economic arguments against minimum wage legislation have usually been refuted by reference to the need of poorer people for larger incomes.

The essential ambiguity of general theoretical systems with respect to public policy, however, has been the real basis of our troubles. So long as a competent economist can bend the existing theory to either side of most viable controversies without violating the rules of professional work, the voice of the economist must be a whisper in the legislative halls.

IV

The economic role of the state has managed to hold the attention of scholars for over two centuries without arousing their curiosity. This judgment that the perennial debate has refused to leave the terrain of abstract discourse is true, I believe, of the continental literature as well as the English and American literature. Economists have refused either to leave the problem alone or to work on it.

Why have not the effects of the regulatory bodies on prices and rates been ascertained, even at the cost of a 1 percent reduction in the literature on how to value assets for rate purposes? Why have not the effects of welfare activities on the distribution of income been determined for an important range of such activities, even at the cost of a 1 percent reduction in denunciations of the invasion of personal liberty? Why has not the degree of success of governments in bringing private and social costs together been estimated, even at the cost of a 1 percent reduction in the literature on consumer surplus? Why have we been content to leave the problem of policy unstudied?

This variously phrased question can be considered to be a request for either a formal theory of state action or a set of empirical studies of the comparative advantages of public and private control.

Consider first the control over economic life as a formal theoretical problem. Why do we not have a theory to guide us in ascertaining the areas of comparative advantage of uncontrolled private enterprise, competitive private enterprise, public regulation, public operation, and the other forms of economic organization? This theory would predict the manner in which the state would conduct various economic activities, such as protecting consumers from monopoly or fraud, assisting distressed industries and areas, or stimulating inventions. The theory might yield rules such as that a competitive system is superior for introducing new products, or public enterprise is superior where there are many parties to a single transaction. That we have not done so is attributable, I conjecture, to two difficulties.

The first difficulty is that the issue of public control had a constantly changing focus: it was the relations of labor and employers one year, the compensation to tenants for improvements on farms and the control of railroad rates the year thereafter. At any one time few areas of economic life were seriously in dispute: most economic activities were uncontroversially private or public. That a single theory should be contrived to guide society in dealing with these various and changing problems was perhaps too great an abstraction to encourage serious efforts.

Moreover, and this is the second difficulty, the standard apparatus of the economist is not clearly appropriate. Ordinary maximizing behavior, with the ordinary rewards and obstacles of economic analysis, does not seem directly applicable to the problem. The bounds of state competence, and the areas of its superiority over variously controlled private action, are difficult to bring within a coherent theoretical system.

In short, the theory of public policy may be a difficult theory to devise, although until we have tried to devise it even this opinion is uncertain.

A usable theory of social control of economic life was not essential, however, to professional study of policy: could not the economist make empirical studies of the effects of various ways of dealing with specific problems? The state regulates machinery in factories: does this reduce accidents appreciably? The state regulated the carriage of emigrants from England and Ireland to the new world—what did the regulations achieve? A thousand prices had been regulated—were they lower or stickier than unregulated prices? The empirical answers would obviously have contributed both to public policy and to the development of a general theory of public and private economy.

Here we must pause, not without embarrassment, to notice that we could ask for empirical studies in areas traditional to economics as well as in the netherland of half economics, half political science. We need not be surprised, I suppose, that we know little of the effects of state regulation, when we also know very little about how oligopolists behave. Marshall's theory that the differences between short- and long-run prices and profits are regulated by the differences between short- and long-run reactions of supply will be 75 years old next year. Despite its immense influence, this theory has yet to receive a full empirical test. If such basic components of modern economic theory have escaped tests for quantitative significance, it is hardly surprising that our antitrust laws, our motor carrier regulation, and our control of insurance company investments have also escaped such tests.

Still, there has been a difference. Empirical tests of economic theories have been made for generations, and with greater frequency and diligence than we encounter in the area of social experiments. Already in 1863 Jevons had ascertained the serious fall in the value of gold consequent upon the Californian and Australian gold discoveries—it was 26 percent over the thirteen-year period, 1849–1862. No such diligence or ingenuity can be found in the study of state controls at that time. A half century later Henry Moore was calculating statistical demand curves; again the study of the effects of public policies was lagging.

The age of quantification is now full upon us. We are now armed with a bulging arsenal of techniques of quantitative analysis, and of a power—as compared to untrained common sense—comparable to the displacement of archers by cannon. But this is much less a cause than a consequence of a more basic development: the desire to measure economic phenomena is now in the ascendant. It is becoming the basic article of work as well as of faith of the modern economist that at a minimum one must establish orders of magnitude, and preferably one should ascertain the actual shapes of economic functions with tolerable accuracy.

The growth of empirical estimation of economic relationships, please notice, did not come as a response to the assault on formal theory by the German Historical School, nor was it a reply to the denunciations of theory by the American Institutionalists. It has been a slow development, contributed to by an earlier development in some natural sciences but mostly by the demonstrated successes of the pioneers of the quantitative method—the Jevons, the Mitchells, the Moores, the Fishers.

It is a scientific revolution of the very first magnitude—indeed I consider the so-called theoretical revolutions of a Ricardo, a Jevons, or a Keynes to have been minor revisions compared to the vast implications of the growing insistence upon quantification. I am convinced that economics is finally at the threshold of its golden age—nay, we already have one foot through the door.

The revolution in our thinking has begun to reach public policy, and soon it will make irresistible demands upon us. It will become inconceivable that the margin requirements on securities markets will be altered once a year without knowing whether they have even a modest effect. It will become impossible for an import-quota system to evade the calculus of gains and costs. It will become an occasion for humorous nostalgia when arguments for private and public performance of a given economic activity are conducted by reference to the phrase, external economies, or by recourse to a theorem on perfect competition.

This is prophecy, not preaching. You have listened to sage advice on what to study and how to study it for well over a century. If you had heeded this advice, you would have accomplished almost nothing, but you would have worked on an immense range of subjects and with a stunning array of approaches. Fortunately you have learned that although such advice is almost inevitable on such occasions as the retirement of an officer of a professional society, it is worth heeding only when it is backed by successful examples. I have no reason to believe that you left your tough-mindedness at home tonight, and I shall respect it. I assert, not that we should make the studies I wish for, but that no one can delay their coming.

I would gloat for one final moment over the pleasant prospects of our discipline. That we are good theorists is not open to dispute: for 200 years our analytical system has been growing in precision, clarity, and generality, although not always in lucidity. The historical evidence that we are becoming good empirical workers is less extensive, but the last half century of economics certifies the immense increase in the power, the care, and the courage of our quantitative researches. Our expanding theoretical and empirical studies will inevitably and irresistibly enter into the subject of public policy, and we shall develop a body of knowledge essential to intelligent policy formulation. And then, quite frankly, I hope that we become the ornaments of democratic society whose opinions on economic policy shall prevail.

NOTES

1. Adam Smith, *The Wealth of Nations*, Modern Library ed., p. 308.

2. See the essay by Viner, "Adam Smith and Laissez Faire," in *Adam Smith 1776–1926* (University of Chicago, 1928).

3. Smith, p. 438.

4. John Ramsay McCulloch, *Principles of Political Economy*, 1st ed. (London: 1825), pp. 144 ff.

5. McCulloch, a somewhat underrated man, again challenged Smith here; see "Navigation Laws," *Edinburgh Review*, May 1823.

6. *The Article on Government* (reprinted from the Supplement to the *Encyclopoedia Britannica* [London: 1829]), p. 7.

7. Ibid., p. 32.

8. Mill's essay elicited a brilliant attack by Macaulay, who turned Mill's argument that every man seeks only his own interests against the plea for universal suffrage:

> That the property of the rich minority can be made subservient to the pleasures of the poor majority will scarcely be denied. But Mr. Mill proposes to give the poor majority power over the rich minority. Is it possible to doubt to what, on his own principles, such an arrangement must lead?

The argument is carried to an interesting prediction: "As for America, we appeal to the twentieth century," "Mill's Essay on Government," in *Critical, Historical and Miscellaneous Essays* (New York: 1873), II, pp. 36–37, 40.

9. Mountifort Longfield, *Lectures on Political Economy* (1834), p. 18.

10. Royal Commission on Railways, *Evidence and Papers Relating to Railways in Ireland* (1866), pp. 126–30, 359–60.

11. *A Letter to Lord Ashley* (London: 1844), pp. 64–65.

12. *Letters on the Factory Act* (London: 1844).

13. He did make some reference to the incompetence of state action: ". . . the great majority of things are worse done by the intervention of government, than the individuals most interested in the matter would do them, or cause them to be done, if left to themselves" [John Stuart Mill, *Principles of Political Economy*, 1st ed. (London: 1848), II, p. 511]. This argument does not play a major role in shaping his attitude, however.

14. Mill, bk. V, ch. 11.

15. Mill's famous essay, *On Liberty*, does little to reduce our uncertainty. It is here that he asserts:

> Despotism is a legitimate mode of government in dealing with barbarians, provided the end be their improvement, and the means justified by actually effecting the ends.
>
> The laws which, in many countries on the Continent, forbid marriage unless the parties can show that they have the means of supporting a family, do not exceed the legitimate powers of the State. . . .
>
> As the principle of the individual liberty is not involved in the doctrine of Free Trade . . . (*The English Philosophers from Bacon to Mill* [Modern Library 1939], pp. 956, 1035, 1024).

It is not easy to avoid the conclusion that for Mill "liberty" was conveniently well correlated with the forms of behavior of which he personally approved.

16. *Memorials of Alfred Marshall* (1925), pp. 274–76, 339 ff.; *Industry and Trade* (1919), pp. 666–72.

17. *Memorials*, p. 338.

18. *Official Papers by Alfred Marshall* (1926), pp. 395–96.

19. Thus McCulloch said of the post office: "It does not seem, though the contrary has been sometimes contended, that the Postoffice could be so well conducted by anyone else as by government: the latter alone can enforce perfect regularity in all its subordinate departments. . . ." (*Dictionary of Commerce* (1854 ed.), article on "Postage").

20. David Roberts, *Victorian Origins of the Welfare State* (New Haven, Conn.: 1960); Oliver MacDonagh, *A Pattern of Government Growth, 1800–60* (London: 1961).

21. W. S. Jevons, *Methods of Social Reform* (London: 1883), pp. 355, 279, 338.

22. Idem, *The State in Relation to Labour* (London: 1882), p. 4.

23. It should be a source of morbid instruction to us, that immediately after laying down this dogmatic rule on how to treat with dangerous machinery, Jevons denounces those who view the economist as a "presumptuous theorist, who is continually laying down hard-and-fast rules for the conduct of other people." [*The State*, p. 8].

24. "Experimental Legislation and the Drink Traffic," *The Contemporary Review* 37 (1880): 192 (reprinted in *Methods of Social Reform*, p. 275). He did not see the potentialities of empirical study in the absence of formal experiment, however,

and denied the feasibility of a statistical approach ("Experimental Legislation," pp. 184–85).

25. A. C. Pigou, *Wealth and Welfare* (London: 1912).

26. Pigou, p. 250.

27. Pigou, p. 253.

28. Pigou, p. 288.

29. The maturing fruit in a later edition, *The Economics of Welfare*, 4th ed. (1932), p. 399.

30. Pigou, *Wealth and Welfare*, p. 274.

31. Henry Sidgwick, *Principles of Political Economy* (London: 1883), pp. 485–86.

32. For example, J. E. Cairnes, *Some Leading Principles of Political Economy* (London: 1873), pp. 258–60.

33. *Principles of Political Economy*, Ashley ed. (London: 1929), p. 402.

34. Alfred Marshall, *Principles of Economics*, 8th ed. (London: 1920), p. 467n.

ECONOMIC COMPETITION AND POLITICAL COMPETITION

· 9 ·

Competition is a central and ubiquitous concept of economic analysis. It is much debated whether there has been a decline of competition in the marketplace, but assuredly no decline has taken place in its role in economic analysis.[1] Although competition, and more generally rivalry, no doubt has a vastly longer history in political than in economic literature, it has received more intensive theoretical and empirical analysis in economics. This paper is devoted to the analogies and contrasts between economic and political competition.

In Part I we present a statement of the standard properties of economic competition, which has a direct and literal application to the behavior of local governments. Here competition is between firms (and in analogy, cities) for the patronage of customers (and in analogy, residents).

In Part II political competition is defined (as is customary) in terms of party competition: the size and number of parties are taken as given, and their consequences for political behavior investigated. Similarity of party size is often believed to favor competition in the sense of parties seeking closer fulfillment of the preferences of voters. The theory of spatial competition is shown to offer ambiguous support for this belief, and to offer little assistance in developing a theory of party sizes or goals with this approach.

The main theme of the paper is developed in Part III—it is that political

From *Public Choice* 13 (Fall 1972). Permission to reprint courtesy of Martinus Nijhoff.

competition, even between parties, basically resembles economic competition. It is argued that even in a democracy no special significance is to be attached to a majority of the vote (or the seats in a legislature). Just as in economic markets, voters in political "markets" may best achieve their preferences through minority parties. The orientation to rational behavior by voters seeking to achieve preferred public policies is shown in Part IV to provide a useful answer to the question: what do political parties maximize? The analysis is extended to a reformulation of the paradox of voting in Part V.

I. Economic Competition
and a Direct Political Analogue

Consider the production of automobiles. To the economist competition denotes the rivalry of the producers of automobiles for the patronage of automobile buyers. If told only that sales of automobiles in 1969 were divided between the firms as follows:

General Motors	47 percent
Chrysler	15 percent
Ford	24 percent
Other	14 percent

the economist cannot draw a rigorous inference with respect to the presence or vigor of competition. The firms may be colluding upon price, and have set it at the monopoly level, or they may be competing vigorously in the following specific sense: no firm would voluntarily sell additional units at the existing price because the additional (marginal) cost of these units would exceed the price.[2]

Several things should be said even at this preliminary level about economic competition:

1. The formal definition—which has not yet been given—turns on the extent of the ability of a firm to influence price. When the firm's influence is zero, the competition is perfect. Competition is usually greater in longer periods (in which new rivals can enter) than in the short run.

2. There are important consequences of competition: the elimination of "profits"—meaning receipts in excess of what the firm can earn in other industries; and the elimination of price discrimination. The com-

petitive industry produces its output with a minimum quantity of resources.

3. The *probability* of the existence of strong competition is believed to be positively correlated with:

    i. the number of rivals;

    ii. their similarity of size, and in particular the smaller the share of industry output possessed by the largest firm, the more vigorous competition is likely to be.

4. A measure of "competition" is afforded by either:

    i. the extent of influence of the firm's output on price (the elasticity of demand); or

    ii. the relative excess of price over marginal cost. These are analytically equivalent if the firm maximizes profits because

$$\frac{\text{price-marginal cost}}{\text{price}} = \frac{-1}{\text{elasticity of demand}}.^3$$

Economists would generally agree that the automobile industry is concentrated, whatever the decision on competition. Concentration is measured in ways we shall refer to later.

This traditional economic definition of competition applies directly and exactly to one area of political life: local government.[4] Consider the competition of local governments for citizens—each city of (say) 25,000 in an area competes for citizens by offering various levels and combinations of public services and taxes. If the city size is not too large (and hence the number of cities too small), we may reproduce the standard conditions and results of economic competition:

1. There will be numerous cities offering each class of municipal services for which a demand exists—e.g., per capita expenditures of $800 per year, few schools, excellent library, etc.

2. The competition of other cities compels each city to supply the services efficiently. Any local party machine will be forced to price (tax) the municipal services at cost.

We may go a step farther and deny the existence of qualitative differences between the competition of private enterprises and public enterprises. There is no element of durable compulsion in the local governments: if any city sets its services or prices at levels to which some of its citizens object, in the long run they can migrate to more congenial governments. The time necessary to reach long-run equilibrium, and the extent of the interim burdens on dissatisfied citizens, will be governed by two circumstances. First, the greater the accuracy with which citizens predict the future services and costs of government, the less the short-run situation can depart from long-run equilibrium. Second, the lower the costs of migration, the less persistent any departure from long-run equilibrium. These factors do not differ in principle from those encountered in the economic theory of long- and short-run decisions (as in long-term investment or occupational choice).

In this regime of local competition, it is not apparent that political parties will have an important role in the political process. The cities will tend to be fairly homogeneous if there are economies in specializing upon one type of city services, as seems probable, or if the citizens prefer to flock with others of similar feather. Multiple local parties are likely to emerge only if new conditions pose policy issues not contemplated by the citizens in making their original municipal choices.

As one moves up to larger cities and to states, the number of rival governments decreases and the conditions for intergovernmental competition are departed from in increasing measure. The reduction in number of cities means that fewer varieties of city services are available. A greater variety of citizens dwell in larger cities because the economies of localization and scale which create large cities require a variegated labor force. The costs of migration presumably also increase—a longer move is necessary on average to change one's public services—so larger departures from long run equilibrium are possible. Even at the international level, however, some element of intergovernmental competition will be found.[5]

II. Party Competition and Its Economic Analogue

The concept of party competition as it is developed in the literature of political science is directed to the closeness of the outcome of elections. A state has a *competitive* party structure when

    1. Victory (in the legislature, say) is won by even the less successful party in a substantial share of elections (25 percent in the original Ranney-Kendall article), or what is related, the average share of votes of the losing party is not *much* less than 50 percent.[6]

    2. The parties do not have long runs of electoral success or failure.[7]

It is commonly asserted that the more competitive the parties in this sense, the more responsive the political system will be to the desires of the majority. In this section we shall examine and question the theory of spatial competition, which gives ambiguous support for this assertion, and in the next section raise

FIGURE 9.1

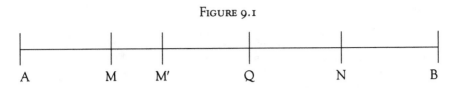

a more fundamental question about the role of a majority in public policy formation.

There is a model of spatial competition in economics due to Harold Hotelling which bears a close resemblance to the foregoing view of party competition.[8] The movement of party platforms and promises *toward* voters, which is one possible direction of definition of political competition, is obviously analogous to the market-oriented movements of two firms located on a road along which customers are distributed. Using a very simple model (with customers distributed uniformly along the road), Hotelling developed an analysis which we briefly restate in political terms.

Let voters (or buyers) be distributed uniformly along a scale of preferences (a road) from A to B (see Figure 9.1). The point A might represent zero expenditures on welfare, the point B, 8 percent of national income. With two parties, collusion such as commercial firms might engage in, would involve locating at points M and N, where each party received the vote of that half of the customers which found the respective platforms (2 percent and 6 percent spent on welfare) more palatable, and divide by agreement the benefits of holding office. The actual law passed would fluctuate randomly between M and N.[9] This—the very maximum of conventional party competition—would be labeled zero competition by the economist because there is no attempt by one party to attract voters from the other. If party M now increased its platform offer to M' (say 2.4 percent of national income for welfare expenditures), it would attract a few voters to the right to Q (the midpoint of the line), who would now find its position closer to that which they prefer.[10] N could retaliate by reducing its platform offer to 5.6 percent—and a process of "competition" would continue until both parties arrived at Q—the paradox which Hotelling presented in his analysis. Again votes would be equally divided, and parties would achieve small majorities in random sequence. The same observed equality of vote as we observed with collusion would now obtain with one form of competitive behavior.

Of course this model is austerely simple. If parties, by moving away from A and B, led citizens at these points to abstain from voting, this would deter the parties' approach to a common platform at Q. If more parties enter, the platform promises will also begin to spread out. This model does not naturally

generalize to deal with parties of different sizes, nor to nonuniform distributions of voter preferences.

The Hotelling form of competition, we observe, is extremely limited in
form. Each party takes the other's location as fixed, even though a sequence of
countermoves should reveal the interdependence of positions to the slightest
intelligence. Nor is there any explanation, if we shift back to economics, of
where the price will be set by the two firms (duopolists). If each firm takes the
output of its rival as fixed, in extension of the assumption it makes about the
rival's location, we would arrive at a price between competitive and monopolist
levels.[11] The corresponding political proposition would presumably be that the
emoluments of the party functionaries—office holders and members of political organizations—would be larger than was needed to attract them from rival
occupations. Such a proposition, however, has shifted the nature of the
political competition from catering to voter preferences to seeking gains from
party electoral success.

If we attribute two reasonable characteristics to the political process,
namely,

1. Only one party can win the election (a self-evident fact that we shall
   deny in the next section),

2. The party machinery is essentially neutral, and its personnel wish
   merely to win elections,

then there is no reason, at this level of abstraction, why there should be more
than one party, which carefully seeks out the position of the median voter and
promises—and delivers—his preference. A rational single party (or tyrant)
which seeks to maximize the emoluments of office will not defy the majority
wish, although it may pocket vast gains from the control of the process—just as
a profit-maximizing monopolist will not deny consumers the product they
desire (at a monopolistic price). Indeed the argument is stronger: if the single
party does not seek the most popular policy, and the monopolist the most
popular product, they reduce the amount of their return (more self-defensive
costs for the tyrant, less profits for the monopolist). The role of competition, at
this level, is not to please voters or customers—it always pays to do that[12]—but
to eliminate unnecessary returns to the party or enterprise functionaries.

Political literature has apparently paid little attention to the return to
party functionaries (spoils system) as an *aspect of political competition*.[13] If this
route is pursued, the main result in economic theory is that the magnitude and
duration of noncompetitive returns to a dominant party (monopolist) will be
governed primarily by the ease of entry of a second party. If the second party
can enter, one would expect it to compete, less by the ideology of party

platform than by the offer of economy and efficiency in performing the desired governmental functions. This threat is itself sufficient to moderate the exactions of a dominant party.

If we add one element of realism to the model, the role of multiple parties will be restored in a measure. Consider the problem of information: how are the desires of the public ascertained? The Hotelling model dismisses this question by its formulation—customers are uniform in intensity of desire, and uniformly distributed along a road (scale of preferences) of known length. In both economic and political life the length of the road and the location of individuals change, and need to be ascertained periodically. The rivalry of parties is then one, and in certain respects an extremely persuasive, method of registering the ruling electoral consensus. On this view, parties are more important, and shifts in political victory more frequent, the more rapidly and unpredictably the preferences of voters change.[14]

In summary, the spatial model of competition sheds little light upon the effects of number and size of parties (or votes) upon the positions taken by parties with respect to voter preferences. Indeed at the level of abstraction at which most discussion of the Hotelling theory has proceeded, there is no reason for the existence of a second party. These limitations arise from the failure to analyze the relationship of voters' preferences to parties and public policies, to which we now turn.

III. The Basic Similarity Between Political and Economic Competition

The analogy between economic competition and nonlocal political competition cannot be carried far before a fundamental difference is encountered: political products (namely, public policies) are usually treated as mutually *exclusive*, whereas economic products (goods and services) are seldom if ever mutually *exclusive*. If we have a social security system with a tax rate of 6 percent on employers, we cannot simultaneously have a system with a different rate. In contrast, the provision of one size and type of house or automobile does not preclude the simultaneous provision of other sizes and types. It is the essence of the political process that its policies be coercive in the sense that many voters may prefer other policies. In economic life such "coercion" arises only when economies of scale prevent an article from being produced to the specifications of an idiosyncratic group. As a result of exclusivity in policies, there is a strong tendency to label the winning of 51 percent of legislative seats a victory and 49 percent a defeat. In economic life the firm which sells 49 percent of a product is no failure, and indeed may be more profitable than a rival selling 51 percent of the product.

From the difference in apparent exclusivity flow certain other differences between political and economic rivalry. Every patron of a business enterprise receives a product, and in the absence of error or fraud it is the product which was covenanted for. The voter for a party may receive nothing: no representative in the government, or one who is unable to achieve the promised policy. Again, the larger the number of enterprises, in general the larger the number of products and the more closely each consumer can match his preferences. The larger the number of political parties, the less the probability that any party will achieve its platform: coalition governments will perhaps be unable to adopt any policy which departs much from the status quo. So goes much political writing.

This approach is unappealing: if nature abhors a vacuum, man at least despises all-or-none alternatives. It is not useful to characterize the outcome of a political rivalry as failure (−1) or success (+1) for a party: in an important sense, political outcomes range continuously from failure to success. Even in an algebraic sense this is true: if a party wins an election by one legislative seat, it is probable that it will soon lose an election, so if success has a time dimension, success is a quantitative, not a qualitative, outcome of political rivalry.

The "outcome" or product of political competition is public policy, legislative and executive and judicial. A voter wishes representatives only as agents, agents to procure and insure the policies the voter prefers. The policy the voter wishes is an actual operating policy: it is not the schedule of enacted personal income tax rates, or even this schedule suitably qualified with loopholes and peculiarities of income definition, but the levels of taxes ultimately collected, taking due account of the degree of vigilance of enforcement. Realized policy is inherently a quantitative notion. The content of policy is determined by appropriations, enforcement, the attitudes of bureaucrats and citizens (who enter enforcement also in the legal process), as well as by the so-called governing legislation.

Full success, 100 percent success, in a policy is presumably achieved when *everyone* favors it. Short of this unanimity, there will be violations and more or less incomplete enforcement, and even serious restrictions upon the legislation. One does not simply pass a law of aid to dependent children; the actual policy depends upon numerous variables: residence requirements, schedule of payments, administration (speed of processing, investigation of claims), appropriations, speed of adjustment to new conditions, and so on. Exclusivity of public policies does not create a basic difference between political and economic competition. The party with 51 percent of the vote in one election can do very little; that with 65 percent in two consecutive elections can do considerably more. At least as a first approximation, an economic firm with 49 percent of output exerts 49/51 as much influence on price as its larger rival. The situation in political parties is not much different.

That political effectiveness is a more or less smoothly increasing function of the size of a party is so important a proposition as to deserve elaboration. In the Appendix a statistical investigation is made of one instance: the effect of minorities which do not use public schools upon the level of public school expenditures. This study offers a measure of support for the present argument: as the minority grows in relative size, the level of expenditures per pupil in public schools *declines*.

A minority that feels intensely the need for a particular policy can pay a sufficient price to obtain it even with normal, legal democratic procedures. The method of payment is primarily vote-trading: the minority may vote for programs it is less opposed to than the one it seeks, and if the minority becomes larger, the number of subcoalitions of the "majority" it must persuade to join it on the desired issue diminishes, and the cost of getting their support becomes less.

Secondly, all political systems contain some element of division of power so a minority will hold a share of minor offices which responds to its relative size. This element is obvious when the system is explicitly federal, as in the United States or Switzerland, but it holds also in centralized states such as England and France. An element of division of power is introduced, for example, by having different terms for various political offices.

Thirdly, the minority, even when each member acts only as an individual, imposes costs upon the majority in enforcing policies to which the minority is opposed. These costs will be larger, the larger the minority and the more intense its opposition. A democratic system cannot, indeed, resolve issues when the minority is (say) one-fifth or more and fervent in its desires: one must resort to partition (Belgium) or civil war (United States) when minority and majority are adamant.

If political effectiveness were not positively and more or less continuously related to party size, it would be impossible to explain important political phenomena. Consider only two:

1. Particular industries and occupations obtain from the state a variety of economic privileges which are injurious to the vast majority of the population. Farm subsidies, oil import quotas, tariffs, and occupational licensing are examples. These small minorities achieve their effectiveness primarily because it is uneconomic for the majority to oppose them.[15]

2. Minority parties often persist for long periods—for example, the Federalists lost power in 1801 but survived for a quarter century. One

explanation (the simple Downsian version) would be that these parties incorrectly predicted voter preferences in a long sequence of elections. It seems much more reasonable to interpret these periods differently: the minority is more effective in achieving its ends as a homogeneous minority than as a more heterogeneous majority.

This second example suggests that persistent minority parties must have one central policy preference to unify them. If they do not have a paramount issue, but instead have many distinctive preferences, they could not engage in vote-trading.

IV. What Should Political Parties Maximize?

When Anthony Downs brought the theory of industrial organization to bear upon political parties, he postulated as the goal of a political party a maximum of votes at the next election.[16] The distinction between a maximum of votes and a maximum plurality was not clearly drawn.[17] Riker proposed an alternative goal: the minimum size necessary to electoral victory, so that the beneficiaries of political power (the members of the successful party) be as a few as possible, and its victims (the nonmembers of this party) be as numerous as possible.[18] We can resolve this question by taking account of the relationship between party strength and political influence argued for in the preceding section.

Two basic postulates may be proposed with respect to political parties:

1. The larger a party's plurality (or majority) in the legislature, the greater its control over the government. The influence function of a party, its probability of determining public policy,[19] say $I(s)$ where s is its share of legislative seats, is a monotonically increasing function of s throughout the entire range of s from 0 to 1. However, there is probably diminishing returns to increments of s beyond some level, so $I'(s) > 0$, $I''(s) < 0$.

2. The larger the share of people (resources) outside the coalition, the greater the opportunity for the use of the machinery of the state to benefit the party members—this is Riker's postulate. The gain to each member of a coalition from a *given* use of political power—say, the passage of a tax or appropriation act—decreases as the ratio of coalition to population rises. This gain function, $G(s)$, therefore decreases monotonically as s rises. If outsiders are chosen properly, the most vulnerable will be admitted last; for example, if a redistribution of wealth from the

FIGURE 9.2

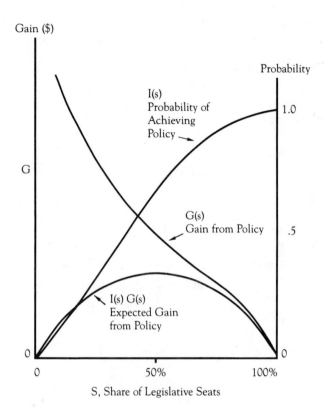

S, Share of Legislative Seats

rich is contemplated, the very richest would be the last to be admitted to the party. Hence $G''(s) < 0$ beyond a certain s_o.

The objective of a political party must then be, for given cost, to maximize the expected gain of its members, or

$$I(s)\ G(s)$$

The functions are illustrated in Figure 9.2. The political party will seek to maximize its *net* gain, which is $I(s)\ G(s)$ *minus* costs, $C(s)$, of achieving the given share of legislative seats. Since the marginal cost of a share of legislative seats is positive and for most party sizes probably increases with s, it serves to reduce the optimum size of party.

Of course this is a much-simplified version of the party decision function, and it could readily be extended. For example, the probability of obtaining desired legislation, I(s), is also a function of the shares of seats held by each other party if there are three or more parties. Again, the basic goal of the party is not to pass legislation in one biennium, but to maximize the present value of all future legislation. The goal of the party, even in these more complex cases, is a direct extension of the present formulation. The merit of this formulation of the goal of parties is precisely that it invites the more complex and subtle analysis which will surely be necessary to understand real political behavior.

V. The Voters' Paradox

The so-called voters' paradox is simply that rational conduct will normally lead to nonvoting, yet the majority of the population (surely by definition, rational) votes. The expected gain from voting is the product of

1. The probability that the vote will change the outcome, and
2. The benefit to the voter of having his preferred party or issue win.

Unless this product exceeds

3. The cost of voting (which includes becoming sufficiently informed to vote appropriately to one's interests),

the rational voter should stay at home.[20] The formulation of an empirical problem should not contain its answer, but in the present instance little more is required. The conventional argument is that the benefit from victory is some finite sum, and that the probability that one's vote will be effective is approximately

$$\frac{1}{\text{Expected Vote Difference between Victory and Defeat}}$$

which in large constituencies is of course in general a negligible quantity (in recent extremely close presidential elections approximately 10^{-6}). This probability is so small that plausible estimates of gain and voting cost lead to nonvoting as rational conduct. The chief escape from this paradox and explanation for the observed turnout of many voters is usually sought in the fulfillment of a sense of civic duty.[21]

The explanation of what it is that coalitions and parties seek to maximize leads us to question this easy argument. If election outcomes are *not* all-or-nothing (49 percent is defeat) and instead influence is a monotonically increasing function of vote share, then the probability that one's vote will make a difference is *unity*, not some infinitesimal fraction. This restatement does not in turn magically dispose of the paradox, because the additional influence achieved by one more vote for one's party is usually "small." The cost of voting is also tolerably "small," however, and no conclusion can be drawn at this level of generality with respect to the rationality of voting.

Perhaps the closest analogy to voting to affect public policy that arises in the private market is the task of changing a product to better satisfy consumers. How does one automobile buyer affect the design of future automobiles, given that large economies of scale require that a substantial number of customers are needed to justify a change in design? Presumably the individual buyer communicates some small message by the type of automobile he chooses from the existing variety, at a definite cost in search and experiment with new goods. It is presumably often rational for the buyer to make a search intended to influence future production,[22] and incur the costs of experimenting with a new product.

The additional influence a party achieves by having $(n+1)$ rather than n votes no doubt varies (and eventually diminishes as n increases), and is larger the larger the number of other parties and the less their intensity of opposition to the policy desired by the given party. It is premature to assert that this self-interest (investment) motive is insufficient to cover the costs of voting for most citizens, so that a utility of voting for its own sake (consumption) needs to be added. The investment motive is rich in empirical implications, and the consumption motive is less well endowed, so we should see how far we can carry the former analysis before we add the latter.

APPENDIX

Let the demand for an average family utilizing the public schools of state i be

$$e_i = f(p, y_i) = p^\ell y_i^\beta, \text{ say.} \tag{1}$$

where e_i = total expenditure per pupil in public schools
y_i = average income per family
p = cost of units of quality of education,

and this cost, p, is assumed to be the same in every state. The actual cost to patrons of public schools will be less than p, however, because some families send their children to parochial and private schools but pay taxes for public schools. As a first approximation, the price to a family using the public schools will be

$$\frac{N_n}{N_c+N_n}\cdot P$$

where N_c is the number of families using Catholic (and private) schools and N_n is the number of families using public schools. Then the demand of families using public schools in state i becomes

$$e_i=\left(\frac{N_n}{N_c+N_n}\right)^{\alpha} P^{\alpha}y_i{}^{\beta}. \qquad (2)$$

If the public school families in a state could choose the level of taxation for schools, they would choose that rate implied by (2). The tax would be proportioned to expenditures per family of all types (since all pay equal taxes by hypothesis), and expenditures per family are proportional to[23]

$$e_i'=\frac{N_n}{N_n+N_c}e_i=\left(\frac{N_n}{N_c+N_n}\right)^{\alpha+1} P^{\alpha}y_i{}^{\beta}. \qquad (3)$$

The elasticity of e_i with respect to $\left(\frac{N_n}{N_n+N_n}=s\right)$ is

$$n_{e's}=1+\alpha<1.$$

To the extent that the political power of the Catholic families is effective, however, taxes are lower, the lower is s, implying that $n_{e's}>0$. The demand effect (equation 3) will lead to a negative elasticity only if α is numerically larger that unity, i.e., if the demand for quality is elastic. Only if the observed elasticity $n_{e's}$ significantly exceeds unity, therefore, can we infer that the direct political influence of the Catholics dominates the demand effect. There is also some question as to how families without present or prospective school age children should be introduced explicitly into the analysis.[24]

For the forty-eight states in existence during the school year, 1954–55, we have calculated the regression equation

$$\log e_i'=a+b\log s+c\log y$$

For the forty-eight states we obtain the following results with e'_i measured by total public expenditures per (public plus private) pupil[25]

$$\log e_i = -4.74 + 1.09 \log s + 1.22 \log y, \quad (R^2 = .659) \qquad (4)$$
$$ (3.12) \qquad (9.03)$$

the t-values being given below the regression coefficients. If we measure e'_i as total expenditure per household, we obtain

$$\log e'_i = -4.64 + 1.96 \log s + 1.20 \log y. \quad (R^2 = .590) \qquad (4.1)$$
$$ (5.18) \qquad (8.01)$$

Both equations yield an elasticity of e' with respect to s greater than unity, and significantly so in the second equation, so it appears that the political power of the non-Catholics increases with their share of the population, and overwhelms the influence of subsidy from the Catholics.

NOTES

1. See the survey by G. J. Stigler, "Perfect Competition, Historically Contemplated," in *Essays in the History of Economics* (Chicago: 1965).

2. Competition can also involve style, durability, horsepower, etc., but there is a deep symmetry in the formal theory, so we ignore these other dimensions of competition.

3. The elasticity of demand—the percentage change in quantity divided by the percentage change in price with which it is associated along a demand curve—is *negative*, and hence the minus sign on the right side of the equation.

4. See Charles M. Tiebout, "A Pure Theory of Local Expenditures," *Journal of Political Economy* (October 1956).

5. More mobile occupations and groups will receive selective attention: witness the concern in Great Britain during the 1960s over the "brain drain."

6. This first condition is generally invoked. See A. Ranney and W. Kendall, "The American Party System," *American Political Science Review* (June 1954). For references to the later literature, see D. G. Pfeiffer, "The Measurement of Inter-Party Competition and Systematic Stability," *American Political Science Review* (June 1957), and R. I. Hofferbert, "Classification of American Party Systems," *Journal of Politics* (August 1964).

7. See J. Schlesinger, "A Two-Dimensional Scheme of American Party Systems," *American Political Science Review* (1955).

8. See H. Hotelling, "Stability in Competition," reprinted in *Readings in Price*

Theory (edited by G. Stigler and K. Boulding); also A. Smithies, "Optimum Location in Spatial Competition," *Journal of Political Economy* (June 1941).

9. Or with rigid 50 percent shares of seats, a compromise of N (4 percent) would be reached—virtually a single party result.

10. Since one-fourth of the voters are between N and Q, over a range of 2 percent of spending, voters in a range of .2 of spending or 1/10 of 1/4 = 1/40 of all voters would shift to M, and the vote would be M', 52.5 percent, N, 47.5 percent.

11. See George Stigler, *The Theory of Price* (New York: 1966), ch. 12. A more interesting economic model would allow each firm to open several stores, but in deference to the analogy to the political process we pursue, this option is not explored.

12. If the monopolist is also a censor (imposing his own tastes), he may make a less preferred product that pleases *him*, but only at a cost in profits. A comparable sentence holds for the tyrant, assuming that he wishes to maximize his utility rather than his emoluments (e.g., set lower welfare expenditures to please himself than the public wishes).

13. James Q. Wilson, "The Economy of Patronage," *Journal of Political Economy* (1961), in fact implicitly postulates noncompetitive conditions in much of his discussion.

14. The closeness of the platforms of the parties could be measured by the stability of the share of votes received by each party, just as in economic competition this measure is used to measure consumer loyalty. In the two-party case, the shares of the parties are s and $(1-s)$ and the variance of the share of either party is $ns(1-s)$, where n is the number of elections. A popular economic measure of *concentration* is the Herfindahl index,

$$H = \sum s^2.$$

i.e., the sum of the squares of the shares of the firms, which has a maximum value of 1 and a minimum value of $1/n$ with n enterprises. With two parties,

$$H = 2s^2 - 2s + 1,$$

so the sum of the variances of the shares is:

$$2ns(1-s) = (1-H)n.$$

This measure of concentration readily generalizes for more than two parties or firms. For a discussion of the economic measures of concentration, see G. J. Stigler, *The Organization of Industry*, ch. 4; and G. Rosenbluth, "Measures of Concentration," in *Business Concentration and Price Policy* (National Bureau of Economic Research, 1955).

15. See George Stigler, "The Theory of Economic Regulation," *The Bell Journal of Economics and Management Science* (Spring 1971).

16. *An Economic Theory of Democracy* (New York: 1957), pp. 31, 35.

17. This distinction is elaborated by M. J. Hinich and P. C. Ordeshook, "Plurality

Maximization v. Vote Maximization: A Spatial Analysis with Variable Participation," *American Political Science Review* (September 1970).

18. *The Theory of Political Coalitions* (New Haven: 1962).

19. The "probability of determining public policy" is easily definable only for the set of alternatives under a single, one-dimensional policy choice. In complex choices, it may not be useful to distinguish influence and the policy achieved.

20. See, for example, A. Downs, *An Economic Theory of Democracy*, pp. 36–50, 260–76; and W. H. Riker and P. C. Ordeshook, "A Theory of the Calculus of Voting," *American Political Science Review* (March 1968).

21. Four of the five satisfactions offered by Riker and Ordeshook are of this sort; the fifth is that going to the polling station may be pleasurable; ibid., p. 28.

22. More precisely, if the variety of automobiles was fixed forever, a given amount of search would be undertaken by the buyer. If desired changes in future products can be encouraged, larger amount of search is justified. See my *The Organization of Industry*, p. 178.

23. If E is total expenditure on public education, e_i is proportional to

$$\frac{E}{N_n}.$$

the factor of proportionality being $1/\lambda$, where λ is school children per family. Taxes per family are proportional to

$$e' = \frac{E}{N_n + N_c} = \frac{E}{N_n} \cdot \frac{N_n}{N_n + N_c} = \frac{e_i N_n}{N_n + N_c}.$$

24. They need not be introduced if each state has a similar family life-child pattern, but their omission will bias the results if older families systematically migrate to communities providing less school service.

25. In both equation (4) and (4.1) income per household is calculated for 1950. Our use of pupil enrollments rather than adult population to measure s is preferable because those numerous Catholic families which use public schools are then implicitly reclassified.

THE PROCESS AND
PROGRESS OF ECONOMICS

· 10 ·

In the work on the economics of information which I began twenty some years ago, I started with an example: how does one find the seller of automobiles who is offering a given model at the lowest price? Does it pay to search more, the more frequently one purchases an automobile, and does it ever pay to search out a large number of potential sellers? The study of the search for trading partners and prices and qualities has now been deepened and widened by the work of scores of skilled economic theorists.

I propose on this occasion to address the same kinds of questions to an entirely different market: the market for new ideas in economic science. Most economists enter this market in new ideas, let me emphasize, in order to obtain ideas and methods for the applications they are making of economics to the thousand problems with which they are occupied: these economists are not the suppliers of new ideas but only demanders. Their problem is comparable to that of the automobile buyer: to find a reliable vehicle. Indeed, they usually end up buying a used, and therefore tested, idea.

Those economists who seek to engage in research on the new ideas of the science—to refute or confirm or develop or displace them—are in a sense both buyers and sellers of new ideas. They seek to develop new ideas and persuade the science to accept them, but they also are following clues and promises and explorations in the current or preceding ideas of the science. It is very costly to

Nobel Memorial Lecture, December 8, 1982. Copyright 1982 by the Nobel Foundation.

enter this market: it takes a good deal of time and thought to explore a new idea far enough to discover its promise or its lack of promise. The history of economics, and I assume of every science, is strewn with costly errors: of ideas, so to speak, that wouldn't run far or carry many passengers. How have economists dealt with this problem? That is my subject.

I begin by distinguishing the prescientific stage of a discipline from its scientific stage. A science is an integrated body of knowledge, and it is pursued and developed by a group of interacting practitioners called scientists. The validation and extension of that body of knowledge is the intellectual goal of the scientists, although of course the pursuit of that goal in turn serves whatever personal goals such as prestige, reputation, and income the scientists seek. These are only definitions, but I hope they are not strained or un-natural ones.

The prescientific stage is characterized in part by the incompleteness of the body of knowledge, but that is only a relative matter since no science is ever complete. This prescientific stage is also characterized by absence of a set of interacting practitioners who are devoting a large part of their lives to the accumulation of knowledge, and hence it is characterized by the absence of cumulative progress.

I. PRESCIENTIFIC ECONOMICS: MERCANTILISM

We will find it useful to spend a short time with the large body of writing called mercantilism. This literature ranges over several centuries, and over England and Western Europe. The literature comprises hundreds of pamphlets and books, and includes participants of the stature of John Locke and William Petty. I must confess at once that I have little direct knowledge of that literature, for I have concentrated my historical work upon the period which followed. However, three major studies of mercantilism are reassuringly agreed upon the characteristics I wish to discuss. The studies are Edgar Furniss's book, *The Position of the Laborer in a System of Nationalism* (1920), Jacob Viner's famous essay, "English Theories of Foreign Trade Before Adam Smith" (1930),[1] and Eli Heckscher's masterly treatise, *Mercantilism* (1934).

A first characteristic of all three surveys of mercantilism is that they almost totally lack a time dimension. Furniss will document a statement by references to two tracts written more than a century apart. With the very first doctrine of mercantilism—that it was vitally important to have an excess of exports over imports—Viner begins a sequence of illustrative quotations with Richard Leicester who wrote in 1381. (Of course if one were allowed to go out of economics it would be easy to continue the sequence of praises of an export balance a full six centuries through 1981 and probably another six centuries through the year 2581!) Heckscher also seldom finds it necessary to notice the temporal sequence of two writers.

A second characteristic is that most mercantilists propose their own views without any attempt to utilize or improve upon the work of other mercantilists. There were sharp controversies, of course, but no regular pattern of sequences of criticisms and responses. These writings, one may note, were almost always briefs for special interests.

The third characteristic is almost a corollary of the first two: there was no cumulative improvement in the doctrines being propounded. I quote Viner:

> In many respects, indeed, as the mercantilist argument became more elaborate and involved, it became more objectionable from the point of view of modern doctrine, and, except with reference to the bullionist doctrines, a strong argument could be presented in defense of the thesis that the mass of ordinary tracts on trade in the first half of the eighteenth century showed a more extreme and confused adherence to the fallacies of mercantilism than did the writings of the sixteenth and early seventeenth centuries.... Insofar as trade theory was concerned, such progress as occurred was due almost solely to a small group of capable writers, able to analyse economic problems more acutely and logically than their predecessors, but not able to make a marked impression upon their contemporaries or even to attract their attention.[2]

The process of analysis simply was not cumulative: there was little advantage in studying foreign trade if one were born in 1680 instead of 1580.

I am now prepared to come to the rescue of an economist who needs little rescuing: Adam Smith. A considerable number of economists, and a few considerable economists, have emphasized the fact that Smith had many gifted predecessors and almost all or perhaps exactly all of his ideas are to be found expressed, and sometimes well expressed, by these predecessors. Some economists therefore wish to give the title of founder of economics to earlier writers such as Cantillon. This line of argument, in my view, misses the point.

It was Smith who provided so broad and authoritative an account of the known economic doctrine that henceforth it was no longer permissible for any subsequent writer on economics to advance his own ideas while ignoring the state of general knowledge. A science consists of interacting practitioners, and henceforth no one could decently ignore Smith's own work, and in due time the work of Malthus, Ricardo, and the galaxy of economists who populated the first half of the nineteenth century.

The change came fast. Smith himself did not interact with any writers on economics after 1776, and of course even in his treatise he cooly ignored his leading rival, Sir James Steuart. Five years after the first edition of the *Essay on Population* (1798), by contrast, Malthus was making fundamental concessions in response to Godwin and other critics. The age of economic science had begun.

How complete the transformation of economics has become may be illustrated by an episode earlier in this century. A. C. Pigou, holding the chair in economics that his predecessor, Alfred Marshall, had made the most prestigious in the world, committed an error in stating the theory of external diseconomies. He asserted that when a firm contemplated entry into a competitive industry which is subject to rising supply prices of its inputs, that firm would make a socially inefficient decision because it would ignore the effect of its entrance into the industry in raising the prices other firms would have to pay for inputs. The error involves a confusion of transfer payments with social costs. The error appeared in his famous treatise, *Wealth and Welfare*, in 1912.

Allowing for the distractions created by the First World War, major economists soon devoted themselves to the problem. The two most famous refutations, by Dennis Robertson and Frank Knight, came in 1924,[3] but the essential point had been made earlier by J. M. Clark and Allyn A. Young.[4] Under these attacks even Pigou, the most remote of scholars, capitulated. The era had already begun when only the detected errors of unimportant economists are spared a prompt refutation.

II. Economic Science: The Environmental View

The politics and economics of mercantilistic policy were the determinants of the issues in the mercantilist literature. Indeed the prescientific age of any discipline is dominated by the practical concerns of the society in which it is cultivated. It is an easy step to the view that the main problems of a discipline, even after it becomes an organized science, are posed directly by the paramount problems and policies of the society in which it is pursued.

Wesley Clair Mitchell went so far as to attempt to present a systematic history of economic thought in terms of the responses of each generation to its environment:

> One of the results of any survey of the development of economic doctrines is to show that in large measure the important departures in economic theory have been intellectual responses to changing current problems; that is, the economic theorists who have counted most in the development of thought have been men who have been deeply concerned with problems that troubled their generation.

As examples, he told us

Malthus's problem of population was as obviously an intellectual reflection of current events as Adam Smith's "obvious and simple system of natural liberty."

The description of the course of English politics in Parliament shows that Ricardo got this problem [how to determine the way in which the produce of the country was divided]—his appreciation of its importance—not in his study, but by following current events. It should also be noticed that Ricardo got his peculiar conception of what the problem of distribution is directly from the Parliamentary struggle.[5]

Yet when Mitchell reached the 1870s and the rise of the marginal utility theory, he abandoned the attempt to find environmental changes to which economic theory was responding. He attributed the abandonment to the difficulty of achieving understanding of and detachment toward more recent work, not the failure of his hypothesis.[6]

The central task of an empirical science such as economics is to provide general understanding of events in the real world, and ultimately all of its theories and techniques must be instrumental to that task. That is very different from saying, however, that it must be responsive to the contemporaneous conditions and problems of the society in which it is situated.

If the problems of economic life changed frequently and radically, and lacked a large measure of continuity in their essential nature, there could not be a science of economics. An essential element of a science is the cumulative growth of knowledge, and that cumulative character could not arise if each generation of economists faced fundamentally new problems calling for entirely new methods of analysis. The change of problems and methods would also undermine the training of economists: if the young studied under the old, the young could be confident that they were learning things that were rapidly becoming obsolete. A science requires for its very existence a set of fundamental and durable problems.

In economics the most fundamental of these central problems is the theory of value. The theory of value must explain how the comparative values of different goods and services are established. Until that problem is solved, it is not possible to analyze for scientific purposes what will be produced and in what quantities, how the resources will be employed in producing the menu of outputs, and how the resources will be valued. Without a theory of value the economist can have no theory of international trade nor possibly a theory of money. This central problem of value does not change in its essential content if one seeks to explain values in rural or urban societies, or in agricultural or industrial societies. Indeed, if the problem of value were so chameleonlike as to alter its nature whenever the economic or political system altered, each epoch in economic life would require its own theory, and short epochs would get short-lived theories.

If an empirical science requires for its very existence a set of fundamental and persistent phenomena, that is not the only kind of phenomena with which it will deal. It will continuously be confronted with new circumstances which call for more than a routine application of standard knowledge. Thus the energy crisis of the 1970s has provided much employment to economists, but it has not called for important changes in economic science.

An empirical science has a second, and vastly more important, interest in and responsiveness to, contemporary problems: its received theory will at times be incapable of dealing with these problems. When England began the long term importation of grain at the time of the Napoleonic wars, and pressed hard upon its domestic production capacities, the economists introduced the law of diminishing returns in dealing with the price of grain. It would be difficult to deny a role to the environment in the appearance of this law. So much for the origin of that theory: it would not help us one whit in understanding Edgeworth's famous analysis of this law in 1911 to look at his economic environment. The important place that diminishing returns has achieved in economics is due precisely to the fact that its usefulness was not limited to Ricardo's analysis of agriculture in Great Britain.

The responsiveness of economics to environmental problems will naturally be more complete and more prompt, the more urgent the problems of the day. The response will also be more complete, the less developed the relevant body of economic analysis. The responsiveness of macroeconomics to contemporary events is notorious. Keynes's conquest in the 1930s was due to the fact that the neoclassical theory could not account for the persistent unemployment of that decade. A generation later, persistent inflation even with less than full employment was equally decisive in ending Keynes's supremacy. If and when macroeconomics produces a good theory of the business cycle, its responsiveness to environmental changes will diminish sharply.

A viable and healthy science requires both the persistent and almost timeless theories that naturally ignore the changing conditions of their society and the unsettled theories that encounter much difficulty in attempting to explain current events. Without the base of persistent theory, there would be no body of slowly evolving knowledge to constitute the science. Without the challenges of unsolved, important problems, the science would become sterile.

One final observation: there is no simple or known relationship between environmental changes and changes in economic analysis. During the Industrial Revolution, economists adopted the law of diminishing returns but ignored the most sustained and widespread growth of output that the world had yet observed. The vast governmental income redistribution programs of the last hundred years have only recently attracted the attention of economic theorists. The scholars who create economic theory do not read the newspapers regularly or carefully during working hours.

III. The Omniscient Scholar?

Once a science becomes well populated, has achieved a secure academic base, and is equipped with the machinery of intellectual exchange—journals, learned societies, and conferences—it is presented with a stream of proposals for new directions or new methods for research. Indeed, the science itself carefully fosters the output of new ideas. Robert K. Merton has shown in his fundamental studies of the reward structure of science that immense value is attached to priority in the development of successful new ideas.[7]

And yet ideas will be proposed which are ignored at the time, but at some later date are accepted (almost invariably after an independent rediscovery) as important to the science. This phenomenon repeatedly called forth the rebukes of Schumpeter in his great *History of Economic Analysis*. Here are examples of men who, Schumpeter believed, quite correctly, to be "writing above their time":

> Longfield's merits may be summed up by saying that he overhauled the whole of economic theory and produced a system that would have stood up well in 1890.
>
> [John Stuart Mill] even went so far as to compare [John] Rae's performance on accumulation with Malthus' performance on population. And all this, written in what was to be for forty years the most influential textbook on economics, was insufficient to introduce Rae to the profession or to rouse any curiosity concerning the rest of his book![8]

Of course Schumpeter, than whom no economist was more sophisticated, gave some sensible reasons for these acts of neglect of genius, but he failed to give the most important reason of all.

In every period of the active pursuit of a science, new ideas are continually being proposed. Any new idea—a new conceptualization of an existing problem, a new methodology, or the investigation of a new area—cannot be fully mastered, developed into the stage of a tentatively acceptable hypothesis, and possibly exposed to some empirical tests, without a large expenditure of time, intelligence, and research resources. That is fact one. Fact two is that the overwhelming majority of these new ideas will prove to be sterile—in fact, quite possibly all the new ideas of a period of years will prove to be sterile. Only afterward, with the fullness of knowledge that history sometimes provides, can we identify the truly fertile ideas of a period.

Some men have superb instincts as to which of the new ideas of the time will repay intensive exploration, but no one is infallible. Even the greatest of economists pursue some problems that take them nowhere. In the last months of his life, Ricardo was still attempting to fashion a precise measure of value, and not advancing one inch. John Stuart Mill and Léon Walras devoted much energy to the propagation of the proposal of nationalization of unanticipated future increments of land values—not the first time or the last that someone proposed nationalizing a sum with an expected value no larger than zero. Jevons could not get over the idea that cycles in sunspots left their tracks on commercial cycles. The great Pareto took a detour through the question of the order in which people consumed various products, out of a belief that this was related to the order of integration of a partial differential equation.

Not only great economists, but all economists who pursue anything, pursue will-o'-the-wisps for periods of time that are painful to consider in retrospect. In the 1930s, the area variously known as industrial organization and microeconomics-with-evidence, was offered the following major research hypotheses:

1. The ownership and the effective control of large corporations have become separated.

2. The phenomenon of product differentiation calls for fundamental changes in the theory of the firm and the industry. (The theory of monopolistic competition.)

3. Prices do not respond downward to changes in supply and demand, perhaps because a particular expectation with respect to rivals' behavior creates a kink in the firm's demand curve.

4. The economist is able to construct criteria of the satisfactory, or alternatively the unsatisfactory, performance of an industry, where the satisfaction of the economist should be shared by society. (The theory of workable competition.)

These were not the only new research proposals: the annual output of new theories of oligopoly was supplemented by searches for truth through the feeding and wining of business leaders.

Each of the four research proposals I have listed received a good deal of attention: none lost its fashionable appeal to at least some highly competent economists for at least five or ten years, and indeed not one is a cold corpse today. But it is also true that not one of them has been absorbed into the mainstream of price theory as a regular and significant part of the analysis of the workings of markets and industries. Quite possibly one could find that Schumpeter followed several of these detours for at least a short distance. Of course some important new ideas (such as that of Hotelling on exhaustible resources and Ramsey on optimal pricing) were being neglected. To err is not only human but also scientific.

IV. The Continuity of Scientific Change

"Nature does not move in jumps," says the proverb, and a science also progresses through time without making large jumps. This continuity is often illustrated by two kinds of evidence.

One evidence of scientific continuity that has been adduced by Robert Merton is the existence of multiple and nearly simultaneous independent discoveries of a theory by several scientists. The popular examples in economics are the discovery of the theory of rent by Edward West and Thomas Robert Malthus in 1815, and the publication of the theory of utility in the early 1870s by Jevons, Menger, and Walras. In each case, the new idea was presumably appropriate to the development of economics at the time: the rent theory allowed the construction of a theory of the distribution of income; and the utility theory led naturally to the marginal productivity theory and the generalization of the theory of utility-maximizing behavior.[9]

This continuity is also used to explain the not uncommon phenomenon of the failure of a man of genius to get acceptance of his ideas from his contemporaries, even though later generations will applaud the performance. Augustin Cournot, for example, was an important scholar in one of the leading intellectual centers of Europe, but he could not persuade economists in 1838 that the mathematical theory of maxima and minima was a useful tool for economic analysis.

I would find it more persuasive to establish the continuity of scientific development by a close examination of the evolution of important concepts in economics. but that route does not seem appropriate to the occasion.[10] Candor compels me to note that the route of close historical study would not be easy to follow because it would require definite answers to the questions: what is a large change in a science? What is a rapid change in a science?

Gary Becker has suggested that a substantial resistance to the acceptance of new ideas by scientists can be explained by two familiar economic concepts. One is the concept of specific human capital: the established scholar possesses a valuable capital asset in his command over a particular body of knowledge. That capital would be reduced if his knowledge were made obsolete by the general acceptance of a new theory. Hence, established scholars should, in their own self-interest, attack new theories, possibly even more than they do in the absence of joint action. The second concept is risk aversion, which leads young scholars to prefer mastery of established theories to seeking radically different theories. Scientific innovators, like adventurers in general, are probably not averse to risk, but for the mass of scholars in a discipline, risk aversion is a strong basis for scientific conservatism. We will find the specific human capital theory illustrated in the episodes to which I shall soon turn.

No one can describe the precise characteristics or content of a new piece of scientific work that will find ready and eager reception from the scientists of a period. Indeed, if knowledge sufficient to identify the theories that will succeed were possessed, it would be of immense value in finding and developing those theories and would therefore be the key to scientific fame. To the scientist such knowledge would be much more valuable than an accurate method of predicting stock prices! Even without such a priceless key to the understanding of scientific innovation, it is interesting to examine several routes by which a scientific idea makes its way into the work of economics. I illustrate two of these routes by subjects on which I have worked.

Acceptance Without Struggle: The Economics of Information

Economists have always known that the extent and accuracy of the knowledge of the economic actor had influence, and often a decisive influence, on his behavior and therefore on the behavior of markets.

One striking example of this critical role of information is provided by the theory of oligopoly. The first formulation of the problem of oligopoly as a specific problem in economic theory was made by Cournot, whose long failure to get acceptance I have already mentioned. It was essential, in explaining how each of two rivals in a market would behave, to attribute to each some belief about the behavioral pattern of the other. Cournot made the assumption that each assumed that the rival did nothing in response to his own actions. The later theories of oligopoly all rest upon different assumptions concerning patterns of behavior which each seller attributes to his rivals. A dozen other areas of economic analysis, such as the workings of the labor market and the role of advertising, also rest squarely on assumptions about information of the economic actors. In this tradition, the amount of information possessed by individuals in any market was arbitrarily postulated rather than derived from economic principles. The consensus was that consumers knew little, traders on organized exchanges a great deal; investors were either gullible or omniscient. Even the powerful and luminous essay by Friedrich von Hayek on "The Use of Knowledge in Society,"[11] had not addressed the principles of acquisition of knowledge.

I proposed (in 1961) the use of the standard economic theory of utility-maximizing behavior to determine how much information people would acquire with special attention to the prices at which they would buy and sell, and a year later made an application of the analysis to labor markets. There is one interesting feature of the subsequent history of the reception of this work by economists to which I wish to call attention.

The proposal to study the economics of information was promptly and widely accepted, and without even a respectable minimum of controversy.

Within a decade and a half, the literature had become so extensive and the theorists working in the field so prominent, that the subject was given a separate classification in the *Index of Economic Articles*, and more than a hundred articles a year are now devoted to this subject.

The absence of controversy certainly was no tribute to the definitiveness of my exposition. I had chosen fixed sample rather than sequential analysis, which a majority of later economists prefer. I had not presented a general equilibrium solution in which the behavior of both sides of a market is analyzed, and that step proved difficult to take. I had done little with information on quality and other variables, in contrast to price, although I soon extended the approach to a different kind of information in the theory of oligopoly. I had not applied the theory to the problem of unemployment, a literature initiated by an important paper by Armen Alchian.[12] All I had done was to open a door to a room that contained many fascinating and important problems.

The absence of controversy was due instead to the fact that no established scientific theory was being challenged by this work: in fact, all I was challenging was the neglect of a promising subject. Moreover, the economics of information was susceptible to study by quite standard techniques of economic analysis. The theory immediately yielded results which were intuitively or observationally plausible. Here was a Chicago theory that didn't even annoy socialists!

Acceptance by Necessity: The Economics of Regulation

The work on the economics of regulation has entered economics by a different route.

The modern era of economists' interest in the economic workings of the state may be dated from the influential work of Anthony Downs, *An Economic Theory of Democracy* (1957), and James Buchanan and Gordon Tullock, *The Calculus of Consent* (1962). Although I had read these works with deep interest and admiration, my own work on regulation at first followed a different, more empirical route.

An examination of the economic literature had revealed no serious professional attempt to measure the impact of public regulation in areas with long histories: the regulation of rates of electrical utilities; the review of new issues by the Securities and Exchange Commission; and the antitrust policy of the United States. The investigations of these problems, strongly reinforced by related work of colleagues and students, gradually forced me to confront a question that should have been obtrusively obvious at once: why does the state engage in its regulatory activities?

The answer (at least for an economist) seemed to lie much less in the theorems of welfare economics or the prescriptions of traditional political science, than in the systematic examination of the self-interest of the various participants in political life. These participants, to be sure, operated under different rules and constraints than the traders in markets, but that did not argue against using that powerful tool of economic analysis, the theory of utility-maximizing behavior. Once the economist can identify the costs and returns from various actions, this theory allows him to make predictions of behavior that have been reasonably successful.

This approach proved to be highly uncongenial to many economists. My teacher, Frank Knight, had often expressed the belief that many economists still share, that the actors (and especially the voters) in political life are ignorant, emotional, and usually irrational. In a famous, unpublished speech he ended a parable with the words: "Truth in society is like strychnine in the individual body, medicinal in specific conditions and minute doses; otherwise and in general, a deadly poison." These economists believe that voters are myopic and forgetful, and that political institutions are designed or perverted to allow the public servants to pursue chiefly their own interests. Another and perhaps larger group of economists is critical of the utility-maximizing approach for the opposite reason: that it appears to be an attack on the chief instrument for purposive social improvement that a society possesses: the state.

Nevertheless the economic theory of regulation is achieving a substantial scientific prosperity. Its findings with respect to both the operation and the origins of regulatory policies directed to particular industries (such as the securities markets, transportation, and occupational licensing) command a substantial support. To be sure, the explanatory triumphs have not been overwhelming, and indeed the theory itself is still relatively primitive. The main reason for the considerable acceptance of the approach is that fundamental rule of scientific combat: it takes a theory to beat a theory. No amount of skepticism about the fertility of a theory can deter its use unless the skeptic can point to another route by which the scientific problem of regulation can be studied successfully.

There is an interesting asymmetry in the success of this literature in dealing with the two problems into which the theory is commonly divided: why are regulatory policies adopted and abandoned; and what are their effects? Economists have been much more successful in measuring effects of policies than in explaining their adoption. The explanation is that one can choose the effects of a policy to study, and usually more easily measured effects are chosen for study. One has no such options when addressed with the question: why did the United States adopt an antitrust policy in 1890?

Thus studies of effects of regulatory policies have usually been concerned with the effects upon prices and outputs, although the effects desired by the supporters of these policies have probably been upon the distribution of income. The panoply of regulatory measures can be used to effect vast income redistributions, and these redistributions of income do not appear explicitly in the budget of the state. The frequent exclusion of new entrants from a field, for example, leads to smaller outputs, higher prices, and higher profits for the protected enterprises, and allows these benefits to increase with the growth of the protected area. If these income transfers are as large as fragmentary evidence suggests, the theory of regulation may well become a full partner of tax and expenditure theory in public finance.

Acceptance by Trial by Combat?

Is it exceptional of the theories I have been discussing that neither was subjected to direct trial by combat with an alternative theory? We speak so often of the competition of ideas: how is that competition conducted?

The direct confrontation of two alternative theories, each seeking to explain the same body of observable phenomena, is not common in economics.[13] (It is perhaps encountered more often in macroeconomics than in microeconomics.) Two modern examples from microeconomics will illustrate the proposition that economists seldom choose between directly rival theories on the basis of critical empirical tests:

1. The doctrine of limit pricing by oligopolists asserted that the firms in an industry would set prices at such a level as to discourage or prevent entry of additional firms into an industry. The theory had a long prehistory under the name of potential competition, but it was given an explicit formulation by Sylos-Labini, Joe Bain, and Franco Modigliani.[14] This version gave rise to a substantial literature, but at no time was a direct empirical test made of this theory as against explicit alternative theories of oligopoly behavior.

2. The Pigovian theory of external economies was challenged directly by Ronald Coase, who in effect argued that the Pigovian theory had assumed noneconomic behavior on the part of the economic actors in a wide class of phenomena.[15] This challenge was met for a time by a considerable number of counterarguments, but these arguments were addressed to the logic of what has come to be known as the Coase theorem. No explicit comparison of the explanatory powers of the Coasian and Pigovian approaches has been undertaken.

Why did not the profession seek directly to test these theories, and, for that matter, the four theories of the 1930s that I characterized as largely unsuccessful innovations? Some part of the answer may lie in the fact that formal empirical tests of economic theories have historically been scarce, although they are increasing in frequency, but I would not press this answer. Instead, the testing procedure—the trial by combat—takes a different form.

It is seldom that a theory in economics has a well-defined domain of applicability. It may have been created to explain a specific class of events—the pricing by oligopolists when entry is possible, in the first illustration above—but it always has a wider domain of possible applicability. The specification of a critical test which, if conducted correctly on a sufficient scale, will decide the combat between two alternative theories, is seldom possible over the whole range of the domains of the two theories.

Economists have therefore generally chosen to decide between the alternative theories by the process of using each to explore a variety of problems. How does the limit theory of oligopoly pricing, for example, handle the process of growth of an industry or the phenomenon of vertical integration? How does the Coasian theory illuminate the structure of the law of torts or the economics of professional sports? These explorations are a form of testing of the theories: they test the fertility of the theories (or at least the intellectual fertility of economists), and the varied applications are partial empirical tests of the theories. Gradually a consensus emerges among the economists working on the subject: the theory becomes a part of the standard analytical corpus or it dies of neglect.

V. CONCLUSION

Our list of factors which influence the receptivity of a science to new ideas could easily be extended.

In particular, it would be useful to examine the question of whether the attractiveness of the public policy positions associated with a theory has an effect upon the applicability of the theory. The textbooks on methodology lecture us on the need to separate positive and normative theories. The study of economics tells us that few if any theories lead unequivocally to one set of policy implications. So science and policy should be separated. Are they? I believe that the separation has been far from complete, especially in the short run, but this is not the occasion to undertake the substantial study necessary to support the belief.

Again, the institutional organization of economic research is a potential influence upon the receptiveness of a science to new ideas. The powerful institutional position of Schmoller and the German Historical School no doubt played a role in the slow development of economic science in Germany after 1870. The dominant role of Cambridge University in economics from Marshall to Keynes surely was not favorable to the receptiveness of new ideas from outsiders. I believe that the shift of the center of economics to the United States was due in some part to the failure of the English economists to share fully in the quantitative study of economics.

Even if I extended this list of potential determinants of scientific choice, and documented each more fully than I have, I would still have kept my promise not to tell you the detailed characteristics of the successful new theories in economic science. I do not lament this failure.

The fascination of scientific work does not lie in the craftsmanlike utilization of the tools of a science. It is admirable for the gymnast to put his splendidly disciplined body through intricate maneuvers, and it is no doubt equally admirable for the scientist to put his disciplined mind through a sequence of complex analytical or experimental maneuvers. The great fascination of scientific endeavor, however, is precisely in the speculative pursuit of new ideas that will widen the horizon of our understanding of the world. This endeavor is not that of a graceful intellectual gymnast: on the contrary, the scientist is stumbling about in a jungle of ideas or facts that seem to defy system or logic, and usually he fails to emerge with anything but scratches. The dangers of the search include the chance that a gifted rival will reach the goal, and the danger is not reduced by the fact that the rivalry is conducted under what for able and ambitious competitors are usually chivalrous rules. Still, learning more about how this search for new knowledge proceeds is itself a worthy search for new knowledge, and we shall not abandon it.

Notes

1. Reprinted in *Studies in the Theory of International Trade* (Harper, 1937).

2. *Studies in the Theory of International Trade*, p. 109.

3. D. H. Robertson, "Those Empty Boxes," *Economic Journal* (1924); F. H. Knight, "Some Fallacies in the Interpretation of Social Cost," *Quarterly Journal of Economics* (1924), both reprinted in *Readings in Price Theory* (American Economic Association, Irwin, 1952).

4. J. M. Clark, review of *Wealth and Welfare*, *American Economic Review* 3 (1913):624; and A. A. Young, review of *Wealth and Welfare*, *Quarterly Journal of Economics* 27 (1913): 682–84.

5. *Types of Economic Theory* (New York: Augustus Kelley, 1967), I, pp. 13, 235, 286.

6. Ibid, II, p. 2.

7. *The Sociology of Science* (Chicago: University of Chicago Press, 1973), esp. ch. 14.

8. *History of Economic Analysis* (New York: Oxford University Press, 1954), pp. 465, 496.

9. I have presented elsewhere an alternative interpretation of Merton's theory of multiple discoveries which emphasized even more than he does how essential it is that science be "ready" for a new idea: see "Merton on Multiples, Denied and Affirmed,"

Transactions of the New York Academy of Sciences, 1980, reprinted in *The Economist as Preacher* (Chicago: University of Chicago Press, 1982).

10. For a fascinating case study in another discipline, see Nicholas Fisher, "Avogadro and the Historians," *History of Science* (June and September, 1982).

11. *American Economic Review* (September 1945).

12. "Information Costs, Pricing, and Resource Unemployment," in *Employment and Inflation Theory*, ed. by E. S. Phelps (Norton, 1970).

13. I once made such a direct confrontation of the theory of the kinked oligopoly demand curve and more traditional theories, finding no evidence to support the existence of a kink. The theory has disappeared from professional work but lives in every textbook. See "The Literature of Economics: The Case of the Kinked Oligopoly Demand Curve," *Economic Inquiry* (1978), reprinted in *The Economist as Preacher*.

14. Paolo Sylos-Labini, *Oligopoly and Technical Progress* (Harvard University Press, 1962); Joe S. Bain, "A Note on Pricing in Monopoly and Oligopoly," American Economic Review (1949); Franco Modigliani, "New Developments on the Oligopoly Front," *Journal of Political Economy* (June 1958).

15. "The Problem of Social Cost," *Journal of Law and Economics* (1961).

STIGLER'S
CONTRIBUTIONS
TO INDUSTRIAL
ORGANIZATION
◆ ◆ ◆

◆ *PART* ◆ *THREE* ◆

A Theory
of Oligopoly[1]

· 11 ·

No one has the right, and few the ability, to lure economists into reading another article on oligopoly theory without some advance indication of its alleged contribution. The present paper accepts the hypothesis that oligopolists wish to collude to maximize joint profits. It seeks to reconcile this wish with facts, such as that collusion is impossible for many firms and collusion is much more effective in some circumstances than in others. The reconciliation is found in the problem of policing a collusive agreement, which proves to be a problem in the theory of information. A considerable number of implications of the theory are discussed, and a modest amount of empirical evidence is presented.

I. The Task of Collusion

A satisfactory theory of oligopoly cannot begin with assumptions concerning the way in which each firm views its interdependence with its rivals. If we adhere to the traditional theory of profit-maximizing enterprises, then behavior is no longer something to be assumed but rather something to be deduced. The firms in an industry will behave in such a way, given the demand-

From the *Journal of Political Economy* 72, no. 1 (February 1964). Copyright 1964 by the University of Chicago.

and-supply functions (including those of rivals), that their profits will be maximized.

The combined profits of the entire set of firms in an industry are maximized when they act together as a monopolist. At least in the traditional formulation of the oligopoly problem, in which there are no major uncertainties as to the profit-maximizing output and price at any time, this familiar conclusion seems inescapable. Moreover, the result holds for any number of firms.

Our modification of this theory consists simply in presenting a systematic account of the factors governing the feasibility of collusion, which like most things in this world is not free. Before we do so, it is desirable to look somewhat critically at the concept of homogeneity of products, and what it implies for profit-maximizing. We shall show that collusion normally involves much more than "the" price.

Homogeneity is commonly defined in terms of identity of products or of (what is presumed to be equivalent) pairs of products between which the elasticity of substitution is infinite. On either definition it is the behavior of buyers that is decisive. Yet it should be obvious that products may be identical to any or every buyer while buyers may be quite different from the viewpoint of sellers.

This fact that every transaction involves two parties is something that economists do not easily forget. One would therefore expect a definition of homogeneity also to be two-sided: if the products are what sellers offer, and the purchase commitments are what the buyers offer, full homogeneity clearly involves infinite elasticities of substitution between both products and purchase commitments. In other words, two products are homogeneous to a buyer if he is indifferent between all combinations of x of one and (say) $20 - x$ of the other, at a common price. Two purchase commitments are homogeneous to a seller if he is indifferent between all combinations of y of one and (say) $20 - y$ of the other, at a common price. Full homogeneity is then defined as homogeneity both in products (sellers) and purchase commitments (buyers).

The heterogeneity of purchase commitments (buyers), however, is surely often at least as large as that of products within an industry, and sometimes vastly larger. There is the same sort of personal differentia of buyers as of sellers—ease in making sales, promptness of payment, penchant for returning goods, likelihood of buying again (or buying other products). In addition there are two differences among buyers which are pervasive and well recognized in economics:

1. The size of purchase, with large differences in costs of providing lots of different size.

2. The urgency of purchase, with possibly sufficient differences in elasticity of demand to invite price discrimination.

It is one thing to assert that no important market has homogeneous transactions, and quite another to measure the extent of the heterogeneity. In a regime of perfect knowledge, it would be possible to measure heterogeneity by the variance of prices in transactions; in a regime of imperfect knowledge, there will be dispersion of prices even with transaction homogeneity.[2]

The relevance of heterogeneity to collusion is this: it is part of the task of maximizing industry profits to employ a price structure that takes account of the larger differences in the costs of various classes of transactions. Even with a single, physically homogeneous product the profits will be reduced if differences among buyers are ignored. A simple illustration of this fact is given in the Appendix; disregard of differences among buyers proves to be equivalent to imposing an excise tax upon them, but one which is not collected by the monopolist. A price structure of some complexity will usually be the goal of collusive oligopolists.

II. THE METHODS OF COLLUSION

Collusion of firms can take many forms, of which the most comprehensive is outright merger. Often merger will be inappropriate, however, because of diseconomies of scale,[3] and at certain times and places it may be forbidden by law. Only less comprehensive is the cartel with a joint sales agency, which again has economic limitations—it is ill suited to custom work and creates serious administrative costs in achieving quality standards, cost reductions, product innovations, etc. In deference to American antitrust policy, we shall assume that the collusion takes the form of joint determination of outputs and prices by ostensibly independent firms, but we shall not take account of the effects of the legal prohibitions until later. Oligopoly existed before 1890, and has existed in countries that have never had an antitrust policy.

The colluding firms must agree upon the price structure appropriate to the transaction classes which they are prepared to recognize. A complete profit-maximizing price structure may have almost infinitely numerous price classes: the firms will have to decide upon the number of price classes in the light of the costs and returns from tailoring prices to the diversity of transactions. We have already indicated by hypothetical example (see Appendix) that there are net profits to be obtained by catering to differences in transactions. The level of collusive prices will also depend upon the conditions of entry into the industry as well as upon the elasticities of demand.

Let us assume that the collusion has been effected, and a price structure agreed upon. It is a well-established proposition that if any member of the agreement can secretly violate it, he will gain larger profits than by conforming to it.[4] It is, moreover, surely one of the axioms of human behavior that all agreements whose violation would be profitable to the violator must be enforced. The literature of collusive agreements, ranging from the pools of the 1880s to the electrical conspiracies of recent times, is replete with instances of the collapse of conspiracies because of "secret" price cutting. This literature is biased: conspiracies that are successful in avoiding an amount of price cutting which leads to collapse of the agreement are less likely to be reported or detected. But no conspiracy can neglect the problem of enforcement.

Enforcement consists basically of detecting significant deviations from the agreed-upon prices. Once detected, the deviations will tend to disappear because they are no longer secret and will be matched by fellow conspirators if they are not withdrawn. If the enforcement is weak, however—if price cutting is detected only slowly and incompletely—the conspiracy must recognize its weakness: it must set prices not much above the competitive level so the inducements to price cutting are small, or it must restrict the conspiracy to areas in which enforcement can be made efficient.

Fixing market shares is probably the most efficient of all methods of combatting secret price reductions. No one can profit from price cutting if he is moving along the industry demand curve,[5] once a maximum profit price has been chosen. With inspection of output and an appropriate formula for redistribution of gains and losses from departures from quotas, the incentive to secret price cutting is eliminated. Unless inspection of output is costly or ineffective (as with services), this is the ideal method of enforcement, and is widely used by legal cartels. Unfortunately for oligopolists, it is usually an easy form of collusion to detect, for it may require side payments among firms and it leaves indelible traces in the output records.

Almost as efficient a method of eliminating secret price cutting is to assign each buyer to a single seller. If this can be done for all buyers, short-run price cutting no longer has any purpose. Long-run price cutting will still be a serious possibility if the buyers are in competition: lower prices to one's own customers can then lead to an expansion of their share of their market, so the price cutter's long-run demand curve will be more elastic than that of the industry. Long-run price cutting is likely to be important, however, only where sellers are providing a major cost component to the buyer.

There are real difficulties of other sorts to the sellers in the assignment of buyers. In general the fortunes of the various sellers will differ greatly over time: one seller's customers may grow three-fold, while another seller's customers shrink by half. If the customers have uncorrelated fluctuations in demand, the various sellers will experience large changes in relative outputs in the short run.[6] Where the turnover of buyers is large, the method is simply impracticable.

Nevertheless, the conditions appropriate to the assignment of customers will exist in certain industries, and in particular the geographical division of the market has often been employed. Since an allocation of buyers is an obvious and easily detectible violation of the Sherman Act, we may again infer that an efficient method of enforcing a price agreement is excluded by the antitrust laws. We therefore turn to other techniques of enforcement, but we shall find that the analysis returns to allocation of buyers.

In general the policing of a price agreement involves an audit of the transaction prices. In the absence or violation of antitrust laws, actual inspection of the accounting records of sellers has been employed by some colluding groups, but even this inspection gives only limited assurance that the price agreement is adhered to.[7] Ultimately there is no substitute for obtaining the transaction prices from the buyers.

An oligopolist will not consider making secret price cuts to buyers whose purchases fall below a certain size relative to his aggregate sales. The ease with which price cutting is detected by rivals is decisive in this case. If p is the probability that some rival will hear of one such price reduction, $1-(1-p)^n$ is the probability that a rival will learn of at least one reduction if it is given to n customers. Even if p is as small as 0.01, when n equals 100 the probability of detection is .634, and when n equals 1000 it is .99996. No one has yet invented a way to advertise price reductions which brings them to the attention of numerous customers but not to that of any rival.[8]

It follows that oligopolistic collusion will often be effective against small buyers even when it is ineffective against large buyers. When the oligopolists sell to numerous small retailers, for example, they will adhere to the agreed-upon price, even though they are cutting prices to larger chain stores and industrial buyers. This is a first empirical implication of our theory. Let us henceforth exclude small buyers from consideration.

The detection of secret price cutting will of course be as difficult as interested people can make it. The price cutter will certainly protest his innocence, or, if this would tax credulity beyond its taxable capacity, blame a disobedient subordinate. The price cut will often take the indirect form of modifying some nonprice dimension of the transaction. The customer may, and often will, divulge price reductions, in order to have them matched by others, but he will learn from experience if each disclosure is followed by the withdrawal of the lower price offer. Indeed the buyer will frequently fabricate wholly fictitious price offers to test the rivals. Policing the collusion sounds very much like the subtle and complex problem presented in a good detective story.

There is a difference: in our case the man who murders the collusive price will receive the bequest of patronage. The basic method of detection of a price cutter must be the fact that he is getting business he would otherwise not obtain. No promises of lower prices that fail to shift some business can be really effective—either the promised price is still too high or it is simply not believed.

Our definition of perfect collusion, indeed, must be that no buyer changes sellers voluntarily. There is no competitive price cutting if there are no shifts of buyers among sellers.

To this rule that price cutting must be inferred from shifts of buyers there is one partial exception, but that an important one. There is one type of buyer who usually reveals the price he pays, and does not accept secret benefices: the government. The system of sealed bids, publicly opened with full identification of each bidder's price and specifications, is the ideal instrument for the detection of price cutting. There exists no alternative method of secretly cutting prices (bribery of purchasing agents aside). Our second empirical prediction, then, is that collusion will always be more effective against buyers who report correctly and fully the prices tendered to them.[9]

It follows from the test of the absence of price competition by buyer loyalty—and this is our third major empirical prediction—that collusion is severely limited (under present assumptions excluding market sharing) when the significant buyers constantly change identity. There exist important markets in which the (substantial) buyers do change identity continuously, namely, in the construction industries. The building of a plant or an office building, for example, is an essentially nonrepetitive event, and rivals cannot determine whether the successful bidder has been a price cutter unless there is open bidding to specification.

The normal market, however, contains both stability and change. There may be a small rate of entry of new buyers. There will be some shifting of customers even in a regime of effective collusion, for a variety of minor reasons we can lump together as "random factors." There will often be some sharing of buyers by several sellers—a device commending itself to buyers to increase the difficulty of policing price agreements. We move then to the world of circumstantial evidence, or, as it is sometimes called, of probability.

III. The Conditions for Detecting Secret Price Reductions

We shall investigate the problem of detecting secret price cutting with a simplified model, in which all buyers and all sellers are initially of equal size. The number of buyers per seller—recalling that we exclude from consideration all buyers who take less than (say) 0.33 percent of a seller's output—will range from 300 down to perhaps 10 or 20 (since we wish to avoid the horrors of full bilateral oligopoly). A few of these buyers are new, but over moderate periods of time most are "old," although some of these old customers will shift among suppliers. A potential secret price cutter has then three groups of customers who would increase their patronage if given secret price cuts: the old customers of rivals; the old customers who would normally leave him; and new customers.

Most old buyers will deal regularly with one or a few sellers, in the absence of secret price cutting. There may be no secret price cutting because a collusive price is adhered to, or because only an essentially competitive price can be obtained. We shall show that the loyalty of customers is a crucial variable in determining which price is approached. We need to know the probability that an old customer will buy again from his regular supplier at the collusive price, in the absence of secret price cutting.

The buyer will set the economies of repetitive purchase (which include smaller transaction costs and less product testing) against the increased probability of secret price cutting that comes from shifting among suppliers. From the viewpoint of any one buyer, this gain will be larger the larger the number of sellers and the smaller the number of buyers, as we shall show below. The costs of shifting among suppliers will be smaller the more homogeneous the goods and the larger the purchases of the buyer (again an inverse function of his size). Let us label this probability of repeat purchases p. We shall indicate later how this probability could be determined in a more general approach.

The second component of sales of a firm will be its sales to new buyers and to the floating old customers of rivals. Here we assume that each seller is equally likely to make a sale, in the absence of price competition.

Let us proceed to the analysis. There are n_0 "old" buyers and n_n new customers, with $n_n = \lambda n_0$ and n_s sellers. A firm may look to three kinds of evidence on secret price cutting, and therefore by symmetry to three potential areas to practice secret price cutting.

1. *The behavior of its own old customers.* It has, on average, n_0/n_s such customers, and expects to sell to $m_1 = p n_0/n_s$ of them in a given round of transactions, in the absence of price cutting. The variance of this number of customers is

$$\sigma_1{}^2 = \frac{(1-p)p n_0}{n_s}.$$

The probability of the firm losing more old customers than

$$\frac{(1-p)n_0}{n_s} + k\sigma_1$$

is given by the probability of values greater than k. The expected number of these old customers who will shift to any one rival is, say,

$$m_2 = \frac{1}{n_s - 1}\left[\frac{(1-p)n_0}{n_s} + k\sigma_1\right],$$

with a variance

$$\sigma_2^2 = \frac{n_s - 2}{(n_s - 1)^2}\left[\frac{(1-p)n_0}{n_s} + k\sigma_1\right].$$

The probability that any rival will obtain more than $m_2 + r\sigma_2$ of these customers is determined by r. We could now choose those combinations of k and r that fix a level of probability for the loss of a given number of old customers to any one rival beyond which secret price cutting by this rival will be inferred. This is heavy arithmetic, however, so we proceed along a less elegant route.

Let us assume that the firm's critical value for the loss of old customers, beyond which it infers secret price cutting, is

$$\frac{(1-p)n_0}{n_s} + \sigma_1 = \frac{(1-p)n_0}{n_s}\left[1 + \sqrt{\left(\frac{p}{1-p}\frac{n_s}{n_0}\right)}\right] = \frac{(1-p)n_0}{n_s}(1+\theta),$$

that is, one standard deviation above the mean. Any one rival will on average attract

$$m_2 = \frac{1}{n_s - 1}\left[\frac{(1-p)n_0}{n_s} + \sigma_1\right]$$

of these customers, with a variance of

$$\sigma_2^2 = \frac{n_s - 2}{(n_s - 1)^2}\left[\frac{(1-p)n_0}{n_s} + \sigma_1\right].$$

Let the rival be suspected of price cutting if he obtains more than $(m_2 + \sigma_2)$ customers, that is, if the probability of any larger number is less than about 30 percent. The joint probability of losing one standard deviation more than the average number of old customers and a rival obtaining one standard deviation more than his average share is about 10 percent. The average sales of a rival are n_0/n_s, ignoring new customers. The maximum number of buyers any seller can obtain from one rival without exciting suspicion, minus the number he will on average get without price cutting $([1-p]n_0/n_s[n_s - 1])$, expressed as a ratio to his average sales, is

$$\frac{[\theta(1-p)n_0/(n_s-1)n_s+\sigma_2]}{n_0/n_s}.$$

This criterion is tabulated in Table 11.1.
The entries in Table 11.1 are measures of the maximum additional sales

TABLE 11.1

PERCENTAGE GAINS IN SALES FROM UNDETECTED PRICE CUTTING BY A FIRM

Criterion I: $\dfrac{1}{(n_s-1)}\left[\theta(1-p)+\sqrt{\dfrac{n_s(n_s-2)(1-p)(1+\theta)}{n_0}}\right]$ $\theta=\sqrt{\dfrac{p}{1-p}}\dfrac{n_s}{n_0}$

Probability of Repeat Sales (p)	No. of Buyers (n_0)	No. of Sellers					
		2	3	4	5	10	20
p=0.95	20	6.9	11.3	11.3	11.4	11.8	12.7
	30	5.6	8.9	8.8	8.8	9.0	9.6
	40	4.9	7.5	7.4	7.4	7.5	7.9
	50	4.4	6.6	6.5	6.4	6.5	6.8
	100	3.1	4.4	4.3	4.3	4.2	4.4
	200	2.2	3.0	2.9	2.8	2.8	2.8
	400	1.5	2.1	2.0	1.9	1.8	1.8
p=0.90	20	9.5	14.8	14.7	14.6	14.8	15.7
	30	7.8	11.7	11.5	11.4	11.4	12.0
	40	6.7	10.0	9.7	9.6	9.5	9.9
	50	6.0	8.8	8.6	8.4	8.3	8.6
	100	4.2	6.0	5.8	5.6	5.4	5.5
	200	3.0	4.1	3.9	3.8	3.6	3.6
	400	2.1	2.8	2.7	2.6	2.4	2.4
p=0.80	20	12.6	19.3	18.9	18.7	18.6	19.4
	30	10.3	15.4	15.0	14.7	14.5	15.0
	40	8.9	13.1	12.7	12.5	12.2	12.5
	50	8.0	11.6	11.2	11.0	10.6	10.8
	100	5.7	8.0	7.7	7.4	7.1	7.1
	200	4.0	5.5	5.3	5.1	4.8	4.7
	400	2.8	3.8	3.6	3.5	3.2	3.2
p=0.70	20	14.5	22.3	21.8	21.5	21.2	21.9
	30	11.8	17.8	17.3	17.0	16.6	16.9
	40	10.2	15.2	14.8	14.5	14.0	14.2
	50	9.2	13.5	13.1	12.8	12.3	12.4
	100	6.5	9.3	9.0	8.7	8.2	8.2
	200	4.6	6.5	6.2	6.0	5.6	5.5
	400	3.2	4.5	4.3	4.2	3.8	3.7

obtainable by secret price cutting (expressed as a percentage of average sales) from any one rival beyond which that rival will infer that the price cutting is taking place. Since the profitability of secret price cutting depends upon the amount of business one can obtain (as well as upon the excess of price over marginal cost), we may also view these numbers as the measures of the incentive to engage in secret price cutting. Three features of the tabulation are noteworthy:

a. The gain in sales from any one rival by secret price cutting is not very sensitive to the number of rivals, given the number of customers and the probability of repeat sales. The aggregate gain in sales of a firm from price cutting—its total incentive to secret price cutting—is the sum of the gains from each rival, and therefore increases roughly in proportion to the number of rivals.

b. The incentive to secret price cutting falls as the number of customers per seller increases—and falls roughly in inverse proportion to the square root of the number of buyers.

c. The incentive to secret price cutting rises as the probability of repeat purchases falls, but at a decreasing rate.

We have said that the gain to old buyers from shifting their patronage among sellers will be that it encourages secret price cutting by making it more difficult to detect. Table 11.1 indicates that there are diminishing returns to increased shifting: the entries increase at a decreasing rate as p falls. In a fuller model we could introduce the costs of shifting among suppliers and determine p to maximize expected buyer gains. The larger the purchases of a buyer, when buyers are of unequal size, however, the greater is the prospect that his shifts will induce price cutting.

In addition it is clear that, when the number of sellers exceeds two, it is possible for two or more firms to pool information and thus to detect less extreme cases of price cutting. For example, at the given probability levels, the number of old customers that any one rival should be able to take from a firm was shown to be at most

$$(1-p)\frac{n_0(1+\theta)}{n_s-1},$$

with variance

$$\frac{(n_s - 2)(1 - p)(1 + \theta)}{(n_s - 1)^2} n_0.$$

At the same probability level, the average number of old customers that one rival should be able to take from T firms is at most

$$\frac{T(1 - p)n_0}{n_s - T}\left(1 + \frac{\theta}{\sqrt{T}}\right),$$

with the variance

$$\frac{(n_s - T - 1)}{(n_s - T)^2}(1 - p)\left(1 + \frac{\theta}{\sqrt{T}}\right)n_0 T.$$

Each of these is smaller than the corresponding expression for one seller when expressed as a fraction of the customers lost by each of the firms pooling information.

There are of course limits to such pooling of information: not only does it become expensive as the number of firms increases, but also it produces less reliable information, since one of the members of the pool may himself be secretly cutting prices. Some numbers illustrative of the effect of pooling will be given at a later point.

2. *The attraction of old customers of other firms is a second source of evidence of price cutting.* If a given rival has not cut prices, he will on average lose $(1 - p)$ (n_0/n_s) customers, with a variance of σ_1^2. The number of customers he will retain with secret price cutting cannot exceed a level at which the rivals suspect the price cutting. Any one rival will have little basis for judging whether he is getting a fair share of this firm's old customers, but they can pool their information and then in the aggregate they will expect the firm to lose at least $(1 - p)$ $(n_0/n_s) - 2\sigma_1$ customers, at the 5 percent probability level. Hence the secret price cutter can retain at most $2\sigma_1$ of his old customers (beyond his average number), which as a fraction of his average sales (ignoring new customers) is

$$\frac{2\sigma_1}{n_0/n_s} = 2\sqrt{\frac{(1 - p)pn_s}{n_0}}.$$

This is tabulated as Table 11.2.

If the entries in Table 11.2 are compared with those in Table 11.1,[10] it is found that a price cutter is easier to detect by his gains at the expense of any

TABLE 11.2

OLD CUSTOMERS THAT A SECRET PRICE CUTTER CAN RETAIN,
AS A PERCENTAGE OF AVERAGE SALES

Criterion II: $2\sqrt{\dfrac{p(1-p)}{2}\dfrac{n_s}{n_0}}$

Probability That Old Customer Will Remain Loyal (p)	No. OF OLD CUSTOMERS PER SELLER (n_0/n_s)			
	10	20	50	100
0.95	13.8	9.7	6.2	4.4
.90	19.0	13.4	8.5	6.0
.85	22.6	16.0	10.1	7.1
.80	25.3	17.9	11.3	8.0
.75	27.4	19.4	12.2	8.7
.70	29.0	20.5	13.0	9.2
.65	30.2	21.3	13.5	9.5
.60	31.0	21.9	13.9	9.8
.55	31.5	22.2	14.1	10.0
0.50	31.6	22.4	14.1	10.0

one rival than by his unusual proportion of repeat sales. This second criterion will therefore seldom be useful.

3. *The behavior of new customers is a third source of information on price cutting.* There are n_n new customers per period,[11] equal to λn_0. A firm expects, in the absence of price cutting, to sell to

$$m_3 = \frac{1}{n_s}\lambda n_0$$

of these customers, with a variance of

$$\sigma_3{}^2 = \left(1 - \frac{1}{n_s}\right)\frac{\lambda n_0}{n_s}.$$

If the rivals pool information (without pooling, this area could not be policed effectively), this firm cannot obtain more than $m_3 + 2\sigma_3$ customers without being deemed a price cutter, using again a 5 percent probability criterion. As a percentage of the firm's total sales, the maximum sales above the expected number in the absence of price cutting are then

$$\frac{2\sigma_3}{n_0(1+\lambda)/n_s}=\frac{2}{1+\lambda}\sqrt{\frac{(n_s-1)\lambda}{n_0}}.$$

We tabulate this criterion as Table 11.3.

Two aspects of the incentive to cut prices (or equivalently the difficulty of detecting price cuts) to new customers are apparent: the incentive increases rapidly with the number of sellers[12] and the incentive increases with the rate of entry of new customers. As usual the incentive falls as the absolute number of customers per seller rises. If the rate of entry of new buyers is 10 percent or more, price cutting to new customers allows larger sales increases without detection that can be obtained by attracting customers of rivals (compare Tables 11.1 and 11.3).

Of the considerable number of directions in which this model could be enlarged, two will be presented briefly.

The first is inequality in the size of firms. In effect this complication has already been introduced by the equivalent device of pooling information. If we tabulate the effects of pooling of information by K firms, the results are equivalent to having a firm K times as large as the other firms. The number of old customers this large firm can lose to any one small rival (all of whom are equal in size) is given, in Table 11.4, as a percentage of the average number of old customers of the small firm; the column labeled $K=1$ is of course the case analyzed in Table 11.1.

The effects of pooling on the detection of price cutting are best analyzed by comparing Table 11.4 with Table 11.1. If there are 100 customers and 10 firms (and $p=0.9$), a single firm can increase sales by 5.4 percent by poaching on one rival, or about 50 percent against all rivals (Table 11.1). If 9 firms combine, the maximum amount the single firm can gain by secret price cutting is 28.9 percent (Table 11.4). With 20 firms and 200 customers, a single firm can gain 3.6 percent from each rival, or about 30 percent from 9 rivals; if these rivals merge, the corresponding figure falls to 14.0 percent. The pooling of information therefore reduces substantially the scope for secret price cutting.

This table exaggerates the effect of inequality of firm size because it fails to take account of the fact that the number of customers varies with firm size, on our argument that only customers above a certain size relative to the seller are a feasible group for secret price cutting. The small firm can find it attractive to cut prices to buyers which are not large enough to be potential customers by price cutting for the large seller.

The temporal pattern of buyers' behavior provides another kind of information: what is possibly due to random fluctuation in the short run cannot

Table 11.3

Maximum Additional New Customers (as a Percentage of
Average Sales) Obtainable by Secret Price Cutting

Criterion III: $\dfrac{2}{1+\lambda}\sqrt{\dfrac{\lambda(n_s-1)}{n_0}}$

Rate of Appearance of New Buyers (λ)	No. of Old Buyers (n_0)	No. of Sellers					
		2	3	4	5	10	20
1/100	20	4.4	6.3	7.7	8.9	13.3	19.3
	30	3.6	5.1	6.3	7.2	10.8	15.8
	40	3.1	4.4	5.4	6.3	9.4	13.6
	50	2.8	4.0	4.8	5.6	8.4	12.2
	100	2.0	2.8	3.4	4.0	5.9	8.6
	200	1.4	2.0	2.4	2.8	4.2	6.1
	400	1.0	1.4	1.7	2.0	3.0	4.3
1/10	20	12.9	18.2	22.3	25.7	38.6	56.0
	30	10.5	14.8	18.2	21.0	31.5	45.8
	40	9.1	12.9	15.8	18.2	27.3	39.6
	50	8.1	11.5	14.1	16.3	24.4	35.4
	100	5.8	8.1	10.0	11.5	17.2	25.1
	200	4.1	5.8	7.0	8.1	12.2	17.7
	400	2.9	4.1	5.0	5.8	8.6	12.5
1/5	20	16.7	23.6	28.9	33.3	50.0	72.6
	30	13.6	19.2	23.6	27.2	40.8	59.3
	40	11.8	16.7	20.4	23.6	35.4	51.4
	50	10.5	14.9	18.3	21.1	31.6	46.0
	100	7.4	10.5	12.9	14.9	22.4	32.5
	200	5.3	7.4	9.1	10.5	15.8	23.0
	400	3.7	5.3	6.4	7.4	11.2	16.2
1/4	20	17.9	25.3	31.0	35.8	53.7	78.0
	30	14.6	20.7	25.3	29.2	43.8	63.7
	40	12.6	17.9	21.9	25.3	38.0	55.1
	50	11.3	16.0	19.6	22.6	33.9	49.3
	100	8.0	11.3	13.9	16.0	24.0	34.9
	200	5.7	8.0	9.8	11.3	17.0	24.7
	400	4.0	5.7	6.9	8.0	12.0	17.4

TABLE 11.4

PERCENTAGE GAINS IN SALES FROM UNDETECTED PRICE CUTTING
BY A SMALL FIRM

$$\text{Criterion IV: } \frac{1}{n_s-K}\left[\theta(1-p)\sqrt{K}+\sqrt{\frac{n_sK(1-p)(n_s-K-1)(1+\theta/\sqrt{K})}{n_0}}\right]$$

$$\theta=\sqrt{\frac{p}{1-p}\frac{n_s}{n_0}}$$

Probability of Repeat Sales (p)	No. of Firms (n_s-K+1)	Buyers per Small Seller (n_0/n_s)	SIZE OF LARGE FIRM (K)			
			1	2	5	9
$p=0.9$	2	10	9.5	13.4	21.2	28.5
		30	5.5	7.7	12.2	16.4
		50	4.2	6.0	9.5	12.7
	3	10	11.7	15.8	23.9	31.4
		30	6.3	8.7	13.3	17.6
		50	4.8	6.6	10.2	13.5
	4	10	9.7	13.1	19.7	25.7
		30	5.2	7.1	10.9	14.4
		50	4.0	5.4	8.3	11.0
	10	10	5.4	7.2	10.7	14.0
		30	2.9	3.9	5.9	7.7
		50	2.2	2.9	4.5	5.9
$p=0.8$	2	10	12.6	17.9	28.3	37.9
		30	7.3	10.3	16.3	21.9
		50	5.7	8.0	12.6	17.0
	3	10	15.4	21.0	32.1	42.3
		30	8.4	11.6	18.0	23.9
		50	6.4	8.9	13.8	18.4
	4	10	12.7	17.3	26.3	34.7
		30	6.9	9.5	14.7	19.5
		50	5.3	7.3	11.3	15.0
	10	10	7.1	9.5	14.4	18.9
		30	3.8	5.2	8.0	10.6
		50	2.9	4.0	6.1	8.1

with equal probability be due to chance if repeated. Thus the maximum expected loss of old customers to a rival in one round of transactions is (at the 1σ level)

$$\frac{n_0}{(n_s-1)n_s}(1-p)(1+\theta),$$

but for T consecutive periods the maximum expected loss is (over T periods)

$$\frac{T}{n_s-1}(1-p)\frac{n_0}{n_s}[1+\theta\sqrt{T}],$$

with a variance of

$$\sigma_b{}^2=\frac{(n_s-2)}{(n_s-1)^2}T(1-p)\frac{n_0}{n_s}[1+\theta\sqrt{T}].$$

This source of information is of minor efficacy in detecting price cutting unless the rounds of successive transactions are numerous—that is, unless buyers purchase (enter contracts) frequently.

Our approach has certain implications for the measurement of concentration, if we wish concentration to measure likelihood of effective collusion. In the case of new customers, for example, let the probability of attracting a customer be proportional to the firm's share of industry output (s). Then the variance of the firm's share of sales to new customers will be $n_n s(1-s)$, and the aggregate for the industry will be

$$C=n_n\sum_1^r s(1-s)$$

for r firms. This expression equals $n_n(1-H)$, where

$$H=\Sigma s^2$$

is the Herfindahl index of concentration. The same index holds, as an approximation, for potential price cutting to attract old customers.[13]

The foregoing analysis can be extended to nonprice variables, subject to two modifications. The first modification is that there be a definite joint profit-maximizing policy upon which the rivals can agree. Here we may expect to encounter a spectrum of possibilities, ranging from a clearly defined optimum

TABLE 11.5

RESIDUALS FROM REGRESSION OF ADVERTISING RATES ON CIRCULATION[a]

No. of Evening Papers	n	Mean Residual (logarithm)	Standard Deviation of Mean
One	23	0.0211	0.0210
With morning paper	10	− .0174	.0324
Without morning paper	13	.0507	.0233
Two	30	−0.0213	0.0135

SOURCE: American Association of Advertising Agencies, *Market and Newspaper Statistics*, vol. 8a (1939).

[a] The regression equation is

$$\log R = 5.194 - 1.688 \log c + .139 (\log c)^2,$$
$$\quad\quad\quad (.620) \quad\quad (.063)$$

where R is the 5 M milline rate and c is circulation.

policy (say, on favorable legislation) to a nebulous set of alternatives (say, directions of research).[14] Collusion is less feasible, the less clear the basis on which it should proceed. The second modification is that the competitive moves of any one firm will differ widely among nonprice variables in their detectability by rivals. Some forms of nonprice competition will be easier to detect than price cutting because they leave visible traces (advertising, product quality, servicing, etc.) but some variants will be elusive (reciprocity in purchasing, patent licensing arrangements). The common belief that nonprice competition is more common than price competition is therefore not wholly in keeping with the present theory. Those forms that are suitable areas for collusion will have less competition; those which are not suitable will have more competition.

IV. SOME FRAGMENTS OF EVIDENCE

Before we seek empirical evidence on our theory, it is useful to report two investigations of the influence of numbers of sellers on price. These investigations have an intrinsic interest because, so far as I know, no systematic analysis of the effect of numbers has hitherto been made.

The first investigation was of newspaper advertising rates, as a function of the number of evening newspapers in a city. Advertising rates on a milline basis are closely (and negatively) related to circulation, so a regression of rates on circulation was made for fifty-three cities in 1939. The residuals (in logarithmic form) from this regression equation are tabulated in Table 11.5. It will be observed that rates are 5 percent above the average in one-newspaper towns and 5 percent below the average in two-newspaper towns, and the towns with one evening paper but also an independent morning paper fall nearly midway between these points. Unfortunately there were too few cities with more than two evening newspapers to yield results for larger numbers of firms.

The second investigation is of spot commercial rates on AM radio stations in the four states of Ohio, Indiana, Michigan, and Illinois. The basic equation introduces, along with number of rivals, a series of other factors (power of station, population of the county in which the station is located, etc.). Unfortunately the number of stations is rather closely correlated with population ($r^2 = .796$ in the logarithms). The general result, shown in Table 11.6, is similar to that for newspapers: the elasticity of price with respect to number of rivals is quite small ($-.07$). Here the range of stations in a county was from one to thirteen.

Both studies suggest that the level of prices is not very responsive to the actual number of rivals. This is in keeping with the expectations based upon our model, for that model argues that the number of buyers, the proportion of

TABLE 11.6

REGRESSION OF AM SPOT COMMERCIAL RATES (TWENTY-SIX TIMES)
AND STATION CHARACTERISTICS, 1961 ($n = 345$)

Independent Variables[a]	Regression Coefficient	Standard Error
1. Logarithm of population of county, 1960	.238	0.026
2. Logarithm of kilowatt power of station	.206	.015
3. Dummy variables of period of broadcasting:		
a) Sunrise to sunset	−.114	.025
b) More than (a), less than 18 hours	−.086	.027
c) 18–21 hours	−.053	.028
4. Logarithm of number of stations in county	−.074	0.046
	$R^2 = .743$	

SOURCE: "Spot Radio Rates and Data," *Standard Rate and Data Service, Inc.* 43, no. 5 (May 1961).
[a] Dependent variable: logarithm of average rate, May 1, 1961 (dollars).

TABLE 11.7

PROFITABILITY AND CONCENTRATION DATA

Industry[a]	CONCENTRATION (1954) Share of Top 4	H[b]	AVERAGE RATE OF RETURN (1953–1957) All Assets	Net Worth	Ratio of Market Value to Book Value (1953–1957)
Sulfur mining (4)	98	0.407	19.03	23.85	3.02
Automobiles (3)	98	.369	11.71	20.26	2.30
Flat glass (3)	90	.296	11.79	16.17	2.22
Gypsum products (2)	90	.280	12.16	20.26	1.83
Primary aluminum (4)	98	.277	6.87	13.46	2.48
Metal cans (4)	80	.260	7.27	13.90	1.60
Chewing gum (2)	86	.254	13.50	17.06	2.46
Hard-surface floor coverings (3)	87	.233	6.56	7.59	0.98
Cigarettes (5)	83	.213	7.23	11.18	1.29
Industrial gases (3)	84	.202	8.25	11.53	1.33
Corn wet milling (3)	75	.201	9.17	11.55	1.48
Typewriters (3)	83	.198	3.55	5.39	0.84
Domestic laundry equipment (2)	68	.174	9.97	17.76	1.66
Rubber tires (9)	79	.171	7.86	14.02	1.70
Rayon fiber (4)	76	.169	5.64	6.62	0.84
Carbon black (2)	73	.152	8.29	9.97	1.40
Distilled liquors (6)	64	0.118	6.94	7.55	0.77

[a] The number of firms is given in parentheses after the industry title. Only those industries are included for which a substantial share (35 percent or more) of the industry's sales is accounted for by the firms in the sample, and these firms derive their chief revenues (50 percent or more) from the industry in question.
[b] H is Herfindahl index.

new buyers, and the relative sizes of firms are as important as the number of rivals.

To turn to the present theory, the only test covering numerous industries so far devised has been one based upon profitability. This necessarily rests upon company data, and it has led to the exclusion of a large number of industries for which the companies do not operate in a well-defined industry. For example, the larger steel and chemical firms operate in a series of markets in which their position ranges from monopolistic to competitive. We have required of each

TABLE 11.8

RANK CORRELATIONS OF MEASURES OF PROFITABILITY
AND MEASURES OF CONCENTRATION

	MEASURE OF PROFITABILITY		
Measure of Concentration	Rate of Return on All Assets	Ratio of Return on Net Worth	Rate of Market Value to Book Value
Share of output produced by four largest firms	.322	.507	.642
Herfindahl index (H)	.524	.692	.730

industry that the earnings of a substantial fraction of the companies in the industry (measured by output) be determined by the profitability of that industry's products, that is, that we have a fair share of the industry and the industry's product is the dominant product of the firms.

Three measures of profitability are given in Table 11.7: (1) the rate of return on all capital (including debt), (2) the rate of return on net worth (stockholders' equity); (3) the ratio of market value to book value of the common stock.

In addition, two measures of concentration are presented: (1) the conventional measure, the share of output produced by the four leading firms; and (2) the Herfindahl index, H.

The various rank correlations are given in Table 11.8. The various concentration measures, on the one hand, and the various measures of profitability, on the other hand, are tolerably well correlated.[15] All show the expected positive relationship. In general the data suggest that there is no relationship between profitability and concentration if H is less than 0.250 or the share of the four largest firms is less than about 80 percent. These data, like those on advertising rates, confirm our theory only in the sense that they support theories which assert that competition increases with number of firms.

Our last evidence is a study of the prices paid by buyers of steel products in 1939, measured relative to the quoted prices (Table 11.9). The figure of 8.3 for hot-rolled sheets, for example, represents an average of 8.3 percent reduction from quoted prices, *paid by buyers*, with a standard deviation of 7.3 percent of quoted prices. The rate of price cutting is almost perfectly correlated with the standard deviation of transaction prices, as we should expect: the less perfect the market knowledge, the more extensive the price cutting.

In general, the more concentrated the industry structure (measured by the

A Theory of Oligopoly

TABLE 11.9

PRICES OF STEEL PRODUCTS, 1939, AND INDUSTRY STRUCTURE, 1938

Product Class	PRICES, 2ND QUARTER, 1939 (PERCENT)		Herfindahl Index	Output in 1939 Relative to 1937
	Average Discount from List Price	Standard Deviation		
Hot-rolled sheets	8.3	7.3	0.0902	1.14
Merchant bars	1.2	4.5	.1517	0.84
Hot-rolled strip	8.5	8.3	.1069	0.56
Plates	2.6	4.8	.1740	0.85
Structural shapes	3.2	4.3	.3280	0.92
Cold-rolled strip	8.8	9.8	.0549	0.88
Cold-rolled sheets	5.8	5.0	.0963	1.14
Cold-finished bars	0.9	3.4	0.0964	0.83

SOURCE: Prices: "Labor Department Examines Consumers' Prices of Steel Products," *Iron Age*, April 25, 1946; industry structure: 1938 capacity data from *Directory of Iron and Steel Works of the United States and Canada*; output: *Annual Statistical Report, Amerian Iron and Steel Institute* (New York: 1938, 1942).

Herfindahl index), the larger were the price reductions. Although there were no extreme departures from this relationship, structural shapes and hot-rolled strip had prices somewhat lower than the average relationship, and cold-finished bars prices somewhat higher than expected, and the deviations are not accounted for by the level of demand (measured by 1939 sales relative to 1937 sales). The number of buyers could not be taken into account, but the BLS (Bureau of Labor Statistics) study states:

> The extent of price concessions shown by this study is probably understated because certain very large consumers in the automobile and container industries were excluded from the survey. This omission was at the request of the OPA which contemplated obtaining this information in connection with other studies. Since a small percentage of steel consumers, including these companies, accounts for a large percentage of steel purchased, prices paid by a relatively few large consumers have an important influence upon the entire steel price structure. Very large steel consumers get greater reductions from published prices than smaller consumers, often the result of competitive bidding by the mills for the large volume of steel involved. One very large steel consumer, a firm that purchased over 2 percent of the total consumption of hot- and cold-rolled sheets in 1940, refused to give purchase prices. This firm wished to protect its suppliers, fearing that "certain transactions might

be revealed which would break confidence" with the steel mills. However, this company did furnish percent changes of prices paid for several steel products which showed that for some products prices advanced markedly, and in one case, nearly 50 percent. The great price advances for this company indicate that it was receiving much larger concessions than smaller buyers.[16]

These various bits of evidence are fairly favorable to the theory, but they do not constitute strong support. More powerful tests will be feasible when the electrical equipment triple-damage suits are tried.[17] The great merit of our theory, in fact, is that it has numerous testable hypotheses, unlike the immortal theories that have been traditional in this area.

Appendix

The importance of product heterogeneity for profit-maximizing behavior cannot well be established by an a priori argument. Nevertheless, the following simple exposition of the implications for profitability of disregarding heterogeneity may have some heuristic value. The analysis, it will be observed, is formally equivalent to that of the effects of an excise tax on a monopolist.

Assume that a monopolist makes men's suits, and that he makes only one size of suit. This is absurd behavior, but the picture of the sadistic monopolist who disregards consumer desires has often made fugitive appearances in the literature so the problem has some interest of its own. The demand curve of a consumer for suits that fit, $f(p)$, would now be reduced because he would have to incur some alteration cost a in order to wear the suit. His effective demand would therefore decline to $f(p+a)$. Assume further that the marginal cost of suits is constant (m), and that it would be the same if the monopolist were to make suits of various sizes.

The effect on profits of a uniform product—uniform is an especially appropriate word here—can be shown graphically (Figure 11.1). The decrease in quantity sold, with a linear demand curve, is

$$MB = \frac{1}{2}af'(p).$$

The decrease in the price received by the monopolist is

$$DN = \frac{MB}{f'(p)} - a = -\frac{a}{2},$$

FIGURE 11.1

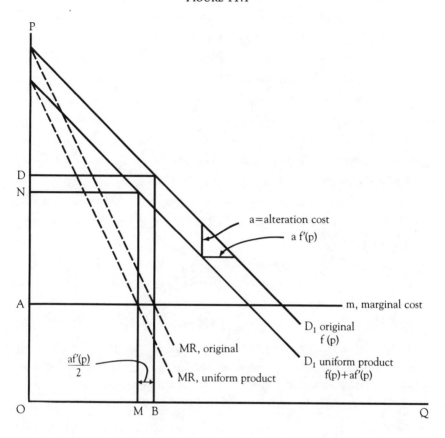

Simple Monopoly	Uniform Product Monopoly
Price=OD	Price=ON
Quantity=OB	Quantity=OM
Profits=OB×AD	Profits=OM×AN

so if π is profit per unit, and q is output, the relative decline in total profit is approximately

$$\frac{\Delta\pi}{\pi}+\frac{\Delta q}{q}$$

or

$$\frac{MB}{OB}+\frac{ND}{AD}.$$

Since

$$OB=\frac{f(m)}{2}$$

$$AD=-\frac{p}{\eta},$$

where η is the elasticity of demand, the relative decline of profits with a uniform product is

$$\frac{af'(p)}{f(m)}+\frac{a\eta}{2p}=\frac{a\eta}{2p}+\frac{a\eta}{2p}=\frac{a\eta}{p}.$$

The loss from imposed uniformity is therefore proportional to the ratio of alteration costs to price.

Our example is sufficiently unrealistic to make any quantitative estimate uninteresting. In general one would expect an upper limit to the ratio a/p, because it becomes cheaper to resort to other goods (custom tailoring in our example), or to abandon the attempt to find appropriate goods. The loss of profits of the monopolist will be proportional to the average value of a/p, and this will be smaller, the smaller the variation in buyers' circumstances.

Still, monopolists are lucky if their long-run demand curves have an elasticity only as large as -5, and then even a ratio of a to p of $1/40$ will reduce their profits by 12 percent. The general conclusion I wish to draw is that a monopolist who does not cater to the diversities of his buyers' desires will suffer a substantial decline in his profits.

Notes

1. I am indebted to Claire Friedland for the statistical work and to Harry Johnson for helpful criticisms.

2. Unless one defines heterogeneity of transactions to include also differences in

luck in finding low price sellers; see my "Economics of Information," *Journal of Political Economy* (June 1961).

3. If the firms are multiproduct, with different product structures, the dis-economies of merger are not strictly those of scale (in any output) but of firm size measured either absolutely or in terms of variety of products.

4. If price is above marginal cost, marginal revenue will be only slightly less than price (and hence above marginal cost) for price cuts by this one seller.

5. More precisely, he is moving along a demand curve which is a fixed share of the industry demand, and hence has the same elasticity as the industry curve at every price.

6. When the relative outputs of the firms change, the minimum cost condition of equal marginal costs for all sellers is likely to be violated. Hence industry profits are not maximized.

7. The literature and cases on "open-price associations" contain numerous refer-ences to the collection of prices from sellers (see Federal Trade Commission, *Open-Price Trade Associations* [Washington: 1929], and cases cited).

8. This argument applies to size of buyer relative to the individual sellers. One can also explain the absence of higgling in small transactions because of the costs of bargaining, but this latter argument turns on the absolute size of the typical transac-tion, not its size relative to the seller.

9. The problem implicitly raised by these remarks is why all sales to the govern-ment are not at collusive prices. Part of the answer is that the government is usually not a sufficiently large buyer of a commodity to remunerate the costs of collusion.

10. For example, take $p=.95$. The entry for 10 customers per seller is 13.8 in Table 11.2—this is the maximum percentage of average sales that can be obtained by price reductions to old customers. The corresponding entries in Table 11.1 are 6.9 (2 sellers, 20 buyers), 8.9 (3 and 30), 7.4 (4 and 40), 6.4 (5 and 50), 4.2 (10 and 100), etc. Multiplying each entry in Table 11.1 by (n_s-1), we get the maximum gain in sales (without detection) by attracting customers of rivals, and beyond 2 sellers the gains are larger by this latter route. Since Table 11.1 is based upon a 10 percent probability level, strict comparability requires that we use 1.6σ, instead of 2σ, in Table 11.2, which would reduce the entries by one-fifth.

11. Unlike old customers, whose behavior is better studied in a round of transac-tions, the new customers are a flow whose magnitude depends much more crucially on the time period considered. The annual flow of new customers is here taken (relative to the number of old customers) as the unit.

12. And slowly with the number of sellers if customers per seller are held constant.

13. A similar argument leads to a measure of concentration appropriate to poten-tial price cutting for old customers. Firm i will lose

$$(1-p)n_0s_i$$

old customers, and firm j will gain

$$(1-p)n_0\frac{s_i s_j}{1-s_i}$$

of them, with a variance

$$(1-p)n_0\frac{s_i s_j}{1-s_i}\left(1-\frac{s_j}{1-s_i}\right).$$

If we sum over all i ($\neq j$), we obtain the variance of firm j's sales to old customers of rivals

$$(1-p)n_0 s_j(1+H-2s_j),$$

to an approximation, and summing over all j, we have the concentration measure,

$$(1-p)n_0(1-H).$$

The agreement of this measure with that for new customers is superficial: that for new customers implicitly assumes pooling of information and that for old customers does not.

14. Of course, price itself usually falls somewhere in this range rather than at the pole. The traditional assumption of stationary conditions conceals this fact.

15. The concentration measures have a rank correlation of .903. The profitability measures have the following rank correlations:

	Return on All Assets	Ratio of Market to Book Value
Return on net worth	.866	.872
Ratio of market to book value	.733	—

16. See "Labor Department Examines Consumers' Prices of Steel Products," op. cit., p. 133.

17. For example, it will be possible to test the prediction that prices will be higher and less dispersed in sales on public bids than in privately negotiated sales, and the prediction that price cutting increases as the number of buyers diminishes.

THE DOMINANT FIRM AND
THE INVERTED UMBRELLA*

· 12 ·

When United States Steel Corporation was founded in 1901, it contained plants producing a large share of the nation's output of basic steel and fabricated steel products. The share of output of steel ingots was 66 percent in 1901. During the next two decades the firm's share of output fell gradually, reaching 46 percent in 1920 and 42 percent in 1925. Declines (usually of lesser magnitude) took place in the company's share of other products. These facts are not in serious dispute.

The interpretation of the facts enjoys no such unanimity. Two rival hypotheses for the formation of the combine will be tested in this note.

The first hypothesis is that a large, perhaps primary, purpose of the merger was to sell securities to untutored investors. The book value of assets of the constituent firms was written up from some $700 million to $1.4 billion when the new corporation was formed, and the common stock then issued is a classic example of watered stocks in the literature of corporation finance.

On this view it was incidental to the motives for the merger whether any

From the *Journal of Law and Economics* 8 (October 1965). Copyright 1965 by the University of Chicago.

* Aaron Director proposed the study, and Richard West, then a graduate student, performed the work under my negligent eye. Director refuses coauthorship, on grounds I find unconvincing; West has been given no chance to do so, on the ground that he has since become a professor and will now hire research assistants. As the middleman in this venture, I assume no credit and all blame.

TABLE 12.1

Market Value of Investment of $10,000[a] Plus Reinvested Dividends from July, 1901[b]

Year	U.S. Steel	Bethlehem	Colorado	Crucible	Lackawanna	Republic	Sloss-Sheffield	Average Excluding U.S. Steel
1901	$ 10,672		$10,000	$ 10,000		$10,000	$10,000	$10,000
1902	9,606		9,427	10,383		9,240	9,905	9,739
1903	7,814		5,813	5,761		6,756	10,952	7,320
1904	3,599		3,199	2,139		3,678	10,994	5,002
1905	9,529	$ 13,851a	4,544	4,683		10,347	35,832	13,851
1906	10,707	13,102	4,884	4,839	$12,920a	13,595	28,184	12,920
1907	11,839	7,196	3,226	3,365	10,835	14,697	29,432	11,458
1908	13,890	9,503	2,930	2,652	7,172	9,948	28,054	10,043
1909	24,801	17,405	4,398	4,335	10,123	16,699	49,518	17,080
1910	26,688	11,945	3,166	4,900	8,470	15,949	38,343	13,796
1911	32,020	15,364	3,436	5,574	7,884	15,587	29,163	12,835
1912	31,374	16,648	3,037	7,331	7,681	13,921	32,789	13,568
1913	25,924	13,956	2,876	5,904	7,300	10,673	14,837	9,258
1914	29,990	18,817	2,532	6,857	6,691	11,195	16,190	10,380
1915	31,062	83,187	3,254	15,978	9,594	16,177	21,305	24,916
1916	47,455	209,845	4,324	29,865	15,750	23,363	28,302	51,908
1917	78,599	215,746d	5,144	37,195	23,649	49,767	35,684	61,198
1918	76,881	154,121	5,189	29,043	23,740	54,020	46,601	52,119
1919	84,081	193,172	6,028	56,543	26,552	60,497	58,411	66,867
1920	73,490	185,991	4,247	146,756e	24,100	61,714	62,892	80,950
1921	60,148	114,594	3,511	56,206	13,493	31,741	29,955	41,583
1922	84,009	185,844	3,124	84,936	27,032c	49,501	39,919	65,059
1923	90,150	125,899	3,712	70,833		30,204	38,904	53,910
1924	101,039	115,453	6,234	61,158		31,686	53,041	53,514

Sources: Stock quotations from *Financial and Commercial Chronicle*, 1901–1924. Dividends and splits from *Poor's Manual of Industrials* 1920, 1924.
[a] For firms entering after 1901 (Bethlehem and Lackawanna) the average market value, excluding U.S. Steel, was employed as the amount of initial investment.
[b] Prices used in calculating values of stock are the averages of the high-lows for the first four Fridays in the month of July of each year, unless otherwise stated.
[c] Lackawanna merged with Bethlehem.
[d] In 1917 Bethlehem declared a 200 percent stock dividend in "Common B." All values between 1917–1922 were calculated on the basis of two types of Common—"old Common" and "Common B." In 1922 the two types were merged.
[e] During 1920 Crucible declared three stock dividends: 50 percent (April 30), 16⅔ percent (July 31), 14½ percent (August 31). In order to take account of the last two stock dividends the price used in calculating the 1920 value was an average of the high-lows of March 30, June 30, September 30 and December 30.

important economies in production or any important monopoly power in the market was achieved. If U.S. Steel was not more efficient, or if it could not control entry, its share would decline with time, and the higher prices it may have set would provide an umbrella under which more efficient rivals would flourish and their shares would gradually increase. This aspect of the theory was not elaborated, because the focus was on the promotional profits in the original stock sales.[1]

The second hypothesis is that provided by the theory of the dominant firm. This theory assumes that U.S. Steel was formed for the monopoly power it achieved. The dominant firm will set a profit-maximizing price such that its marginal cost equals marginal revenue based upon *its* demand curve (the industry demand curve minus the amount supplied by others). The profit to be maximized is long run (actually, the sum of discounted future profits) so account will be taken of the rate at which rivals enter and expand. Nevertheless, the dominant firm will find, usually, that it is profitable to yield up some share of the industry, for higher prices may more than offset the decline in share.[2]

Neither theory denies the decline in share, which after all is a well-known historical fact. They differ on the wisdom of purchasing the stock of U.S. Steel when it was first offered: the former theory says this was an unwise purchase; the latter does not.

The purpose of this note is to investigate the financial returns to investors in U.S. Steel common stock and in that of other steel companies. On the former theory, the investors should have purchased stock in other steel companies; on the latter theory, U.S. Steel should have done as well as other steel companies.[3]

The financial returns of an investor are in principle easily determined:

1. Buy a block of stock in a company at a given date—say $10,000 worth.

2. Reinvest all cash dividends in the stock.

3. Calculate the market value of the stock (including stock dividends) at any desired subsequent date.

This is in effect our procedure,[4] and it yields the returns reported in Table 12.1.

The experience of investors in the various companies whose stocks were traded is presented graphically in Figure 12.1. The current market value of the shares obtained with an initial investment of $10,000, and with reinvestment of all earnings, is given for each year from 1901 to 1925. Since the figure is semi-logarithmic in scale, rates of increase can be read directly. The figure is sufficient to reach the main conclusion: the stockholders of U.S. Steel did better than those of any of the other companies except Bethlehem Steel. The

FIGURE 12.1

MARKET VALUE OF INVESTMENT OF $10,000
PLUS REINVESTED DIVIDENDS FROM JULY, 1901

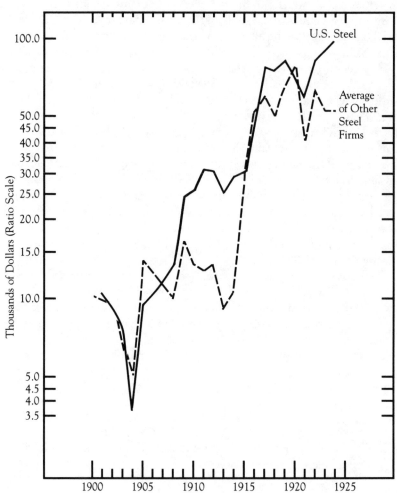

SOURCE: Table 12.1.

average value of the investments in the other companies was below that of U.S. Steel in sixteen of the eighteen years after 1905. At the end of the period the accumulated market value of U.S. Steel was twice that of the average of the other companies.

The evidence seems conclusive that the exploitation of stockholders by promoters did not take place. The formation of United States Steel Corporation must therefore be viewed as a master stroke of monopoly promotion; and it is churlish of the literature to complain at the $62 million of stock given to the Morgan syndicate for bringing it about.

NOTES

1. Perhaps the most influential statement of this hypothesis was made by Dewing, *Financial Policy of Corporations*, vol. 2, bk. IV, ch. 4, 924–26 (4th ed., 1941).

2. This version is explicit in Stigler, "Monopoly and Oligopoly by Merger," in Papers and Proceedings of the Sixty-second Annual Meeting of the American Economic Association, *American Economic Review* 40, no. 23 (May 1950).

3. It is not certain as to whether U.S. Steel stock should have done precisely as well, or better or worse. This depends fundamentally on whether the costs of U.S. Steel were greater or less than those of other companies.

4. The calculations depart in one respect from this description. The mean July price of the stock is used in calculating the number of shares purchased by reinvestment of dividends during a year, except when stock rights are issued. In this latter case the rights are valued as of the time they were exercisable, and reinvested at current prices.

The stocks whose quotations begin in later years are brought into the average in the first available year, with an investment equal to the average value of the current investments in other companies (excluding U.S. Steel).

THE ECONOMIC EFFECTS
OF THE ANTITRUST LAWS*

· 13 ·

The task I have set is to form a quantitative notion of the effects of the antitrust laws. The task is formidable. A Congress which had goodwill toward scholars would have exempted from the Sherman Act not a collection of special pleaders, as has been our historical practice, but a random sample of industries. A world more favorable to scholars would have had many United States, some of which had antitrust policies. (Our federal nation could have been almost that favorable, but the state antitrust laws have been pushed nearly into oblivion by the federal laws.) In our statistically inefficient world, the investigator must somehow disentangle the effects of one battalion of an army of forces that have been influencing the American economy in the past 75 years.

Many students have undertaken our task, and diverse estimates of the effects of our antitrust laws may be found in the literature. These estimates have invariably been made by one procedure. The scholar studies the history of our policy and in the light of his knowledge of our economy—and perhaps of other economies—he makes a summary judgment. The defect of the procedure is that the link between the survey of experience and the conclusion is not explicit, so different scholars reach different conclusions. Yet it should be

From the *Journal of Law and Economics* 9 (October 1966). Copyright 1966 by the University of Chicago.

* I wish to express my gratitude to Claire Friedland for much of the statistical work; and important contributions were made by Mrs. Belle Cole, Ruth Westheimer, and Barry Herman.

the fundamental attribute of a measurement procedure that different men can use it to achieve similar results. Until such procedures are available, there is no tendency for the measurements to improve—each man's work remains independent of all other's work. The main purpose of this paper is to seek improvable procedures.

I. SIMPLE ANTITRUST LAWS

Let us begin with an antitrust law that seems easy to assess: it is the provision of the Panama Canal Act that no company violating the Sherman Act be permitted to ship goods through the canal.[1] This act, we assume, has not had any effect upon the methods of shipments used by monopolists, let alone upon the extent of competition, and for several reasons:

1. An instance of enforcement would surely have received much publicity, so presumably none has occurred.
2. It is inconceivable that none of the many violators of the Sherman Act ever used the canal.
3. The attorney-general gave to the canal authorities an interpretation of the provision which implied that it could be ignored.[2]

I do not wish to quarrel with this universal presumption that the provision never influenced the movement of monopolized goods. I do not wish to emphasize the fact that this presumption is a poor substitute for evidence. The provision could have frightened monopolists into using the railroads, and the only way we can eliminate this possibility is by studying the comparative shipments of firms which were and were not prosecuted under the antitrust laws. Perhaps the problem is too small to justify the extensive labor such research would entail, but until this research is done, we possess a presumption, not a finding. The central weakness of the antitrust literature has been its reliance on presumptions—and in cases vastly more important and uncertain than the trifling question with which I begin.

A slightly more significant antitrust law is that no man may serve as director of two companies if at least one has assets of $1 million or more and the two companies compete with one another.[3] The logic of the law is that joint directors could effect collusive schemes between two companies more easily than conspiring officers or directors.

As a matter of history, the law has been invoked in formal complaints on 23 occasions up to January 1965.[4] The one instance leading to a court decision concerned Sidney Weinberg who was a director of Sears, Roebuck & Co. and

TABLE 13.1

INTERLOCKING DIRECTORATES, GREAT BRITAIN, 1964

Industry	Companies	Number of Directors	Number of Overlapping Directors
Aircraft	13	130	1
Boots and Shoes	50	290	0
Rubber Products: Tires	8	63	0
Cement	29	194	1

SOURCE: *The Stock Exchange Official Year-Book* (1964).

B. F. Goodrich Co., both of which sold a variety of similar consumer goods at retail.[5] The economic merits of the case were negligible.

Let me now begin the empirical study of the effects of antitrust laws. England has no such law. The number of joint directors of companies in the same industry is extraordinarily small, however (see Table 13.1). I am prepared to conclude that our prohibition of interlocking directorships has not had a noticeable effect upon corporate directorates. It therefore is unnecessary to examine the more basic question: would the existence of many interlocking directorates lead to a decrease of competition?[6]

II. THE EFFECTS UPON CONCENTRATION

We turn now to the first main purpose of the antitrust laws, the prevention of monopoly. This goal was sought by two routes: the prohibition of attempts to monopolize in Section 2 of the Sherman Act; and the prohibition of mergers that tend to reduce competition.

We require both a measure of concentration and—when we consider mergers—a measure of the effects of mergers on concentration. We adopt the Herfindahl index—the sum of the squares of the shares of industry output possessed by each firm. It is a comprehensible measure of firm sizes (with a maximum value of 1 for the index with monopoly and a minimum of $1/n$ with n firms of equal size). That the Herfindahl index is suited to the study of mergers deserves a fuller explanation.

Let us consider a simple way in which the impact of a merger upon the concentration of an industry can be measured.[7] Take, for example, the largest firm and calculate its growth, as a share of the industry, by the percentages of industry output acquired by merger at different dates. If we assume that the acquired firms would have maintained their shares of industry output in the absence of merger, we may directly calculate the contribution of internal growth and mergers to the growth of the leading firm. For example, the leading English cement producer, the Associated Portland Cement Companies, Ltd., acquired, between 1900 and 1960, approximately 125 percent of industry capacity, but had a market share of 70 percent in 1960. Internal growth would then be reckoned at −55 percent of industry output.

The sum of shares acquired by merger by all firms is unfortunately a meaningless number. There is a problem of duplication: let A have 40 percent, B, 20 percent and C, 10 percent of industry output. If B acquired C (10 percent) and then A acquires B (30 percent), the sum (40 percent) is greater than if A acquired B and C directly. This duplication can of course be avoided by counting each constituent firm only once. More important, the numbers have no scale. If there are 1,000 identical firms, and each of 100 acquires 9, the sum of merged shares is 90 percent, although concentration is negligible (4 percent for the largest 4 firms). Or if 2 firms with shares of 10 percent and 90 percent, respectively, each acquires a firm with 10 percent, the measure of the effect of merger would be the same.

The Herfindahl index, which can be derived from general arguments on the probability of successful collusion,[8] is a more appropriate measure of the sum of merger activity in the industry. If firms with shares p_1 and p_2 combine, the Herfindahl index rises by

$$(p_1-p_2)^2-p_1{}^2-p_2{}^2=2p_1p_2.$$

In the 1,000-firms industry above, the Herfindahl index would rise, after the 900 firms were acquired, to .01 from its previous level of .001. If a firm with 90 percent of output acquires a firm with 10 percent, the Herfindahl index rises .18 from .82 to 1, whereas a merger of 2 firms each with 10 percent raises the index by only .02.

The basic test of the effectiveness of our policies to prevent monopoly and high concentration must of course be: has it made concentration in American industry lower than it would otherwise be? An answer is sought along three lines: comparisons of the United States with other countries which have no antitrust law; comparisons of periods before and after passage of antitrust laws; and comparisons of industries exempt from and subject to the antitrust laws.

1. The Comparison with England

The English economy is one source of information about an economy in which there is no public policy against concentration of control. The English economy operates in an otherwise similar legal environment and in approxiimately the same state of technology. Its smaller size in general tends to lead to higher concentration than we observe in the United States because the optimum size of enterprise is roughly the same in the two countries.[9] Since our economy has grown from perhaps twice the size of the British economy in 1900 to four times the British size in 1965, we should expect *national* concentration in America to be lower and to be declining relative to British concentration. However, for cement and steel, where regional data are available, we compare a region in the United States with England to reduce the bias. More work is required in this area.[10]

Comparisons have been made of the history of concentration in seven industries in the United States and England since approximately 1900. Seven industries will scarcely support any general conclusion, and the comparison is presented primarily for methodological purposes. The reason the sample is so small is that it has proven to be rather difficult to piece out tolerably reliable estimates for all the British and some American industries. The output of each American automobile company has long been reported by weeks, for example, but even approximate outputs began to be reported on a regular basis in England less than twenty years ago.

The data for these industries (automobiles, cement, cigarettes, flat glass, soap and detergents, steel, tires) are given in the Appendix; they are summarized graphically in Figure 13.1.

1. The automobile industry has been more highly concentrated in the United States than in the United Kingdom for the entire period studied.

2. The cement industry has been much more highly concentrated in the United Kingdom than in the United States (Lehigh Valley). Concentration has not risen over time in the United States.

3. The cigarette industry is concentrated in the United States, but at a much lower level since the dissolution of American Tobacco. Since 1911 the concentration in Great Britain has been much higher than in the United States.

4. The American glass industry in the 1950s was less concentrated than the British industry (which is a monopoly). Concentration has risen in the United States since the 1920s, however, to a high level.

5. The soap industry is substantially more highly concentrated in the United Kingdom than in the United States, but concentration is fairly high in the United States.

6. The steel industry (ingots) was fairly highly concentrated in the United States after U.S. Steel was formed, but it has declined steadily and substantially. Nevertheless, it is above the level in the United Kingdom.

FIGURE 13.1

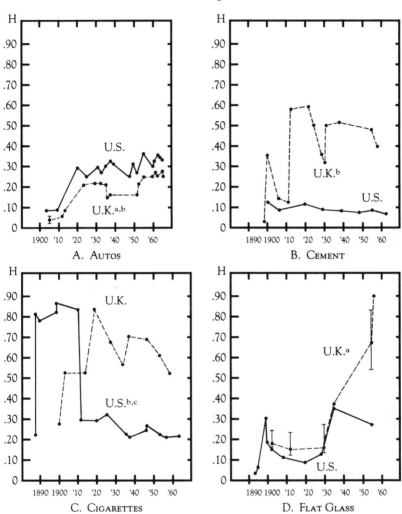

A. AUTOS

B. CEMENT

C. CIGARETTES

D. FLAT GLASS

FIGURE 13.1—Continued

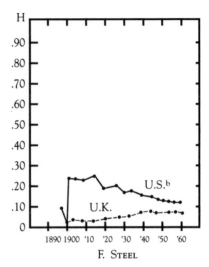

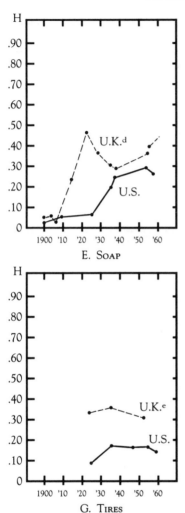

E. SOAP

F. STEEL

G. TIRES

SOURCE: Tables 13.4 to 13.18.

[a] Where a range of estimates is shown in the appendix tables, this is indicated by a vertical line the midpoint of which is connected to adjacent points; the "best estimate," rather than midpoint, is employed whenever given in the tables.

[b] The values for "premerger" Herfindahls given in the tables are plotted in the year previous to the merger year.

[c] Shares of domestic consumption, 1900 and prior years; shares of production, 1900 to 1947; shares of domestic consumption, 1947 on.

[d] Shares of household and industrial consumption, 1954 and prior years; shares of household consumption only, 1954 and 1961.

[e] Based on value of domestic consumption in Table 13.18.

TABLE 13.2

DISTRIBUTION OF LARGE MANUFACTURING AND MINING ACQUISITIONS
BY TYPE AND BY PERIOD OF ACQUISITION

Type of Merger	1948–1953		1954–1959		1960–1964	
	Number	Percentage	Number	Percentage	Number	Percentage
Horizontal	18	31.0	78	24.8	42	12.0
Vertical	6	10.3	43	13.7	59	17.0
Conglomerate:						
Market Extension	4	6.9	20	6.4	24	6.9
Product Extension	27	46.6	145	46.2	184	52.9
Other	3	5.2	28	8.9	39	11.2
Total	58	100.0	314	100.0	348	100.0

SOURCE: Bureau of Economics, Federal Trade Commission.

7. The rubber tire industry is highly concentrated in the United Kingdom but concentration is declining somewhat; concentration is substantially lower in the United States, and has had no trend since the 1930s.

These instances are compatible with the hypothesis (which I presently favor) that the Sherman Act was a modest deterrent to high concentration.[11] The underlying statistical tables (see Appendix) suggest that mergers to achieve very high concentration (H > .3) were more common in England than in the United States. These hypotheses can, of course, eventually be tested against a much larger body of data: the test is improvable.

2. The Decline of Horizontal Mergers

A second and more comprehensive set of data look to the impact of the 1950 antimerger amendment to the Clayton Act. These data concern the number of horizontal mergers engaged in by the 200 leading companies in manufacturing and mining. The basic data are presented in Table 13.2.

These merger data suggest that the 1950 antimerger statute has been a powerful discouragement to horizontal mergers. The fraction of horizontal mergers by large companies has fallen to low levels. Even this Federal Trade Commission count of horizontal mergers is heavily biased toward this type of merger: two companies were considered in the same industry and market if even a small fraction of their sales overlapped. There are also no important mergers recorded since 1950 in the seven American industries in Tables 13.4 to 13.17.

Unfortunately, the extent of horizontal mergers in earlier times has not been measured—it seems incredible but it is true that all forms of merger are combined in the standard merger series. (In our seven industries horizontal mergers were more frequent and important before than after 1950; see Table 13.20. The deficiency in the statistical history of mergers is of course remediable.

3. The Exempt Areas

The industries exempt from the antitrust laws are still another potential source of information, but a reluctant source. Most exempt industries are subjected to regulation of other sorts, and presumably have economic characteristics which distinguish them from nonexempt unregulated industries.

The insurance industry (or industries) are a fairly simple example of exempt industries. The exemption is not unqualified, but no merger cases have been brought against insurance companies, and the impact of the 1950 merger statute is presumably negligible.[12] Nevertheless, the level of concentration is low in the life and fire-and-casualty branches of the industry, and merger activity has been quite minor. The data for fire and casualty insurance companies is given in Table 13.21; they may be summarized:

Year	Herfindahl Index	Contributions of Mergers from Previous Date
1945	.0163	
1953	.0164	.0000
1963	.0189	.0024

Almost as low concentration is found in a typical industrial state.[13]

The ambiguity in such evidence is that we have no standard of comparable nonexempt industries. Still, the levels of concentration and of mergers in insurance have been so low that it is virtually impossible to conceive of a pattern (of sharply falling concentration) in the nonexempt industries, such that the insurance industry would corroborate our previous finding on the substantial effects of the 1950 merger act.

III. The Effects upon Collusion

The main thrust of the Sherman Act was against conspiracies in restraint of trade, and the judgment of its successes must rest largely on its achievements in this direction. No type of legislative endeavor, however, is harder to measure in its effects than a prohibition of actions which can be concealed.

Through 1963, there were some 957 completed antitrust cases reported in the Commerce Clearing House (CCH) Bluebooks in which some element of conspiracy was charged.[14] Of these cases, the Department of Justice won exactly 756, or slightly over three-quarters of the total. In addition, a large number of Federal Trade Commission cases involving collusion have been brought. We can equally well hail the numerous cases (and equally the victories) as evidence of the beneficial effect of the Sherman Act, or as evidence of its failure. What we want, of course, is a census of collusion, detected and undetected, and a census with and without an antitrust law.

Our difficulty rests on one fundamental fact: we do not have a generally acceptable theory of oligopoly. If we had such a theory, it would tell us what the determinants of successful collusion are, and we could then investigate the effects of the Sherman Act upon these determinants. When the event we wish to study is clandestine, we cannot rely upon direct observation.

I believe that my theory of oligopoly is a useful tool for this study, precisely because it seeks to isolate the determinants and forms of successful collusion— or rather, the determinants of successful cheating and hence unsuccessful collusion. The argument turns on the problem of getting reliable information on the observance of collusive agreements: invoices and sellers and buyers, and even physical shipments, may lie. And where an agreement cannot be en- forced, it will not be obeyed.

On this view, certain methods of collusion are highly efficient. The most efficient is the joint sales agency, for then price cutting is impossible and any large, hidden movement of goods is also virtually impossible. This plausible position is supported by the European cartel experience:

> This method (by which the cartel has access to the records of each member), no matter how rigorously it is administered, nevertheless does not give a complete guarantee against evasions of the cartel policy. Rather, it is a popular, recurring complaint that one cannot detect clever violations, es- pecially concealed price reductions. This leads the cartels in ever rising numbers to the establishment of a *common selling agency* as the only wholly reliable protection against evasion. It is not an individual incident, but rather wholly typical, that one of the oldest and best organized Austrian cartels, the

plate glass syndicate, explained when a common selling bureau was established that without this device even the severest controls would not prevent price cutting or the exceeding of quotas.[15]

It is relevant to observe that marine insurance was exempted from the antitrust laws by the Merchant Marine Act of 1920. A syndicate of domestic and some foreign companies was formed, and their business was assigned to the syndicate, in which each of the member insurance companies had a quota of participation. No member may deal directly in this market except by permission of, and at rates set by, the syndicate—a strict joint sales agency system.[16]

Somewhat less efficient collusion is achieved by the assignment of customers, whether individually or by geographic area or otherwise. There is still a possible inducement to secret price cutting: in the long run, the favored customers may grow relative to their rivals who purchase from another seller who abides by the cartel price. Actual shipments to nonassigned customers are usually detectable, as in the case of joint sales agencies.

Both the joint sales agency and the assignment of customers are obvious to the buyers and therefore they are likely to be called to the attention of the antitrust division and, once suspected, their existence is easily proven. No such ease of detection exists with the lesser forms of collusion, such as price agreements, but these lesser forms also are much less easily enforced.[17]

The types of collusion I call efficient (joint sales agencies and assignment of customers) are more likely found to be in violation of the antitrust laws than the other types of collusion. This is almost necessarily true, since the efficient types of collusion are per se offenses, whereas the inefficient types of collusion include a fair number of innocuous trade association activities and other uncertain extensions of the law. The hypothesis is, in fact, readily tested: in an analysis of a small sample of the two types of cases, we obtain the results in Table 13.3. The sample is small so that the test is weak (the results could arise by chance with probability .2) but the sample could readily be enlarged.

This line of argument may be, and I hope is, plausible, but it is not yet persuasive. Two things are needed. The first is a substantial testing of the oligopoly theory that underlies this argument. A systematic empirical test has so far eluded me. The second omission is a showing that the "nonefficient" forms of collusion are substantially less efficient than the "efficient" forms. This latter defect can be partially remedied, I believe, by the following procedure.

A series of cartel cases have been brought for a variety of reasons, including the contagious property of a prominent case in a large industry of eliciting parallel complaints. I hypothesize that the interval between inception of a scheme and its detection will be shorter for the more efficient techniques. If so, the act has reduced the comparative gain, and hence the comparative frequency, of these forms of collusion. A small number of cases has been analyzed, and the pattern is in keeping with the hypothesis.[18]

TABLE 13.3

ANALYSIS OF COLLUSION CASES BY TYPE AND OUTCOME[a]

Type	Government Wins	Defendant Wins	Total
Efficient	9	4	13
Inefficient	9	8	17
Total	18	12	

SOURCE: The Federal Anti-Trust Laws, with summary of cases instituted by the United States (1951); supplementary information necessary for assigning cartels to "efficient" and "inefficient" classes was obtained from U.S. Courts, Federal Anti-Trust Decisions (vols. 1–12).

[a] Cases identified by Commerce Clearing House (CCH) number are as follows (only one of a group of closely related cases is included): "Efficient" cases, nos. 14, 18, 24, 34, 83, 239, 240, 254, 277, 282, 348, 349, and 355; "Inefficient" cases, nos. 21, 66, 76, 215, 218, 227, 241, 243, 244, 246, 248, 265, 273, 274, 284, 331, and 343.

Types of Collusion	Number	Period from Inception of Alleged Collusion to Complaint
Efficient	7	21.6 (±3.9) months
Inefficient	10	56.7 (±2.4) months

The accumulation of more such cases (many are available) and more fundamentally the rigorous testing of the underlying oligopoly theory would greatly strengthen this argument.

IV. CONCLUSION

The substantive findings of this study are meager and undogmatic:

1. The Sherman Act appears to have had only a very modest effect in reducing concentration.
2. The 1950 Merger Act has had a strongly adverse effect upon horizontal mergers by larger companies.
3. The Sherman Act has reduced the availability of the most efficient methods of collusion and thereby reduced the amount and effects of collusion.

Discussions of methodology are usually offered as a substitute when an author has lacked the imagination to devise strong tests and the diligence to compile a large body of evidence, and I apologetically follow this tradition. I do not claim that any reasonable man must accept the above conclusions, for even the strongest (on the effects of the antimerger statute) is not overpowering in the volume or pointedness of the evidence. I do claim that each of the findings is improvable, and the extension of this work will shrink the range of defensible conclusions.

APPENDIX

The concentration data in the following tables are based upon a variety of industry histories, trade journals, the financial press, and so on. The references which are given after Table 13.21 are only to the main sources. Especially in the earlier years a considerable amount of indirect estimation is necessary, so the figures are only approximate. The estimates of the shares of medium-size and small companies are especially rough; however, variations in the estimated shares of these companies have an almost negligible effect on an industry's Herfindahl index. The share of the largest company in the terminal year is included in the tables beginning with the earliest Herfindahl year in which its share exceeded 25 percent.

Mergers are defined here to include the acquisition of 50 percent or more of the common stock of one company by another and the creation of formal joint sales arrangements. Unless otherwise indicated, the Herfindahl index shown for a given year is based on company shares after all mergers taking place in that year.

With the exception of cement and steel, for which capacity shares were employed, wherever possible the Herfindahl indexes are based on company shares of domestic consumption (as approximated by production plus imports, less exports). Where it was necessary to employ some other basis (for example, production shares) the magnitude of exports or imports is indicated in the footnotes if either was considerable.

NOTES

1. 37 Stat. 567 (1912), 15 U.S.C. § 31 (1964).
2. 30 Ops. Attorney General 355 (1915).
3. 38 Stat. 732 (1914), 15 U.S.C. § 19 (1964).

4. Staff of Subcomm. no. 5, House Comm. on the Judiciary, 89th Cong., 1st Sess., Interlocks in Corporate Management 57 (Comm. Print 1965).

5. United States v. Sears, Roebuck & Co., 111 F. Supp. 614 (D.C.N.Y. 1953).

6. Interlocking directorates are a clumsy technique, even when one desires to coordinate the activities of two firms, so I would not expect their presence or absence to have a significant relationship to the extent of competition among firms.

7. See Stigler, "The Statistics of Monopoly and Merger," *Journal of Political Economy* 64, no. 33.

8. See my article, "A Theory of Oligopoly," *Journal of Political Economy* 72, no. 44 (1964).

9. So, at least, argues Florence, *The Logic of British and American Industry* 22–29 (1953), as to relative optimum sizes in the two countries.

10. The 1954 ratios of U.S. to U.K. industry size are: automobiles, 8.8 (1955); cement, 1.0; cigarettes, 3.6; glass, 7.0; soap, 8.9; steel, 5.1; tires, 6.0.

11. The industries favorable to the hypothesis that the Sherman Act has served to keep down concentration are cement and cigarettes, with glass, soap and tires pointing more weakly the same way. The automobile and steel industries support the opposite interpretation. Since 1911, merger has not been a major source of high concentration in the United States.

12. The industry is exempt to the extent (1) that states regulate the industry, and (2) certain forbidden acts, such as concerted boycotts, are not engaged in. The Antitrust Division believes mergers of insurance companies are exempt if the states have so-called Little Clayton Acts; see Hearings Pursuant to S. Res. 57 Before the Subcommittee on Antitrust and Monopoly of the Senate Committee on the Judiciary, The Insurance Industry, 86th Cong., 1st Sess., pt. 2, at 931 (1960).

13. Thus the Herfindahl ratio in Illinois in 1963 was .0232 for fire and casualty insurance.

14. The tabulation of cases has been made by Michael Marks in an unpubished study.

15. Kestner, Der Organizationszwang 153 (1912).

16. Hearings Pursuant to S. Res. 57, *supra* note 12, at pts. 2 and 9. The cartel agreement is reprinted in pt. 9 at 5555 to 5633.

17. With one important exception. The government as buyer usually uses bidding techniques which make secret price cuts impossible. Hence, collusive systems usually work best against government buyers.

18. The cases analyzed have Commerce Clearing House (CCH) case numbers: 18, 24, 34, 83, 277, 348, and 349 in the efficient class; 66, 76, 215, 218, 244, 265, 273, 274, 284, and 343 in the inefficient class.

TABLE 13.4
U.S. Auto Industry: Contributions of Mergers and Concentration Measures for Selected Dates[a]

Selected Dates	H	GM Share 1931–1964	Contributions of Mergers to ΔH	Remarks
1904	.076			
1908			.0179	GM formed
1909-10	.090		.0022	U.S. Motors formed
1912			.0001	Chevrolet-Little
1916			.0090	GM-Chevrolet
1917			.0001	Maxwell-Chalmers
1918			.0020	GM–Scripps Booth
1920	.279			
1922			.0018	Ford-Lincoln
1925	.243			
1928			.0059	Dodge-Chrysler
			.0002	Hupp-Chandler
1929	b			
1931	.284	.433		
1932	.261	.412		
1935	.292	.384		
1937	.283	.406		
1938	.307	.448		
1939	.297	.437		
1948	.253	.406		
1950	.298	.454		
1952	.275[a]	.418		
1953			.0004	Kaiser-Willys
1954			.0006	Hudson-Nash
			.0008	Studebaker-Packard
1955	.363	.508		
1960	.286	.436		
1961	.315	.466		
1962	.352[b]	.519		
1963	.342	.510		
1964	.331	.491		

[a] Based on production shares prior to 1925; based on shares of new car registrations, including imports, 1925 and after.

[b] Herfindahl indexes based on production shares, and hence comparable with U.K. figures, are as follows: 1929=.218 (exports=10 percent of production, imports negligible); 1952=.278 (exports and imports=4 percent and 1 percent, respectively, of production); 1962=.383 (exports and imports=3 percent and 5 percent, respectively, of production).

TABLE 13.5

U.K. Auto Industry: Contributions of Mergers and Concentration
Measures for Selected Dates, Based on Shares of Production[a]

Selected Dates	H	Morris-BMC Share 1924–1964	Contributions of Mergers to ΔH	Remarks
1905	.02-.05			
1910			.0012 max	BSA-Daimler
1912	.065			
1913	.084			
1919			.0008 max.	Talbot & Darracq form STD
1921			.0018	Sunbeam-STD
1924	.202	.305		
1926–27			.0133	Morris-Wolseley
1928			.0006	Humber-Hillman
1929	.212	.350		
1931			.0002 max.	Rolls-Royce–Bentley
1932	.208	.334		
1935	.198	.315	.0026 max.	Rootes-STD
1937	.147	.233	.0016	Morris-Riley
1938	.160	.235		
1945			.0030	Standard-Triumph
1947			.0002 max.	Aston Martin–Lagonda
1952	.158 premerger	.197		
	.235 postmerger	.394	.0776 max.	Austin & Morris form BMC
1955	.253	.390	.0007	Rootes-Singer
1960	.253[b]	.365		
1961	.275	.385		
1962	.261	.377		
1963	.273	.385		
1964	.253	.368		
1966			.0168[c]	BMC-Jaguar

[a] Exports as percent of production were as follows: 1913, 6 percent; 1924, 10 percent; 1929, 13 percent; 1932, 16 percent; 1935 and 1937, 14 percent; 1938, 13 percent; 1952, 61 percent; 1955, 38 percent; 1960, 40 percent; 1961, 36 percent; 1962, 43 percent; 1963, 38 percent; 1964, 36 percent. Retained imports as percent of production were 16 percent in 1913, 9 percent in 1924 and 12 percent in 1929; in every later year for which a Herfindahl index is given above, retained imports were less than 5 percent.

[b] In 1960 shares of domestic sales for the top two and top five companies were 70 percent and 90 percent, respectively; production shares employed above for the top two and top five were 67 percent and 96 percent, respectively.

[c] Based on shares of domestic market. Source: Wall Street Journal, July 12, 1966, p. 1.

Max.=Maximum estimate, i.e., companies taken as equal in size when no other information is available.

TABLE 13.6

U.S. CEMENT INDUSTRY (LEHIGH VALLEY[a]): CONTRIBUTIONS OF MERGERS AND
CONCENTRATION MEASURES FOR SELECTED DATES, BASED ON PLANT CAPACITY

Selected Dates	H	Contributions of Mergers to ΔH	Remarks
1900[b]	.132		
1902		.0203	Lehigh-Saylor
1904		.0083	Atlas-Keystone
1905		.0025	Alpha-National
1907	.092		
1912		.0019	Alpha-Catskill
1920	.118		
1924		.0058	Lehigh-Tidewater
1925		.0004	North American (Security)–Helderberg
		.0008	Dexter–Penn-Allen
1926		.0057	Lehigh-Bath
		.0040	Penn. Dixie–Penn. Cem.
		.0007	North American (Security)–Acme
1928[c]		.0022	International-Phoenix
1929	.086		
1939	.079		
1948	.072		
1954		.0025	Martin-Lawrence
1955	.080	.0024	Allentown–Valley Forge
1963	.072		

[a] Eastern Pennsylvania, New York east of Buffalo, New Jersey, Maryland and extreme eastern West Virginia.

[b] In most cases, capacities interpolated between dates of first shipments and 1907.

[c] FTC dates control beginning 1925 for International-Phoenix.

TABLE 13.7

U.K. CEMENT INDUSTRY: CONTRIBUTIONS OF MERGERS AND CONCENTRATION
MEASURES FOR SELECTED DATES, BASED ON PLANT CAPACITY

Selected Dates	H	APCM Share 1900–1959	Contributions of Mergers to ΔH	Remarks
1900	.028 premerger	.088 (White)		Before APCM formed
	.359 postmerger	.594	.3317	After APCM formed
1907	.142	.361		
1912	.119 premerger	.322		Before BPCM formed
	.565 postmerger	.750	.4446	BPCM formed and acquired by APCM
1922	.576	.753	.0475	APCM-Kent
1924	.501	.700	.0466	APCM-Humber
1928	.368	.580	.0199	Red Δ formed
			.0004	East-Lewes
1931	.331 premerger	.549		Before Red Δ acquisition
	.498 postmerger	.701	.1673	After Red Δ acquisition (and Tunnell-Clyde merger, contribution= .0004)
1933–34[a]			.0147	Formation of Alpha
1936[a]			.0002	Rugby-Bachelor
1938	.512	.700	.1650	APCM-Alpha
1955	.480	.667	.0022	Rugby-Nelson
1959	.395	.598		

[a] Employs 1938 shares.

TABLE 13.8

U.S. CIGARETTE INDUSTRY: CONTRIBUTIONS OF MERGERS AND
CONCENTRATION MEASURES FOR SELECTED DATES, BASED ON NUMBER OF
CIGARETTES CONSUMED DOMESTICALLY[a]

Selected Dates	H	Reynolds Tob. Co. Share 1921–1963[b]	Contributions of Mergers to ΔH	Remarks
1890	.207 premerger .234[a] premerger .812 postmerger .925[a] postmerger		.6050 } .6911[a] }	Allen & Ginter, W. S. Kimball, Goodwin, Kinney, W. Duke form Amer. Tob. Co. and acquire S. F. Hess
1891	.779			
1892			.0906	S. Hernsheim–Amer.
1894			.0391	H. Ellis–Amer.
1898			.0912	Drummond-Amer.
1899			.1482	Amer. acquisition of Monopol, National, W. R. Irby, and Liggett & Myers
1900	.809 .860[a]		.0082 .0121	S. Anargyros–Amer. J. Bollman–Amer.
1901			.0230 .0109	Brown-Amer. C. V. Winfree–Amer.
1903			.0338 .0104	Wells, Whitehead–Am. Craft-American
1911[a]	.831		−.5292	Breakup of Am. Tob.
1912[a]	.302		.0003	Formation of Tob. Products Corp.
1916[a]			.0004	Schinasi–Tob. Products Corp.
1917[a]			.0004	Prudential–Tob. Products Corp.
1918[a]			.0004	Falk–Tob. Products
1921[a]	.286	.354		
1923[a]			.0186	Tob. Products Corp.– American
1925[a]	.318	.416		
1935[a]	.212	.282		
1937[a]	.197	.281		
1944[a]			.0021	Axton-Fisher–Phillip Morris
1947	.242[a] .256	.283 .301		
1954	.216[a] .221	.247 .251	.0011	Benson & Hedges–Phillip Morris
1958	.198[a] .202	.281 .287		
1963	.221	.344		

[a] For 1911 through 1944 figures are based on shares of total output. In other years, alternative figures given based on total output wherever indicated by "a"; Exports as percent of total output for selected years are as follows: 1890, 11 percent; 1900, 31 percent; 1912, 14 percent; 1921, 14 percent; 1935, 3 percent; 1947, 9 percent.

[b] The American Tobacco Co. share slightly exceeded that of the Reynolds Tobacco Co. in 1947 and 1954 and varied between 80 and 96 percent of production from 1890 (postmerger) to 1911 (predissolution).

TABLE 13.9

U.K. CIGARETTE INDUSTRY: CONTRIBUTIONS OF MERGERS AND
CONCENTRATION MEASURES FOR SELECTED DATES, BASED ON SHARES OF
DOMESTIC CONSUMPTION[a]

Selected Dates	H	Imperial Share 1900–1959	Contributions of Mergers to ΔH	Remarks
1900[b]	.281	.516 (Wills)		Before formation of Imperial Tobacco Co.
1901–02[b]			.2259	Formation of Imperial and acquisition of Ogden
1903[b, c]	.507	.710		After formation of Imperial
1915[c]	.507	.710		
1920	.830	.910		
1926			.0235	Imperial-Ardath
1928	.670	.814		
1932[d]			.0494	Imperial-Gallaher
1933[d]	.565	.738		
1934[d]			.0398	Jackson group to Imperial via Gallaher
1937[d]			.0034	Robinson to Imperial via Gallaher
1938[d]	.712	.841	.0336	Imperial-Walters
1946[d]			−.0857	Imperial interest in Gallaher reduced to less than 50 percent
1947	.690	.824		
1952			.0001 max.	Carreras-Dunhill
1952–53			.0136 max.	Imperial–John Wood, Charlesworth & Austin, Express Tobacco (via Ardath)
1954	.612	.772		
1955			.0003 max.	Gallaher–Benson & Hedges
1958			.0002	Carreras-Rothmans
1959	.496	.652		
1960			.0044	Imperial-Phillips (via Ardath)
1961			.0168	Gallaher-Wix

[a] 1947 and prior year shares are based primarily on consumption in lbs.; later year shares are based on consumption in value terms; in 1954 cigarettes were 84.0 percent of all U.K. manufactured tobacco production by weight and 86.7 percent of production in value terms.

[b] Based on estimated shares in 1903, hence entire difference between H for 1900 and H for 1903 is necessarily due to 1901–2 merger contribution.

[c] Identical 1903 and 1915 estimates for H reflect unchanged Imperial share as estimates for smaller companies are only approximate.

[d] From 1932 to 1946 Imperial owned 51 percent of the equity of Gallaher, whereas after 1946 Imperial owned less than 50 percent (42.5 percent in 1956), hence Imperial is considered above as having acquired Gallaher in 1932 and divested itself of Gallaher in 1946; if Imperial and Gallaher are considered independent throughout, H for 1933=.516, H for 1938=.641 and the *only* entries in the merger contribution column from 1932 through 1946 would read as follows: .0019 Jackson-Gallaher; .0002 Robinson-Gallaher; and .0318 Imperial-Walters.

Max.=employs maximum estimates of acquired company shares where no exact information available.

TABLE 13.10

U.S. FLAT GLASS INDUSTRY[a]: CONTRIBUTIONS OF MERGERS AND
CONCENTRATION MEASURES FOR SELECTED DATES, BASED ON SHARES OF
VALUE OF PRODUCTION[b]

Selected Dates	H	L-O-F Share[c] 1935-1954	PPG Share[c] 1900-1954	Contributions of Mergers to ΔH	Remarks
1895	.035 premerger .066 postmerger			.0306	After PPG joined with 4 other plate companies but before formation of American Glass Co.
1895-1899				.2376	American Glass Co. formed
1899	.304				
1900	.192		.242	−.0545	Breakup of Amer. Glass into Amer. Window Glass Co. and independent companies
1901				.0182[d]	Independent Glass Co. formed
1902	.158[e]		.225	.0056[d]	Federation (Coop) formed
1904				d	Breakup of Indep. & Federation (Coop)
				.0006	Mississippi Glass Co.-Appert Glass and Rolland Glass
1909	.106		.234		
1910				f	
1912				.0119	Formation of Johnston Brokerage Agency
1913				.0059	Formation of U.S. Window & sales contract with PPG
1919	.094		.229		
1920				.0027	Formation of National Plate
1925				.0003	Libbey-Owens–Fairfield
1928				.0027	Libbey-Owens–Adamston
1929	.136		.298		
1930				.0104	L-O and Edw. Ford form L-O-F
				.0109	PPG-Standard

TABLE 13.10—Continued

Selected Dates	H	L-O-F Share[c] 1935–1954	PPG Share[c] 1900–1954	Contributions of Mergers to ΔH	Remarks
1931				.0138	L-O-F acquires Ottowa, Ill. plants of Nat'l Plate
1932				.0017	Mississippi–Highland–Western
1933				−.0049	L-O-F divestiture of Adamston
1935[e]	.346	.424	.399	.0024	Formation of Fourco
				.0131[g]	L-O-F acquisition of Vitrolite and sales contract with Blue Ridge
1936				.0005	Amer.–Baker Bros.
1948				−.0006	Blackford split-off from Fourco
1954	.280	.380	.340		

[a] Sheet, plate, and rolled glass; excludes laminated glass and products of purchased glass.

[b] Prior to 1935 a complex and indirect procedure was necessary. Company capacities were used to estimate company shares of plate, sheet, and rolled glass, which in turn were estimated separately by production processes (hand v. machine, Colburn v. Fourcault machine, and so on) from production data.

The Herfindahl index for 1902 calculated directly from production is estimated to be between .164 and .176

In 1935, when there was considerable idle capacity in sheet and plate, the Herfindahl index on the basis employed in earlier years is estimated to be approximately .260.

Imports as percent of production were as follows: 1895, approx.=17 percent; 1899=8.4 percent; 1909=5.0 percent; 1919, negligible; 1929=5.0 percent; 1935, negligible; 1954=5.5 percent. Exports were 5.0 percent in 1919 and less than 5 percent in other Herfindahl years.

[c] As shares of L-O-F and PPG are almost identical in 1935 and 1954, both companies' shares are shown here for those years. Shares of the American (Window) Glass Co. in the period when it was the dominant firm are as follows: 1899=.499; 1900=.359 (after split-off of independent companies); 1902=.256.

[d] Contributions of 1901 and 1902 mergers are excluded from Table 13.20 calculations as inadequate information is available to estimate effect of dissolution of both companies in 1904.

[e] See note [b] above.

[f] Formation of Imperial Window Glass Co. in April 1909 omitted as company was dissolved in Nov. 1910 and hence operated only in the 1909–10 blast.

[g] Exact date of L-O-F sales contract with Blue Ridge is not available; 1935 is earliest year when contract known to be in operation.

TABLE 13.11

U.K. FLAT GLASS: CONTRIBUTIONS OF MERGERS AND CONCENTRATION
MEASURES FOR SELECTED DATES, BASED ON SHARES OF
DOMESTIC CONSUMPTION

Selected Dates		H	Pilkington Share 1904 to 1955	Contributions of Mergers to ΔH	Remarks
1901				.0051	Pilkington-Ravenhead
1904	best est.	.190	.288		
	range[a, c]	.170–.232	.216–.360		Includes cartel of continental companies exporting plate to U.K. as one company[d]
1913	best est.	.154	.364		
	range[a, c]	.121–.221	.273–.455		Cartel above ended[d]
1930	best est.	.168	.373		
	range[a]	.135–.256	.255–.492		Includes Belgian sheet & plate cartels and German sheet & plate cartels and Czech sheet cartel each as one company[d]
1935		.370[b]	.584		ditto[d]
1954	range:[a, b]				
	max. est.	.725–.834	.844–.912		[d]
	range:[a, c]				
	min. est.	.533–.748	.699–.859		[d]
1955[e]		.904	.950	.1793–.0699[a, b] .3512–.1557[a, c]	Pilkington-Chance

[a] Employs extreme estimates of company shares of rolled glass, for which no information is available.

[b] Evaluates output at export prices.

[c] Evaluates output at import prices, including tariff.

[d] Imports as percent of consumption were as follows: 1904, 75 percent; 1913, 68 percent, 1930, 33 percent; 1935, 30 percent; 1954, negligible.

[e] Pilkington began purchase of Chance stock in 1936; complete ownership was achieved in 1955. Exact year when majority interest achieved is not available; Pilkington directors appear on the Chance Board of Directors for the first time in 1951.

TABLE 13.12

U.S. SOAP INDUSTRY:[a] CONTRIBUTIONS OF MERGERS AND CONCENTRATION
MEASURES FOR SELECTED DATES, BASED ON SHARES OF VALUE OF OUTPUT

Selected Dates	H	P & G Share 1935–1958	Contribution of Mergers to ΔH	Remarks
1900	.030			
1903			.0046	P & G–Schultz & Co.
1909	.068			
1910			.0049	P & G–D.S. Brown
1919			.0002	Palmolive-Crystal
			.0002	B.T. Babbitt–Mendelson
1925	.088			
1926			.0051	Palmolive-Peet
1927			.0124	P & G– Wm. Waltke
			.0019	P & G–Rub-No-More
1928			.0290	Colgate–Palmolive Peet
			.0033	P & G–Globe
1929			.0043	P & G–Duz Co.
1930			.0082	Colgate-Palm-Peet–Kirkman
			.0106	P & G–James S. Kirk
1933			.0007	P & G– Hewitt Brothers
1935	.198	.357		
1936			.0024	P & G–Cincinnati Soap Co.
1937	.259[b]	.432		
1939			.0112	Lever–Gold Dust
1951	[b]			
1954	.288	.500		
1955			.0002	Purex–Old Dutch
1956			.0004	Purex-Manhattan
1957			.0088	Lever–Monsanto's "All" division
1958	.253	.452	.0002	Purex-Wrisley
1964			.0008	Purex-Fels

[a] 1957 SIC definition, but excludes alkaline detergents and glycerine. 1937 and before includes shaving preparations. 1909 and before includes glycerine and 1900 includes candles, to the extent produced in soap establishments of large companies.

[b] 1951 H based on shares of household soap and detergent output (i.e., excluding industrial)= .314; comparable figure for 1937=.245.

TABLE 13.13

U.K. SOAP INDUSTRY: CONTRIBUTIONS OF MERGERS AND CONCENTRATION
MEASURES FOR SELECTED DATES, BASED ON SHARES OF
DOMESTIC CONSUMPTION IN TONS[a]

Selected Dates	H	Lever Share 1915–1961	Contribution of Mergers to ΔH	Remarks
1899			.0024	Lever–Benj. Brooks
1900	.057			
1905	.063			
1906			.0040	Lever-Vinolia
			.0040	Lever–Hodgson & Simpson
1907	.045			
1908			.0142	Lever-Hudson
1910–12[b]			.0459	Lever–Thomas, Cook & Others
1911			.0027	Crosfield & Gossage form Crossage
1913[c]			.0896	Lever-Crossage
1915[c]	.228	.460		
1917			.0603	Lever-Watson
1919[c]			.0128	Lever-Price (Gibbs)
1920			.0384	Lever-Knight
1921	.462	.670		
1925			.0922	Lever-BOCM
1929	.376	.600		
1935	.308	.535		
1938	.300	.515		
1954[d]	.350	.523		
	.391[e]	.543		
1961[d]	.432[e]	.594	.0044	Lever-Pinoya

[a] See Table 13.14 for 1900 through 1921 on production shares basis, in tons, for selected years.

[b] Excludes Knight and Watson as Lever had obtained less than 50 percent interest in 1910–1912.

[c] De facto merger of Lever and Crossage dated 1913, year in which Lever acquired 50 percent interest; 1915 H=.170 and merger contribution=.1378 if merger dated 1919, year Lever acquired full control.

[d] Estimated H based on the value shares in 1954 and 1961=.384 and .430 resp. (synthetic detergents weighted 1.5, following Edwards and Puplett "soap equivalent" concept).

[e] In terms of shares of household consumption only, that is, excludes industrial.

TABLE 13.14

U.K. SOAP INDUSTRY: CONTRIBUTIONS OF MERGERS AND CONCENTRATION
MEASURES FOR SELECTED DATES, BASED ON SHARES OF
PRODUCTION IN TONS 1900–1921

Selected Dates	H	Lever Share 1915 and 1921	Contribution of Mergers to ΔH[a]	Remarks
1900	.059			
1905	.078			
1907	.056			
1911			.0130	Crosfield & Gossage form Crossage
1913[b]			.1729[b]	Lever-Crossage
1915 max. est.	.364	.593		
min. est.	.313	.548		
1921	.535	.725		

[a] Computed on production shares basis only for mergers involving Crosfield & Gossage (Crossage), i.e., companies other than Lever with large export trade. See Table 13.13 for other merger contributions.

[b] Merger contribution=.2112 if merger dated 1919. See Table 13.13, footnote c.

TABLE 13.15

U.S. STEEL INDUSTRY: CLEVELAND-DETROIT, CHICAGO, PITTSBURGH-
YOUNGSTOWN & EASTERN DISTRICTS[a]—CONTRIBUTIONS OF MERGERS AND
CONCENTRATION MEASURES FOR SELECTED DATES, BASED ON INGOT CAPACITY[b]

Selected Dates[c]	H	U.S. Steel Share 1901–1960	Contributions of Mergers to ΔH[d]	Remarks
1899	.084[e]		.0001	Formation of Republic
1900			.0003	Formation of Crucible
1901	.021 premerger	.206 (Carnegie)		
	.233 postmerger	.472	.2117	Formation of U.S. Steel[f]
1902			.0248	U.S. Steel–Union Steel
1903			.0010	U.S. Steel–Troy Steel
1904	.232	.471	.0130	U.S. Steel–Clairton Steel
1908	.225	.463		
1911			.0003	Crucible-Midland
1916	.240	.475	.0017	Bethlehem-Pennsylvania
1917			.0002	Bethlehem-American
1919			.0002	Wheeling Steel & Iron– LaBelle Iron Works Whitaker Glessner
1920	.178	.405		
1922			.0043	Bethlehem-Lackawanna
1923			.0077	Bethlehem–Midvale Steel & Ordnance (Coatesville & Johnston plants)
			.0018	Youngstown Sheet & Tube– Brier Hill Steel–Steel & Tube Co. of Amer.
1926	.206	.419		
1927			.0002	American Rolling Mill– Forged Steel Wheel
1928			.0004	Republic Iron & Trumbell Steel
1929			.0002	Amer. Rolling–Ashland
			.0004	Formation of Nat'l Steel: Weirton Steel, Great Lakes
1930	.177	.377	.0038	Formation of Republic Steel: Republic Steel & Iron, Central Alloy Steel, Don- ner Steel & Bourne Fuller
			.0003	Amer. Rolling Mill–Sheffield Steel
1934			.0002	Amer. Rolling Mill–Scullin Steel
1935	.183	.382	.0023	Republic-Corrigan- McKinney

TABLE 13.15—Continued

Selected Dates[c]	H	U.S. Steel Share 1901–1960	Contributions of Mergers to ΔH[d]	Remarks
1936			.0001	Amer. Rolling Mill–Rustless Iron & Steel
1938	.163	.350		
1942			.0014	Jones & Laughlin–Otis
1944			.0003	Jones & Laughlin–Electric Weld Tube Division
1945	.156	.336		
1946			−.0124	U.S. Steel divestiture of Farrel & Mingo works to Sharon Steel & Wheeling Steel resp.
			.0005	Republic–Defense Plant Corp. So. Chicago plant
1948	.143	.312		
1951	.138	.304		
1954	.130	.291		
1957	.125	.276	.0003	Jones & Laughlin–Rotary Electric
1960	.122	.266		

[a] The American Iron and Steel Institute in its *Directory of Iron and Steel Works of the United States and Canada* (1954, 1957) divides the United States into six districts according to the principal regional markets which are served by states producing steel. We have excluded steel facilities in the southern and western districts comprising the following states: Alabama, Alaska, Colorado, California, Georgia, Nebraska, North Carolina, Oklahoma, Oregon, South Carolina, Tennessee, Utah, Virginia, and the Canal Zone. The source for capacities by state between 1911–1960 is the American Iron and Steel Institute's Annual Statistical Report (1911–1960). The American Iron and Steel Institute's *Directory of Steel Works and Rolling Mills in the United States and Canada* for 1901, 1904 and 1908 provided state totals for these years. Capacity by state was interpolated for the intervening years where necessary.

Company notes regarding exclusion of southern and western facilities:

1. U.S. Steel: Excluded are steel ingot capacities of the Tennessee Coal, Iron & Railway Co. from 1907 on; Columbia Steel Co., 1930 on; and the Geneva Steel Co., 1946 on.
2. Bethlehem: Excluded are ingot capacities of the Pacific Coast Steel Corp. and the Southern California Iron and Steel Manufacturing Co. from 1930 on.
3. Republic: Excluded are plant at Birmingham, Ala., in 1901 and 1904, and the Gulf States Steel Co. from 1937 on.
4. Armco: Since 1945, firm total excludes plants of Sheffield Steel Corp. in Sand Springs, Okla., and Houston, Texas.

[b] That is, based on shares of productive capacity in tons.

[c] Herfindahls were computed for all years between 1900 and 1960 in which the AISI published directories.

[d] Mergers are recorded for the following largest firms in the industry: U.S. Steel, Bethlehem, Republic, Youngstown Sheet and Tube, Jones and Laughlin, National, Inland, Wheeling, Crucible, Pittsburgh, Armco and Sharon.

[e] The Herfindahl for 1899 is based on capacities included in the 1901 directory but reflects the size of firms prior to the formation of the U.S. Steel Corporation (1901), the Crucible Steel Co. (1900), and Republic Iron and Steel Co. (1899), and after the incorporation of the Federal Steel Co. (1898), the National Steel Co. (1899), and the American Steel & Wire Co. of N. J. (1899).

[f] Incorporating the following steel-producing companies: Carnegie, Federal Steel, National Steel, American Steel and Wire Co., National Tube, American Steel Hoop Co., American Sheet and Steel Co., American Bridge Co.

TABLE 13.16

U.K. STEEL INDUSTRY: CONTRIBUTIONS OF MERGERS AND CONCENTRATION
MEASURES FOR SELECTED DATES, BASED ON INGOT CAPACITY[a]

Selected Dates	H	Contributions of Mergers to ΔH	Remarks
1900	.036		
1902		.0022	Guest Keen–Nettlefords
			Alfred Baldwin–Wright Butler
			John Brown–Thomas Firth
1903	.040	.0030	Dorman Long–Northeastern Steel Formation of
			Stewarts & Lloyds
1905		.0060	Beardmore–Mossend Steel Works
			South Durham–Cargo Fleet
1908	.035		
1910		.0056	South Durham–Palmers Shipbuilding & Iron
1913	.032		
1915		.0026	David Colville–Clydebridge Steel & Glengarnock
			Iron & Steel
1916		.0007	Steel, Peech & Tozer–Samuel Fox
1917		.0021	Steel, Peech & Tozer–Frodingham
			Richard Thomas–Cwmfelin Iron & Steel
1918		.0034	Formation of United Steel Cos.
			Baldwins–Brymbo Steel
1920	.037	.0012	John Summers–Shelton Iron & Steel
			Guest, Keen & Nettlefords–John Lysaght
			Stewarts & Lloyds–Alfred Hickman
1925		.0017	Richard Thomas–Grovesend Steel & Tinplate
1928	.042		
1929		.0015	Formation of English Steel
1930		.0061	Formation of Lancashire Steel
			Formation of Colvilles
			Formation of British (Guest, Keen & Baldwins) Iron
			& Steel
			Dorman Long–Bolchow Vaughan
1932	.051		
1936		.0070	Colvilles–Lanarkshire Steel & Steel Co. of Scotland
1938	.067		
1944	.068	.0030	Formations of Richard Thomas & Baldwins
1947[b]	.070	−.0033	Formation of Steel Co. of Wales through Guest,
			Keen & Baldwins divestiture of Margum & Port
			Talbot
1953		.0003	Firth Brown–Beardmore
1954[b]	.068	.0005	Tube Investments–Parkgate Iron & Steel
1957	.067		
1960	.065		

[a] Except for 1900 and 1913, when shares of output in tons were employed, company shares are based on furnace capacity per heat without adjustment for differences in heats per week or number of operating weeks in the year.

[b] Figures for 1947 are prenationalization. Figures for 1954 are based on 1954 shares of companies denationalized between 1953 and 1957.

TABLE 13.17

U.S. RUBBER TIRES AND TUBES INDUSTRY: CONTRIBUTIONS OF MERGERS AND
CONCENTRATION MEASURES FOR SELECTED DATES, BASED ON VALUE OF
DOMESTIC CONSUMPTION PLUS EXPORTS[a]

Selected Dates	H	Contributions of Mergers to ΔH	Remarks
1912		.0226	Goodrich-Diamond
1915		.0061	Fisk-Federal
1923		.0007	Lee-Republic
1925	.089		
1926		.0002	Seiberling-Portage
1929		.0030	Goodrich-Hood
1930		.0096	Goodrich-Miller
1931		.0373	U.S. Rubber–Gillette U.S. Rubber–Samson
1935	.168	.0119	Goodyear–Kelly-Springfield
1939		.0116	U.S. Rubber–Fisk
1945		.0007	General-Penna
1947	.163		
1954	.165		
1958	.141		

[a] Exports as percent value of production were as follows: 1925, 3.7 percent; 1935, 3.5 percent; 1947, 8.3 percent; 1954, 4.4 percent; 1958, 3.7 percent.

TABLE 13.18

U.K. RUBBER TIRES & TUBES INDUSTRY: CONTRIBUTIONS OF MERGERS AND
CONCENTRATION MEASURES FOR SELECTED DATES, BASED ON VALUE OF
DOMESTIC CONSUMPTION PLUS EXPORTS[a]

Selected Dates	H	Dunlop Share 1924 to 1952	Contributions of Mergers to ΔH	Remarks
1912				Large-scale tire output begins
1924	.363	.584		Before import tariff
1925			.0899	Dunlop-Macintosh
1927				Import tariff imposed
1933			.0070	BTR-IRGP&T (Palmer)
			.0171	Dunlop-India
			.0009	BTR-Stepney
1935	.355	.571		
1938			.0001	North British–U.S. Rubber (Dominion)
1947			.0007	Dunlop-Tyres (Scotland)
1952	.271	.465		
1953			.0056	Dunlop-Simons (Tyresoles)

[a] That is, imports plus U.K. production. Exports as percent of production plus imports were as follows: 1924, 16 percent; 1935, 22 percent; 1952, 25 percent—see Table 13.19 for alternative figures based on domestic consumption.

TABLE 13.19

U.K. RUBBER TIRES & TUBES INDUSTRY: CONTRIBUTIONS OF MERGERS AND
CONCENTRATION MEASURES FOR SELECTED DATES, BASED ON VALUE OF
DOMESTIC CONSUMPTION[a]

Selected Dates	H	Dunlop Share 1924 to 1952	Contributions of Mergers to ΔH	Remarks
1924	.334[b]	.557		
1925			.0813	Dunlop-Macintosh
1933			.0095	BTR-IRGP&T (Palmer)
			.0121	Dunlop-India
			.0014	BTR-Stepney
1935	.355[b, d]	.571		
1938			.0001	North British–U.S. Rubber (Dominion)
1947			.0004	Dunlop-Tyres (Scotland)
1952	.301[c]	.497		
1953			.0070	Dunlop-Simons (Tyresoles)

[a] That is, imports and production less estimated exports.

[b] Exports assumed to be in proportion to production for U.K. companies in 1924 and 1935.

[c] Figures for 1952 are for actual supply to home market; that is, exports not estimated as in other years; 1952 figure comparable with 1935 and 1924 is .271.

[d] Same as H based on share of imports plus U.K. production in Table 13.18 as imports negligible in this year.

TABLE 13.20

CONTRIBUTIONS OF MERGERS AND INTERNAL GROWTH TO CHANGES IN
CONCENTRATION FOR SELECTED PERIODS, U.S. & U.K.

	(1) Period[a]	(2) ΔH	(3) Contribution of Mergers to ΔH	(4) Contribution of Internal Growth to ΔH=Col. (2) less Col. (3)
Autos, U.S.	1904–1920	.203	.031	.172
	1920–1939[b]	.018	.008	.010
	1939–1952	−.022	.000	−.022
	1952–1964	.056	.002	.054
Autos, U.K.	1905–1924[c]	.167	.003	.164
	1924–1938	−.042	.018	−.060
	1938–1952	.075	.081	−.006
	1952–1964	.018	.001	.017
Cement, U.S.	1900–1920	−.014	.033	−.047
	1920–1939	−.039	.020	−.059
	1939–1955	.001	.005	−.004
	1955–1963	−.008	.000	−.008
Cement, U.K.	1900–1922[d]	.548	.824	−.276
	1922–1938	−.064	.414	−.478
	1938–1955	−.032	.002	−.034
	1955–1959	−.085	.000	−.085
Cigarettes, U.S.	1890–1921[e]	.052	.631[g]	−.579
	1921–1937[e]	−.089	.019	−.108
	1937–1954[e]	.019	.003	.016
	1954–1963[f]	.000	.000	.000
Cigarettes, U.K.	1900–1920	.549	.226	.323
	1920–1938	−.118	.150	−.268
	1938–1954[h]	−.100	−.072	−.028
	1954–1959	−.116	.000	−.116
Flat Glass, U.S.	1895–1919[d]	.059	.232	−.173
	1919–1935	.252	.053	.199
	1935–1954	−.066	.000	−.066
Flat Glass, U.K.	1904–1935[i]	.180	.000	.180
	1935–1955[j]	.534	.070–.351	.183–.464
Soap, U.S.	1900–1925	.058	.010	.048
	1925–1937	.171	.078	.093
	1937–1954	.029	.011	.018
	1954–1958	−.035	.010	−.045
Soap, U.K.	1900–1921	.405	.272	.133
	1921–1938	−.162	.092	−.254
	1938–1954	.050	.000	.050
	1954–1961[k]	.037	.004	.033

TABLE 13.20—Continued

	(1) Period[a]	(2) ΔH	(3) Contribution of Mergers to ΔH	(4) Contribution of Internal Growth to ΔH=Col. (2) less Col. (3)
Steel, U.S.	1899–1920	.094	.253	−.159
	1920–1938	−.015	.022	−.037
	1938–1954	−.033	−.010	−.023
	1954–1960	−.008	.000	−.008
Steel, U.K.	1900–1920[l]	.001	.027	−.026
	1920–1938	.030	.016	.014
	1938–1954	.001	.000	.001
	1954–1960	−.003	.000	−.003
Tires, U.S.	1925–1935	.079	.062	.017
	1935–1954	−.003	.012	−.015
	1954–1958	−.024	.000	−.024
Tires, U.K.[m]	1924–1935	−.008	.115	−.123
	1935–1952	−.084	.001	−.085

SOURCE: Tables 13.4 to 13.19.

[a] The dates below were chosen to break the data, so far as possible, into the following four periods:

1. Initial Herfindahl year to earliest post–World War I year. With the exception of industries in which important mergers took place in the 1890s, the initial year is 1900, or the earliest year thereafter for which it was possible to compute a Herfindahl index.

2. Earliest post–World War I year to latest pre–World War II year.

3. Latest pre–World War II year to mid-1950s.

4. Mid-1950s to terminal Herfindahl year.

[b] See note [a], Table 13.4.

[c] Employs average of minimum and maximum estimates for H in 1905.

[d] Employs premerger figure in initial year.

[e] Based on shares of cigarette production.

[f] Based on shares of cigarettes consumed domestically.

[g] Production share figure employed for 1890 formation of American Tobacco.

[h] See note [a], Table 13.9.

[i] Employs "best estimate" in Table 13.11 for 1904.

[j] Employs extreme estimates in Table 13.11 for 1955 merger.

[k] Figures for 1961 adjusted to basis of earlier years by 1954 ratio of H including industrial to H excluding industrial.

[l] See note [a], Table 13.16.

[m] Based on value of domestic consumption plus exports in Table 13.18.

TABLE 13.21

U.S. FIRE AND CASUALTY INSURANCE COMPANIES, STOCK AND MUTUAL,
CONTRIBUTIONS OF MERGERS AND CONCENTRATION MEASURES FOR SELECTED
DATES, 1945–1963, BASED ON NET PREMIUMS WRITTEN[a]

Selected Dates	H	Contributions of Mergers to ΔH	Remarks
1945	.0163		
1947		.000002	Employers Mutual of Wausau–Hudson Mohawk
1951		.00003	Nationwide–National Casualty
1953	.0164		
1954		.000002	Employers Group–Halifax Insurance
		.00011	Fireman's Fund–National Surety
		.000006	Fire Ass'n of Phila.–Eureka Cas.
1956		.00027[b]	Continental Cas.–Nat'l Fire of Hartford
		.00012	Amer. Ins. of Newark–Amer. Auto Insurance
		.000007	Fire Ass'n of Phila.–Gen'l Cas. of Wisc.
1957		.00063	America Fore–Fireman's (Loyalty) Group
1958		.00010	America Fore-Loyalty–Yorkshire
		.000005	Fire Ass'n of Phila.–Hoosier Cas.
1959		.00004	Commercial Union–North British
		.000002	Northern Ins.–Maine Bonding and Casualty
1960		.00001	Employers–Northern Assurance
		.000004	Springfield-Monarch–Standard Ins. of Tulsa
		.000006	Springfield-Monarch–Freeport Ins.
1961	.0154[c]	.000002	Reliance–Standard Fire of New York
		.00006	Reliance–Standard Accident
		.00008	Royal-Globe–London and Lancashire
1962		.00003	General Accident–Camden Fire
		.000005	St. Paul F & M–Birmingham Fire and Cas.
		.00007	U.S. Fidel. & Guar.–Merchants Fire Assurance
		.00003	Nationwide–Commercial Standard
1963	.0189[d]	.00003	James S. Kemper–Economy Fire and Cas.
		.00025[b]	Cont'l-Nat'l Fire–American Casualty
		.00047	Fireman's Fund–Amer. Ins. of Newark
		.000007	Great Amer.–First Ins. of Hawaii
		.00007	Maryland Casualty–Northern Insurance

[a] Excludes factory mutuals, reciprocal and Lloyds companies.
[b] If accident and health excluded=.00012.
[c] 1961 H, excluding accident and health=.0168.
[d] Comparable figure for state of Illinois, 1963=.0232.

PRINCIPAL SOURCES FOR TABLES 13.4 TO 13.21

U.S. Automobile Industry:

Automotive Industries (periodical).
Automotive News and *Automotive News Almanac* (periodicals).
Edwards, *Dynamics of the United States Automobile Industry* (1965).
Epstein, *The Automobile Industry: Its Economic and Commercial Development* (1928).
Federal Trade Commission, *Report on Motor Vehicle Industry* (1939)
Kennedy, *The Automobile Industry: The Coming of Age of Capitalism's Favorite Child* (1941).
Seltzer, *A Financial History of the American Automobile Industry* (1928).
Temporary National Economic Committee, *Investigation of Concentration of Economic Power*, Monograph no. 27, The Structure of Industry (1941).
Ward's Automotive Year Book (various years).

U.K. Automobile Industry:

Andrews and Brunner, *The Life of Lord Nuffield* (1955).
Buchanan, *Mixed Blessing: The Motor in Britain* (1958).
Maxcy and Silberston, *The Motor Industry* (1959).
Silberston, "The Motor Industry 1955–1964," *Oxford University Institute of Economics and Statistics Bulletin* no. 27 (1965): 253.
Society of Motor Manufacturers and Traders, Ltd., *The Motor Industry of Great Britain* (various years).
Youngson, *The British Economy, 1920–1957* (1960).

U.S. Cement Industry:

American Portland Cement Association, *Directory of Portland Cement Manufacturers in the U.S.*
Federal Trade Commission, *Report of Federal Trade Commission on Price Bases Inquiry: Basing Point Formula and Cement Prices* (1932).
Lesley, *History of the Portland Cement Industry in the United States* (1924).
Pit and Quarry (periodical).
Federal Trade Commission, *Cement Industry* (1933).

U.K. Cement Industry:

Davis, *Portland Cement* (1909).
Cembureau, *World Cement Directory* (1961).

U.S. Cigarette Industry:

Cox, *Competition in the American Tobacco Industry, 1911–1932* (1933).
Jacobstein, *The Tobacco Industry in the United States* (1907).
Jones, *The Trust Problem in the United States* (1924).
Nicholls, *Price Policies in the Cigarette Industry* (1951).
Printer's Ink: Jan. 28, 1944; Feb. 2, 1945; Feb. 1, 1946; Jan. 31, 1947; Jan. 23, 1948; Apr. 1, 1949; Jan. 13, 1950; Jan. 5, 1951; Nov. 18, 1952; Jan. 9, 1953; Jan. 15, 1954; Dec. 31, 1954; Dec. 30, 1955; Dec. 28, 1956; Dec. 27, 1957; Dec. 26, 1958; Dec. 25, 1959; Dec. 23, 1960.
Bureau of Corporations, *Report of the Commissioner of Corporations on the Tobacco Industry*, pts. I, II, and III (1909, 1911, and 1915).

U.K. Cigarette Industry:

Gt. Brit. Monopolies Commission, *Report on the Supply of Cigarettes and Tobacco and of Cigarette and Tobacco Machinery*, Cmd. no. 218 (1961).
Gt. Brit. Board of Trade, Standing Committee on Trusts, *Tobacco Industry*, Cmd. no. 558 (in vol. 23 of Parliamentary Papers) (1920).

U.S. Flat Glass:

Glass Factory Year Book and Directory (1927, 1930, 1949, 1963, 1965).
American Glass Trade Directory (1909–1913).
Davis, *The Development of the American Glass Industry* (1949).
Fortune, May, 1955, and May, 1956.
National Glass Budget, Nov. 11, 1899; Oct. 19, 1901; Oct. 26, 1901; Jan. 25, 1902; Mar. 22, 1902.
Glass Factory Directory (1916, 1919, 1939, 1943).
Stocking and Watkins, *Monopoly and Free Enterprise* (1951).
Tariff Commission, *Flat Glass and Related Glass Products* (1937).

U.K. Flat Glass:

Barker, *Pilkington Brothers and the Glass Industry* (1960), and correspondence with Professor Barker. Pilkington Brothers Ltd., correspondence.

U.S. Soap Industry:

1925 and prior years:

Bureau of the Census, *Census of Manufacturers 1910 and 1925*. Establishment data adjusted to company basis employing information on establishment locations from various industrial manuals and company histories.

1935 and after:

A. C. Nielsen Co. data: *Advertising Age*, Mar. 30, 1964; Oct. 24, 1963; Nov. 30, 1963; Jan. 28, 1963; Dec. 26, 1960.
Lief, *It Floats* (1958).
Procter and Gamble Company, *Into a Second Century with Procter and Gamble* (1955).

U.K. Soap Industry:

Corlett, *The Economic Development of Detergents* (1958).
Gt. Brit. Parliament, Standing Committee on Trusts, *Report on the Soap Industry*, Cmd. no. 1126 (in vol. 16 of Parliamentary Papers) (1921).
Puplett, *Synthetic Detergents* (1957).
Redfern, *The Story of the C.W.S.* (1913).
Wilson, *The History of Unilever* (1954).

U.S. Steel Industry:

American Iron and Steel Institute, *Directory of Iron and Steel Works in the United States and Canada* (various years).

U.K. Steel Industry:

1938 and prior years:

Burn, *Economic History of Steelmaking, 1867–1939* (1940).
Iron and Coal Trades Review, supplement, Mar. 30, 1900, and Feb. 12, 1904.
Ryland's Directory of Ironmongers of Great Britain (various years).

1939 and later years:

British Iron and Steel Federation, *Statistical Year Book*. After 1954 the title changed to *Iron and Steel: Annual Statistics*.

U.S. Tire Industry:

Allen, *The House of Goodyear* (1936).
Gaffey, *The Productivity of Labor in the Rubber Tire Manufacturing Industry* (1940).
Lief, *The Firestone Story* (1951).
Sobel, *Economic Impact of Collective Bargaining Upon the Rubber Tire Industry* (1951) [unpublished dissertation in University of Chicago Library].

Wolf and Wolf, *Rubber: A Story of Glory and Greed* (1936).
Ziegler, *Current Cases in Business* (1964).

U.K. Tire Industry:

Allen, *The Industrial Development of Birmingham and the Black Country, 1860–1927* (1929).
Allen, *The House of Goodyear* (1936).
Donnithorne, *British Rubber Manufacturing* (1958).
Dunning, *American Investment in British Manufacturing Industry* (1958).
Gt. Brit. Monopolies Commission, *Report on the Supply and Export of Pneumatic Tyres* (1955).
History of the Rubber Industry (Schidrowitz and Dawson, eds., 1952).
Palmerton, *Market for Rubber Products in the United Kingdom* (1922).

U.S. Fire and Casualty Insurance Industry:

Best's insurance reports, fire, marine and miscellaneous (various years).
Insurance Year Book (various years up to 1955); insurance by states of fire and marine, casualty, surety, and miscellaneous lines (after 1955).
The Spectator Desk Directory of Insurance (1964).

GENERAL REFERENCES FOR TABLES 13.4 TO 13.21

United States

The Structure of American Industry (Adams, ed., 3rd ed., 1961).
Federal Trade Commission, *Report on Corporate Mergers and Acquisitions* (1955).
Bureau of the Census, *Census of Manufactures* (various years).
Department of Commerce, *Foreign Commerce and Navigation of the United States* (various years).
Commerce Clearing House, records of antitrust cases. [Record in United States v. Procter and Gamble Co., 356 U.S. 677 (1957).]
Temporary National Economic Committee and Bureau of the Census, various concentration studies.

United Kingdom

Allen, *British Industries and Their Organization* (3rd ed., 1951).
National Institute of Economic and Social Research, *Economic and Social Study*, no. 15 (Burn, ed., 1958).
Cook, *Effects of Mergers* (1958).

Evely and Little, Concentration in British Industry (1960).
Fitzgerald, Industrial Combination in England (1927).
Gt. Brit. Board of Trade, The Report on the Census of Production (various years).
Gt. Brit. Customs and Excise Dept. Statistical Office, Annual Statement of Trade of the United Kingdom with foreign countries and British possessions (various years).
Macrosty, The Trust Movement in British Industry (1907).
Maizels and Leak, The Structure of British Industry, Journal of the Royal Statistical Society (Series A) 108 (1945):142.
Mennell, Takeover: The Growth of Monopoly in Britain, 1951–61 (1962).
Rees, Trusts in British Industry, 1914–1921 (1922).

What Can
Regulators Regulate?
The Case of Electricity*

· 14 ·

The literature of public regulation is so vast that it must touch on everything, but it touches seldom and lightly on the most basic question one can ask about regulation: Does it make a difference in the behavior of an industry?

This impertinent question will strike anyone connected with a regulated industry as palpably trivial. Are not important prices regulated? Are not the routes of a trucker and an airline prescribed? Is not entry into public utility industries limited? Is not an endless procession of administrative proceedings aging entrepreneurs and enriching lawyers?

But the innumerable regulatory actions are conclusive proof, not of effective regulation, but of the desire to regulate. And if wishes were horses, one would buy stock in a harness factory.

The question of the influence of regulation can never be answered by an enumeration of regulatory policies. A thousand statutes now forbid us to do things that we would not dream of doing even if the statutes were repealed: we would not slay our neighbor, or starve our children, or burn our house for the insurance, or erect an abattoir in the back yard. Whether the statutes really have an appreciable effect on actual behavior can only be determined by examining the behavior of people not subject to the statutes.

From the *Journal of Law and Economics* 5 (October 1962). Copyright 1962 by the University of Chicago.

* In collaboration with Claire Friedland.

An order to a trucker not to haul goods between cities A and B is even more difficult to assess. He may not wish to have this route, in analogy to the laws governing our personal behavior. But let him wish with all his heart to have it, and be denied; there still will be no economic effect of the regulation if others are allowed, in adequate number, to have the desired route.

The point at issue may be restated in the language of economics. An industry's output and price are normally governed primarily by the basic economic and technological determinants of supply and demand: by whether the demand curve is D_1 or D_2, and the supply curve S_1 or S_2 (see Figure 14.1). Regulation will affect price and output only if it shifts the curves or the point on a curve where the industry operates. Does regulation introduce shifts in curves of the magnitude of S_1 to S_2 or S_1 to S'_2? Then its effect will be negligible. Does regulation shift the effective operating point from P_1 to P_2? Then its effect will again be negligible.

The test of the economic effect of regulation is essentially independent of the content of the formal regulations. No degree of care in analyzing the regulations, or even their administration, will tell us whether they rubber-stamp or slightly heckle the state of affairs or substantially alter it.

What does one mean in saying that regulation has had large or small effects? He means that of the observed economic behavior in a certain industrial sector, a large or small part can be explained only by recourse to regulation. Consider these examples:

1. Is the decline of railroading due in any important part to ICC regulations? If in other economies with rising incomes and extensive adoption of automobiles and trucks the railroad traffic shows a pattern similar to ours, then regulation has not been the primary influence.

2. Do utility commissions reduce the differential in prices of utility services to large and small buyers? If in a group of unregulated markets we observe a mean ratio of rates of large to small buyers of m_{nr}, and in regulated markets a ratio of m_r, do m_{nr} and m_r differ significantly? If of the total variance among markets in the ratio of large to small buyers only 2 percent can be explained by regulation, the regulations have negligible impact.

3. Do regulatory bodies succeed in preventing monopoly profits? We take it that they will usually prevent such profits from appearing ex-plicitly in accounting statements. Whether they go beyond this may be judged, for example, by the fortunes of investors in stocks of regulated companies over periods extending from pre-regulation on, compared with those of investors in similar but unregulated enterprises.

These summary remarks will deceive no informed person as to the analytical and empirical complexity of the task of isolating the effects of regulation. They

FIGURE 14.1

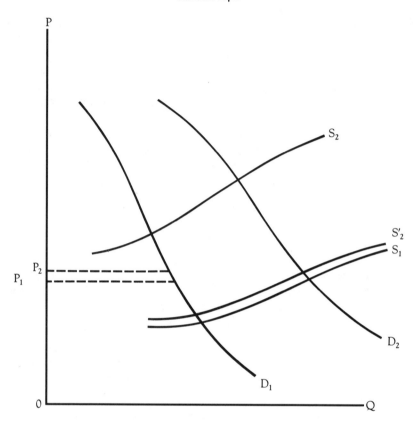

are intended only to suggest why one does not read the regulations to reach the answer.

We propose now to make an investigation of one regulated industry to explore techniques and hopefully reach tentative results. This is the electric utility industry. Here we face three major problems: (1) What firms are regulated? (2) What effects of regulation shall we study, and how shall we measure them? (3) How do we explain our findings?

I. When Is a Firm Regulated?

Every enterprise producing and distributing electricity has been regulated since its founding by way of charter limitations and franchises; its use of public thoroughfares was enough to insure this. It would therefore be possible to say that there is no unregulated sector to provide a base for judging the effects of regulation. This statement would not be acceptable to the professional writers on public utilities: they hail the beginnings of effective regulation with the establishment of the public service commissions in New York and Wisconsin in 1907.[1]

Yet these specialists have assuredly not faced the problem of measuring the effects of regulation, so their judgments are suspect. Indeed, if we accepted their judgments our problem would be solved, for they never question the importance of (effective!) regulation.

There is no substitute for an objective measure of regulation, and the one we choose is the creation of a special state commission endowed with the power to regulate rates of electric utilities.[2] It may be complained that some of these commissions were long ineffective, or that municipal regulation was effective earlier in some states. Such assertions can only be tested by a study invoking another criterion of the existence of regulation: the year the commission issued its first rate order upheld by the courts, the year the commission first spent $100,000 or published 100 pages of orders, etc. But it is intrinsic to the problem that there be an independent criterion of regulation, and that findings on effectiveness be conditional on acceptance of that criterion. There is a strict analogy with the problem of estimating the influence of monopoly, where the result is conditioned by the criterion of monopoly (concentration ratio, number of firms, etc.).

The classification of states by the existence of regulatory commissions with jurisdiction over electric utilities is given in the Appendix in Table 14.9. The beginning of regulation by this criterion varied as shown in the accompanying tabulation. Two-thirds of the states had commissions by 1915, three-quarters by 1922.

	States
Before 1910	6
1910–20	29
1920–30	1
1930–40	3
1940–50	2
1950–60	2

II. The Effects of Regulation on Rates and Returns

There are two basic purposes of the public regulation of prices: the curtailment of the exercise of monopoly power and the elimination of certain forms of price

TABLE 14.1

AVERAGE REVENUE PER KWH,

STATES WITH AND WITHOUT REGULATION, 1912–1937

	REGULATED[a]		UNREGULATED	
Year	States	Revenue (cents)	States	Revenue (cents)
1912	6	2.30	41	2.99
1917	31	1.88	16	3.20
1922	33	2.44	12	3.87
1927	35	2.85	10	4.21
1932	34	2.91	8	3.69
1937	34	2.32	6	3.04

[a] A state is considered regulated in a given year if commission regulation was established three years previously.

discrimination. There will no doubt be other effects on prices, including unintended effects such as the short term rigidity of price commonly associated with regulation, but we shall concentrate upon these basic purposes. Our analysis of effects will be limited to the period up to 1937, simply because by that time 39 states had regulating commissions. By that date every unregulated state had at least two adjoining states with regulatory commissions, and even a showing of no difference in rates would be ambiguous: it could be argued that the threat of regulation was always latent in the unregulated states. This position does not seem wholly convincing to us—in a sense the threat of regulation was operative as soon as the Interstate Commerce Commission was created—but the small number of unregulated states after 1937 offers statistical support for this terminus.

The Level of Rates

We shall make little use of the direct comparison of the average level of rates in regulated and unregulated states, of which a sample summary is given in Table 14.1.[3] The ambiguity of simple differences may be illustrated by the data for 1917. In this year the average revenue per kwh was 1.88 cents in regulated states and 3.20 cents in unregulated states, which might suggest that regulation lowered rates by almost 40 percent. But we can classify the rates of these states in several years (see Table 14.2). This classification makes clear the fact that rates were lower on average in the regulating states, not only *after* but also *before* regulation.

TABLE 14.2

	Number of States	AVERAGE RATE		
		1917	*1912*	*1907*
States instituting regulation before 1912	6	1.88	2.30	2.76
States instituting regulation from 1912 to 1917	25	1.88	2.30	2.93
States not regulating before 1917	16	3.20	4.07	4.34

The basic fact is, of course, that regulation is associated with economic characteristics which also exert direct, independent influence on rates—the size and urbanization of the population, the extent of industrialization, etc. To isolate the effects of regulation we must take direct account of these economic factors. We do so by the following procedure.

The main determinants of the level of rates for an unregulated monopolist would be the size of the market and its density (which affect both production and distribution costs), the price of fuel, and the incomes of consumers. We approximate the market size and density by the population in cities with 25,000 or more population; the fuel costs by an equivalent Btu cost and by the proportion of power derived from hydroelectric sources; and consumer incomes by per capita state income. We fit the equation,

$$\log p = a + b \log U + c \log p_F + dH + e \log Y + fR,$$

where p =average revenue per kwh, in cents;

U =population in cities over 25,000 (in thousands);

p_F =price of fuel (in dollars per Btu equivalent ton of bituminous coal);

H =proportion of power from hydroelectric sources;

Y =per capita state income, in dollars;

R =dummy variable, 0 if an unregulated state, 1 if a regulated state.

The results of fitting this equation to 1922 data are presented in Table 14.3. The regression of millions of kw's of output, in logarithms, on these variables is also added.

The effects of regulation may be expressed in two ways: by the regression coefficient in the dummy variable representing regulation or by the difference in the coefficient of multiple determination including and excluding regulation. By either standard, regulation had no effect upon the level of rates in 1922.

For the other census years we use the abbreviated regression equations

TABLE 14.3
REGRESSION EQUATIONS OF AVERAGE REVENUE PER KWH AND OUTPUT ON URBAN POPULATION, COST OF FUEL, PER CAPITA INCOME, PROPORTION OF HP FROM HYDROELECTRIC, AND REGULATION, 47 STATES, 1922

Dependent Variable	Constant Term	Regression Coefficients and Their Standard Errors					R^2	
		Urban Population	Cost of Fuel	Per Capita Income[a]	Proportion of HP from Hydroelectric	Regulation	Including Regulation	Excluding Regulation
Average revenue per kwh	.0918	-.0592 (.0248)[a]	.0604 (.1665)	.230 (.204)	-.498 (.083)	-.0109 (.0068)	.567	.540
Output	-.166	.395 (.052)	-.577 (.349)	.718 (.428)	.491 (.174)	.0172 (.0143)	.694	.684

[a] Linear interpolations between averages for the following years: 1919–1921 [Maurice Leven, *Income in the Various States* (1925)]; 1929–1931 [U.S. Office of Business Economics, *Personal Income by States Since 1929*, Supplement to the Survey of Current Business, 1956].

TABLE 14.4

REGRESSION EQUATION OF AVERAGE REVENUE PER KWH ON URBAN POPULATION, PER CAPITA INCOME, PROPORTION OF HYDROELECTRIC POWER AND REGULATION, 1912–1937

Year	Number of States	Constant Term	REGRESSION COEFFICIENTS AND THEIR STANDARD ERRORS				R^2	
			Urban Population	Per Capita Income[a]	Proportion Hydroelectric[b]	Regulation	Including Regulation	Excluding Regulation
I. All Sales								
1912	47	.663	-.0291 (.0134)	—	-.552 (.062)	.0028 (.0590)	.654	.654
1922	47	.730	-.0533 (.0240)	—	-.508 (.081)	-.0708 (.0596)	.546	.531
1932	42	.380	-.0478 (.0144)	.141 (.090)	-.336 (.058)	-.0630 (.0409)	.580	.554
1937	39	.323	-.0486 (.0157)	.123 (.121)	-.257 (.059)	-.102 (.043)	.496	.413
II. Sales to Domestic Customers								
1932	42	1.036	-.0044 (.0125)	-.0804 (.0781)	-.132 (.050)	-.0371 (.0358)	.286	.266
1937	39	.726	-.0223 (.0130)	.0187 (.1002)	-.146 (.409)	-.0337 (.0358)	.271	.251
III. Sales to Commercial and Industrial Customers								
1932	42	.622	-.0496 (.0149)	—	-.349 (.059)	-.0306 (.0391)	.546	.539
1937	39	.572	-.0520 (.0159)	—	-.262 (.061)	-.0925 (.0417)	.493	.422

[a] Per capita income variable introduced only in years in which annual data are available.
[b] In 1912 and 1922, ratio of HP capacity of water wheels and turbines to HP capacity of all prime movers; in 1932 and 1937, ratio of kw capacity of hydroelectric to kw capacity of all generators.

summarized in Table 14.4. No effect of regulation is observable through 1932. The 1937 equation does display a regulation effect, but it is localized in the sales to commercial and industrial consumers—the class of consumers that regulation was *not* designed to protect. We believe even this modest 1937 effect would be eliminated by a fuller statistical analysis.[4]

We conclude that no effect of regulation can be found in the average level of rates.

The Rate Structure

We have examined two aspects of the rate structure for possible influences of regulation. The first is the ratio of monthly bills of domestic consumers for larger amounts of electricity relative to smaller amounts. Here our expectation was that the regulatory bodies would recognize the greater potential political popularity of low rates for the numerous consumers who buy small quantities. The evidence is essentially negative (Table 14.5): in only one of four comparisons was the ratio of monthly bills significantly different in regulated states from unregulated states.[5] The quantity rate structure for domestic consumers seems independent of the existence of regulation.

A second aspect of the rate structure where regulation might be expected to be influential is in the comparative charges to domestic and industrial

TABLE 14.5

DIFFERENTIALS BY SIZE OF MONTHLY CONSUMPTION, 1924 AND 1936

Year	Class of States	Number of States	Average Ratio of Larger to Smaller Monthly Bills
A. 100 and 25 kwh per Month Bills			
1924	Regulated	29	3.02
	Unregulated	10	3.25
1936	Regulated	30	2.79
	Unregulated	9	2.86
B. 250 and 100 kwh per Month Bills			
1924	Regulated	29	1.90
	Unregulated	10	2.15
1936	Regulated	30	1.83
	Unregulated	9	1.82

SOURCE: U.S. Federal Power Commission, "Trends in Residential Rates from 1924 to 1936" (Washington, D.C.: 1937), table 11. The observations are unweighted average rates for cities of over 50,000 population in each state.

TABLE 14.6

AVERAGE RATIO OF DOMESTIC TO INDUSTRIAL PRICE PER KWH

	1917	1937
Regulated states	1.616 (29 states)	2.459 (32 states)
Unregulated states	1.445 (16 states)	2.047 (7 states)

buyers. The regulatory bodies would reduce domestic rates relative in industrial rates if they sought to reduce discrimination; the industrial users presumably have better alternative power sources and therefore more elastic demands. Or, again as a political matter, the numerous domestic users might be favored relative to the industrial users. To test this expectation, the average ratio of charges per kwh to domestic users to charges to industrial users was calculated for two years (see Table 14.6). The ratios are therefore directly opposite to those which were expected. But a scatter diagram analysis reveals that the ratio of domestic to industrial rates depends primarily upon the average number of kwh sold to domestic customers divided by the average number of kwh sold to industrial customers, and the relationship does not differ between regulated and unregulated states.[7] Again no effect of regulation is detectable.

Stockholder Experience

The final area to which we look for effects of regulation is investors' experience. Our basic test is this: Did investors in companies which were not regulated, or were regulated for only a few years, do better than investors in companies which were regulated from an early date?

To answer this question, we invest $1,000 in each electrical utility in 1907, reinvest all dividends and cash value of rights, and calculate the accumulated investment in 1920.[8] The year 1907 was chosen as the first date to reduce the possible impact of expectations of regulation, and even this date—which is later than we would like—reduced the number of companies we could trace to 20. The basic data are given in Table 14.7.

The pattern of increases in market values appears erratic. A simple regression of market value as a function of the increase in dollar sales of the utility system and the number of years of regulation is presented in Table 14.8. There is thus a slight, statistically significant effect of regulation on market values.[9]

TABLE 14.7

MARKET VALUE IN 1920 OF INVESTMENT OF $1,000 IN 1907
(20 ELECTRIC COMPANIES)

Year of Regulation	Company	Market Value in 1920	Relative Change in Sales 1907– 1920 (percent)
1887	*Massachusetts:*		
	Edison Electric Illuminating Co. of Boston	$1,689	246
	Lowell Electric Light Corporation	1,485	295
	New Bedford Gas & Edison Light Co.	1,528	164
	Edison Electric Illuminating Co. of Brockton	2,310	558
1907	*New York:*		
	Buffalo General Electric Co.	2,632	718
	Kings County Electric Light & Power Co.	2,356	279
	N.Y. and Queens Electric Light & Power Co.	1,059	225
1909	*Michigan:*		
	Detroit Edison Co.	4,273	1,412
	Houghton County Electric Light Co.	1,959	130
1910	*Maryland:*		
	Consolidated Gas, Electric Light & Power Co. (Baltimore)	6,547	286
	New Jersey:		
	Public Service Corp. of New Jersey	1,546	206
1911	*Ohio:*		
	Columbia Gas and Electric Co.	3,952	999
	Connecticut:		
	Hartford Electric Light Co.	2,028	728
	California:		
	Pacific Gas and Electric Co.	2,051	212
1913	*Illinois:*		
	Commonwealth Edison Co.	2,179	299
1914	*Pennsylvania:*		
	Philadelphia Electric Co.	4,254	296
Not regulated in 1920	Galveston-Houston Electric Co.	1,001	262
	Northern Texas Electric Co.	4,861	272
	El Paso Electric Co.	4,046	281
	Tampa Electric Co.	2,830	183

TABLE 14.8

REGRESSION EQUATIONS OF MARKET VALUE IN 1918 AND 1920 OF
$1,000 INVESTMENT IN 1907, ON GROWTH IN SALES AND REGULATION[a]
(20 ELECTRIC COMPANIES)

Terminal Year (t)	Constant Term	Growth in Sales	Regulation	R^2
1918	3.28	.332	−.015	.16
		(.227)	(.010)	
1920	3.27	.395	−.017	.21
		(.232)	(.010)	

[a] Market values in logarithms; growth in sales=log $(sales_t/sales_{1907})$.

III. CONCLUSION

Our study was undertaken primarily to investigate the feasibility of measuring the effects of regulation, but our inability to find any significant effects of the regulation of electrical utilities calls for some explanation. This finding is contingent upon our criteria of regulation and of the areas in which we sought effects, but both of these criteria are accepted by much of the literature of public utility economies.

The ineffectiveness of regulation lies in two circumstances. The first circumstance is that the individual utility system is not possessed of any large amount of long run monopoly power. It faces the competition of other energy sources in a large proportion of its product's uses, and it faces the competition of other utility systems, to which in the long run its industrial (and hence many of its domestic) users may move. Let the long run demand elasticity of one utility system be on the order of −8; then the system faces demand and marginal revenue curves such as those displayed in Figure 14.2. Given the cost curves we sketch, price will be MP.[10]

The second circumstance is that the regulatory body is incapable of forcing the utility to operate at a specified combination of output, price, and cost. As we have drawn the curves, there is no market price that represents the announced goal of competitive profits; let us assume that the commission would set a price equal to average cost at some output moderately in excess of output OM, say at R. Since accounting costs are hardly unique, there is a real question of whether the regulatory body can even distinguish between costs of MS and MP. Let the commission be given this knowledge; then the utility can reduce costs below MS by reducing one or more dimensions of the services

FIGURE 14.2

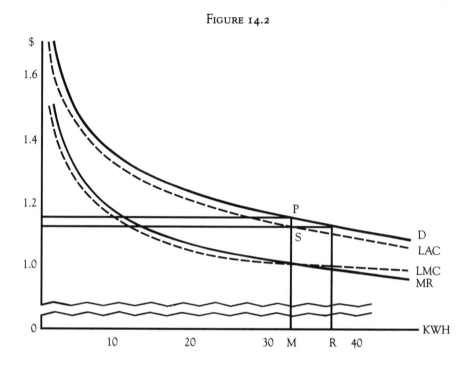

which are really part of its output: peak load capacity, constancy of current, promptness of repairs, speed of installation of service. It can also manipulate its average price by suitable changes in the complex rate structure (also with effects on costs). Finally, recognize that the cost curve falls through time, and recognize also the inevitable time lags of a regulatory process, and the possibility becomes large that the commission will proudly win each battlefield that its protagonist has abandoned except for a squad of lawyers. Since a regulatory body cannot effectively control the daily detail of business operations, it cannot deal with variables whose effect is of the same order of magnitude in their effects on profits as the variables upon which it does have some influence.

The theory of price regulation must, in fact, be based upon the tacit assumption that in its absence a monopoly has exorbitant power. If it were true that pure monopoly profits in the absence of regulation would be 10 or 20 percent above the competitive rate of return, so prices would be on the order of 40 to 80 percent above long run marginal cost, there might indeed be some possibility of effective regulation. The electrical utilities do not provide such a possibility.

NOTES

1. L. S. Lyon and V. Abramson, *Government and Economic Life* (1940): 636; Twentieth Century Fund, *Electric Power and Government Policy* (1948): 65, 235.

2. In our statistical work we measure regulation from three years after the creation of the commission, on impressionistic evidence of the lag involved in organizing the commission, hence all statements regarding, for example, states regulated in 1917 should be interpreted to refer to states initiating regulation no later than 1914.

3. The complete average rates are reported in the Appendix in Table 14.10. These average revenues per kilowatt hour involve the following adjustments of census data: for 1907 to 1922 revenues include sales by private electric companies to ultimate consumers, domestic and industrial, plus net sales to out-of-state companies, municipal electric companies, and electric railroads, but exclude intercompany sales within states. Kwh figures are for kwh's generated by private electric companies plus net purchases of kwh's from electric railroads or out-of-state electric companies. For 1927 to 1937 revenue and kwh data are for current sold to ultimate consumers, including gross sales to electric railroads but excluding all sales to other electric companies.

4. The regression coefficient of regulation becomes non-significant if we shift from measuring urban population by the logarithm of population in cities over 25,000. A set of alternative regressions, reported in Tables 14.12 and 14.13, are also relevant; these equations employ total output and output per customer as independent variables, and thus raise identification questions which led to their replacement by those in the text, but seem worth reporting.

5. In 1924 the ratio of bills for 250 and 100 kwh is barely significant at the 5 percent level; the difference is opposite to that predicted as resulting from regulation.

6. The 1917 difference is significantly different from zero at the 5 percent level; the 1937 difference at the 10 percent level.

7. In 1937, 6 of 7 unregulated states had kwh per domestic buyer divided by kwh per industrial buyer above the mean of all states, but only 7 of 29 regulated states had ratios above the mean.

8. A separate termination in 1918 yields the same results.

9. An analysis of variance was also made of Table 14.7, grouping states into four classes, by year of regulation: 1887, 1907–1910, 1911–1914, not regulated in 1920. No significant effect of regulation was found.

10. An elasticity of -8 implies that a utility will set prices 14 percent above marginal cost. In the constant cost case, given a capital/sales ratio of 4, rates of return will exceed the competitive level by 3½ percent.

Appendix

Table 14.9
Dates of Creation of State Commission Electric Rate Jurisdiction

State	Date of Electric Rate Jurisdiction	State	Date of Electric Rate Jurisdiction
Alabama	1915[a, b]	Nevada	1911
Arizona	1912	New Hampshire	1911[f, c]
Arkansas	1935[c, d]	New Jersey	1910
California	1911	New Mexico	1941[o]
Colorado	1913[e]	New York	1907[f]
Connecticut	1911[f, g]	North Carolina	1913
Delaware	1949	North Dakota	1919
Florida	1951	Ohio	1911[j]
Georgia	1907	Oklahoma	1913[p]
Idaho	1913	Oregon	1912
Illinois	1913	Pennsylvania	1914[f]
Indiana	1913	Rhode Island	1912
Iowa	[h, i]	South Carolina	1922[q]
Kansas	1911[j]	South Dakota	[h]
Kentucky	1934	Tennessee	1919
Louisiana	1934[k]	Texas	[h]
Maine	1913	Utah	1917
Maryland	1910	Vermont	1908
Massachusetts	1887[g, l]	Virginia	1914[r]
Michigan	1909[j]	Washington	1911
Minnesota	[h]	West Virginia	1913
Mississippi	1956	Wisconsin	1907
Missouri	1913[f, g]	Wyoming	1915[g]
Montana	1913	Washington, D.C.	1913
Nebraska	[m, n]		

Sources: State laws, statutes, Public Utility Commission reports; Bonbright and Co. and F.P.C. Surveys, and correspondence with commission, unless otherwise noted.
[a] No jurisdiction to change existing contracts.
[b] No jurisdiction over contracts with municipalities.
[c] Approves changes in rates only (i.e., new rates).
[d] "Concurrent jurisdiction" with municipalities. Commission hears appeals.
[e] 1921 Court decision: no authority in cities controlling public utilities under home-rule amendment of 1912. Denver (a home-rule city) voted to surrender control to commission in early 1950s. Number of home-rule cities in which commission has no jurisdiction is given as 13 in 1954.
[f] Sets maximum rates only.
[g] Power to investigate upon complaint only.
[h] None through 1960.
[i] Authority outside cities, 1954.
[j] Municipalities fix rates; commission hears appeals only.
[k] Power to fix rates in New Orleans, and other cities voting to surrender control, from 1921 on, subject to optional powers of municipalities. Primary control shifted from municipalities to state commission in 1934.
[l] Barnes, I., "Public Utility Control in Massachusetts," 1930, p. 96. Requirement to furnish information to Gas and Electric Commission begins 1908.
[m] None in cities through 1960.
[n] Most companies are public.
[o] Commission had jurisdiction in cities under 10,000 population from 1921 on.
[p] Right to change rates fixed by municipal franchise established by 1915 court decisions.
[q] Jurisdiction over maximum electric rates, on complaint, granted in 1910, but no rate cases reported. In 1922, power of commission extended to allow fixing of rates on own motion. 1922 report indicates jurisdiction over electric utilities considered "recent" by commission.
[r] Excludes services rendered to a municipal corporation in 1914. In 1918, power strengthened so that utilities cannot change rates without commission approval.

TABLE 14.10

AVERAGE REVENUE PER KWH BY STATE, IN CENTS, 1907–1937

State	1907	1912	1917	1922	1927	1932	1937
Maine	1.90	1.42	1.51	1.62	2.06	1.96	2.03
New Hampshire	2.36	1.69	1.78	3.92	4.39	3.80	3.03
Vermont	2.62	1.91	2.21	1.89	a	a	a
Massachusetts	4.66	3.96	2.82	3.23	3.74	3.79	3.05
Rhode Island	4.50	3.44	2.32	2.32	a	a	a
Connecticut	3.50	3.53	2.64	3.25	3.46	3.56	2.81
New York	2.19	2.22	1.86	2.09	2.58	3.05	2.21
New Jersey	4.17	2.71	2.50	3.22	4.04	3.97	3.03
Pennsylvania	3.49	2.22	1.50	2.15	2.40	2.55	1.96
Ohio	3.38	2.75	1.85	2.36	2.60	2.73	2.01
Indiana	3.18	2.86	2.42	3.02	2.89	3.11	2.24
Illinois	2.94	2.28	1.93	2.24	2.62	2.68	2.20
Michigan	2.22	1.89	1.46	2.01	2.40	2.67	1.94
Wisconsin	3.67	2.36	1.82	2.43	2.77	3.18	2.41
Minnesota	2.74	2.76	1.74	2.85	3.14	3.15	2.63
Iowa	5.44	5.23	1.29	1.94	3.72	3.79	2.66
Missouri	3.57	3.56	2.86	3.10	2.83	2.64	2.22
North Dakota	5.69	6.52	7.05	6.73	8.02	6.01	4.36
South Dakota	3.35	4.03	5.41	5.58	7.27	5.65	4.33
Nebraska	4.44	4.41	3.11	3.59	3.57	3.24	2.78
Kansas	2.20	1.77	2.08	2.68	3.27	3.29	2.66
Virginia	3.05	2.40	1.72	1.88	2.44	2.65	2.22
West Virginia	2.44	2.32	1.55	1.36	a	a	1.59
North Carolina	2.70	1.08	1.34	2.12	1.30	1.79	1.59
South Carolina	1.07	.86	.48	1.01	1.54	1.65	a
Georgia	1.23	1.45	1.13	1.27	1.97	2.19	a
Florida	5.94	4.91	4.54	5.24	5.51	4.59	3.90
Kentucky	4.01	3.65	3.38	3.55	3.20	3.12	2.30
Tennessee	3.61	2.78	.70	2.04	2.40	1.90	1.99
Alabama	2.92	2.22	.79	1.22	1.66	1.69	a
Mississippi	4.08	3.38	3.66	4.66	4.67	3.59	a
Arkansas	5.84	5.50	4.01	4.33	4.46	3.22	2.64
Louisiana	4.53	3.86	3.27	5.26	3.05	2.55	2.06
Oklahoma	4.32	4.37	3.24	3.39	3.26	3.12	2.36
Texas	4.82	4.38	2.94	3.18	3.09	2.82	2.36
Montana	1.57	.84	.74	.81	a	a	a
Idaho	4.85	1.22	1.37	.70	2.00	2.06	1.56
Wyoming	5.51	5.08	3.32	4.97	5.17	4.49	3.64
Colorado	2.57	2.49	2.09	2.85	3.39	4.10	3.10
New Mexico	5.66	4.93	4.93	5.32	7.15	a	a
Arizona	5.72	3.12	2.65	2.59	2.53	a	a
Utah	9.01	1.42	.98	4.41	a	a	a
Nevada	1.14	1.34	1.46	1.65	2.54	2.70	2.47
Washington	1.06	2.57	1.66	1.41	1.51	1.45	1.44
Oregon	1.94	2.09	2.11	1.39	2.09	2.10	1.89
California	1.97	1.39	1.29	1.57	2.18	2.20	1.82

SOURCE: U.S. Bureau of the Census, Census of Electrical Industries, quinquennial.
a Not presented separately to avoid disclosure of information for individual establishments. Where data for two or more adjoining states are presented, the combined data were used provided the states in the combination had the same regulation status in the year under consideration. Rates for combinations employed are as follows: Vermont and Rhode Island, 1927=3.44, 1932=3.54, 1937=2.81; Montana and Utah, 1927=1.08, 1932=1.94, 1937=1.13; Delaware, Maryland, and Washington, D.C., 1907=3.68, 1912=3.22, 1917=2.01, 1922=2.52, 1937=1.95; Delaware, Maryland, Washington, D.C., and West Virginia, 1927=2.39, 1932=2.35. Combinations of Delaware with adjoining states do not meet the above criterion but are included because Delaware's rated horsepower capacity is less than 10 percent (in 1927) of the total for either combination.

TABLE 14.11

AVERAGE REVENUE PER KWH BY STATE AND TYPE OF CUSTOMER,
IN CENTS, 1932 AND 1937

State	DOMESTIC		COMMERCIAL AND INDUSTRIAL	
	1932	1937	1932	1937
Maine	6.4	5.3	1.4	1.5
New Hampshire	7.3	5.6	2.9	2.4
Vermont and Rhode Island	7.0[a]	5.8[a]	2.7[a]	2.2[a]
Massachusetts	6.1	5.3	3.0	2.4
Connecticut	5.5	4.6	2.8	2.3
New York	6.2	5.0	2.4	1.8
New Jersey	7.3	5.5	3.1	2.4
Pennsylvania	5.9	4.6	2.0	1.6
Ohio	5.4	3.9	2.2	1.6
Indiana	6.0	4.7	2.5	1.8
Illinois	5.3	4.3	2.0	1.8
Michigan	4.4	3.5	2.2	1.6
Wisconsin	5.4	3.8	2.6	2.0
Minnesota	5.7	4.1	2.6	2.2
Iowa	6.6	5.0	2.8	2.1
Missouri	4.9	3.9	2.2	1.8
North Dakota	7.0	4.7	5.4	4.2
South Dakota	7.1	5.1	4.9	3.9
Nebraska	5.7	4.6	2.7	2.3
Kansas	5.5	4.9	2.5	2.1
Delaware, Maryland, and Washington, D.C.	[b]	3.8[a]	[b]	1.6[a]
Delaware, Maryland, Washington, D.C., and West Virginia	5.0[a]	—	1.9[a]	—
Virginia	5.6	4.1	2.0	1.8
West Virginia	[b]	4.4	[b]	1.3
North Carolina	5.8	3.8	1.4	1.4
South Carolina	5.6	[a]	1.4	[a]
Georgia	5.4	[a]	1.8	[a]
Florida	6.7	5.3	3.6	3.2
Kentucky	6.2	4.2	2.5	1.9
Tennessee	6.2	3.4	1.4	1.7
Alabama	5.3	[a]	1.4	[a]
Mississippi	6.6	[a]	3.0	[a]
Arkansas	7.3	5.7	2.6	2.2
Louisiana	7.6	5.7	1.9	1.6
Oklahoma	6.3	5.3	2.6	1.9
Texas	6.2	4.8	2.3	1.9
Montana and Utah	4.8[a]	4.0[a]	1.6[a]	.9[a]
Idaho	3.6	3.1	1.7	1.3
Wyoming	6.8	6.1	3.8	3.0
Colorado	6.1	5.5	3.4	2.5
New Mexico	[a]	[a]	[a]	[a]
Arizona	[a]	[a]	[a]	[a]
Nevada	5.0	4.2	2.3	2.1
Washington	2.7	2.7	1.3	1.2
Oregon	3.2	2.8	1.7	1.6
California	4.3	3.8	1.8	1.5

SOURCE: U.S. Bureau of the Census, Census of Electrical Industries, quinquennial.

[a] Not presented separately to avoid disclosure of information for individual establishments. See Table 14.10, footnote, for criterion for inclusion.

[b] See combined data for Delaware, Maryland, Washington, D.C., and West Virginia.

TABLE 14.12

REGRESSION EQUATIONS OF AVERAGE REVENUE PER KWH[a] ON OUTPUT,
OUTPUT PER CUSTOMER, INCOME, AND REGULATION, 1907–1937

				REGRESSION COEFFICIENTS AND THEIR STANDARD ERRORS			R^2	
Year	Number of States	Constant Term	Output[b]	Output per Customer[d]	Per Capita Income[e]	Regulation	Including Regulation	Excluding Regulation
1907	45	.502	.0039 (.0427)	−.628 (.072)	.0882 (.1279)	—	c	.737
1912	47	.648	−.0237 (.0649)	−.702 (.089)	.0497 (.2032)	.0112 (.0816)	.701	.701
1917	47	1.061	−.0268 (.0357)	−.631 (.060)	−.138 (.141)	.0269 (.0346)	.850	.848
1922	47	.928	−.0155 (.0282)	−.692 (.051)	−.0662 (.1055)	.0283 (.0350)	.890	.889
1927	45	1.157	−.0274 (.0188)	−.664 (.048)	−.118 (.071)	.0029 (.0252)	.921	.921
1932	38	.772	−.0383 (.0167)	−.700 (.049)	.0479 (.0548)	−.0219 (.0195)	.907	.903
1937	38	.655	−.0456 (.0145)	−.672 (.047)	.0876 (.0545)	−.0210 (.0180)	.921	.917

[a] Cents, in logarithms.
[b] Millions of kwh, in logarithms.
[c] Not computed because only Massachusetts was regulated.
[d] Thousands of kwh, in logarithms.
[e] Dollars, in logarithms.

TABLE 14.13

REGRESSION EQUATIONS OF AVERAGE REVENUE PER KWH[a] ON OUTPUT,
OUTPUT PER CUSTOMER, AND INCOME, BY TYPE OF CUSTOMER, 1932 AND 1937

	Number of States	Constant Term	Output[b]	Output per Customer[c]	Per Capita Income[d]	Regulation	Including Regulation	Excluding Regulation
							R^2	
Year							Including Regulation	Excluding Regulation
I. Sales to Domestic Customers								
1932	37	.628	−.0492 (.0145)	−.807 (.068)	.0407 (.0509)	−.0140 (.0193)	.843	.840
1937	38	.522	−.0520 (.0110)	−.807 (.056)	.0835 (.0450)	−.0270 (.0145)	.882	.870
II. Sales to Commercial and Industrial Customers								
1932	37	.969	−.0382 (.0312)	−.694 (.120)	—	−.0565 (.0362)	.630	.603
1937	38	.870	−.0541 (.0278)	−.602 (.113)	—	−.0380 (.0352)	.668	.657

[a] Cents, in logarithms.
[b] Millions of kwh, in logarithms.
[c] Thousands of kwh, in logarithms.
[d] Dollars, in logarithms.

THE THEORY OF
ECONOMIC REGULATION

· 15 ·

The state—the machinery and power of the state—is a potential resource or threat to every industry in the society. With its power to prohibit or compel, to take or give money, the state can and does selectively help or hurt a vast number of industries. That political juggernaut, the petroleum industry, is an immense consumer of political benefits, and simultaneously the underwriters of marine insurance have their more modest repast. The central tasks of the theory of economic regulation are to explain who will receive the benefits or burdens of regulation, what form regulation will take, and the effects of regulation upon the allocation of resources.

Regulation may be actively sought by an industry, or it may be thrust upon it. A central thesis of this paper is that, as a rule, regulation is acquired by the industry and is designed and operated primarily for its benefit. There are regulations whose net effects upon the regulated industry are undeniably onerous; a simple example is the differentially heavy taxation of the industry's product (whiskey, playing cards). These onerous regulations, however, are exceptional and can be explained by the same theory that explains beneficial (we may call it "acquired") regulation.

Two main alternative views of the regulation of industry are widely held. The first is that regulation is instituted primarily for the protection and benefit

From the Bell Journal of Economics and Management Science 2, no. 1 (Spring 1971). Permission to reprint courtesy of the Rand Journal of Economics.

of the public at large or some large subclass of the public. In this view, the regulations which injure the public—as when the oil import quotas increase the cost of petroleum products to America by $5 billion or more a year—are costs of some social goal (here, national defense) or, occasionally, perversions of the regulatory philosophy. The second view is essentially that the political process defies rational explanation: "politics" is an imponderable, a constantly and unpredictably shifting mixture of forces of the most diverse nature, comprehending acts of great moral virtue (the emancipation of slaves) and of the most vulgar venality (the congressman feathering his own nest).

Let us consider a problem posed by the oil import quota system: why does not the powerful industry which obtained this expensive program instead choose direct cash subsidies from the public treasury? The "protection of the public" theory of regulation must say that the choice of import quotas is dictated by the concern of the federal government for an adequate domestic supply of petroleum in the event of war—a remark calculated to elicit up-roarious laughter at the Petroleum Club. Such laughter aside, if national defense were the goal of the quotas, a tariff would be a more economical instrument of policy: it would retain the profits of exclusion for the treasury. The nonrationalist view would explain the policy by the inability of consumers to measure the cost to them of the import quotas, and hence their willingness to pay $5 billion in higher prices rather than the $2.5 billion in cash that would be equally attractive to the industry. Our profit-maximizing theory says that the explanation lies in a different direction: the present members of the refining industries would have to share a cash subsidy with all new entrants into the refining industry.[1] Only when the elasticity of supply of an industry is small will the industry prefer cash to controls over entry or output.

This question, why does an industry solicit the coercive powers of the state rather than its cash, is offered only to illustrate the approach of the present paper. We assume that political systems are rationally devised and rationally employed, which is to say that they are appropriate instruments for the fulfillment of desires of members of the society. This is not to say that the state will serve any person's concept of the public interest: indeed the problem of regulation is the problem of discovering when and why an industry (or other group of likeminded people) is able to use the state for its purposes, or is singled out by the state to be used for alien purposes.

I. What Benefits Can a State Provide to an Industry?

The state has one basic resource which in pure principle is not shared with even the mightiest of its citizens: the power to coerce. The state can seize money by the only method which is permitted by the laws of a civilized society, by taxation. The state can ordain the physical movements of resources and the economic decisions of households and firms without their consent. These powers provide the possibilities for the utilization of the state by an industry to increase its profitability. The main policies which an industry (or occupation) may seek of the state are four.

The most obvious contribution that a group may seek of the government is a direct subsidy of money. The domestic airlines received "air mail" subsidies (even if they did not carry mail) of $1.5 billion through 1968. The merchant marine has received construction and operation subsidies reaching almost $3 billion since World War II. The education industry has long shown a masterful skill in obtaining public funds: for example, universities and colleges have received federal funds exceeding $3 billion annually in recent years, as well as subsidized loans for dormitories and other construction. The veterans of wars have often received direct cash bonuses.

We have already sketched the main explanation for the fact that an industry with power to obtain governmental favors usually does not use this power to get money: unless the list of beneficiaries can be limited by an acceptable device, whatever amount of subsidies the industry can obtain will be dissipated among a growing number of rivals. The airlines quickly moved away from competitive bidding for air mail contracts to avoid this problem.[2] On the other hand, the premier universities have not devised a method of excluding other claimants for research funds, and in the long run they will receive much-reduced shares of federal research monies.

The second major public resource commonly sought by an industry is control over entry by new rivals. There is considerable, not to say excessive, discussion in economic literature of the rise of peculiar price policies (limit prices), vertical integration, and similar devices to retard the rate of entry of new firms into oligopolistic industries. Such devices are vastly less efficacious (economical) than the certificate of convenience and necessity (which in-cludes, of course, the import and production quotas of the oil and tobacco industries).

The diligence with which the power of control over entry will be exercised by a regulatory body is already well known. The Civil Aeronautics Board has not allowed a single new trunk line to be launched since it was created in 1938. The power to insure new banks has been used by the Federal Deposit Insurance Corporation to reduce the rate of entry into commercial banking by 60 percent.[3] The interstate motor carrier history is in some respects even more striking, because no even ostensibly respectable case for restriction on entry can be developed on grounds of scale economies (which are in turn adduced to limit entry for safety or economy of operation). The number of federally licensed common carriers is shown in Figure 15.1: the immense growth of the

FIGURE 15.1
CERTIFICATES FOR INTERSTATE MOTOR CARRIERS

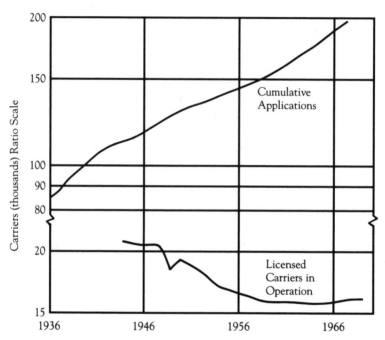

SOURCE: Table 15.5.

freight hauled by trucking common carriers has been associated with a steady secular decline of numbers of such carriers. The number of applications for new certificates has been in excess of 5,000 annually in recent years: a rigorous proof that hope springs eternal in an aspiring trucker's breast.

We propose the general hypothesis: every industry or occupation that has enough political power to utilize the state will seek to control entry. In addition, the regulatory policy will often be so fashioned as to retard the rate of growth of new firms. For example, no new savings and loan company may pay a dividend rate higher than that prevailing in the community in its endeavors to attract deposits.[4] The power to limit selling expenses of mutual funds, which is soon to be conferred upon the Securities and Exchange Commission, will serve to limit the growth of small mutual funds and hence reduce the sales costs of large funds.

One variant of the control of entry is the protective tariff (and the corresponding barriers which have been raised to interstate movement of goods and people). The benefits of protection to an industry, one might think, will usually be dissipated by the entry of new domestic producers, and the question naturally arises: why does the industry not also seek domestic entry controls? In a few industries (petroleum) the domestic controls have been obtained, but not in most. The tariff will be effective if there is a specialized domestic resource necessary to the industry; oil-producing lands is an example. Even if an industry has only durable specialized resources, it will gain if its contraction is slowed by a tariff.

A third general set of powers of the state which will be sought by the industry are those which affect substitutes and complements. Crudely put, the butter producers wish to suppress margarine and encourage the production of bread. The airline industry actively supports the federal subsidies to airports; the building trade unions have opposed labor-saving materials through building codes. We shall examine shortly a specific case of interindustry competition in transportation.

The fourth class of public policies sought by an industry is directed to price fixing. Even the industry that has achieved entry control will often want price controls administered by a body with coercive powers. If the number of firms in the regulated industry is even moderately large, price discrimination will be difficult to maintain in the absence of public support. The prohibition of interest on demand deposits, which is probably effective in preventing interest payments to most nonbusiness depositors, is a case in point. Where there are no diseconomies of large scale for the individual firm (e.g., a motor trucking firm can add trucks under a given license as common carrier), price control is essential to achieve more than competitive rates of return.

Limitations upon political benefits

These various political boons are not obtained by the industry in a pure profit-maximizing form. The political process erects certain limitations upon the exercise of cartel policies by an industry. These limitations are of three sorts.

First, the distribution of control of the industry among the firms in the industry is changed. In an unregulated industry each firm's influence upon price and output is proportional to its share of industry output (at least in a simple arithmetic sense of direct capacity to change output). The political decisions take account also of the political strength of the various firms, so small firms have a larger influence than they would possess in an unregulated industry. Thus, when quotas are given to firms, the small firms will almost always receive larger quotas than cost-minimizing practices would allow. The original quotas under the oil import quota system will illustrate this practice (Table 15.1). The smallest refiners were given a quota of 11.4 percent of their

TABLE 15.1
IMPORT QUOTAS OF REFINERIES AS PERCENT OF DAILY INPUT OF PETROLEUM
(DISTRICTS I–IV, JULY 1, 1959–DEC. 31, 1959)

Size of Refinery (thousands of barrels)	Percent Quota
0–10	11.4
10–20	10.4
20–30	9.5
30–60	8.5
60–100	7.6
100–150	6.6
150–200	5.7
200–300	4.7
300 and over	3.8

SOURCE: Hearing, Select Committee on Small Business, U.S. Congress, 88th Cong., 2nd Sess., Aug. 10 and 11, 1964, p. 121.

daily consumption of oil, and the percentage dropped as refinery size rose.[5] The pattern of regressive benefits is characteristic of public controls in industries with numerous firms.

Second, the procedural safeguards required of public processes are costly. The delays which are dictated by both law and bureaucratic thoughts of self-survival can be large: Robert Gerwig found the price of gas sold in interstate commerce to be 5 to 6 percent higher than in intrastate commerce because of the administrative costs (including delay) of Federal Power Commission reviews.[6]

Finally, the political process automatically admits powerful outsiders to the industry's councils. It is well known that the allocation of television channels among communities does not maximize industry revenue but reflects pressures to serve many smaller communities. The abandonment of an unprofitable rail line is an even more notorious area of outsider participation.

These limitations are predictable, and they must all enter into the calculus of the profitability of regulation of an industry.

An illustrative analysis

The recourse to the regulatory process is of course more specific and more complex than the foregoing sketch suggests. The defensive power of various other industries which are affected by the proposed regulation must also be taken into account. An analysis of one aspect of the regulation of motor trucking will illustrate these complications. At this stage we are concerned only with the correspondence between regulations and economic interests; later we shall consider the political process by which regulation is achieved.

The motor trucking industry operated almost exclusively within cities before 1925, in good part because neither powerful trucks nor good roads were available for long-distance freight movements. As these deficiencies were gradually remedied, the share of trucks in intercity freight movements began to rise, and by 1930 it was estimated to be 4 percent of ton-miles of intercity freight. The railroad industry took early cognizance of this emerging competitor, and one of the methods by which trucking was combatted was state regulation.

By the early 1930s all states regulated the dimensions and weight of trucks. The weight limitations were a much more pervasive control over trucking than the licensing of common carriers because even the trucks exempt from entry regulation are subject to the limitations on dimensions and capacity. The weight regulations in the early 1930s are reproduced in the Appendix (Table 15.6). Sometimes the participation of railroads in the regulatory process was incontrovertible: Texas and Louisiana placed a 7,000-pound payload limit on trucks serving (and hence competing with) two or more railroad stations, and a 14,000-pound limit on trucks serving only one station (hence, not competing with it).

We seek to determine the pattern of weight limits on trucks that would emerge in response to the economic interests of the concerned parties. The main considerations appear to be the following:

1. Heavy trucks would be allowed in states with a substantial number of trucks on farms: the powerful agricultural interests would insist upon this. The 1930 Census reports nearly 1 million trucks on farms. One variable in our study will be, for each state, trucks per 1,000 of agricultural population.[7]

2. Railroads found the truck an effective and rapidly triumphing competitor in the shorter hauls and hauls of less than carload traffic, but much less effective in the carload and longer-haul traffic. Our second variable for each state is, therefore, length of average railroad haul.[8] The longer the average rail haul is, the less the railroads will be opposed to trucks.

3. The public at large would be concerned by the potential damage done to the highway system by heavy trucks. The better the state highway system, the heavier the trucks that would be permitted. The percentage of each state's highways that had a high-type surface is the third variable. Of course good highways are more likely to exist where the

TABLE 15.2

REGRESSION ANALYSIS OF STATE WEIGHT LIMITS ON TRUCKS
(T VALUES UNDER REGRESSION COEFFICIENTS)

Dependent Variable	N	Constant	X_3	X_4	X_5	R^2
X_1	48	12.28 (4.87)	0.0336 (3.99)	0.0287 (2.77)	0.2641 (3.04)	0.502
X_2	46	10.34 (1.57)	0.0437 (2.01)	0.0788 (2.97)	0.2528 (1.15)	0.243

X_1 = Weight limit on four wheel trucks (thousands of pounds), 1932–33
X_2 = Weight limit on six wheel trucks (thousands of pounds), 1932–33
X_3 = Trucks on farms per 1,000 agricultural labor force, 1930
X_4 = Average length of railroad haul of freight (miles), 1930
X_5 = Percent of state highways with high type surface, Dec. 31, 1930

SOURCES: X_1 and X_2: *The Motor Truck Red Book and Directory*, 1934 ed., pp. 85–102, and U.S. Dept. of Agric., Bur. of Public Roads, Dec. 1932.

X_3: *Census of Agriculture*, 1930, Vol. IV.

X_4: A.A.R.R., Bur. of Railway Economics, *Railway Mileage by States*, Dec. 31, 1930, and U.S.I.C.C., *Statistics of Railways in the U.S.*, 1930.

X_5: *Statistical Abstract of the U.S.*, 1932.

potential contribution of trucks to a state's economy is greater, so the causation may be looked at from either direction.

We have two measures of weight limits on trucks, one for 4-wheel trucks (X_1) and one for 6-wheel trucks (X_2). We may then calculate two equations,

$$X_1 \text{ (or } X_2) = a + bX_3 + cX_4 + dX_5,$$

where X_3 = trucks per 1000 agricultural labor force, 1930,
X_4 = average length of railroad haul of freight traffic, 1930,
X_5 = percentage of state roads with high-quality surface, 1930.

(All variables are fully defined and their state values given in Table 15.7.)
The three explanatory variables are statistically significant, and each works in the expected direction. The regulations on weight were less onerous: the larger the truck population in farming, the less competitive the trucks were to railroads (i.e., the longer the rail hauls), and the better the highway system (see Table 15.2).

The foregoing analysis is concerned with what may be termed the industrial demand for governmental powers. Not every industry will have a significant demand for public assistance (other than money!), meaning the prospect of a substantial increase in the present value of the enterprises even if the governmental services could be obtained gratis (and of course they have costs to which we soon turn). In some economic activities entry of new rivals is extremely difficult to control—consider the enforcement problem in restricting the supply of domestic servants. In some industries the substitute products cannot be efficiently controlled—consider the competition offered to bus lines by private carpooling. Price fixing is not feasible where every unit of the product has a different quality and price, as in the market for used automobiles. In general, however, most industries will have a positive demand price (schedule) for the services of government.

II. The Costs of Obtaining Legislation

When an industry receives a grant of power from the state, the benefit to the industry will fall short of the damage to the rest of the community. Even if there were no deadweight losses from acquired regulation, however, one might expect a democratic society to reject such industry requests unless the industry controlled a majority of the votes.[9] A direct and informed vote on oil import quotas would reject the scheme. (If it did not, our theory of rational political processes would be contradicted.) To explain why many industries are able to employ political machinery to their own ends, we must examine the nature of the political process in a democracy.

A consumer chooses between rail and air travel, for example, by voting with his pocketbook: he patronizes on a given day that mode of transportation he prefers. A similar form of economic voting occurs with decisions on where to work or where to invest one's capital. The market accumulates these economic votes, predicts their future course, and invests accordingly.

Because the political decision is coercive, the decision process is fundamentally different from that of the market. If the public is asked to make a decision between two transportation media comparable to the individual's decision on how to travel—say, whether airlines or railroads should receive a federal subsidy—the decision must be abided by everyone, travellers and nontravellers, travellers this year and travellers next year. This compelled universality of political decisions makes for two differences between democratic political decision processes and market processes.

1. The decisions must be made simultaneously by a large number of persons (or their representatives): the political process demands simultaneity of decision. If A were to vote on the referendum today, B

tomorrow, C the day after, and so on, the accumulation of a majority decision would be both expensive and suspect. (A might wish to cast a different vote now than last month.)

The condition of simultaneity imposes a major burden upon the political decision process. It makes voting on specific issues prohibitively expensive: it is a significant cost even to engage in the transaction of buying a plane ticket when I wish to travel; it would be stupendously expensive to me to engage in the physically similar transaction of voting (i.e., patronizing a polling place) whenever a number of my fellow citizens desired to register their views on railroads versus airplanes. To cope with this condition of simultaneity, the voters must employ representatives with wide discretion and must eschew direct expressions of marginal changes in preferences. This characteristic also implies that the political decision does not predict voter desires and make preparations to fulfill them in advance of their realization.

2. The democratic decision process must involve "all" the community, not simply those who are directly concerned with a decision. In a private market, the nontraveller never votes in rail versus plane travel, while the huge shipper casts many votes each day. The political decision process cannot exclude the uninterested voter: the abuses of any exclusion except self-exclusion are obvious. Hence, the political process does not allow participation in proportion to interest and knowledge. In a measure, this difficulty is moderated by other political activities besides voting which do allow a more effective vote to interested parties: persuasion, employment of skilled legislative representatives, etc. Nevertheless, the political system does not offer good incentives like those in private markets to the acquisition of knowledge. If I consume ten times as much of public service A (streets) as of B (schools), I do not have incentives to acquire corresponding amounts of knowledge about the public provision of these services.[10]

These characteristics of the political process can be modified by having numerous levels of government (so I have somewhat more incentive to learn about local schools than about the whole state school system) and by selective use of direct decision (bond referenda). The chief method of coping with the characteristics, however, is to employ more or less full-time representatives organized in (disciplined by) firms which are called political parties or machines.

The representative and his party are rewarded for their discovery and fulfillment of the political desires of their constituency by success in election and the perquisites of office. If the representative could confidently await reelection whenever he voted against an economic policy that injured the society, he would assuredly do so. Unfortunately virtue does not always command so high a price. If the representative denies ten large industries their special subsidies of money or governmental power, they will dedicate themselves to the election of a more complaisant successor: the stakes are that important. This does not mean that every large industry can get what it wants or all that it wants: it does mean that the representative and his party must find a coalition of voter interests more durable than the anti-industry side of every industry policy proposal. A representative cannot win or keep office with the support of the sum of those who are opposed to: oil import quotas, farm subsidies, airport subsidies, hospital subsidies, unnecessary navy shipyards, an inequitable public housing program, and rural electrification subsidies.

The political decision process has as its dominant characteristic infrequent, universal (in principle) participation, as we have noted: political decisions must be infrequent and they must be global. The voter's expenditure to learn the merits of individual policy proposals and to express his preferences (by individual and group representation as well as by voting) are determined by expected costs and returns, just as they are in the private marketplace. The costs of comprehensive information are higher in the political arena because information must be sought on many issues of little or no direct concern to the individual, and accordingly he will know little about most matters before the legislature. The expression of preferences in voting will be less precise than the expressions of preferences in the marketplace because many uninformed people will be voting and affecting the decision.[11]

The channels of political decision-making can thus be described as gross or filtered or noisy. If everyone has a negligible preference for policy A over B, the preference will not be discovered or acted upon. If voter group X wants a policy that injures non-X by a small amount, it will not pay non-X to discover this and act against the policy. The system is calculated to implement all strongly felt preferences of majorities and many strongly felt preferences of minorities but to disregard the lesser preferences of majorities and minorities. The filtering or grossness will be reduced by any reduction in the cost to the citizen of acquiring information and expressing desires and by any increase in the probability that his vote will influence policy.

The industry which seeks political power must go to the appropriate seller, the political party. The political party has costs of operation, costs of maintaining an organization and competing in elections. These costs of the political process are viewed excessively narrowly in the literature on the financing of elections: elections are to the political process what merchandizing is to the process of producing a commodity, only an essential final step. The party maintains its organization and electoral appeal by the performance of costly services to the voter at all times, not just before elections. Part of the costs of services and organization are borne by putting a part of the party's workers on the public payroll. An opposition party, however, is usually essential insurance for the voters to discipline the party in power, and the opposition party's costs are not fully met by public funds.

The industry which seeks regulation must be prepared to pay with the two things a party needs: votes and resources. The resources may be provided by campaign contributions, contributed services (the businessman heads a fund-raising committee), and more indirect methods such as the employment of party workers. The votes in support of the measure are rallied, and the votes in opposition are dispersed, by expensive programs to educate (or uneducate) members of the industry and of other concerned industries.

These costs of legislation probably increase with the size of the industry seeking the legislation. Larger industries seek programs which cost the society more and arouse more opposition from substantially affected groups. The tasks of persuasion, both within and without the industry, also increase with its size. The fixed size of the political "market," however, probably makes the cost of obtaining legislation increase less rapidly than industry size. The smallest industries are therefore effectively precluded from the political process unless they have some special advantage such as geographical concentration in a sparsely settled political subdivision.

If a political party has in effect a monopoly control over the governmental machine, one might expect that it could collect most of the benefits of regulation for itself. Political parties, however, are perhaps an ideal illustration of Demsetz's theory of natural monopoly.[12] If one party becomes extortionate (or badly mistaken in its reading of effective desires), it is possible to elect another party which will provide the governmental services at a price more closely proportioned to the costs of the party. If entry into politics is effectively controlled, we should expect one-party dominance to lead that party to solicit requests for protective legislation but to exact a higher price for the legislation.

The internal structure of the political party, and the manner in which the perquisites of office are distributed among its members, offer fascinating areas for study in this context. The elective officials are at the pinnacle of the political system—there is no substitute for the ability to hold the public offices. I conjecture that much of the compensation to the legislative leaders takes the form of extrapolitical payments. Why are so many politicians lawyers? Because everyone employs lawyers, so the congressman's firm is a suitable avenue of compensation, whereas a physician would have to be given bribes rather than patronage. Most enterprises patronize insurance companies and banks, so we may expect that legislators commonly have financial affiliations with such enterprises.

The financing of industry-wide activities such as the pursuit of legislation raises the usual problem of the free rider.[13] We do not possess a satisfactory theory of group behavior—indeed this theory is the theory of oligopoly with one addition: in the very large number industry (e.g., agriculture) the political party itself will undertake the entrepreneurial role in providing favorable legislation. We can go no further than the infirmities of oligopoly theory allow, which is to say, we can make only plausible conjectures such as that the more concentrated the industry, the more resources it can invest in the campaign for legislation.

Occupational Licensing

The licensing of occupations is a possible use of the political process to improve the economic circumstances of a group. The license is an effective barrier to entry because occupational practice without the license is a criminal offense. Since much occupational licensing is performed at the state level, the area provides an opportunity to search for the characteristics of an occupation which give it political power.

Although there are serious data limitations, we may investigate several characteristics of an occupation which should influence its ability to secure political power:

1. *The size of the occupation.* Quite simply, the larger the occupation, the more votes it has. (Under some circumstances, therefore, one would wish to exclude noncitizens from the measure of size.)

2. *The per capita income of the occupation.* The income of the occupation is the product of its numbers and average income, so this variable and the preceding will reflect the total income of the occupation. The income of the occupation is presumably an index of the probable rewards of successful political action: in the absence of specific knowledge of supply and demand functions, we expect licensing to increase each occupation's equilibrium income by roughly the same proportion. In a more sophisticated version, one would predict that the less the elasticity of demand for the occupation's services, the more profitable licensing would be. One could also view the income of the occupation as a source of funds for political action, but if we view political action as an investment this is relevant only with capital-market imperfections.[14]

The average income of occupational members is an appropriate variable in comparisons among occupations, but it is inappropriate to comparisons of one occupation in various states because real income will be approximately equal (in the absence of regulation) in each state.

3. *The concentration of the occupation in large cities.* When the occupation organizes a campaign to obtain favorable legislation, it incurs expenses in the solicitation of support, and these are higher for a diffused occupation than a concentrated one. The solicitation of support is

complicated by the free-rider problem in that individual members cannot be excluded from the benefits of legislation even if they have not
shared the costs of receiving it. If most of the occupation is concentrated
in a few large centers, these problems (we suspect) are much reduced in
intensity: regulation may even begin at the local governmental level. We
shall use an orthodox geographical concentration measure: the share of
the occupation in the state in cities over 100,000 (or 50,000 in 1900 and
earlier).

4. *The presence of a cohesive opposition to licensing.* If an occupation
deals with the public at large, the costs which licensing imposes upon
any one customer or industry will be small and it will not be economic for
that customer or industry to combat the drive for licensure. If the injured
group finds it feasible and profitable to act jointly, however, it will oppose
the effort to get licensure, and (by increasing its cost) weaken, delay, or
prevent the legislation. The same attributes—number of voters, wealth,
and ease of organization—which favor an occupation in the political
arena, of course, favor also any adversary group. Thus, a small occupation
employed by only one industry which has few employers will have
difficulty in getting licensure; whereas a large occupation serving everyone will encounter no organized opposition.

An introductory statistical analysis of the licensing of select occupations
by states is summarized in Table 15.3. In each occupation the dependent
variable for each state is the year of first regulation of entry into the occupation. The two independent variables are: (1) the ratio of the occupation to the
total labor force of the state in the census year nearest to the median year of
regulation; (2) the fraction of the occupation found in cities over 100,000 (over
50,000 in 1890 and 1900) in that same year. We expect these variables to be
negatively associated with year of licensure, and each of the nine statistically
significant regression coefficients is of the expected sign.

The results are not robust, however: the multiple correlation coefficients
are small, and over half of the regression coefficients are not significant (and in
these cases often of inappropriate sign). Urbanization is more strongly associated than size of occupation with licensure.[15] The crudity of the data may be a
large source of these disappointments: we measure, for example, the characteristics of the barbers in each state in 1930, but fourteen states were licensing
barbers by 1910. If the states which licensed barbering before 1910 had
relatively more barbers, or more highly urbanized barbers, the predictions
would be improved. The absence of data for years between censuses and before
1890 led us to make only the cruder analysis.[16]

In general, the larger occupations were licensed in earlier years.[17] Veteri-
narians are the only occupation in this sample who have a well-defined set of

TABLE 15.3

INITIAL YEAR OF REGULATION AS A FUNCTION OF RELATIVE SIZE OF
OCCUPATION AND DEGREE OF URBANIZATION

Occupation	Number of States Licensing	Median Census Year of Licensing	REGRESSION COEFFICIENTS (AND T-VALUES)		R^2
			Size of Occupation (relative to labor force)	Urbanization (share of occupation in cities over 100,000)[a]	
Beauticians	48	1930	−4.03 (2.50)	5.90 (1.24)	0.125
Architects	47	1930	−24.06 (2.15)	−6.29 (0.84)	0.184
Barbers	46	1930	−1.31 (0.51)	−26.10 (2.37)	0.146
Lawyers	29	1890	−0.26 (0.08)	−65.78 (1.70)	0.102
Physicians	43	1890	0.64 (0.65)	−23.80 (2.69)	0.165
Embalmers	37	1910	3.32 (0.36)	−4.24 (0.44)	0.007
Registered Nurses	48	1910	−2.08 (2.28)	−3.36 (1.06)	0.176
Dentists	48	1900	2.51 (0.44)	−22.94 (2.19)	0.103
Veterinarians	40	1910	−10.69 (1.94)	−37.16 (4.20)	0.329
Chiropractors	48	1930	−17.70 (1.54)	11.69 (1.25)	0.079
Pharmacists	48	1900	−4.19 (1.50)	−6.84 (0.80)	0.082

SOURCES: The Council of State Governments, "Occupational Licensing Legislation in the States," 1952, and U.S. Census of Population, various years.
[a] 50,000 in 1890 and 1900.

customers, namely livestock farmers, and licensing was later in those states with large numbers of livestock relative to rural population. The within-occupation analyses offer some support for the economic theory of the supply of legislation.

A comparison of different occupations allows us to examine several other variables. The first is income, already discussed above. The second is the size of the market. Just as it is impossible to organize an effective labor union in only one part of an integrated market, so it is impossible to regulate only one part of the market. Consider an occupation—junior business executives will do—which has a national market with high mobility of labor and significant mobility of employers. If the executives of one state were to organize, their scope for effective influence would be very small. If salaries were raised above the competitive level, employers would often recruit elsewhere so the demand elasticity would be very high.[18] The third variable is stability of occupational membership: the longer the members are in the occupation, the greater their financial gain from control of entry. Our regrettably crude measure of this variable is based upon the number of members aged 35–44 in 1950 and aged 45–54 in 1960: the closer these numbers are, the more stable the membership of the occupation. The data for the various occupations are given in Table 15.4.

The comparison of licensed and unlicensed occupations is consistently in keeping with our expectations: (1) the licensed occupations have higher incomes (also before licensing, one may assume); (2) the membership of the licensed occupations is more stable (but the difference is negligible in our crude measure); (3) the licensed occupations are less often employed by business enterprises (who have incentives to oppose licensing); (4) all occupations in national markets (college teachers, engineers, scientists, accountants) are unlicensed or only partially licensed. The size and urbanization of the three groups, however, are unrelated to licensing. The interoccupational comparison therefore provides a modicum of additional support for our theory of regulation.

III. Conclusion

The idealistic view of public regulation is deeply imbedded in professional economic thought. So many economists, for example, have denounced the ICC for its prorailroad policies that this has become a cliché of the literature. This criticism seems to me exactly as appropriate as a criticism of the Great Atlantic and Pacific Tea Company for selling groceries, or as a criticism of a politician for currying popular support. The fundamental vice of such criticism is that it misdirects attention: it suggests that the way to get an ICC which is not subservient to the carriers is to preach to the commissioners or to the people who appoint the commissioners. The only way to get a different commission would be to change the political support for the Commission, and reward commissioners on a basis unrelated to their services to the carriers.

Until the basic logic of political life is developed, reformers will be ill equipped to use the state for their reforms, and victims of the pervasive use of

Table 15.4
Characteristics of Licensed and Unlicensed Professional Occupations, 1960

Occupation	Median Age (years)	Median Education (years)	Median Earnings (50–52 wks.)	Instability Of Membership[a]	Percent Not Self-Employed	Percent in Cities over 50,000	Percent of Labor Force
Licensed:							
Architects	41.7	16.8	$ 9,090	0.012	57.8%	44.1%	0.045%
Chiropractors	46.5	16.4	6,360	0.053	5.8	30.8	0.020
Dentists	45.9	17.3	12,200	0.016	9.4	34.5	0.128
Embalmers	43.5	13.4	5,990	0.130	52.8	30.2	0.055
Lawyers	45.3	17.4	10,800	0.041	35.8	43.1	0.308
Prof. Nurses	39.1	13.2	3,850	0.291	91.0	40.6	0.868
Optometrists	41.6	17.0	8,480	0.249	17.5	34.5	0.024
Pharmacists	44.9	16.2	7,230	0.119	62.3	40.0	0.136
Physicians	42.8	17.5	14,200	0.015	35.0	44.7	0.339
Veterinarians	39.2	17.4	9,210	0.169	29.5	14.4	0.023
Average	43.0	16.3	8,741	0.109	39.7	35.7	0.195
Partially Licensed:							
Accountants	40.4	14.9	6,450	0.052	88.1	43.5	0.698
Engineers	38.3	16.2	8,490	0.023	96.8	31.6	1.279
Elem. School Teachers	43.1	16.5	4,710	[b]	99.1	18.8	1.482
Average	40.6	15.9	6,550	0.117[c]	94.7	34.6	1.153
Unlicensed:							
Artists	38.0	14.2	5,920	0.103	77.3	45.7	0.154
Clergymen	43.3	17.0	4,120	0.039	89.0	27.2	0.295
College Teachers	40.3	17.4	7,500	0.085	99.2	36.0	0.261
Draftsmen	31.2	12.9	5,990	0.098	98.6	40.8	0.322
Reporters & Editors	39.4	15.5	6,120	0.138	93.9	43.3	0.151
Musicians	40.2	14.8	3,240	0.081	65.5	37.7	0.289
Natural Scientists	35.9	16.8	7,490	0.264	96.3	32.7	0.221
Average	38.3	15.5	5,768	0.115	88.5	37.6	0.242

Source: U.S. Census of Population, 1960.

[a] 1 − R where R=ratio: 1960 age 45–54 to 1950 age 35–44.

[b] Not available separately; Teachers N.E.C. (incl. secondary school and other)=0.276

[c] Includes figure for Teachers N.E.C. in note [b].

the state's support of special groups will be helpless to protect themselves. Economists should quickly establish the license to practice on the rational theory of political behavior.

Notes

1. The domestic producers of petroleum, who also benefit from the import quota, would find a tariff or cash payment to domestic producers equally attractive. If their interests alone were consulted, import quotas would be auctioned off instead of being given away.

2. See Keyes, L. S., *Federal Control of Entry into Air Transportation* (Cambridge, Mass.: Harvard University Press, 1951), pp. 60ff.

3. See Peltzman, S., "Entry in Commercial Banking," *Journal of Law and Economics* (October 1965).

4. The Federal Home Loan Bank Board is the regulatory body. It also controls the amount of advertising and other areas of competition.

5. The largest refineries were restricted to 75.7 percent of their historical quota under the earlier voluntary import quota plan.

6. Gerwig, R. W., "Natural Gas Production: A Study of Costs of Regulation," *Journal of Law and Economics* (October 1962): 69–92.

7. The ratio of trucks to total population would measure the product of (1) the importance of trucks to farmers, and (2) the importance of farmers in the state. For reasons given later, we prefer to emphasize (1).

8. This is known for each railroad, and we assume that (1) the average holds within each state, and (2) two or more railroads in a state may be combined on the basis of mileage. Obviously both assumptions are at best fair approximations.

9. If the deadweight loss (of consumer and producer surplus) is taken into account, even if the oil industry were in the majority it would not obtain the legislation if there were available some method of compensation (such as sale of votes) by which the larger damage of the minority could be expressed effectively against the lesser gains of the majority.

10. See Becker, G. S., "Competition and Democracy," *Journal of Law and Economics* (October 1958).

11. There is an organizational problem in any decision in which more than one vote is cast. If because of economies of scale it requires a thousand customers to buy a product before it can be produced, this thousand votes has to be assembled by some entrepreneur. Unlike the political scene, however, there is no need to obtain the consent of the remainder of the community, because they will bear no part of the cost.

12. Demsetz, H., "Why Regulate Utilities?," *Journal of Law and Economics* (April 1968).

13. The theory that the lobbying organization avoids the "free rider" problem by

selling useful services was proposed by Thomas G. Moore ("The Purpose of Licensing," *Journal of Law and Economics* [October 1961]) and elaborated by Mancur Olson (*The Logic of Collective Action* [Cambridge, Mass.: Harvard University Press, 1965]). The theory has not been tested empirically.

14. Let n=the number of members of the profession and y=average income. We expect political capacity to be in proportion to (ny) so far as benefits go, but to reflect also the direct value of votes, so the capacity becomes proportional to $(n^a y)$ with $a > 1$.

15. We may pool the occupations and assign dummy variables for each occupation; the regression coefficients then are:

size of occupation relative to labor force:	-0.450 (t=0.59)
urbanization :	-12.133 (t=4.00).

Thus urbanization is highly significant, while size of occupation is not significant.

16. A more precise analysis might take the form of a regression analysis such as:

Year of licensure=constant
    $+b_1$ (year of critical size of occupation)
    $+b_2$ (year of critical urbanization of occupation),

where the critical size and urbanization were defined as the mean size and mean urbanization in the year of licensure.

17. Lawyers, physicians, and pharmacists were all relatively large occupations by 1900, and nurses also by 1910. The only large occupation to be licensed later was barbers; the only small occupation to be licensed earlier was embalmers.

18. The regulation of business in a partial market will also generally produce very high supply elasticities within a market: if the price of the product (or service) is raised, the pressure of excluded supply is very difficult to resist. Some occupations are forced to reciprocity in licensing, and the geographical dispersion of earnings in licensed occupations, one would predict, is not appreciably different than in unlicensed occupations with equal employer mobility. Many puzzles are posed by the interesting analysis of Arlene S. Holen in "Effects of Professional Licensing Arrangements on Interstate Labor Mobility and Resource Allocation," *Journal of Political Economy* 73 (1915), pp. 492–98.

APPENDIX

TABLE 15.5

COMMON, CONTRACT, AND PASSENGER MOTOR CARRIERS, 1935–1969[a]

Year Ending	CUMULATIVE APPLICATIONS			OPERATING CARRIERS	
	Grandfather	New	Total	Approved Applications[c]	Number in Operation[b]
Oct. 1936	82,827	1,696	84,523	—	—
1937	83,107	3,921	87,028	1,114	—
1938	85,646	6,694	92,340	20,398	—
1939	86,298	9,636	95,934	23,494	—
1940	87,367	12,965	100,332	25,575	—
1941	88,064	16,325	104,389	26,296	—
1942	88,702	18,977	107,679	26,683	—
1943	89,157	20,007	109,164	27,531	—
1944	89,511	21,324	110,835	27,177	21,044
1945	89,518	22,829	112,347		20,788
1946	89,529	26,392	115,921		20,632
1947	89,552	29,604	119,156		20,665
1948	89,563	32,678	122,241		20,373
1949	89,567	35,635	125,202		18,459
1950	89,573	38,666	128,239		19,200
1951	89,574	41,889	131,463		18,843
1952	(89,574)[d]	44,297	133,870		18,408
1953	"	46,619	136,192		17,869
1954	"	49,146	138,719		17,080
1955	"	51,720	141,293		16,836
June 1956	"	53,640	143,213		16,486
1957	"	56,804	146,377		16,316
1958	"	60,278	149,851		16,065
1959	"	64,171	153,744		15,923
1960	"	69,205	158,778		15,936
1961	"	72,877	162,450		15,967
1962	"	76,986	166,559		15,884
1963	"	81,443	171,016		15,739
1964	"	86,711	176,284		15,732
1965	"	93,064	182,637		15,755
1966	"	101,745	191,318		15,933
1967	"	106,647	196,220		16,003
1968	"	f	f		16,230[e]
1969	"	f	f		16,318[e]

SOURCE: U.S. Interstate Commerce Commission *Annual Reports*.

[a] Excluding brokers and within-state carriers.

[b] Property carriers were the following percentages of all operating carriers: 1944, 93.4 percent; 1950, 92.4 percent; 1960, 93.0 percent; 1966, 93.4 percent.

[c] Estimated.

[d] Not available; assumed to be approximately constant.

[e] 1968 and 1969 figures are for number of carriers required to file annual reports.

[f] Not available comparable to previous years; applications for permanent authority *disposed of* (i.e., from new and pending files) 1967–69 are as follows: 1967, 7,049; 1968, 5,724; 1969, 5,186.

TABLE 15.6

WEIGHT LIMITS ON TRUCKS, 1932–33,[a] BY STATES

(BASIC DATA FOR TABLE 15.2)

State	MAXIMUM WEIGHT (IN LBS.)		State	MAXIMUM WEIGHT (IN LBS.)	
	4-wheel[b]	6-wheel[c]		4-wheel[b]	6-wheel[c]
Alabama	20,000	32,000	Nebraska	24,000	40,000
Arizona	22,000	34,000	Nevada	25,000	38,000
Arkansas	22,200	37,000	New Hampshire	20,000	20,000
California	22,000	34,000	New Jersey	30,000	30,000
Colorado	30,000	40,000	New Mexico	27,000	45,000
Connecticut	32,000	40,000	New York	33,600	44,000
Delaware	26,000	38,000	No. Carolina	20,000	20,000
Florida	20,000	20,000	No. Dakota	24,000	48,000
Georgia	22,000	39,600	Ohio	24,000	24,000
Idaho	24,000	40,000	Oklahoma	20,000	20,000
Illinois	24,000	40,000	Oregon	25,500	42,500
Indiana	24,000	40,000	Pennsylvania	26,000	36,000
Iowa	24,000	40,000	Rhode Island	28,000	40,000
Kansas	24,000	34,000	So. Carolina	20,000	25,000
Kentucky	18,000	18,000	So. Dakota	20,000	20,000
Louisiana	13,400	N.A.	Tennessee	20,000	20,000
Maine	18,000	27,000	Texas	13,500	N.A.
Maryland	25,000	40,000	Utah	26,000	34,000
Massachusetts	30,000	30,000	Vermont	20,000	20,000
Michigan	27,000	45,000	Virginia	24,000	35,000
Minnesota	27,000	42,000	Washington	24,000	34,000
Mississippi	18,000	22,000	West Va.	24,000	40,000
Missouri	24,000	24,000	Wisconsin	24,000	36,000
Montana	24,000	34,000	Wyoming	27,000	30,000

[a] Red Book figures are reported (p. 89) as "based on the state's interpretations of their laws [1933] and on physical limitations of vehicle design and tire capacity." Public Roads figures are reported (p. 167) as "an abstract of state laws, including legislation passed in 1932."

[b] 4-wheel: The smallest of the following 3 figures was used: (a) Maximum gross weight (as given in Red Book, pp. 90–91); (b) Maximum axle weight (as given in Red Book, pp. 90–91), multiplied by 1.5 (see Red Book, p. 89); (c) Maximum gross weight (as given in Red Book, p. 93). Exceptions: Texas and Louisiana—see Red Book, p. 91.

[c] 6-wheel: Maximum gross weight as given in Public Roads, p. 167. These figures agree in most cases with those shown in Red Book, p. 93, and with Public Roads maximum axle weights multiplied by 2.5 (see Red Book, p. 93). Texas and Louisiana are excluded as data are not available to convert from payload to gross weight limits.

TABLE 15.7

INDEPENDENT VARIABLES (BASIC DATA FOR TABLE 15.2, CONTINUED)

State	Trucks on Farms per 1,000 Agricultural Labor Force	Average Length of Railroad Haul of Freight (miles)[a]	Percent of State Highways with High-type Surface[b]
Alabama	26.05	189.4	1.57
Arizona	79.74	282.2	2.60
Arkansas	28.62	233.1	1.72
California	123.40	264.6	13.10
Colorado	159.50	244.7	0.58
Connecticut	173.80	132.6	7.98
Delaware	173.20	202.7	21.40
Florida	91.41	184.1	8.22
Georgia	32.07	165.7	1.60
Idaho	95.89	243.6	0.73
Illinois	114.70	207.9	9.85
Indiana	120.20	202.8	6.90
Iowa	98.73	233.3	3.39
Kansas	146.70	281.5	0.94
Kentucky	20.05	227.5	1.81
Louisiana	31.27	201.0	1.94
Maine	209.30	120.4	1.87
Maryland	134.20	184.1	12.90
Massachusetts	172.20	144.7	17.70
Michigan	148.40	168.0	6.68
Minnesota	120.40	225.6	1.44
Mississippi	29.62	164.9	1.14
Missouri	54.28	229.7	2.91
Montana	183.80	266.5	0.09
Nebraska	132.10	266.9	0.41
Nevada	139.40	273.2	0.39
New Hampshire	205.40	129.0	3.42
New Jersey	230.20	137.6	23.30
New Mexico	90.46	279.0	0.18
New York	220.50	163.3	21.50
No. Carolina	37.12	171.5	8.61
No. Dakota	126.40	255.1	0.01
Ohio	125.80	194.2	11.20
Oklahoma	78.18	223.3	1.42
Oregon	118.90	246.2	3.35
Pennsylvania	187.60	166.5	9.78
Rhode Island	193.30	131.0	20.40
So. Carolina	20.21	169.8	2.82
So. Dakota	113.40	216.6	0.04
Tennessee	23.98	191.9	3.97
Utah	101.70	235.7	1.69
Vermont	132.20	109.7	2.26
Virginia	71.88	229.8	2.86
Washington	180.90	254.4	4.21
West Virginia	62.88	218.7	8.13
Wisconsin	178.60	195.7	4.57
Wyoming	133.40	286.7	0.08

[a] *Average length of RR haul of (revenue) freight*=Average distance in miles each ton is carried=ratio of number of ton-miles to number of tons carried for each state. Average length of haul was obtained by weighting average length of haul of each company by the number of miles of line operated by that company in the state (all for Class I RR's).

[b] *Percentage of state roads with high-quality surface:* Where high-quality (high-type) surface consists of bituminous macadam, bituminous concrete, sheet asphalt, Portland cement concrete, and block pavements. All state rural roads, both local and state highway systems, are included.

STIGLER'S CONTRIBUTIONS TO THE HISTORY OF ECONOMIC THOUGHT

◆ ◆ ◆ ◆

◆ *PART* ◆ *FOUR* ◆

Perfect Competition, Historically Contemplated

· 16 ·

No concept in economics—or elsewhere—is ever defined fully, in the sense that its meaning under every conceivable circumstance is clear. Even a word with a wholly arbitrary meaning in economics, like "elasticity," raises questions which the person who defined it (in this case, Marshall) never faced: for example, how does the concept apply to finite changes or to discontinuous or stochastic or multiple-valued functions? And of course a word like "competition," which is shared with the whole population, is even less likely to be loaded with restrictions or elaborations to forestall unfelt ambiguities.

Still, it is a remarkable fact that the concept of competition did not begin to receive explicit and systematic attention in the main stream of economics until 1871. This concept—as pervasive and fundamental as any in the whole structure of classical and neoclassical economic theory—was long treated with the kindly casualness with which one treats of the intuitively obvious. Only slowly did the elaborate and complex concept of perfect competition evolve, and it was not until after the First World War that it was finally received into general theoretical literature. The evolution of the concept and the steps by which it became confused with a perfect market, uniqueness of equilibrium, and stationary conditions are the subject of this essay.

From the *Journal of Political Economy* 65, no. 1 (February 1957). Copyright 1957 by the University of Chicago.

The Classical Economists

"Competition" entered economics from common discourse, and for long it connoted only the independent rivalry of two or more persons. When Adam Smith wished to explain why a reduced supply led to a higher price, he referred to the "competition [which] will immediately begin" among buyers; when the supply is excessive, the price will sink more, the greater "the competition of the sellers, or according as it happens to be more or less important to them to get immediately rid of the commodity."[1] It will be noticed that "competition" is here (and usually) used in the sense of rivalry in a race—a race to get limited supplies or a race to be rid of excess supplies. Competition is a process of responding to a new force and a method of reaching a new equilibrium.

Smith observed that economic rivals were more likely to strive for gain by under- or overbidding one another, the more numerous they were:

> The trades which employ but a small number of hands, run most easily into such combinations.
>
> If this capital [sufficient to trade in a town] is divided between two different grocers, their competition will tend to make both of them sell cheaper, than if it were in the hands of one only; and if it were divided among twenty, their competition would be just so much the greater, and the chance of their combining together, in order to raise the price, just so much the less.[2]

This is all that Smith has to say of the number of rivals.

Of course something more is implicit, and partially explicit, in Smith's treatment of competition, but this "something more" is not easy to state precisely, for it was not precise in Smith's mind. But the concept of competition seemed to embrace also several other elements:

1. The economic units must possess tolerable knowledge of the conditions of employment of their resources in various industries. "This equality [of remuneration] can take place only in those employments which are well known, and have been long established in the neighbourhood."[3] But the necessary information was usually available: "Secrets . . ., it must be acknowledged, can seldom be long kept; and the extraordinary profit can last very little longer than they are kept."[4]

2. Competition achieved its results only in the long run: "This equality in the whole of the advantages and disadvantages of the different employments of labour and stock, can take place only in the ordinary, or what may be called the natural state of those employments."[5]

3. There must be freedom of trade; the economic unit must be free

to enter or leave any trade. The exclusive privileges or corporations which exclude men from trades, and the restrictions imposed on mobility by the settlement provisions of the poor law, are examples of such interferences with "free competition."

In sum, then Smith had five conditions of competition:

1. The rivals must act independently, not collusively.
2. The number of rivals, potential as well as present, must be sufficient to eliminate extraordinary gains.
3. The economic units must possess tolerable knowledge of the market opportunities.
4. There must be freedom (from social restraints) to act on this knowledge.
5. Sufficient time must elapse for resources to flow in the directions and quantities desired by their owners.

The modern economist has a strong tendency to read more into such statements than they meant to Smith and his contemporaries. The fact that he (and many successors) was willing to call the ownership of land a monopoly—although the market in agricultural land met all these conditions—simply because the total supply of land was believed to be fixed is sufficient testimony to the fact that he was not punctilious in his language.[6]

Smith did not state how he was led to these elements of a concept of competition. We may reasonably infer that the conditions of numerous rivals and of independence of action of these rivals were matters of direct observation. Every informed person knew, at least in a general way, what competition was, and the essence of this knowledge was the striving of rivals to gain advantages relative to one another.

The other elements of competition, on the contrary, appear to be the necessary conditions for the validity of a proposition which was to be associated with competition: the equalization of returns in various directions open to an entrepreneur or investor or laborer. If one postulates equality of returns as the equilibrium state under competition, then adequacy of numbers and independence of rivals are not enough for equilibrium. The entrepreneur (or other agents) must know what returns are obtainable in various fields, he must be allowed to enter the fields promising high rates of return, and he must be given time to make his presence felt in these fields. These conditions were thus prerequisites of an analytical theorem, although their reasonableness was no doubt enhanced by the fact that they corresponded more or less closely to observable conditions.

This sketch of a concept of competition was not amplified or challenged in any significant respect for the next three-quarters of a century by any important member of the English school. A close study of the literature, such as I have not made, would no doubt reveal many isolated passages on the formal properties or realism of the concept, especially when the theory was applied to concrete problems. For example, Senior was more interested in methodology than most of his contemporaries, and he commented:

> But though, under free competition, cost of production is the regulator of price, its influence is subject to much occasional interruption. Its operation can be supposed to be perfect only if we suppose that there are no disturbing causes, that capital and labour can be at once transferred, and without loss, from one employment to another, and that every producer has full information of the profit to be derived from every mode of production. But it is obvious that these suppositions have no resemblance to the truth. A large portion of the capital essential to production consists of buildings, machinery, and other implements, the results of much time and labour, and of little service for any except their existing purposes.... Few capitalists can estimate, except upon an average of some years, the amounts of their own profits, and still fewer can estimate those of their neighbours.[7]

Senior made no use of the concept of perfect competition hinted at in this passage, and he was wholly promiscuous in his use of the concept of monopoly.

Cairnes, the last important English economist to write in the classical tradition, did break away from the Smithian concept of competition. He defined a state of free competition as one in which commodities exchanged in proportion to the sacrifices (of labor and capital) in their production.[8] This condition was amply fulfilled, he believed, so far as capital was concerned, for there was a large stock of disposable capital which quickly flowed into unusually remunerative fields.[9] The condition was only partly fulfilled in the case of labor, however, for there existed a hierarchy of occupational classes ("noncompeting industrial groups") which the laborer found it most difficult to ascend.[10] Even the extra rewards of skill beyond those which paid for the sacrifices in obtaining training were a monopoly return.[11] This approach was not analytically rigorous—Cairnes did not tell how to equate the sacrifices of capitalists and laborers—nor was it empirically fruitful.

Cairnes labeled as "industrial competition" the force which effects the proportioning of prices to psychological costs which takes place to the extent that the products are made in one noncompeting group, and he called on the reciprocal demand theory of international trade to explain exchanges of products between noncompeting groups. Hence we might call industrial competition the competition within noncompeting groups, and commercial competition that between noncompeting groups. But Sidgwick and Edgeworth attribute the opposite concepts to Cairnes: commercial competition is competition within an industry, and industrial competition requires the ability of resources to flow between industries.[12] Their nomenclature seems more appropriate; I have not been able to find Cairnes's discussion of commercial competition and doubt that it exists.[13]

THE CRITICS OF PRIVATE ENTERPRISE

The main claims for a private-enterprise system rest upon the workings of competition, and it would not have been unnatural for critics of this system to focus much attention on the competitive concept. They might have argued that Smith's assumptions were not strong enough to insure optimum results or that, even if perfect competition were formulated as the basis of the theory, certain deviations from optimum results (such as those associated with external economies) could occur. The critics did not make this type of criticism, however, possibly simply because they were not first-class analysts; and for this type of development we must return to the main line of theorists, consisting mostly of politically conservative economists.

Or, at another pole, the critics might simply have denied that competition was the basic form of market organization. In the nineteenth century, however, this was only a minor and sporadic charge.[14] The Marxists did not press this point; both the labor theory of value and the doctrine of equalization of profit rates require competition.[15] The early Fabian essayists were also prepared to make their charges rest upon the deficiencies in the workings of competition rather than its absence.[16] The charge that competition was nonexistent or vanishing did not become commonplace until the end of the nineteenth century.

The critics, to the extent that they took account of competition at all, emphasized the evil tendencies which they believed flowed from its workings. It would be interesting to examine their criticisms systematically with a view to their treatment of competition; it is my impression that their most common, and most influential, charge was that competition led to a highly objectionable, and perhaps continuously deteriorating, distribution of income by size.[17] In their explanations of the workings of a competitive economy the most striking deficiency of the classical economists was their failure to work out the theory of the effects of competition on the distribution of income.

THE MATHEMATICAL SCHOOL

The first steps in the analytical refinement of the concept of competition were made by the mathematical economists. This stage in the history of the concept is of special interest because it reveals both the types of advances that were achieved by this approach and the manner in which alien elements were introduced into the concept.

When an algebraically inclined economist seeks to maximize the profits of a producer, he is led to write the equation

$$\text{Profits} = \text{Revenue} - \text{Cost}$$

and then to maximize this expression; that is, to set the derivative of profits with respect to output equal to zero. He then faces the question: How does revenue (say, pq) vary with output (q)? The natural answer is to *define* competition as that situation in which p does not vary with q—in which the demand curve facing the firm is horizontal. This is precisely what Cournot did:

> The effects of competition have reached their limit, when each of the partial productions D_k [the output of producer k] is *inappreciable*, not only with reference to the total production $D = F(p)$, but also with reference to the derivative $F'(p)$, so that the partial production D_k could be subtracted from D without any appreciable variation resulting in the price of the commodity.[18]

This definition of competition was especially appropriate in Cournot's system because, according to his theory of oligopoly, the excess of price over marginal cost approached zero as the number of like producers became large.[19] Cournot believed that this condition of competition was fulfilled "for a multitude of products, and, among them, for the most important products."[20]

Cournot's definition was enormously more precise and elegant than Smith's so far as the treatment of numbers was concerned. A market departed from unlimited competition to the extent that price exceeded the marginal cost of the firm, and the difference approached zero as the number of rivals approach infinity. But the refinement was one-sided; Cournot paid no attention to conditions of entry and so his definition of competition held also for industries with numerous firms even though no more firms could enter.

The role of knowledge was made somewhat more prominent in Jevons's exposition. His concept of competition was a part of his concept of a market, and a perfect market was characterized by two conditions:

> 1. A market, then, is theoretically perfect only when all traders have perfect knowledge of the conditions of supply and demand, and the consequent ratio of exchange; . . .
> 2. . . . there must be perfectly free competition, so that anyone will exchange with any one else upon the slightest advantage appearing. There must be no conspiracies for absorbing and holding supplies to produce unnatural ratios of exchange.[21]

One might interpret this ambiguous second condition in several ways, for the pursuit of advantages is not inconsistent with conspiracies. At a minimum, Jevons assumes complete independence of action by every trader for a corollary of the perfect market in that "in the same market, at any moment, there cannot be two prices for the same kind of article."[22] This rule of a single price (it is called the "law of indifference" in the second edition) excludes price discrimination and probably requires that the market have numerous buyers and sellers, but the condition is not made explicit. The presence of large numbers is clearly implied, however, when we are told that "a single trader. . . must buy and sell at the current prices, which he cannot in an appreciable degree affect."[23]

The merging of the concepts of competition and the market was unfortunate, for each deserved a full and separate treatment. A market is an institution for the consummation of transactions. It performs this function efficiently when every buyer who will pay more than the minimum realized price for any class of commodities succeeds in buying the commodity, and every seller who will sell for less than the maximum realized price succeeds in selling the commodity. A market performs these tasks more efficiently if the commodities are well specified and if buyers and sellers are fully informed of their properties and prices. Possibly also a perfect market allows buyers and sellers to act on differing expectations of future prices. A market may be perfect and monopolistic or imperfect and competitive. Jevons's mixture of the two has been widely imitated by successors, of course, so that even today a market is commonly treated as a concept subsidiary to competition.

Edgeworth was the first to attempt a systematic and rigorous definition of perfect competition. His exposition deserves the closest scrutiny in spite of the fact that few economists of his time or ours have attempted to disentangle and uncover the theorems and conjectures of the *Mathematical Psychics*, probably the most elusively written book of importance in the history of economics. For his allegations and demonstrations seem to be the parents of widespread beliefs on the nature of perfect competition.

The conditions of perfect competition are stated as follows:

> The *field of competition* with reference to a contract, or contracts, under consideration consists of all individuals who are willing and able to recontract about the articles under consideration. . . .
>
> There is free communication throughout a *normal* competitive field. You might suppose the constituent individuals collected at a point, or connected by telephones—an ideal supposition [1881], but sufficiently approximate to existence or tendency for the purposes of abstract science.
>
> A *perfect* field of competition professes in addition certain properties peculiarly favourable to mathematical calculation; . . . The conditions of a *perfect* field are four; the first pair referrible [sic] to the heading *multiplicity* or continuity, the second *dividedness* or fluidity.

1. An individual is free to *recontract* with any out of an indefinite number, . . .

2. Any individual is free to *contract* (at the same time) with an indefinite number; . . . This condition combined with the first appears to involve the indefinite divisibility of each *article* of contract (if any X deal with an indefinite number of Ys he must give each an indefinitely small portion of x); which might be erected into a separate condition.

3. Any individual is free to *recontract* with another independently of, *without the consent* being required of, any third party, . . .

4. Any individual is free to *contract* with another independently of a third party; . . .

The failure of the first [condition] involves the failure of the second, but not *vice versa*; and the third and fourth are similarly related.[24]

The natural question to put to such a list of conditions of competition is: are the conditions necessary and sufficient to achieve what intuitively or pragmatically seems to be a useful concept of competition? Edgeworth replies, in effect, that the conditions are both necessary and sufficient. More specifically, competition requires (1) indefinitely large numbers of participants on both sides of the market; (2) complete absence of limitations upon individual self-seeking behavior; and (3) complete divisibility of the commodities traded.[25]

The rationale of the requirement of indefinite numbers is as follows. With bilateral monopoly, the transaction will be indeterminate—equilibrium can be anywhere on the contract curve.[26] If we add a second buyer and seller, it is shown that the range of permissible equilibriums (the length of the tenable contract curve) will shrink.[27] By intuitive induction, with infinitely many traders it will shrink to a single point; a single price must rule in the market.[28]

Before we discuss this argument, we may take account also of the condition that individual traders are free to act independently. Edgeworth shows that combinations reduce the effective number of traders and that "combiners *stand to gain.*"[29] In effect, then, he must assume that the individual trader not only is free to act independently but will in fact do so.

The proof of the need for indefinite numbers has serious weaknesses. The range of indeterminacy shrinks only because one seller or buyer tries to cut out the other by offering better terms.[30] Edgeworth fails to show that such price competition (which is palpably self-defeating) will occur or that, if it does occur, why the process should stop before the parties reach a unique (competitive) equilibrium. Like all his descendants, he treated the small-numbers case unsatisfactorily.

It is intuitively plausible that with infinite numbers all monopoly power (and indeterminacy) will vanish, and Edgeworth essentially postulates rather than proves this. But a simple demonstration, in case of sellers of equal size, would amount only to showing that

$$\text{Marginal revenue} = \text{Price} + \frac{\text{Price}}{\text{Number of sellers} \times \text{Market elasticity}}$$

and that this last term goes to zero as the number of sellers increases indefinitely.[31] This was implicitly Cournot's argument.

But why do we require divisibility of the traded commodity?

> Suppose a market, consisting of an equal number of masters and servants, offering respectively wages and service; subject to the condition that no man can serve two masters, no master employ more than one man; or suppose equilibrium already established between such parties to be disturbed by any sudden influx of wealth into the hands of the masters. Then there is no *determinate*, and very generally *unique*, arrangement towards which the system tends under the operation of, may we say, a law of Nature, and which would be predictable if we knew beforehand the real requirements of each, or of the average, dealer;. . .[32]

Consider the simple example: a thousand masters will each employ a man at any wage below 100; a thousand laborers will each work for any wage above 50. There will be a single wage rate: knowledge and numbers are sufficient to lead a worker to seek a master paying more than the going rate or a master to seek out a worker receiving less than the market rate. But any rate between 50 and 100 is a possible equilibrium.[33]

It is not the lack of uniqueness that is troublesome, however, for a market can be perfectly competitive even though there be a dozen possible stable equilibrium positions.[34] Rather, the difficulty arises because the demand (or supply) functions do not possess continuous derivatives: the withdrawal of even one unit will lead to a large change in price, so that the individual trader—even though he has numerous independent rivals—can exert a perceptible influence upon price.

The element of market control arising out of the noncontinuity is easily eliminated, of course. If the article which is traded is divisible, then equalities replace inequalities in the conditions of equilibrium: the individual trader can no longer influence the market price. A master may employ a variable amount of labor, and he will therefore bid for additional units so long as the wage rate is below his marginal demand price. A worker may have several employers, and he will therefore supply additional labor so long as any employer will pay more than his marginal supply price. "If the labour of the assistants can be sold by the

274 • ECONOMIC THOUGHT

hour, or other sort of differential dose, the phenomenon of determinate equilibrium will reappear."[35] Divisibility was introduced to achieve determinateness, which it fails to do, but it is required to eliminate monopoly power.

Divisibility had a possible second role in the assumptions, which, however, was never made explicit. If there are infinitely many possessors of a commodity, presumably each must have only an infinitesimal quantity of it if the existing total stock is to be finite. But no economist placed emphasis upon the strict mathematical implications of concepts like infinity, and this word was used to convey only the notion of an indefinitely large number of traders.

The remainder of the mathematical economists of the period did not extend, or for that matter even reach, the level of precision of Edgeworth. Walras gave no adequate definition of competition.[36] Pareto noticed the possible effects of social controls over purchases and sales.[37] Henry Moore, in what may have been the first article on the formal definition of competition,[38] listed five "implicit hypotheses" of competition:

1. Each economic factor seeks a maximum net income.
2. There is but one price for commodities of the same quality in the same market.
3. The influence of the product of any one producer upon the price per unit of the total product is negligible.
4. The output of any one producer is negligible as compared with the total output.
5. Each producer orders the amount of his product without regard to the effect of his act upon the conduct of his competitors.[39]

This list of conditions is noteworthy chiefly because it marked an unsuccessful attempt to revert to the narrower competitive concept of Jevons.

MARSHALL

Marshall as usual refused to float on the tide of theory, and his treatment of competition was much closer to Adam Smith's than to that of his contemporaries. Indeed, Marshall's exposition was almost as informal and unsystematic as Smith's in this area. His main statement was:

We are investigating the equilibrium of normal demand and normal supply in their most general form: we are neglecting those features which are special to particular parts of economic science, and are confining our attention to those broad relations which are common to nearly the whole of it. Thus we assume that the forces of demand and supply have free play in a perfect market; there is no combination among dealers on either side, but each acts for himself: and there is *free competition*; that is, buyers compete freely with buyers, and sellers compete freely with sellers. But though everyone acts for himself, his knowledge of what others are doing is supposed to be sufficient to prevent him from taking a lower price or paying a higher price than others are doing;...[40]

If this quotation suggests that Marshall was invoking a strict concept of competition, we must remember that he discussed the "fear of spoiling the market" and the firms with negatively sloping demand curves in the main chapters on competition[41] and that the only time perfect competition was mentioned was when it was expressly spurned.[42]

Soon he yielded a bit to the trend toward refinement of the concept. Beginning with the third (1895) edition, he explicitly introduced the horizontal demand curve for the individual firm as the normal case and gave it the same mathematical formulation as did Cournot.[43] But these were patchwork revisions, and they were not carried over into the many passages where looser concepts of competition had been employed.

Marshall's most significant contribution was indirect: he gave the most powerful analysis up to his time of the relationship of competition to optimum economic organization (Book V, Chapter xiii, on the doctrine of maximum satisfaction). There he found the competitive results to have not only the well-known qualification that the distribution of resources must be taken as a datum, and the precious exception that only one of several multiple stable equilibriums could be the maximum,[44] but also a new and possibly extremely important exception, arising out of external economies and diseconomies. The doctrine of external economies in effect asserts that in important areas the choices of an individual are governed by only part of the consequences, and inevitably the doctrine opens up a wide range of competitive equilibriums which depart from conventional criteria of optimum arrangement. It was left for Pigou to elaborate, and exaggerate, the importance of this source of disharmonies in *Wealth and Welfare*.

THE COMPLETE FORMULATION: CLARK AND KNIGHT

Only two new elements needed to be added to the Edgeworth conditions for competition in order to reach the modern concept of perfect competition. They pertained to the mobility of resources and the model of the stationary economy, and both were presented, not first,[45] but most influentially, by John Bates Clark.

Clark, in his well-known development of the concept of a static economy, ascribed all dynamic disturbances to five forces:

1. Population is increasing.
2. Capital is increasing.
3. Methods of production are improving.
4. The forms of industrial establishments are changing.
5. The wants of consumers are multiplying.[46]

The main purpose of his treatise was to analyze the stationary economy in which these forces were suppressed, and for this analysis the assumption of competition was basic:

> There is an ideal arrangement of the elements of society, to which the force of competition, acting on individual men, would make the society conform. The producing mechanism actually shapes itself about this model, and at no time does it vary greatly from it.
>
> We must use assumptions boldly and advisedly, making labor and capital absolutely mobile, and letting competition work in ideal perfection.[47]

Although the concepts of a stationary economy and of competition are completely independent of each other, Clark somehow believed that competition was an element of static analysis:

> The statement made in the foregoing chapter that a static state excludes true entrepreneurs' profits does not deny that a legal monopoly might secure to an entrepreneur a profit that would be permanent as the law that should create it—and that, too, in a social condition which, at first glance, might appear to be static. The agents, labor and capital, would be prevented from moving into the favored industry, though economic forces, if they had been left unhindered, would have caused them to move in. This condition, however, is not a true static state, as it has been defined. . . . Industrial groups are in a truly static state when the in-industrial agents, labor and capital, show a *perfect mobility, but no motion.* A legal monopoly destroys at a certain point this mobility. . . .[48]

I shall return to this identification of competition with stationary equilibrium at a later point.

The introduction of perfect mobility of resources as an assumption of competition was new, and Clark offers no real explanation for the assumption. One could simply eliminate his five dynamic influences, and then equilibrium would be reached after a time even with "friction" (or less than instantaneous mobility). Clark was aware of this possible approach but merely said that "it is best to assume" that there is no friction.[49] The only gain in his subsequent work, of course, is the avoidance of an occasional "in the long run."

Mobility of resources had always been an implicit assumption of competition, and in fact the conditions of adequate knowledge of earning opportunities and absence of contrived barriers to movement were believed to be adequate to insure mobility. But there exist also technological limitations to the rate at which resources can move from one place or industry to another, and these limitations were in fact the basis of Marshall's concept of the short-run normal period. Once this fact was generally recognized, it became inevitable that mobility of resources be given an explicit time dimension, although of course it was highly accidental that instantaneous mobility was postulated.

The concept of perfect competition received its complete formulation in Frank Knight's *Risk, Uncertainty and Profit* (1921). It was the meticulous discussion in this work that did most to drive home to economists generally the austere nature of the rigorously defined concept[50] and so prepared the way for the widespread reaction against it in the 1930s.

Knight sought to establish the precise nature of an economy with complete knowledge as a preliminary step in the analysis of the impact of uncertainty. Clark's procedure of eliminating historical changes was shown to be neither necessary nor sufficient: a stationary economy was not necessary to achieve complete competitive equilibrium if men had complete foresight; and it was not sufficient to achieve this equilibrium, because there might still be nonhistorical fluctuations, owing, for example, to drought or flood, which were imperfectly anticipated.[51] Complete, errorless adjustments required full knowledge of all relevant circumstances, which realistically can be possessed only when these circumstances do not change; that is, when the economy is stationary.

The assumptions necessary to competition are presented as part of a list that describes the pure enterprise economy, and I quote those that are especially germane to competition:

> 2. We assume that the members of the society act with complete "rationality." By this we do not mean that they are to be "as angels, knowing good from evil"; we assume ordinary human motives . . .; but they are supposed to "know what they want" and to seek it "intelligently." . . . They are supposed to know absolutely the consequence of their acts when they are performed, and to perform them in the light of the consequences. . . .
>
> 4. We must also assume complete absence of physical obstacles to the making, execution, and changing of plans at will; that is, there must be "perfect mobility" in all economic adjustments, no cost involved in movements or changes. To realize this ideal all the elements entering into eco-

nomic calculations—effort, commodities, etc.—must be continuously variable, divisible without limit. . . . The exchange of commodities must be
virtually instantaneous and costless.

5. It follows as a corollary from number 4 that there is perfect competition. There must be perfect, continuous, costless intercommunication between all individual members of the society. Every potential buyer of a good
constantly knows and chooses among the offers of all potential sellers, and
conversely. Every commodity, it will be recalled, is divisible into an indefinite
number of units which must be separately owned and compete effectually
with each other.

6. Every member of the society is to act as an individual only, in entire
independence of all other persons. . . . And in exchanges between individuals, no interests of persons not parties to the exchange are to be concerned, either for good or for ill. Individual independence in action excludes
all forms of collusion, all degrees of monopoly or tendency to monopoly. . . .

9. All given factors and conditions are for the purposes of this and the
following chapter and until notice to the contrary is expressly given, to
remain absolutely unchanged. They must be free from periodic or progressive
modification as well as irregular fluctuation. The connection between this
specification and number 2 (perfect knowledge) is clear. Under static conditions every person would soon find out, if he did not already know, everything
in his situation and surroundings which affected his conduct. . . .

The above assumptions, especially the first eight, are idealizations or
purifications of tendencies which hold good more or less in reality. They are
the conditions necessary to perfect competition. The ninth, as we shall see, is
on a somewhat different footing. Only its corollary of perfect knowledge
(specification number 2) which may be present even when change takes place
is necessary for perfect competition.[52]

This list of requirements of perfect competition is by no means a statement
of the *minimum* requirements, and in fact no one is able to state the minimum
requirements.

Consider first complete knowledge. If each seller in a market knows any n
buyers, and each seller knows a different (but overlapping) set of buyers, then
there will be perfect competition if the set of n buyers is large enough to
exclude joint action. Or let there be indefinitely many brokers in any market,
and let each broker know many buyers and sellers, and also let each buyer or
seller know many brokers—again we have perfect competition. Since entrepreneurs in a stationary economy are essentially brokers between resource owners
and consumers, it is sufficient for competition if they meet this condition. That
is, resource owners and consumers could dwell in complete ignorance of all
save the bids of many entrepreneurs. Hence knowledge possessed by any one
trader need not be complete; it is sufficient if the knowledge possessed by the
ensemble of individuals in the market is in a sense comprehensive.

And now, mobility. Rigid immobility of every trader is compatible with perfect competition if we wish to have this concept denote only equilibrium which is not affected by the actions of individual traders: large numbers (in any market) and comprehensive knowledge are sufficient to eliminate monopoly power. If we wish perfect competition to denote also that a resource will obtain equal returns in all possible uses, mobility becomes essential, but not for all resources. If one resource were immobile and all others mobile, clearly the returns of all resources in all uses could be equalized. Even if all resources were immobile, under certain conditions free transport of consumers' goods would lead to equalization of returns.[53] Even in the general case in which mobility of resources is required, not all the units of a resource need be mobile. If some units of each resource are mobile, the economic system will display complete mobility for all displacements up to a limit that depends upon the proportion of mobile units and the nature of the displacement.

The condition that there be no costs of movement of resources is not necessary in order to reach maximum output for an economy; under competition only those movements of resources will take place for which the additional return equals or exceeds the cost of movement. But costless movement is necessary if equality is to obtain in the return to a resource in all uses: if the movement between A and B costs $1.00 (per unit of time), the return to a resource at A can vary within $1.00 of either direction of its return at B. Equilibrium could be reached anywhere within these limits (but would be uniquely determined), and this equilibrium would depend upon the historical distribution of resources and consumers.

Next, divisibility. It is not enough to have a large number of informed traders in a market: price must change continuously with quantity if an individual trader is to have only an imperceptible influence upon the market rate, and this will generally require divisibility of the commodity traded. Infinite divisibility, however, is not necessary to eliminate significant control over price by the individual trader, and divisibility of time in the use of a resource is a substitute for divisibility in its quantity. Divisibility, however, is not sufficient to insure uniqueness of equilibriums; even in the simpler problems one must also require that the relevant economic functions display strict monotonicity, but this has nothing to do with competition.

And homogeneity. The formal condition that there be many producers of *a* commodity assumes homogeneity of this commodity (Knight's fifth assumption). Certain forms of heterogeneity are of course unimportant because they are superficial: potatoes need not be of the same size if they are sold by the pound; laborers do not have to be equally efficient if the differences in their productivity are measurable. As these examples may suggest, heterogeneity can be a substitute for divisibility.

The final assumption, concerning collusion, is especially troublesome. If one merely postulates the absence of collusion, then why not postulate also that even two rivals can behave in such a way as to reach competitive equilibrium? Instead, one usually requires that the number of traders be large enough so that collusion will not appear. To determine this number, one must have a theory of the conditions under which collusion occurs. Economists have generally emphasized two barriers to collusion. The first is imperfect knowledge, especially of the consequences of rivalry and of the policy which would maximize profits for the group, and of course neither of these difficulties would arise in the stationary economy with perfect knowledge. The second barrier is the difficulty of determining the division of profits among colluders, and we simply do not know whether this difficulty would increase with the number of traders under the conditions we are examining. Hence it seems essential to assume the absence of collusion as a supplement to the presence of large numbers: one of the assumptions of perfect competition is the existence of a Sherman Act.

It is therefore no occasion for complaint that Knight did not state the minimum requirements for perfect competition; this statement was impossible in 1921, and it is impossible today. The minimum assumptions for a theoretical model can be stated with precision only when the complete theory of that model is known. The complete theory of competition cannot be known because it is an open-ended theory; it is always possible that a new range of problems will be posed in this framework, and then, no matter how well developed the theory was with respect to the earlier range of problems, it may require extensive elaboration in respects which previously it glossed over or ignored.

The analytical appeal of a definition of competition does not depend upon its economy of assumptions, although gratuitously wide assumptions are objectionable.[54] We wish the definition to specify with tolerable clarity—with such clarity as the state of the science affords—a model which can be used by practitioners in a great variety of theoretical researches, so that the foundations of the science need not be debated in every extension or application of theory. We wish the definition to capture the essential general content of important markets, so the predictions drawn from the theory will have wide empirical reliability. And we wish a concept with normative properties that will allow us to judge the efficiency of policies. That the concept of perfect competition has served these varied needs as well as it has is providential.

Concluding Reflections

If we were free to redefine competition at this late date, a persuasive case could be made that it should be restricted to meaning the absence of monopoly power in a market. This is an important concept that deserves a name, and "competition" would be the appropriate name. But it would be idle to propose such a restricted signification for a word which has so long been used in a wide sense, and at best we may hope to denote the narrower concept by a suggestive phrase. I propose that we call this narrower concept *market competition*.

Perfect market competition will prevail when there are indefinitely many traders (no one of which controls an appreciable share of demand or supply) acting independently in a perfect market. A perfect market is one in which the traders have full knowledge of all offer and bid prices. I have already remarked that it was unfortunate that a perfect market was made a subsidiary characteristic of competition, for a perfect market may also exist under monopoly. Indeed, in realistic cases a perfect market may be more likely to exist under monopoly, since complete knowledge is easier to achieve under monopoly.

Market competition can exist even though resources or traders cannot enter or leave the market in question. Hence market competition can rule in an industry which is not in long-run competitive equilibrium and is compatible with the existence of large profits or losses.

It is interesting to note that Chamberlin's definition of "pure" competition is identical with my definition of market competition: "competition unalloyed with monopoly elements."[55] But Chamberlin implied that pure competition could rule in an imperfect market; the only conditions he postulated were large numbers of traders and a standardized commodity. The conditions are incomplete: if 1 million buyers dealt with 1 million sellers of a homogeneous product, each pair dealing in ignorance of all others, we should simply have 1 million instances of bilateral monopoly. Hence pure competition cannot be contrasted with perfect competition, for the former also requires "perfect" knowledge (subject to qualifications I have previously discussed), and for this reason I prefer the term "market competition."

The broad concept of perfect competition is defined by the condition that the rate of return (value of the marginal product) of each resource be equal in all uses. If we wish to distinguish this concept from market competition, we may call it (after the terminology attributed to Cairnes) *industrial competition*. Industrial competition requires (1) that there be market competition within each industry; (2) that owners of resources be informed of the returns obtainable in each industry; and (3) that they be free to enter or leave any industry. In addition, the resources must be infinitely divisible if there is to be strict equality in the rate of return on a resource in all uses.

An industrial competitive equilibrium will obtain continuously if resources are instantaneously mobile or in the long run if they move at a finite time rate. Since the concept of long-run competitive equilibrium is deeply imbedded in modern economic theory, it seems most desirable that we interpret industrial competition as a long-run concept. It may be noticed that a time period did not have to figure explicitly in the pre-Marshallian theory because that theory did not separate and devote special attention to a short-run normal period in which only a portion of the resources were mobile: the basic classical theory was a long-run theory.

The concept of industrial competition has a natural affinity to the static economy even though our definition does not pay any explicit attention to this problem. Rates of return on resources will be equalized only if their owners have complete knowledge of future returns (in the case of durable resources), and it seems improper to assume complete knowledge of the future in a changing economy. Not only is it misleading to endow the population with this gift of prophecy but also it would often be inconsistent to have people foresee a future event and still have that event remain in the future.

One method by which we might seek to adapt the definition to a historically evolving economy is to replace the equalization of rates of return by *expected* rates of return. But it is not an irresistably attractive method. There are troublesome questions of what entrepreneurs seek to maximize under these conditions and of whether risk or uncertainty premiums also enter into their calculations. A more important difficulty is that this formulation implies that the historically evolving industry is in equilibrium in long-run normal periods, and there is no strong reason to believe that such long-run normal periods can be defined for the historically evolving industry. If all economic progress took the form of a secularly smooth development, we could continue to use the Marshallian long-run normal period, and indeed much progress does take this form. But often, and sooner or later always, the historical changes come in vast surges, followed by quiescent periods or worse, and it is harder to assume that the fits and starts can be foreseen with tolerable confidence or that they will come frequently enough to average out within economically relevant time periods.

It seems preferable, therefore, to adapt the concept of competition to changing conditions by another method: to insist only upon the absence of barriers to entry and exit from an industry in the long-run normal period; that is, in the period long enough to allow substantial changes in the quantities of even the most durable and specialized resources. Then we may still expect that some sort of expected return will tend to be equalized under conditions of reasonably steady change, although much work remains to be done before we can specify exactly what this return will be.[56]

The way in which the competitive concept loses precision when historically changing conditions are taken into account is apparent. It is also easily explained: the competitive concept can be no better than the economic theory with which it is used, and until we have a much better theory of economic development we shall not have a much better theory of competition under conditions of nonrepetitive change.

The normative role of the competitive concept arises from the fact that the equality of rate of return on each resource in all uses which defines competition is also the condition for maximum output from given resources. The outputs are measured in market prices, and the maximum is relative to the distribution of ownership of resources. This well-known restriction of the competitive optimum to production, it may be remarked, should be qualified by the fact that the effects of competition on distribution have not been studied. A competitive system affects the distribution of the ownership of resources, and—given a stable distribution of human abilities—a competitive system would probably lead eventually to a stable income distribution whose characteristics are unknown. The theory of this distribution might have substantial normative value.

The vitality of the competitive concept in its normative role has been remarkable. One might have expected that, as economic analysis became more precise and as the range of problems to which it was applied widened, a growing list of disparities between the competitive allocation of resources and the maximum-output allocation would develop. Yet to date there have been only two major criticisms of the norm.[57] The first is that the competitive individual ignores external economies and diseconomies, which—rightly or wrongly—most economists are still content to treat as an exception to be dealt with in individual cases. The second, and more recent, criticism is that the competitive system will not provide the right amount (and possibly not the right types) of economic progress, and this is still an undocumented charge. The time may well come when the competitive concept suitable to positive analysis is not suitable to normative analysis, but it is still in the future.

Finally, we should notice the most common and the most important criticism of the concept of perfect competition—that it is unrealistic. This criticism has been widespread since the concept was completely formulated and underlies the warm reception which the profession gave to the doctrines of imperfect and monopolistic competition in the 1930s. One could reply to this criticism that all concepts sufficiently general and sufficiently precise to be useful in scientific analysis must be abstract: that, if a science is to deal with a large class of phenomena, clearly it cannot work with concepts that are faithfully descriptive of even one phenomenon, for then they will be grotesquely undescriptive of others. This conventional line of defense for all abstract concepts is completely valid, but there is another defense, or rather another form of this defense, that may be more persuasive.

This second defense is that the concept of perfect competition has defeated its newer rivals in the decisive area: the day-to-day work of the economic theorist. Since the 1930s, when the rival doctrines of imperfect and monopolistic competition were in their heyday, economists have increasingly reverted to the use of the concept of perfect competition as their standard model for analysis. Today the concept of perfect competition is being used more widely by the profession in its theoretical work than at any time in the past. The vitality of the concept is strongly spoken for by this triumph.

Of course, this is not counsel of complacency. I have cited areas in which much work must be done before important aspects of the definition of competition can be clarified. My fundamental thesis, in fact, is that hardly any important improvement in general economic theory can fail to affect the concept of competition. But it has proved to be a tough and resilient concept, and it will stay with us in recognizable form for a long time to come.

NOTES

1. *The Wealth of Nations* (Modern Library ed.), pp. 56–57.

2. Ibid., pp. 126 and 342.

3. Ibid., p. 114.

4. Ibid., p. 60.

5. Ibid., p. 115.

6. Ibid., p. 145. Perhaps this is not the ideal illustration of the laxness of the period in the use of the competitive concept, for several readers of this paper have sympathized with this usage. But, to repeat, competition is consistent with a zero elasticity of supply: the fact of windfall gains from unexpected increases in demand is characteristic of all commodities with less than infinitely elastic supplies.

7. N. W. Senior, *Political Economy* (New York: 1939), p. 102.

8. *Some Leading Principles of Political Economy Newly Expounded* (London: 1874), p. 79.

9. Ibid., p. 68.

10. Ibid., p. 72.

11. Ibid., p. 85. Thus Cairnes tacitly labeled all differences in native ability as "monopolistic."

12. Henry Sidgwick, *Principles of Political Economy* (London: 1883), p. 182; F. Y. Edgeworth, *Papers Relating to Political Economy* (London: 1925), II, pp. 280, 311.

13. Karl Marx once distinguished interindustry from intraindustry competition in *Theorien über den Mehrwert* (Stuttgart: 1905), II, pt. 2, p. 14 n.

14. For example, Leslie repeatedly denied that resource owners possessed sufficient knowledge to effect an equalization of the rates of return (see T. E. Cliffe Leslie, *Essays in Political and Moral Philosophy* [London: 1888], pp. 47–48, 81, 158–59, 184–85).

15. See especially vol. III of *Das Kapital* and also F. Engels, *The Condition of the Working-Classes in England*, reprinted in Karl Marx and Friedrich Engels, *On Britain* (London: 1954), pp. 109 ff. The Marxian theory of the increasing concentration of capital was a minor and inconsistent dissent from the main position (see *Capital* [Modern Library ed.], pp. 684 ff.).

16. See *Fabian Essays* (Jubilee ed.; London: 1948), especially those by Shaw and Webb. But the attention devoted to monopoly was increasing, and the essay by Clarke argued that "combination is absorbing commerce" (ibid., p. 84). A few years later the Webbs used a competitive model in their celebrated discussion of "higgling in the market" and then went on to describe the formation of monopolistic structures as defenses erected against the competitive pressures the Webbs did not quite understand (see *Industrial Democracy* [London: 1920], pt. III, ch. ii).

17. A second main criticism became increasingly more prominent in the second half of the nineteenth century: that a private-enterprise system allowed or compelled large fluctuations in employment. For some critics (e.g., Engels), competition was an important cause of these fluctuations.

18. *Mathematical Principles of the Theory of Wealth* (New York: 1929), p. 90. It is sufficient to assume that D_k is small relative to D if one assumes that the demand function is continuous, for then "the variations of the demand will be sensibly proportional to the variations in price so long as these last are small fractions of the original price" (ibid., p. 50).

19. Let the revenue of the firm be $q_i p$, and let all firms have the same marginal costs, MC. Then the equation for maximum profits for one firm would be

$$p+q_i\frac{dp}{dq}=\text{MC}.$$

The sum of n such equations would be

$$np+q\frac{dp}{dq}=n\text{MC},$$

for $nq_i=q$. This last equation may be written,

$$p=\text{MC}-\frac{p}{nE},$$

where E is the elasticity of market demand (ibid., p. 84).

20. Ibid., p. 90.

21. *Theory of Political Economy* (1st ed.; London: 1871), pp. 87 and 86.

22. Ibid., p. 92. This is restated as the proposition that the last increments of an act of exchange (that is, the last exchange in a competitive market) must be proportional to the total quantities exchanged, or that dy exchanges for dx in the same proportion that y exchanges for x, or

$$\frac{dy}{dx}=\frac{y}{x}.$$

It would have been better for Jevons simply to assert that, if x_i exchanges for y_i, then for all i

$$\frac{x_i}{y_i}=\frac{P_y}{P_x}.$$

23. Ibid., p. 111. In the preface to the second edition, where on most subjects Jevons was farseeing, the conceptual treatment of competition deteriorated: "Property is only another name for monopoly... Thus monopoly is limited by competition..." (*Theory* [4th ed.], pp. xlvi–xlvii).

24. *Mathematical Psychics* (London: 1881), pp. 17–19.

25. Edgeworth's emphasis upon recontract, the institution which allows tentative contracts to be broken without penalty, is motivated by a desire to assure that equilibrium will be achieved and will not be affected by the route by which it is achieved. It will not be examined here.

26. Ibid., pp. 20 ff.

27. Ibid., pp. 35 ff.

28. Ibid., pp. 37–39.

29. Ibid., p. 43.

30. "...It will in general be possible for *one* of the Ys (without the consent of the other) to *recontract* with the two Xs, so that for all those three parties the recontract is more advantageous than the previously existing contract" (ibid., p. 35).

31. Let one seller dispose of q_i, the other sellers each disposing of q. Then the seller's marginal revenue is

$$\frac{d(pq_i)}{dq_i}=p+q_i\frac{dp}{dQ}\frac{dQ}{dq_i},$$

where Q is total sales, and $dQ/dq_i=1$. Letting $Q=nq_i=nq$, and writing E for

$$\frac{dQ}{dp}\frac{p}{Q},$$

we obtain the expression in the text.

32. *Mathematical Psychics*, p. 46.

33. Of course, let there be one extra worker, and the wage will be fifty; one extra master, and it will be one hundred.

34. Since chance should operate in the choice of the equilibrium actually attained, it is not proper to say, as Edgeworth does (in a wider context), that the dice will be "loaded with villainy" (ibid., p.50).

35. *Collected Papers Relating to Political Economy* (London: 1925), I, p. 36. One might also seek to eliminate the indeterminateness by appeal to the varying demand-and-supply prices of individual traders; this is the path chosen by Hicks in "Edgeworth, Marshall, and the Indeterminateness of Wages," *Economic Journal* 40 (1930): 45–31.

This, however, is a complicated solution; one must make special hypotheses about the distribution of these demand-and-supply prices.

36. *Elements of Pure Economics*, trans. Jaffé (Homewood, Ill.: 1954), pp. 83 and 185. It is indicative that the word "competition" is not indexed.

37. *Cours d'économie politique* (Lausanne: 1896, 1897), §§ 46, 87, 705, 814; cf. also *Manuel d'économie politique* (2nd ed.; Paris: 1927), pp. 163, 210, 230.

38. "Paradoxes of Competition," *Quarterly Journal of Economics* 20 (1905–6): 209–30. Most of the article is concerned with duopoly.

39. Ibid., pp. 213–14. The fifth statement is held to be a corollary of 3 and 4; but see below.

40. *Principles of Economics* (1st ed.; London: 1890), p. 402. A comparison with the corresponding passage in the eighth edition (op. cit., p. 341) will reveal the curious changes which were later made in the description of competition.

41. *Principles* (8th ed.; London: 1929), pp. 374 and 458.

42. Ibid., p. 540.

43. Ibid., pp. 517 and 849–50.

44. Both of these qualifications were of course recognized by predecessors such as Walras and Edgeworth.

45. In the mathematical exposition of theory it was natural to postulate stable supply and demand functions, and therefore stable technologies and tastes, so one could trace a gradually expanding concept of the stationary economy in Walras, Auspitz and Lieben, and Irving Fisher.

46. *The Distribution of Wealth* (New York: 1899), p. 56.

47. Ibid., pp. 68 and 71.

48. Ibid., p. 76; cf. also p. 78.

49. Ibid., p. 81.

50. Although Pigou was not concerned with the formal definition of competition, he must also be accounted an influential figure in the popularization of the concept of perfect competition. In his *Wealth and Welfare* (1912), he devoted individual chapters to the effects of immobility (with incorrect knowledge as one component) and indivisibility upon the ability of a resource to receive an equal rate of return in all uses (ibid., pt. II, chaps. iv and v).

51. *Risk, Uncertainty and Profit* (New York: 1921), pp. 35–38.

52. Ibid., pp. 76–79; cf. also p. 148.

53. See P. A. Samuelson, "International Factor-Price Equalization Once Again," *Economic Journal* 59 (1949): 181–97; and S. F. James and I. F. Pierce, "The Factor Price Equalization Myth," *Review of Economic Studies* 19 (1951–52): 111–22.

54. They are objectionable chiefly because they mislead some user or abusers of the concept as to its domain of applicability. That dreadful list of assumptions of perfect competition which textbooks in labor economics so often employ to dismiss the marginal productivity theory is a case in point.

55. *The Theory of Monopolistic Competition* (1st ed.; Cambridge, Mass.: 1933), p. 6.

56. It is worth noticing that even under static conditions the definition of the return is modified to suit the facts and that mobility of resources is the basic competitive requirement. Thus we say that laborers move so that the net advantages, not the current money return, of various occupations are equalized. The suggestion in the text is essentially that we find the appropriate definition of net advantages for the historically evolving economy.

57. In a wider framework there have of course been criticisms of the competitive norm with respect to (1) the ability of individuals to judge their own interests, and (2) the ability of a competitive system to achieve a continuously high level of employment of resources.

Bernard Shaw, Sidney Webb and the Theory of Fabian Socialism

· 17 ·

The transition of public policy in England from one of relatively pure laissez-faire to one of collectivism began in the first half of the nineteenth century, and presumably has not yet reached its end. The shift in public opinion and in effective electoral power which lies behind the shift of policy, therefore, cannot have been initiated by the Fabian socialists, who began their labors in 1884. Yet they are commonly credited with a leading role in persuading the intellectual classes of England of the undesirability of organizing economic life on the basis of private enterprise.

The two leading theoreticians of Fabian socialism were Shaw and Webb—indeed one is inclined to say that they were the only theoreticians in the first decades of the Society. Webb's labors in both economic scholarship and politics are well known; at least in this country, there is some tendency to underestimate Shaw's part, simply because his other activities eventually overshadowed as well as displaced his Fabian period. Shaw felt differently:

> Now gentlemen, I am really a political economist. I have studied the thing. I understand Ricardo's law of rent; and Jevons' law of value. I can tell you what in its essence sound economy means for any nation.[1]

The propriety of this claim is better judged at a later point.

I propose to discuss only two aspects of the Fabian movement. The first

From *Proceedings of the American Philosophical Society* 103 (June 1959). Permission to reprint courtesy of the American Philosophical Society.

aspect is the early work in economic theory by Shaw which commands our interest because of its importance as well as its authorship. The second aspect is the precise nature of the theoretical critique of capitalism to which Shaw and Webb devoted their immense talents and energies in the first two decades of the Fabian Society.

I. The Early Shaw

Bernard Shaw was first persuaded of the need for radical economic reform, he tells us, when—in 1882—he accidentally drifted into a London hall and heard one of Henry George's influential lectures for a tax on the rent of land.[2] The study of *Progress and Poverty* soon led Shaw toward socialism. Shaw's incomplete novel, *An Unsocial Socialist*, revealed that within a year after hearing George the conversion to socialism was complete. Shaw's hero, a Sydney Trefusis, abandoned his wife and his inheritance—both of admirable dimensions—to devote his days to long speeches on the iniquities of capitalism and to inciting the rural proletariat to trespass. That this prince of prigs did not choke off socialism in England is itself one indication that the novel was not widely read.

The criticisms of Henry George by English Marxists drove Shaw to the French edition of Volume I of *Das Kapital*. He was captivated without being persuaded of the validity of all its economic theory. These doubts spilled into print in a letter to a weekly, *Justice*, entitled "Who Is the Thief?"[3] It is a tribute to Shaw's penetration that he had found for himself a crucial flaw in Marx's labor theory of value.

Marx's central argument was that the capitalists, by their control over capital equipment and the means of subsistence, forced a worker who added ten shillings of value to ten shillings of material, to work for only three shillings (his assumed subsistence requirement), yielding up seven shillings of surplus value.

> But mark what must ensue. Some rival capitalist, trading in tables on the same principle, will content himself with six shillings profit for the sake of attracting custom. He will sell the table for nineteen shillings; that is, he will allow the purchaser one shilling out of his profit as a bribe to secure his custom. The first capitalist will thus be compelled to lower his price to nineteen shillings also, and presently the competition of brisk young traders, believing in small profits and quick returns, will bring the price of tables down to thirteen shillings and sixpence.[4]

But if the worker is being robbed of seven shillings, then the purchaser is committing thirteen-fourteenths of the theft—every English consumer is the thief. The criticism received no reply.

The assumptions of competition and of surplus value are indeed incompatible, and even today I would like to amend Shaw's argument in only two respects. The competition of capitalists would also take place in the labor market, and force wages up. And, secondly, the customer-thieves are, of course, chiefly the workmen and their families.

The distrust of Marx's value theory was strengthened by an attack made by Philip H. Wicksteed.[5] Using the recently developed marginal utility theory, Wicksteed showed that Marx's theory was illogical. It was illogical because Marx insisted that only socially necessary labor governs values, which introduced surreptitiously the very quality of utility which he had denied as a universal attribute of commodities. The theory was incomplete because it could not cope with the value of commodities which were not freely reproducible (such as old masters) or were monopolized. Wicksteed's own radical leanings (which diminished subsequently) were perhaps revealed by the fact that he did not comment upon the crucial flaw in Marx's theory—the denial of productivity to resources other than labor.

Shaw took upon himself the writing of a good-natured rejoinder to Wicksteed.[6] Ignoring Marx, he rashly attacked the marginal utility theory, a task for which he was unprepared. The attack centered upon the fact that the amount of utility obtained from an increment of a commodity fluctuates widely over time for one man, and varies widely among men, without any corresponding variation in the value of the commodity. The criticism failed to distinguish positions of equilibrium from those of disequilibrium, and Wicksteed had no trouble in disposing of it.[7]

The debate now shifted to a small discussion group, the Hampstead Historic Club, where Shaw and Webb, as well as other critics of capitalism, were joined by two economists, Wicksteed and Edgeworth. For two years Shaw was subjected to training in economic theory by two of the world's leading theoreticians—although one may conjecture that with students such as he the professors learned a fair amount about debating. He emerged a complete convert to Jevons and Ricardo—an odd set of intellectual parents considering Jevons's vast dislike for Ricardo's theory.

The conversion was announced by three notices on *Das Kapital* in *The National Reformer* (1887).[8] They express a deep appreciation of the powerful influence of Marx's denunciation of the injustice of capitalism and of his presentation of a law of historical evolution which gives little more time to capitalistic society. The crucial weakness of the Marxian theory of value proves to be the same point that Wicksteed made, that only relative utilities can account for the observed phenomena of value, and this is tacitly recognized when Marx refers to socially necessary labor.[9]

It will suffice merely to mention Shaw's remaining work, because we shall consider its theoretical content below. The essays on the economic theory of and the transition to socialism in *Fabian Essays* (1889) were his. Thereafter, his economic writings took the form chiefly of Fabian pamphlets,[10] although he also wrote a book on municipal trading.[11] The much later *Intelligent Woman's Guide to Socialism* contains nothing new on our main subject.

Sydney Webb's prodigious literary output seldom lacked relevance to economic theory, but only a few early items are germane to our inquiry.[12] They will be considered in the Fabian critique of the basic logic of a capitalistic (private enterprise) system, to which we now turn.

II. THE ECONOMIC THEORY OF FABIANISM

The main Fabian indictment of private enterprise rested squarely upon the classical theory of the rent of land.

> On Socialism the analysis of the economic action of Individualism bears as a discovery, in the private appropriation of land, of the source of those unjust privileges against which Socialism is aimed. It is practically a demonstration that public property in land is the basic economic condition of Socialism.[13]

The crux of this theory is the assumption that, in a settled country the effective supply of land is fixed. No degree of expansion of the demand for the products of land would call forth an additional acre of land—putting aside normally trifling amounts due to drainage, irrigation, and the like. The aggregate income of the landowners will therefore wax with the growth of population and wealth.

This doctrine had provided the main theoretical support for free trade in grain—the repeal of the Corn Laws in effect greatly increased the supply of land available to meet the demands of British consumers.[14] This was the main goal of policy of the Ricardian school, and one might have expected that once the goal was achieved, the landowner and the rent theory would have receded from the stage of public controversy.

For a time after the repeal of the Corn Laws the criticisms of the private ownership of land abated, but they revived in the latter decades of the century. John Stuart Mill threw his immense prestige behind the Land Tenure Reform Association,[15] and he was succeeded by A. R. Wallace, the codiscoverer of the Darwinian theory. The importance of the absentee rents in the Irish agitation contributed to this revival. The interest in land taxation or nationalization became almost universal after Henry George's triumphal lecture tours beginning in 1882.[16]

Shaw restated the Ricardian rent theory without appreciable modification so far as land is concerned, embellishing it only with his handsome prose.

Shaw's piece on the economics of socialism in the Fabian essays was a straightforward reproduction, on a nonrigorous level, and his tract on *The Impossibility of Anarchism*, where anarchism virtually means competitive private enterprise, turns on the fact that it is intrinsic to economic life that some land is more valuable than others.[17] Webb's acceptance was as complete.[18]

How could one seriously make a heavy indictment of private property in land when free trade had made wheat—and land—cheap? Late Victorian England was an odd place to offer heavy criticism of feudalism. The answer is a complex one. In the first place, the facts were largely ignored and, when recognized, misinterpreted. The famous Fabian Tract, *Facts for Socialists*, estimates rents to be £200,000,000 or one-sixth of the nation's income in the mid-eighties. Aside from a myriad of minor errors, which the incredibly complex English income tax law invited,[19] the Fabians blithely included the value of all buildings in that of land. The true rent of land (urban as well as rural) surely did not exceed £60 million, or a mere 5 percent of income. Moreover, agricultural rents had been declining in absolute amount since the 1870s, and as a share of national income they had probably been declining since 1810. One careful student set the pure agricultural land rents at £6 million at the end of the century.[20]

One could divert attention to urban rents, and the Duke of Bedford made a regular appearance in Fabian publications. Shaw asserted that "town rents have risen oppressively,"[21] and Webb was no doubt the author of *The Unearned Increment*, which dilated upon the unearned increment in London, which even his one-sided manipulations raised only to £6 million per year in the twenty-five years up to 1895.[22]

But no amount of literary skill or empirical absentmindedness can make a Duke of Bedford the archvillain of capitalism. It was necessary to generalize the indictment, and the attempt was made by both men. They sought to include interest on capital with rent on land, and they denounced the unequal distribution of income. Both criticisms, however, had to be based upon the theory of rent, or a second, independent theoretical basis had to be found for explaining the workings of a capitalistic system. The second alternative was not chosen: it is not only intellectually inelegant, but psychologically ineffective, to use several unrelated theoretical principles to launch a program of reform.

Shaw's endeavors to extend the theory of rent to interest, that is, to identify the returns to capital and labor—were relatively crude. The basic method was that of assertion:

> Colloquially, one property with a farm on it is said to be land yielding rent; whilst another, with a railway on it, is called capital yielding interest. But economically there is no distinction between them when they once become

sources of revenue. . .shareholder and landlord live alike on the produce
extracted from their property by the labor of the proletariat.[23]

This argument is, in effect, that all capital instruments incorporate land in
some degree—the unique location and resources of a railroad or a water
company are similar to those of agricultural or urban land. Of course this is
true, and "land" is in fact only an abbreviation, in the classical economics, for
nonproducible, nonhuman resources. But this element of land hardly dominates the vast mass of capital of an economy, which is both fluid in form and
augmentable in quantity, and therefore not obedient to such classical theorems
as that the rent of a piece of land increases with economic progress. Shaw's
dogmatic assertion that capital produces nothing, and interest is a mere
exaction, is simple Marxism, wholly inconsistent with the marginal utility
theory of value he professed.

Webb's attempt to identify rent and interest took a more sophisticated
form. He generalized the rent theory to cover other distributive shares. If rent is
the surplus of the yield of resources on good land over the yield on poor land,
can one not also say that interest is the surplus of return of resources (including
land) on good capital over the yield on decrepit and obsolete capital?

"Economic interest" is the amount of produce over and above "economic
wages" which is obtained through the use of capital, upon land at the margin
of cultivation by the skill of the worst worker employed in the industrial
community, or upon the better land with greater skill, after deduction of the
economic rent of the land and ability.

Economic interest, as here defined, is expressed by a law similar to the
Ricardian law of rent.[24]

Webb argues that most interest is the product of "opportunity and chance."
The basic theorem that the rates of interest on various investments tend to
equality, is conceded only for "the last increment of capital employed in each
case."[25]

It is true that in one sense the rent theory can be generalized to embrace
every form of return—Wicksteed demonstrated in 1894 that the rent theory in
this sense is analytically equivalent to the marginal productivity theory.[26] But
the rent theory, in this sense, is only a device for isolating the contribution of
one productive factor to a product, and has no relevance to the crucial
assumption of fixity of supplies which gave the Ricardian rent theory its
empirical content.

Without this assumption of fixity of supply, there is little substantive
similarity between capital and land. Under competition all forms of investment which yield higher than average rates of return will attract additional

investment until the rate of return is equalized on all, not merely on marginal, increments of investment.

One could seek escape from this conclusion by denying the existence of competition—by arguing that monopolies of various sorts had become so ubiquitous and powerful that most interest was a monopoly return.[27] But Webb placed no emphasis upon such a development. On the contrary, he asserts that "every development toward a freer Individualism must, indeed, inevitably emphasize the power of the owner of the superior instruments of wealth-production to obtain for himself all the advantages of their superiority."

> But the monopoly of which the democracy is here impatient is not that of any single individual, but that of the class itself. What the workers are objecting to is. . . the creation of a new feudal class of industry, . . . who compete, it is true, among themselves, but who are nevertheless able, as a class, to preserve a very real control over the lives of those who depend upon their own daily labor.[28]

In Webb's scheme, indeed monopoly was not even an evil. In *Industrial Democracy* he presents the famous picture of "higgling in the market."[29] The search of consumers for bargains forces down retailers' prices, retailers in turn are compelled to drive down wholesalers' prices, and so on until the competitive pressure "finally crushes the isolated workman at the bottom of the pyramid."[30] Monopolies are devices to obtain some relief from this unrelenting pressure, and, if they succeed in diminishing competition, they treat their workers a *little* better. Here monopoly is a modestly benevolent phenomenon.

In this later volume, Webb alleges a further resemblance between land and capital, but it appears to be ad hoc: the supply of savings is held to be virtually independent of the rate of interest. [31] But even if this were wholly true, it would not yield the Ricardian conclusion that the capitalist necessarily benefits from every advance of society—what happened would depend upon the supply of capital over time.[32]

Both Webb and Shaw seek to extend the rent theory even farther, to include the "rent of ability" of superior workers.[33] It is a most unusual feature of Fabian socialism that it attacked large labor incomes as well as property incomes. Much of the superior earnings of professional men and artists was attributed to the unequal distribution of income, which allowed a few men to prosper by catering to the whims of the rich. Even more was attributed to the "monopoly" of education by the children of property-owning families. The chief remedy proposed was widespread education (which was already developing rapidly), supplemented if necessary by a progressive income tax.

In one respect the analogy between labor and land was closer than that between capital and land: there are natural differences in quality of both men and acres, unlikely to be eliminated under any social system. But the fixity of supply of land finds no parallel in population, and both classical economists and almost all socialists concurred in the absence of any secular increase in wage rates as a society progressed economically. The Fabian doctrine of rents of ability tended both to blur the ethical differences they alleged between wages and other incomes, and to alienate the professional classes from their doctrines, and perhaps these are the reasons this aspect of their theory received little elaboration or emphasis. Still, the socialization of the labor force was latent in this doctrine, and the various hints of compulsion which were dropped[34] are in keeping with the antidemocratic tendencies both Shaw and Webb made explicit in later years.

The final indictment of capitalism, that it generated a cruel and inhuman distribution of income, was no doubt the most influential. The street corner orator was especially clear in Shaw when he reached this theme:

> A New York lady for instance, having a nature of exquisite sensibility, orders an elegant rosewood and silver coffin, upholstered in pink satin, for her dead dog. It is made: and meanwhile a live child is prowling barefooted and hunger-stunted in the frozen gutter outside.[35]

This sort of diatribe—adorned by frequent references to such strange capitalistic institutions as compulsory prostitution—must have been especially effective at the lips of one of the most formidable debaters of his time.

The denunciation of inequality may be viewed as an ethical judgment, to be accepted or rejected according to one's taste. This is not a very useful view, however, for equality is not a basic ethical value in any important western philosophy.[36] One surely wishes to distinguish nominal from real inequality: the difference between the average earnings of a twenty-five year-old lawyer and one twice his age is devoid of ethical significance. If policies are to have purpose and effectiveness, one must isolate the sources of inequality, be they education, natural inheritance, luck, thrift, property inheritance, or a particular government policy. One should seek to quantify the subtle and ambiguous concept of inequality, discover whether it is increasing or decreasing, and invent and analyze alternative methods of dealing with objectionable inequality.

Shaw and Webb discharged a portion, but only a very small portion, of the duties of a responsible proponent of an egalitarian program. Shaw advanced, in fact, three basic arguments for equality of income. The first was simply that there is no other objective basis for distribution:

> Now . . . suppose you think there should be some other standard applied to men, I ask you not to waste time arguing about it in the abstract, but bring it

down to a concrete case at once. Let me take a very obvious case. I am an exceedingly clever man. There can be absolutely no question at all in my case that in some ways I am above the average of mankind in talent. You laugh; but I presume you are not laughing at the fact, but only because I do not bore you with the usual modest cough. . . . Now pick out somebody not quite so clever. How much am I to have and how much is he to have? I notice a blank expression on your countenances. You are utterly unable to answer the question. . . .

It is now plain that if you are going to have any inequalities of income, they must be arbitrary inequalities.[37]

This argument cannot be taken as seriously as it was given. Equality is an unambiguous rule of distribution only when it is applied as unmeaning arithmetic, giving equal sums of income to the day-old baby, the adult worker, and the jailed felon. Conversely, a competitive market does determine, not how much more clever Shaw was than contemporary dramatists, but how much more he produced of what people desired.

Shaw's second argument for equality was professedly "economic":

. . . if you allow the purchasing power of one class to fall below the level of the vital necessities of subsistence, and at the same time allow the purchasing power of another class to rise considerably above it into the region of luxuries, then you find inevitably that those people with that superfluity determine production to the output of luxuries, while at the same time the necessities that are wanted at the other end cannot be sold, and are therefore not produced. I have put it as shortly as possible; but that is the economic argument in favor of equality of income.[38]

That an unequal distribution of income will lead to an unequal distribution of consumption, however, is not an argument for equality. If one believes, as almost everyone always has, that no living person should be denied subsistence (and perhaps much more), then he should favor raising consumption of some people, but the belief does not lead to egalitarianism.

Shaw's final argument for egalitarianism was eugenic; economic barriers prevented marriage from taking place whenever biological urges dictated:

Just consider what occurs at the present time. I walk down Oxford Street, let me say, as a young man. I see a woman who takes my fancy. I fall in love with her. It would seem very sensible, in an intelligent community, that I should take off my hat and say to this lady: "Will you excuse me; but you attract me very strongly, and if you are not already engaged, would you mind taking my name and address and considering whether you would care to marry me?" Now I have no such chance at present. Probably when I meet that woman, she is either a charwoman and I cannot marry her, or else she is a duchess and she will not marry me.[39]

Of this argument I will say only that Shaw was utterly sincere, and that it did not become a Fabian article of faith.

Webb based his analysis of inequality much more directly upon the rent theory.

> Nor is there any doubt or dispute as to the causes of this inequality. The supersession of the Small by the Great Industry has given the main fruits of invention and the new power over nature to a comparatively small proprietary class, upon whom the mass of the people are dependent for leave to earn their living. When it suits any person having the use of land and capital to employ the worker, this is done only on the condition that two important deductions, rent and interest, can be made from his product, for the benefit of two, in this capacity, absolutely unproductive classes—those exercising the bare ownership of land and capital.[40]

That "the most virtuous artisan cannot dodge the law of rent"[41] is the anchor of this indictment of inequality.

The net effect of rent upon the distribution of income among families in late Victorian England is not known. If it parallels modern American experience—and there should be at least a family resemblance—the wealthiest classes received a much more than proportionate share of rents, and so, too, did the lowest income classes, and the intermediate classes received a less than proportionate share.[42] Elimination of rents, therefore, would reduce income inequality at the top of the income distribution and increase it at the lower end. But no matter what one did with rents, the distribution of income would change little.

Only if one includes interest on capital are the possibilities of redistribution large, and here the rent theory was of no avail: one must contrive an entirely new reason for rejecting private property in capital. Of course such reasons can be contrived, but the Fabians did not meet this demand.

III. CONCLUSION

Reformers seldom proportion criticism carefully to evil, but the Fabians must be among the most extreme in their concentration upon a minor and uncharacteristic aspect of capitalism as its major flaw. There is a nonfunctional income to productive resources in fixed supply, and it is roughly—but only very roughly—approximated by rent of land, but it was already trifling in their time and it was on balance (including urban rents) declining relative to national income.

One expects blind slogans and high emotions to carry a mass movement, but the particular clientele of the Fabians was the educated class of Great Britain. That they were as successful as they are reputed to be[43] is suggestive of a proposition for which I believe there is much support: that social problems are the creation of the "intellectual." The intrinsic importance of a complaint against a social system, as judged by later opinion, has little to do with its effectiveness in shifting opinion. If enough able and determined men—and the number in the Fabian group was almost unbelievably small—denounce and denounce again a deficiency, that deficiency becomes grave.[44]

It is less unusual of the Fabian theoreticians that they were not good economists—popular reformers have seldom been. In economics Shaw was merely a clever dilettante. No short sentence could do justice to Webb's large talents, but they did not include a strong command of economic theory. Their limitations prevented them from constructing a coherent program of eco-nomic reform, but it apparently did not decrease the effectiveness of their criticisms of the existing order. Had the leading economists of the period subjected this literature to critical review—instead they simply ignored it—I doubt whether the control over land use would have been an element of modern English socialism.

NOTES

1. Shaw, G. B., "The Case for Equality," p. 11, an address delivered on the first of May, 1913 (1st ed: London, 1913), National Liberal Club Political and Economic Circle, *Transactions*, pt. 85; reprinted in *The Socialism of Shaw*, ed. with introduction by J. Fuchs (New York: Vanguard, 1926), p. 58.

2. Archibald Henderson, *George Bernard Shaw: Man of the Century* (New York: Appleton-Century-Crofts, 1956), p. 215.

3. Signed G. B. S. Larking. Reprinted by R. W. Ellis in *Bernard Shaw and Karl Marx: A Symposium, 1884–1889* (New York: Random House, for R. W. Ellis: Georgian Press, 1930).

4. Ibid., pp. 5–6.

5. Wicksteed was adding to his careers in the Unitarian ministry and literature—he was the translator of Dante—that of economist.

6. G. B. Shaw, *The Jevonian Criticism of Marx* (1885), reprinted in Ellis, op. cit.

7. Wicksteed, "A Rejoinder," reprinted in Ellis, op. cit. Shaw subsequently wrote that his reply proved nothing but his incompetence (Ellis, op. cit., p. 138n).

8. Shaw, reprinted in Ellis, op. cit. The essays contain a remarkable vilification of H. M. Hyndman, the Colonel Blimp of English Marxism.

9. Apropos of the "transformation" problem of which there was promised a solution in the third volume of Das Kapital, Shaw observes that "scientific socialism" means cashing a promissory note of Mr. Engels, dated "London, an Marx' Geburtstag, 5 mai, 1885" (Ellis, op. cit., p. 108).

10. They are identified in E. R. Pease, History of the Fabian Society, appendix IV (new and revised edition; New York: International Publishers, 1926); some are reprinted in The Socialism of Shaw.

11. The Commonsense of Municipal Trading, Fabian Socialist Series, no. 5 (London: A. C. Fifield, 1908). Although the volume is of more interest to political scientists than to economists, it has some remarkably bold analyses resting on the differences between social and private costs. Shaw places extraordinary weight upon the ability of cities to borrow at low interest rates.

12. There seems to be no doubt that Beatrice did not contribute to the work on economic theory. Perhaps one reason was her haste: "I went straight to the club and read right through Marshall's six hundred pages—got up, staggering under it. It is a great book, nothing new—showing the way, not following it." (Diary, July 27, 1890, quoted in Margaret Cole, Beatrice Webb [New York: Harcourt, Brace, 1946].)

13. Shaw, in Fabian Essays, p. 24 (Jubilee edition; London: George Allen & Unwin, 1950), p. 24.

14. Of course economists defended free trade in grain also—as perhaps one should say, directly—on the principle of comparative cost, but this more general theory had no special relevance to the politically strategic commodity, food, nor did it necessarily have a prospering beneficiary, that is, a villain.

15. John Stuart Mill, Dissertations and Discussions (Papers on Land Tenure [London: L. J. Parker & Son, 1859]), p. 5. Mill recognized the validity of the landowners' claim to compensation for any differential taxation, and proposed that only future increments of land values be taken by the state.

16. E. P. Lawrence, Henry George in the British Isles (East Lansing: Michigan State University Press, 1957).

17. Fabian Tract no. 45 (4th ed., 1893). Also Fabian Essays, pp. 165, 167.

18. The rate of interest and the laws of distribution, Quarterly Journal of Economics 2 (1887–88), 188–209; also, "The Rate of Interest," ibid., pp. 469–72.

19. J. C. Stamp, British Incomes and Property (London: P. S. King & Son, 1916).

20. J. R. Thompson, "An Inquiry into the Rent of Agricultural Land," Journal of the Royal Statistical Society 70 (1907): 587 ff.

21. G. B. Shaw, "The Impossibility of Anarchism," p. 9n.

22. Tract no. 30, 1895.

23. Fabian essays, p. 19. He subsequently refers to "a form of rent called interest, obtained by special adaptations of land to production by the application of capital . . ." (ibid., p. 25).

24. "The National Dividend and Its Distribution," in S. and B. Webb, Problems of Modern Industry (London, New York, and Bombay: Longmans, Green, 1898), pp. 218, 219.

25. Ibid., p. 220.

26. Philip Henry Wicksteed, *Coordination of the Laws of Distribution* (London: Macmillan, 1894).

27. It would still not be a rent, in the sense that a reduction in this monopoly return brought about by price fixing or taxation would usually lead to a reduction in the monopolist's output.

28. *Problems of Modern Industry*, p. 237. Also *Fabian Essays*, p. 55.

29. Ibid., pt. III, ch. II.

30. Op cit., p. 671.

31. Ibid., pp. 622 ff.

32. In *Capital and Land* (Fabian Tract no. 7 [7th ed., 1908]) a wholly different criticism of private receipt of interest is advanced by Sidney Oliver. It is to the effect that savings are invested to form concrete capital goods, and when these goods wear out, the goods which replace them are in some mysterious sense not due to the original savings. Shaw uses this argument also in *The Intelligent Woman's Guide to Socialism and Capitalism* (Garden City, N.Y.: Garden City Publ. Co., ca. 1928; London: Constable, 1928).

33. Thus Webb says the Ricardian theory must be extended "to all the instruments of production, as well as to the varying efficiencies of every kind of human labour" ("The Rate of Interest," loc. cit., p. 472; for Shaw's statement, see *Fabian Essays*, pp. 183 ff.).

34. For example, *Fabian Essays*, pp. 55–57. See also E. Halévy, *L'ère des tyrannies* (3rd ed., Paris: Gallimard, ca. 1938), pp. 217–18.

35. *Fabian Essays*, p. 21.

36. For every Shavian parable on the inequities of inequality, one could contrive a counterparable on the inequities of equality; e.g., "Dr. John Upright, the young physician, devoted every energy of his being to the curing of the illnesses of his patients. No hours were too long, no demand on his skill or sympathies too great, if a man or child could be helped. He received £2,000 net each year, until he died at the age of 41 from overwork. Dr. Henry Leisure, on the contrary, insisted that even patients with broken legs be brought to his office only on Tuesdays, Thursdays, and Fridays, between 12:30 and 3:30 P.M. He preferred to take three patients simultaneously, so he could advise while playing bridge, at which he cheated. He received £2,000 net each year, until he retired at the age of 84."

37. "The Case for Equality," in *The Socialism of Shaw*, pp. 53–54.

38. Ibid., p. 60.

39. Ibid., pp. 63–64.

40. "The Difficulties of Individualism," in *Problems of Modern Industry*, pp. 235–36.

41. Ibid., p. 260.

42. See D. Gale Johnson, "Rent Control and the Distribution of Income," *Proceedings of the American Economic Association*, May, 1951, pp. 568–82.

43. Their influence is a difficult question, to which no established answer has yet been given. They are credited with much long-run influence, but little immediate

impact, by H. Pelling, *The Origins of the Labour Party, 1880–1900* (London: Macmillan, 1954; New York: St. Martin's Press, 1954).

44. Of course, to the possibly decisive extent that the distribution of income, rent, theory aside, was the successful element of their indictment, they were only one of many streams of nineteenth-century criticism, and their influence must be assessed correspondingly lower.

ECONOMICS OR ETHICS?

· 18 ·

I. THE ECONOMIST AS PREACHER*

Economists seldom address ethical questions as they impinge on economic theory or economic behavior. They (and I) find this subject complex and elusive in comparison with the relative precision and objectivity of economic analysis. Of course the ethical questions are inescapable: one must have goals in judging policies, and these goals will certainly have ethical content, however well concealed it may be. These lectures will explore some of the problems raised by ethical questions, using the history of economics as an important vehicle in the exploration.

In this first lecture I propose to discuss how economists—primarily great English economists in the main line of development of economics—have advised men and societies on proper conduct. My interest on this occasion is not so much in the advice they have given as in the ethical basis on which this advice has been grounded. Economists have no special professional knowledge

From *The Tanner Lectures on Human Values*, vol. 2 (Salt Lake City: University of Utah Press, 1981). Permission to reprint courtesy of the Trustees of the Tanner Lectures on Human Values.

* I wish to express my gratitude to Gary Becker, Richard Posner, and Stephen Stigler for important assistance, and acknowledge my immense debt to Aaron Director for discussions of these issues both during the preparation of the lectures and in the many years of our friendship. Most of the writing was done while I was a visiting scholar at the Hoover Institution at Stanford University, and I thank Glenn Campbell for providing this attractive setting.

of that which is virtuous or just, and the question naturally arises as to how they are able to deliver confident and distinctive advice to a society that is already well supplied with that commodity.

How Much Preaching?

The first, probably the most important, and possibly the most surprising thing to say about the economist-preachers is that they have done very little preaching. I suppose that it is essential to state what I mean by preaching. I mean simply a clear and reasoned recommendation (or, more often, denunciation) of a policy or form of behavior by men or societies of men. It is hardly desirable to label every nonneutral word as preaching—indeed our language is rather short of words that cannot be used in such a way as to hint of approval or disapproval. During a recent war one economist remarked that he was against "business as usual," and a second was moved to ask whether the speaker was against "business, comma, as usual."

I shall illustrate my loose definition of preaching and many subsequent points by quotations from famous economists, and I digress for a moment to explain their authority to any noneconomists who are present. All but one of the economists I quote were highly intelligent, disciplined men whose views on subjects related to economics deserve your attention and thoughtful consideration, but no more. One, Adam Smith, is differently placed: if on first hearing a passage of his you are inclined to disagree, you are reacting inefficiently; the correct response is to say to yourself: I wonder where I went amiss?

When Adam Smith speaks of the debasement of the currency—which of course proceeds at a much more rapid pace today than it did during his lifetime—he says, "By means of those operations the princes and sovereign states which performed them were enabled, in appearance, to pay their debts and to fulfill their engagements with a smaller quantity of silver than would otherwise have been requisite. It was indeed in appearance only; for their creditors were really defrauded of a part of what was due to them."[1] I consider this to be preaching since "fraud" is not merely a descriptive word. On this mild and I hope reasonable definition of a moral judgment, I have just quoted the only clear example of preaching in the first hundred pages of the Wealth of Nations. The preaching becomes more frequent in Smith's latter pages, but it is almost nonexistent in Ricardo's Principles, quite sparse in Mill's Principles, and virtually nonexistent in Marshall's Principles. Of course these admirable men expressed approval or disapproval of many things with every degree of literary subtlety. It would be easy to compile many remarks like Jevons's that the Morrill Tariff Act of 1861 was "the most retrograde piece of legislation that this [nineteenth] century has witnessed," in which disapproval is at least hinted at.[2]

But these dicta are noteworthy for their scarcity rather than their frequency in the professional works of the economists.

The proposition that economists are not addicted to taking frequent and disputatious policy positions will appear incredible to most noneconomists, and implausible to many economists. The reason, I believe, for this opinion is that in talking to a noneconomist, there is hardly anything in economics except policy for the economist to talk about. The layman is unequipped to discuss with an economist the problems that concern professional economics at any time: he would find that in their professional writing the well-known columnists of *Newsweek* are quite incomprehensible. The typical article in a professional journal is unrelated to public policy—and often apparently unrelated to this world. Whether the amount of policy-advising activity of economists is rising or falling I do not know, but it is not what professional economics is about.

The great economists, then, have not been preoccupied with preaching. Indeed, none has become great because of his preaching—but perhaps I should make an exception for Marx, whom some people rank as a great economist and I rank as an immensely influential one. The fact that the world at large thinks of us as ardent enthusiasts for a hundred policies is not pure error, but it tells more about what the world likes to talk about than what economics is about. The main task of economics has always been to explain real economic phenomena in general terms, and throughout the last two centuries we have adhered to this task with considerable faithfulness, if not always with considerable success.

Preaching to Whom?

It is my impression that the clergy of former times devoted their finest efforts to mending the behavior of individuals, but that in recent times they have sought rather to mend social policy. Whether this impression be right or wrong, economists have seldom spent much time exhorting individuals to higher motives or more exemplary conduct.

Again I return to Mr. Smith. The servants of great joint stock companies such as the East India Company, Smith avers, were concerned only with their own personal fortunes.

> Nothing could be more compleatly foolish than to expect that the clerks of a great counting-house at ten thousand miles distance, and consequently almost quite out of sight, should, upon a simple order from their masters, give up at once doing any sort of business upon their own account, abandon for ever all hopes of making a fortune, of which they have the means in their hands, and content themselves with the moderate salaries which those

masters allow them, and which, moderate as they are, can seldom be augmented, being commonly as large as the real profits of the company trade can
afford. . . . They will employ the whole authority of government, and pervert
the administration of justice, in order to harass and ruin those who interfere
with them in any branch of commerce which, by means of agents, either
concealed, or at least not publickly avowed, they may publickly chuse to
carry on.[3]

After having described these wretchedly venal servants, who exploit both their
masters and their victims, Smith hurries on to say, "I mean not, however, by any
thing which I have here said, to throw any odious imputation upon the general
character of the servants of the East India company, and much less upon that of
any particular persons. It is the system of government, the situation in which
they are placed, that I mean to censure; not the character of those who have
acted in it."[4] So it is social institutions that one should castigate: men respond
to these situations in predictable, and probably unchangeable, ways. This is
not to approve or disapprove of the principle of self-interest that guides men,
although Smith might well have agreed with the remark of Frank H. Knight,
whom we shall later meet more intimately, that anything which is inevitable
is ideal!

Smith's general practice of addressing little preaching to individuals in
their private behavior has continued to this day to be the practice of economists. Of course mortal man cannot wholly abstain from all instruction to the
young, the inferior, and the great, and an enumeration of these acts would be
amusing to you and embarrassing to me. Malthus complained that the lower
classes were excessively attentive to what he termed "the passion between the
sexes," and even John Stuart Mill shared with him a propensity to propose
draconian methods of dealing with the popular implementation of this passion. Alfred Marshall pointed out the unwisdom of gambling with the aid of
the law of diminishing marginal utility, but later, fortunately, Milton Friedman
and Jimmie Savage were able to excuse this activity with the aid of a law of
increasing marginal utility. A vast number of economists have believed that the
sin of myopia with respect to future needs is pervasive. We were once told that a
corporation has no soul to damn or body to kick—a statement that has been
emphatically and prosperously refuted by many politicians to this day. Yet
surely a devil embodied in a person is a much more satisfying object of dislike
and disapproval than some impersonal institution. These lapses of economists
from concern with social rather than individual behavior are forgivable—a
concession to their membership in the human race.

But the lapses are not defensible. Social policies and institutions, not
individual behavior, are the proper object of the economist-preacher's solic-
itude. This orientation is demanded by the very logic of economic theory: we

deal with people who maximize their utility, and it would be both inconsistent and idle for us to urge people not to do so. If we could persuade a monopolist not to maximize profits, then other reformers could persuade resources not to flow to their most remunerative uses, and our theory would become irrelevant.

Preaching Efficiency

In the economists' sermons the dominant theme has been that good policy favors, and bad policy interferes with, the maximizing of income of a society. We shall find other themes, but over the last two hundred years efficiency in the sense of fuller achievement of uncontroversial goals has been the main prescription of normative economists. Let us first look at a major example before turning to an examination of the content and authority of this primary rule of good conduct.

The most sustained application of this principle by Adam Smith was in the attack on interferences with free trade and on mercantilism generally; he devoted one-fourth of his large treatise to this cause. Smith thus asserted that:

> The natural effort of every individual to better his own condition, when suffered to exert itself with freedom and security, is so powerful a principle, that it is alone, and without any assistance, not only capable of carrying on the society to wealth and prosperity, but of surmounting a hundred impertinent obstructions with which the folly of human laws too often incumbers its operations; though the effect of these obstructions is always more or less either to encroach upon its freedom, or to diminish its security.[5]

The argument for free trade was deepened some forty years later by the theory of comparative costs, but the central policy conclusion remained, in Ricardo's words, that "under a system of perfectly free commerce, each country naturally devotes its capital and labour to such employments as are most beneficial to each."[6] This position has been almost universally accepted by economists to this day.

Many other examples, but none more important, of the economists' use of efficiency as the criterion for desirable economic policy could be given. The central element of the criticism of monopoly is that it reduces the efficiency of the use of resources. The central element of the criticism of labor market interferences, such as minimum wage laws or barriers to geographical or occupational mobility, has been their effect on the allocation of resources. An economist is a person who, reading of the confinement of Edmond Dantès in a small cell, laments his lost alternative product.

In Smith's time and for a few decades thereafter the argument for efficiency was embellished with a rhetoric of sacred and inviolable rights of natural liberty. But if the concern with natural liberty was ever strong,[7] it had disappeared by the mid-Victorian age.

The attack on the efficiency of public policies will only be appropriate and convincing when achievement of the goals and costs of the policies are undisputed. If one policy will achieve more of a given goal than a second policy with the same cost in resources, the former policy is clearly superior, and there is no room for argument over ethics. This has indeed been the essential nature of the great majority of the economists' preachings on public policy.

On this reading, the economist-preacher has simply helped to straighten out the issues for a frequently muddled nation. John Stuart Mill explained the misunderstandings that supported mercantilism with his customary lucidity: how common discourse confused money and wealth; how a trader does not consider his venture successful until he has converted his goods into money; how money is par excellence the command over goods in general, ready on the instant to serve any desire as no other commodity can; how the state "derives comparatively little advantage from taxes unless it can collect them in money," and so on. "All these causes conspire to make both individuals and government, in estimating their means, attach almost exclusive importance to money...." But mark well the conclusion: "An absurdity, however, does not cease to be an absurdity when we have discovered what are the appearances which make it plausible...."[8]

And there we have the answer to the question of how the economist can operate so extensively and so easily as a critic of policy when he is not in possession of a persuasive ethical system. The answer is that he needs no ethical system to criticize error: he is simply a well-trained political arithmetician. He lives in a world of social *mistakes*, ancient and modern, subtle and simple, and since he is simply pointing out to the society that what it seeks, it is seeking inefficiently, he need not quarrel with what it seeks.

A world full of mistakes, and capable of producing new mistakes quite as rapidly as the economists can correct the old mistakes! Such well-meaning, incompetent societies need their economic efficiency experts, and we are their self-chosen saviors.

Take away the linen of sophistication in which economists are nowadays dressed, and I believe that this is still the fundamental belief that underlies the large majority of the policy recommendations of our profession. There have indeed been grave income redistribution questions which are receiving increasing attention, but day in and day out for the economist the society's problems are usually problems of efficiency. We live in a mistake-prone world.

I believe that this view of society as a community with acceptable, if not always admirable, goals but possessing only a feeble understanding of efficient methods of achieving them was and is profoundly mistaken.

The mistake in this view should have been evident simply because throughout the period I am discussing there were vigorous controversies over the goals of policy. Indeed, in every literate society, even the most dictatorial, there are critics of the goals of the society. In Ricardo's day, for example, Godwin forcefully argued that the institutions of government and property were among the main causes of social misery. Perhaps Godwin is not an apposite illustration; I suppose that an anarchist is a free trader. Consider, then, Malthus, the first professor of political economy in the history of England, who was a supporter of the very protection of agriculture which was the target of Ricardo's attack.

Malthus argued that a nation specializing in manufactures and trade could easily find that its advantages were eroded by foreign or domestic competition, and in any event could be strongly dependent upon the prosperity of its trading partners. An exclusively agricultural nation could find itself locked into a stagnant feudal social system, or alternatively it could find itself unable to employ capital efficiently once its agricultural plant ceased to grow. Hence Malthus wished a mixed agricultural-commercial system.

I shall not conceal my doubt that Malthus actually demonstrated the superiority of this mixed agricultural-commercial system, but it is surely true that he raised a cloud of complications which were only slowly dealt with by later generations of free traders. Some of these complications concern the determinants of the long-term growth and stability of economies, on which to this day economists have not found confident understanding.

There is a second, and even stronger, reason why the economist—of all people—should be reluctant to characterize a large fraction of political activity as mistaken. The discipline that assumes man to be a reasonably efficient utility maximizer is singularly ill suited to assuming that the political activity of men bears little relationship to their desires. I have argued the theme of intelligent political behavior often enough that I must here limit myself to the barest of remarks.[9] The failure to analyze the political process—to leave it as a curious mixture of benevolent public interest and unintentional blunders—is most unsatisfactory.

Whether one accepts or rejects the high hopes that some of us now entertain for the economic theory of politics, the assumption that public policy has often been inefficient because it was based upon mistaken views has little to commend it. To believe, year after year, decade after decade, that the protective tariffs or usury laws to be found in most lands are due to confusion rather than purposeful action is singularly obfuscatory. Mistakes are indeed made by the best of men and the best of nations, but after a century are we not entitled to question whether the so-called mistakes produce only unintended results?

Alternately stated, a theory that says that a large set of persistent policies are mistaken is profoundly anti-intellectual unless it is joined to a theory of mistakes. It is the most vacuous of "explanatory" principles to dismiss inex-plicable phenomena as mistakes—everything under the sun, or above the sun, can be disposed of with this label, without yielding an atom of understanding.

We economists have traditionally made innumerable criticisms of the inefficiency of various policies, criticisms which have often been to their own (and my own) utter satisfaction. The meager success of these criticisms in changing these policies, I am convinced, stems from the fact that more than narrow efficiency has been involved in almost every case—that inexplicit or incomprehensible goals were served by these policies and served tolerably efficiently. Tariffs were redistributing income to groups with substantial politi-cal power, not simply expressing the deficient public understanding of the theory of comparative costs. We live in a world that is full of mistaken policies, but they are not mistaken for their supporters.

I wish to recur for a moment to the policy of mercantilism, which Smith attributed to the clever machinations of the merchants and traders against the simple, honorable landowners who still constituted the governing class of Great Britain in his time. Smith and his followers should have asked themselves whether simple error could persist, to the large and centuries-long cost of a class intelligent enough to hire the likes of Edmund Burke. I say, with great fear and trembling, that it is more probable that Smith, not the nobility of England, was mistaken as to the cost and benefits of the mercantile system. I say this for his sake: a world of great and permanent error would be a poor place for economics to live.

Preaching Equity

There is one large set of policies which cannot easily be judged merely as to efficiency in reaching widely accepted, comparatively uncontroversial goals: I refer to those which seek to redistribute income. If Nelson and Jones have equal incomes, and a policy takes half of Nelson's income and gives it to Jones, a question of equity will inevitably arise in the minds of everyone except Jones.

For the century from Smith to Jevons, economists were correspondingly discreet in their discussions of income distribution. It may be supposed that Smith thought income distribution was a matter for markets to determine when he said, "To hurt in any degree the interest of any one order of citizens, for no other purpose but to promote that of some other, is evidently contrary to that justice and equality of treatment which the sovereign owes to all the different orders of his subjects."[10] I am inclined to accept this view even though one can find occasional departures such as his proposal to tax the "indolence and vanity of the rich" by having disproportionately heavy tolls on carriages of luxury (II, p. 246), for these departures are few and casual.[11]

The classical school did not depart far from Smith's practice. The evil effects of equality were held to be two: a decrease in incentives to thrift and work; and an increase in the population on Malthus's principles. Ricardo would deny the suffrage to those who would not respect the rights of property.[12] Mill, although he was the author of the comforting thesis that the distribution of wealth, unlike its production, was socially malleable, was unprepared to support a progressive income tax—in his case, because of a fear of the effects of leveling income upon the growth of population as well as because such a tax would be insufferably inquisitorial in administration. Bentham's flirtation with notions of equality flowing from the utilitarian calculus left no imprint on friends, disciples, or tenants.

There was one interesting near exception to this rule of near silence on the redistribution of income. The rent of land, the payment for the use of its "original and indestructible" properties, was by definition a nonfunctional income, so that social control over rent would not affect the use of the land. Hence Mill was the ardent supporter of the nationalization of future incre-ments of land values. But even here Mill wished to compensate present landowners fully.[13]

All this was to change when, but not because, the theory of utility became a centerpiece of economics. In 1881 Edgeworth published *Mathematical Psychics*, in which the utilitarian calculus was presented with magnificent subtlety, imagery, and fruitfulness. A marriage was performed between utility and natural selection, culminating in proposals such as that people below a certain level of capacity should not be allowed to have children,[14] and that the possible correlation of capacity to produce with capacity to enjoy might lead even to the superiority of aristocracy. This effusion was in due time replaced by the classic formulation of the utilitarian rule of taxation, minimum sacrifice. The state should tax the rich *before* the poor, not simply more heavily than the poor, subject to the unexplored dangers of the effects of aggressively progressive taxation on production.[15] Progression followed from the twin assumptions that the marginal utility of income falls as income rises, and there is no systematic relationship between the amount of income a person possesses and his efficiency in converting income into utility.

By 1912 Pigou was prepared to assert as an axiom of welfare economics that "economic welfare is likely to be augmented by anything that, leaving other things unaltered, renders the distribution of the national dividend less unequal."[16] He was still reluctant to engage in extensive direct redistribution, on the ground—so characteristic of this eccentric man—that the poor would not use the funds intelligently: "Women, who cook badly or feed their children on pickles, are not bankrupted out of the profession of motherhood; fathers who invest their sons' activities unremuneratively are not expelled from fatherhood. . . . What has been said, however, . . . should suffice to establish the thesis . . . that the poor, as entrepreneurs of investment in themselves and their children, are abnormally incompetent."[17] Fortunately the intelligence of the poor was rising at a powerful rate, so a few years later Pigou was able to write that, "To charge the whole body of the poorer classes with ignorance and lack of capacity for management would, indeed, be to utter a gross libel."[18] Or was Pigou getting in step with society?

I shall assert what I believe I could document, a steadily rising concern with the distribution of income among economist-preachers during the last one hundred years. Today the consequences of any policy on the distribution of income is the early subject of every appraisal, and egalitarianism is an almost uncontroverted goal of social policy. Two broad statements can be made about the ascendancy of income distribution as the subject of ethical judgments on economic policy.

The first is that the expanding concern of economists with income distribution did not come from within economics. Until recently, the professional literature on income distribution has been sparse, relatively iconoclastic (especially with reference to the possibility of interpersonal comparisons of utility), and noncumulative. It cannot be doubted that the economists have imported egalitarian values into economics from the prevailing ethos of the societies in which they live, and they have not been important contributors to the formation of that ethos. In the English tradition from which I have been drawing my examples, the Fabian socialists were immensely more influential and outspoken supporters of egalitarianism than the neoclassical economists.

The second generalization is that the wide acceptance of the ethical desirability of extensive income redistribution has inhibited the development of a positive theory of income distribution. Such a positive theory would explain how the size distribution of income affected, and was affected by, developments such as rising wealth and education, the roles of taxation and other forms of political action, the institutions of inheritance, and the changing nature of the family. Just such a positive theory is beginning to emerge, and I predict that it will have important effects upon the attitudes of economists toward policies of redistribution. The remarkable circumstance, however, that professional study of income distribution up to recent times was small and noncumulative is attributable to the fact that economists viewed the subject as primarily ethical.

Conclusion

I must bring this sermon on economic sermons to a close. The main lesson I draw from our experience as preachers is that we are well received in the measure that we preach what the society wishes to hear. Perhaps all preachers achieve popularity by this route.

The degree of popularity of a preacher does not necessarily measure his influence as a preacher, let alone as a scholar. In fact one could perhaps argue that the unpopular sermons are the more influential—certainly if the opposite is true, and preachers simply confirm their listeners' beliefs, pulpits should be at the rear of congregations, to make clearer who is leading. Whether economic preachers lead or follow, they need an ethical system to guide their recommendations. I shall address the nature and sources of their ethics in the next lecture.

II. THE ETHICS OF COMPETITION: THE FRIENDLY ECONOMISTS

The system of organization of an economy by private decisions on the allocation of resources and the private determination of the composition and distribution of final outputs is variously known as the market system, the enterprise system, competition, laissez-faire, and by the Marxian word, monopoly-capitalism. This system has been the main method of control of economic life in the last two hundred years in the Western world, but the extent of governmental intervention has increased enormously in both its scope and depth of detail.

In this lecture I plan first to discuss the attitudes of the mainstream of English economists toward this system—the measure and content of their approval and disapproval of the enterprise system. I shall dwell only briefly on the premodern evolution of their attitudes and treat primarily with the modern attitudes toward the market. Thereafter, I shall address the questions of where the economists get their ethics and the effects of these ethical values on their work.

To 1900: The Growth of Caution in the Economists' Defense

Until the mid-nineteenth century, the virtues of the enterprise system were as widely accepted as the belief in its efficiency. Private property turned sand into gold, and no one complained at the loss of the sand or the presence of the gold. The "natural system of liberty" was extended widely. It is true that considerable lists have been compiled of the public tasks which the classical economists assigned to the state to correct or reinforce private actions, but they were not widespread or systematic *programs*, rather a spattering of Band-Aids to be put on the body economic. Malthus denounced systems of equality as part of his population essay and Ricardo ridiculed Robert Owen's parallelograms.[19]

John Stuart Mill was much more ambivalent on the comparative merits of private enterprise and various forms of socialism. The ambivalence was attributable to three sources: his remarkable propensity to understand and state fairly almost any view; the influence of Harriet, the femme fatale of the history of economics; and the astonishing and absurd deficiencies which he assigned to private enterprise. He asserted that perhaps nine-tenths of the labor force had compensation which at best was loosely related to exertion and achievement—indeed so loosely that he expressed indignation that the "produce of labour should be apportioned as we now see it, almost in an inverse ratio to the labour."[20] He felt able to assert that a competitive market could not achieve a shortening of hours of work, even if all the laborers wished it.[21] It has been said that only a highly educated man can be highly mistaken. Mill is no refutation.

Nevertheless, while stating in explicit and implicit ways that political economy did not imply laissez-faire, he initiated a practice that was soon to become widey imitated. After listing several reasons for preferring laissez-faire—chiefly grounded on a desire for individual freedom and development, but grounded also on efficiency—Mill concludes, "few will dispute the more than sufficiency of these reasons, to throw, in every instance, the burthen of making out a strong case, not on those who resist, but on those who recommend, government interference. *Laissez-faire*, in short, should be the general practice: every departure from it, unless required by some great good, a certain evil."[22] The practice of denying laissez-faire as a theorem but asserting its expediency as a general rule soon became, and to this day (I shall later argue) has remained, the set lecture of the economist. Soon Cairnes, Jevons, Sidgwick, Marshall, and J. M. Keynes confirmed the tradition.[23] Monopoly, externalities, ignorance, and other reasons for departing from laissez-faire accumulated, but as individual exceptions to a general rule.

This compromise, in which Pure Science was silent but Heavy Presumption favored laissez-faire, troubles me more than it has most economists. A science is successful in the measure that it explains in general terms the behavior of the phenomena within its self-imposed boundaries. Let me give an example: the science should be able to tell us the effects of a minimum wage law on the employment and compensation of all workers, the effects on consumers through price changes, and so on. The standard analysis, to be specific, predicts that a minimum wage law reduces the incomes of the least capable workers and of the community at large, and various other effects.

One could say that the theory does not lead to an unambiguous rejection of minimum wage laws because of limitations imposed by the economist's framework: for example, monopsony in the labor market or ignorance of workers leads to inefficient market results. Then, however, the economist should analyze the effects reached under (say) minimum wage laws and laissez-faire with monopsony, and reach a definite result or no result. In either event, no *presumption* is established.

Alternatively, the theory may be deemed inconclusive for reasons lying outside the economists' domain; in particular, social values not recognized by the theory may reverse the conclusion.[24] For example, a desired income redistribution (or some other social value) may be achieved by the minimum wage law. Thus the apparent beneficiaries of a minimum wage law are the workers above the minimum wage, and indeed that is the reason the AFL-CIO supports the law. Or the workers in a high-wage area may be protected from the competition of a low-wage area, preserving a desired distribution of population.

Very well, let these or other reasons be sufficient to explain the informed passage and continuance of the minimum wage law by the community. Is it not then a fair request of economic theory that it include these results in its study of the minimum wage law? Why shouldn't the full range of consequences important to the society be important to the economist? Unless we invoke consequences outside the scope of rational inquiry—say, that the law favors believers in the true God, without further identification—it is not easy to live with both a pure science of economic phenomena and a set of nonderivative presumptions about practice. Of course the neglect of values other than efficiency may be defended on grounds of scientific division of labor, even though no other science seems inclined to study the neglected share. In any event, one wonders again where the presumption comes from.

I suspect the answer to these questions is that the economists have decided, possibly implicitly and silently, that the other values that might overcome the efficiency presumption are usually weak or conflicting, or even reinforce the conclusion based upon the studied effects. I am in no position to quarrel with this as a working philosophy: no matter how full the explanation of why we have minimum wages—and it is a study we should broaden—I predict that we economists will not like the law. But the working philosophy should not parade as science.

Marginal Productivity Ethics

The decline in open, unconditional praise of the enterprise system by economists suffered one important interruption at the end of the nineteenth century. The occasion was the discovery and widespread adoption of the marginal productivity theory.

The marginal productivity theory states that in competitive equilibrium each productive factor receives a rate of compensation equal to the value of its marginal or additional contribution to the enterprise that employs it. If the productive factor is a laborer, and he works as (say) a service worker with negligible capital equipment, in equilibrium his wage will equal simply the amount of revenue his services add to the enterprise. If, as is usually the case, the product of all factors is commingled, the marginal product may be manifested as a slighty larger crop or a more reliable machine or some other salable attribute.

If you declare to a layman that a certain individual is paid his marginal product, after explaining perhaps more clearly than I have what a marginal product is, and then add, "Isn't that simply outrageous?," I predict that this layman will be amazed by your comment. In any event, several economists who were among the founders and disseminators of the marginal productivity theory did take exactly the view that the value of the marginal product of a person was the just rate of his remuneration.

The most famous exponent of this view was John Bates Clark. In his magnum opus, *The Distribution of Wealth* (1899), he stated:

> The welfare of the laboring classes depends on whether they get much or little; but their attitude toward other classes—and therefore the stability of the social state—depends chiefly on the question, whether the amount they get, be it large or small, is what they produce. If they create a small amount of wealth and get the whole of it, they may not seek to revolutionize society; but if it were to appear that they produce an ample amount and get only part of it, many of them would become revolutionists, and all would have the right to do so. . . .
>
> Having first tested the honesty of the social state, by determining whether it gives to every man his own [product], we have next to test its beneficence, by ascertaining whether that which is his own is becoming greater or smaller.[25]

T. N. Carver of Harvard was also an exponent of productivity ethics:

> But if the number of a particular kind of laborers is so small and the other factors are so abundant that one more laborer of this particular kind would add greatly to the product of the combination, then it is not inaccurate to say that his physical product is very high. That being the case, his value is very high. This, therefore, is the principle which determines how much a man is worth, and consequently, according to our criterion of justice, how much he ought to have as a reward for his work.[26]

I have not sought to discover how many economists joined in this ethical justification of competition. I believe that many economists did so, not so often by explicit avowal as by the implicit acceptance of the propriety of marginal productivity as the basis for remuneration. Pigou, for example, wished to define an exploitive wage, and he chose as his definition a wage which fell below the value of the marginal product of the worker.[27]

This literature is usually referred to as "naive productivity ethics," with the adjective serving not to distinguish it from some other more sophisticated ethical system but to express disapproval. The classic statement of this disapproval is the famous essay by Frank Knight, "The Ethics of Competition" (1923).[28] Four charges are made against the claims of the competitive system to be just:

> 1. An economic system molds the tastes of its members, so the system cannot be defended on the ground that it satisfies demand efficiently.[29]
>
> 2. The economic system is not *perfectly* efficient: there are indivisibilities, imperfect knowledge, monopoly, externalities, etc.[30]
>
> 3. The paramount defect of the competitive system is that it distributes income largely on the basis of inheritance and luck (with some minor influence of effort). The inequality of income increases cumulatively under competition.[31]
>
> 4. Viewed (alternatively) as a game, competition is poorly fashioned to meet acceptable standards of fairness, such as giving everyone an even start and allowing a diversity of types of rivalries.

When I first read this essay a vast number of years ago, as a student writing his dissertation under Professor Knight's supervision, you should not be surprised to hear that I thought his was a conclusive refutation of "productivity ethics." When I reread it a year or so ago, I was shocked by the argumentation. Knight made a series of the most sweeping and confident empirical judgments (such as those underlying the first and third charges) for which he could not have even a cupful of supporting evidence. Moreover, why was it even relevant, with respect to his second charge, that real-world markets are not perfectly competitive in his special sense: one can define a perfect standard to judge imperfect performance, and assuredly real-world performance under any form of economic organization will be less than perfect by any general criterion. Knight kept referring to the objections to competitive results under any "acceptable ethical system" but never told us what such a system contained in the way of ethical content. His own specific judgments do not seem compelling, as when he asserted that "no one contends that a bottle of old wine is ethically worth as much as a barrel of flour." Dear Professor Knight, please forgive your renegade student, but I do so contend, if it was a splendid year for claret.

I shall have more to say about acceptable ethical positions shortly, but for the moment I wish only to assert that the appeal of productivity ethics for income distribution commands wide support not only from the public but also from the economists when they are watching their sentiments rather than their words. Ethical values cannot be counted by a secret ballot referendum, but the support for a productivity ethic is indeed widespread. Even Marx, like Pigou, defined surplus value as the part of a worker's product that he was not paid. The fact that more than skill and effort go into remuneration—that in Knight's example bearded women get good circus jobs simply by not shaving—is not enough to dismiss productivity ethics.

The Ethics of Economists

I have postponed as long as possible the question: where do economists get their ethical systems? My answer is: wherever they can find one.

One occasional source has been a widely acceptable philosophical system. The most important such system in the history of economics has been utilitarianism, which was strongly influential on Bentham's circle, Sidgwick, Marshall, Pigou, and above all Edgeworth. I have already referred to Edgeworth's *Mathematical Psychics* (1881), which is in good part a reproduction of his earlier monograph, *New and Old Methods of Ethics* (1877). Edgeworth presents the utilitarian ethic in full grandeur:

> 'Mécanique Sociale' may one day take her place along with 'Mécanique Celeste,' throned each upon the double-sided height of one maximum principle, the supreme pinnacle of moral as of physical science. As the movements of each particle, constrained or loose, in a material cosmos are continually subordinated to one maximum sum-total of accumulated energy, so the movements of each soul, whether selfishly isolated or linked sympathetically, may continually be realizing the maximum energy of pleasure, the Divine love of the universe.[32]

Edgeworth's calculus and Sidgwick's *Methods of Ethics* represent the high point of the utilitarian ethics in neoclassical economics.

It proved to be a major obstacle to the explicit use of the utilitarian ethic that it required additional information, particularly about the efficiency of different persons in producing utility, that admitted of no objective determination. Recall that Edgeworth was led to recognize the possibility that an aristocracy might be the best of all societies.

Even when the difficulty of comparing utilities could be overcome, and it was generally overcome by consensus rather than by argument or evidence, the systematic ethic led to an embarrassing consequence. Let me explain by example.

When one traces out the applications of a general ethical system one encounters problems such as one that Alfred Marshall faced. He examined the properties of good excise taxes in a chapter suitably entitled "Theories of Changes in Normal Demand and Supply in Relation to the Doctrine of Maximum Satisfaction."[33] According to the utilitarian theory, it is more desirable, Marshall stated, to tax necessaries rather than luxuries because the demand for necessaries is less elastic and therefore an excise tax will occasion a smaller loss of consumer utility (surplus).[34] Of course he rejected this recommendation of regressive taxation because it ignored ability to pay taxes.

It might be argued that if Marshall had properly weighted the marginal utility of income of the poor as greater than that of the rich, he would be freed of embarrassment. Possibly, although he would then have needed to compare the magnitudes of utilities with taxation of luxuries and taxation of necessaries. In any event, other embarrassing implications are readily found, for example, that the utilitarian goal would imply cosmopolitan income redistribution.

And that is the trouble with a comprehensive ethical system: it leads to conclusions which are unpopular with the community and therefore unpopular with the economists. I believe, although I have not undertaken the substantial task of verifying, the proposition that wherever an ethical system has clashed with widespread social values, the economists have abandoned the implications of the ethical system. If that is indeed the case, it strongly argues for the acceptance of the community's values with whatever inconsistencies they contain.

John Rawls once proposed a way out of this impasse—a method of deriving general ethical values that were both inductive and capable of consistent application. His proposal was as follows. Select a set of competent judges and ask them to decide many and varied specific conflicts that arise between individuals in the society. Given their decisions, seek an explication or principle that correctly predicts these decisions on average and call that principle the ethical principle. Any implicit ethical principles that had been followed by the competent judges would be recovered by this procedure. One might complain at the elitist nature of the procedure, and a fundamental question is of course whether any principles would be found to exist.[35] Rawls's later and influential presentation of a modified utilitarian theory of justice has no such inductive basis, which suggests that he also found an inductive ethics difficult to systematize, and possibly difficult to accept.[36]

If economists have been content to base their goals upon the ruling views of the educated classes, as I believe to be the case, that is not quite the same thing as saying that they have simply taken an implicit opinion poll on ethical values and either accepted the majority view or distributed themselves in proportion to the frequencies of views held by these classes. Their own discipline has had its own influence.

Members of other social sciences often remark, in fact I must say complain, at the peculiar fascination that the logic of rational decision-making exerts upon economists. It is such an interesting logic: it has answers to so many and varied questions, often answers that are simultaneously reasonable to economists and absurd to others. The paradoxes are not diminished by the delight with which economists present them. How pleased Longfield must have been when he showed that if, in periods of acute shortage, the rich bought grain and sold it at half price to the poor, the poor were not helped. How annoyed the ecclesiastical readers of Smith must have been to learn that the heavy subsidization of clerical training served only to lower the income of curates. How outraged even some economists are with Becker's "rotten kid theorem," which demonstrates that altruistic treatment of a selfish person forces him to behave as an unselfish person would.

Economic logic centers on utility-maximizing behavior by individuals. Such behavior may be found in every area of human behavior—and my just-mentioned colleague, Gary Becker, has analyzed it with striking results in areas such as crime, marriage and divorce, fertility, and altruistic behavior—but the central application of economic theory has been in explicit markets. The power of self-interest, and its almost unbelievable delicacy and subtlety in complex decision areas, has led economists to seek a large role for explicit or implicit prices in the solution of many social problems.

As a result, in a period of rapid and extensive movement away from reliance on competitive markets to allocate resources and to distribute income, economists have not led the trend but rather followed it at substantial distance. They have sought persistently to employ prices to abate pollution or to ration energy or to incite safety conditions. They have been at the forefront of what presently appears to be a modest policy of deregulation of certain areas of economic behavior.

It would take a wiser person than I to determine which shares of this market orientation of economists are due to professional training, to attachment to a demonstrably efficient machinery for allocating resources that is largely (but not completely) independent of the goals being sought, and to ethical values in the market organization of economic activity. But this last component, the ethical attractiveness of voluntary exchange, plays at least some part in our attitudes, and I shall give an example of its role.

Market transactions are voluntary and repetitive. These traits are much less marked in political transactions, or military transactions, although perhaps not in religious transactions. Because the market transactions are voluntary, they must benefit at least one party and not injure the other. Because they are repetitive, they (usually) make deceit and nonfulfillment of promises unprofitable. A reputation for candor and responsibility is a commercial asset—on the enterprise's balance sheet it may be called goodwill.

Nothing in rational behavior precludes the formation of habits which economize on decision-making costs. One such habit according to Marshall is probity: "The opportunities for knavery are certainly more numerous than they were; but there is no reason for thinking that men avail themselves of a larger proportion of such opportunities than they used to do. On the contrary, modern methods of trade imply habits of trustfulness on the one side and power of resisting temptation to dishonesty on the other, which do not exist among a backward people."[37] A still stronger, and much earlier, extension of the same argument was made by Smith:

> Whenever commerce is introduced into any country, probity and punctuality always accompany it. These virtues in a rude and barbarous country are almost unknown. Of all the nations in Europe, the Dutch, the most commercial, are the most faithful to their word. The English are more so than the Scotch, but much inferiour to the Dutch, and in the remote parts of this country they (are) far less so than in the commercial parts of it. This is not at all to be imputed to national character, as some pretend. There is no natural reason why an Englishman or a Scotchman should not be as punctual in performing agreements as a Dutchman. It is far more reduceable to self interest, that general principle which regulates the actions of every man, and which leads men to act in a certain manner from views of advantage, and is as deeply implanted in an Englishman as a Dutchman. A dealer is afraid of losing his character, and is scrupulous in observing every engagement. When a person makes perhaps 20 contracts in a day, he cannot gain so much by endeavouring to impose on his neighbours, as the very appearance of a cheat would make him lose. Where people seldom deal with one another, we find that they are somewhat disposed to cheat, because they can gain more by a smart trick than they can lose by the injury which it does their character. They whom we call politicians are not the most remarkable men in the world for probity and punctuality. Ambassadors from different nations are still less so: they are praised for any little advantage they can take, and pique themselves a good deal on this degree of refinement. The reason of this is that nations treat with one another not above twice or thrice in a century, and they may gain more by one piece of fraud than by having a bad character. France has had this character with us ever since the reign of Lewis XIVth, yet it has never in the least hurt either its interest or splendour.[38]

I do not know whether in actual fact the participants in economic transactions behave more honestly than those in diplomatic exchanges or in primitive barter, but I am reasonably confident that Marshall and Smith also did not know when they wrote these passages, whatever they have learned since. But I do believe that they, and most modern economists, accept the substance of their position on commercial morality.

This belief is based not upon some poll of opinion but on our daily practice. Modern economists almost invariably postulate transactions free of fraud or coercion. This postulate is partially presented in mathematical versions as the budget equation, which states that for each economic agent the sum of values received equals the sum of values given up. No transaction

therefore leaves anyone worse off, ex ante, than he was before he entered it—
almost a definition of a noncoercive transaction.

There is no inherent reason for us to make this assumption, and two good
reasons for not doing so. The first reason for including fraud and coercion in
economics is that they are probably impossible to distinguish from honorable
dealing. Assume that I take a shortcut home through a park each night, and
once a week on average I am robbed of my trousers—I have learned not to carry
money. Is this not a voluntary transaction in which I pay a toll of one-fifth of a
pair of trousers per day for access to the shortcut? Assume that I sell to you a
plot of land which you erroneously believe to cover an oil pool, and I know the
truth. Am I being fraudulent? If so, modify the circumstances so that you know
there is oil and I don't. Clearly we find situations in which the presence of fraud
is rejected by half the population.

Second, even when fraud or coercion is unambiguous in the eyes of the
society, that is no reason to believe that ordinary economic analysis is inapplicable. Fraudulent securities will be supplied in such quantity that their
marginal costs, including selling costs, equal their marginal revenue. One
would not expect criminals to earn more than they could obtain in legitimate
callings, proper allowance being made for all costs of doing business. The
ordinary propositions of economics hold for crime.

I conclude that we economists have customarily excluded fraud and
coercion because we have thought they they are not empirically significant
elements in the ordinary economic transactions of an enterprise economy.

Although economists have displayed a larger affection for the system of
private enterprise than has the remainder of the educated public, this is not to
say that prevalent social views have no influence on technical economic
writing. Consider the enormous attention that is devoted to monopoly in
modern economic theory, an attention so vast that it has virtually taken
possession of the literature on industrial organization. The evidence that
monopoly is important is negligible, and the evidence that it is a quite minor
influence on the workings of the economy is large. I have slowly been ap-
proaching the view of Schumpeter, that the eminent role of monopoly in
economic literature is due to the influence of general social views.[39]

What Is Ethics?

Economists, I have just said, believe that economic transactions are
usually conducted on a high level of candor and responsibility, because it is in
the interest of the parties to behave honorably in repetitive transactions.
Hence honesty pays.

Against this view we may set that of Archbishop Richard Whately, himself
something of an economist as well as a noted logician and divine. The man

who acts on the principle that honesty is the best policy, said His Grace, is a man who is not honest.[40] He did not elaborate, but the meaning is clear: he who behaves honestly because it is remunerative is simply an amoral calculator; an honest man is one whose principles of right conduct are adopted independently of their consequences for him.

If every person in a society shared the utilitarian goal of maximum utility for the society, all would presumably behave honestly because there is a large deadweight loss to society in erecting defenses against dishonesty and punishing its manifestations. If even one person did not share this ethic, it might well pay him to engage in acts of dishonesty—indeed it would hardly pay the society to take defensive steps against him or her. One may therefore conclude that honesty would be a utilitarian ethic for the society as a whole, even though honesty did not pay (was not utilitarian) for an individual.

Do people possess ethical beliefs which influence their behavior in ways not dictated by, and hence in conflict with, their own long-run utility-maximizing behavior? This question is not free of ambiguity: if we allow unlimited altruism in the individual's utility function, we are back to social utilitarianism. Less to avoid this result than to attain a position that seems empirically defensible, I shall assume that the altruism is strong within the family and toward close friends and diminishes with the social distance of the person— very much the position Adam Smith advanced in his *Moral Sentiments*.[41] This interpretation does not determine the answer to the question whether people act on ethical principles. Indeed it eliminates the easy answer, "of course, they give to charity."

The question of the existence of effective ethical values is of course an empirical question, and in principle it should be directly testable. I recall reading of an experiment in which stamped and addressed but unsealed envelopes with small sums of money were scattered in the streets, and records were compiled of which envelopes were mailed to the designated recipient. My faint recollection is that more envelopes were mailed when the designated recipient was a charity, but that most sums were appropriated by the finders.

One could quarrel at the design of this test, as I recall it, for it gave no information on the finders: perhaps those who were conversing with their clergymen when the envelope was found behaved differently from those who were conversing with their bookies. Still, it is an interesting line of inquiry, one that would be a better employment of the recent doctorates in philosophy than the employments which are reported.

Let me predict the outcome of the systematic and comprehensive testing of behavior in situations where self-interest and ethical values with wide verbal allegiance are in conflict. Much of the time, most of the time in fact, the self-interest theory (as I interpreted it on Smithian lines) will win. In a set of cases that is not negligible and perhaps not random with respect to social characteristics of the actors, the self-interest hypothesis will fail—at least without a subtle and unpredictable interpretation of self-interest.

I predict this result because it is the prevalent one found by economists not only within a wide variety of economic phenomena, but in their investigations of marital, childbearing, criminal, religious, and other social behavior as well. We believe that man is a utility-maximizing animal—apparently pigeons and rats are also—and to date we have not found it informative to carve out a section of his life in which he invokes a different goal of behavior. In fact, the test I have just proposed has very little potential scope, I shall argue, because most ethical values do not conflict with individual utility-maximizing behavior.

I pursue this dangerous line of thought in my final lecture.

III. The Ethics of Competition: The Unfriendly Critics

In the century following the appearance of the *Wealth of Nations*, the pace of economic progress accelerated to levels never before achieved on so continuous and comprehensive a scale. The technology, the economy, the lives, and even the politics of the Western world underwent profound and lasting changes. The standard of living reached continually higher levels, longevity increased, and education spread over the entire society.

It was to be expected that the radical changes accompanying this astonishing economic development would arouse deep opposition and bitter criticism from some groups. Important figures in the cultural circles of Great Britain were soon nostalgic for a romantic past. Robert Southey, the poet laureate, viewed the earlier cottage system and the factory system through bifocal spectacles with rose and black tints, respectively:

> . . . we remained awhile in silence, looking upon the assemblage of dwellings below. Hence, and in the adjoining hamlet of Millbeck, the effects of manufactures and of agriculture may be seen and compared. The old cottages are such as the poet and the painter equally delight in beholding. Substantially built of the native stone without mortar, dirtied with no white-lime, and their long low roofs covered with slate, if they had been raised by the magic of some indigenous Amphion's music, the materials could not have adjusted themselves more beautifully in accord with the surrounding scene: and time has still further harmonized them with weather-stains, lichens and moss, short grasses and short fern, and stone-plants of various kinds. The ornamented chimneys, round or square, less adorned than those which, like litte turrets, crest the houses of the Portuguese peasantry; and yet not less happily suited to their place, the hedge of clipt box beneath the windows, the rose bushes beside the door, the little patch of flower ground, with its tall

holly-hocks in front; the garden beside, the beehives, and the orchard with its bank of daffodils and snowdrops (the earliest and the profusest in these parts), indicate in the owners some portion of ease and leisure, some regard to neatness and comfort, some sense of natural and innocent and healthful enjoyment. The new cottages of the manufacturers are . . . upon the manufacturing pattern . . . naked, and in a row.

How is it, said I, that everything which is connected with manufactures presents such features of unqualified deformity? From the largest of Mammon's temples down to the poorest hovel in which his helotry are stalled, these edifices have all one character. Time cannot mellow them; nature will neither clothe nor conceal them; and they remain always as offensive to the eye as to the mind![42]

Of the innumerable voices that joined in this swelling chorus, I shall briefly notice two.

Thomas Carlyle, who gave the dismal science this name, wrote with his customary passion:

And yet I will venture to believe that in no time, since the beginnings of Society, was the lot of those same dumb millions of toilers so entirely unbearable as it is even in the days now passing over us. It is not to die, or even to die of hunger, that makes a man wretched; many men have died; all men must die,—the last exit of us all is in a Fire-Chariot of Pain. But it is to live miserable we know not why; to work sore and yet gain nothing; to be heartworn, weary, yet isolated, unrelated, girt in with a cold universal Laissez-faire; it is to die slowly all our life long, imprisoned in a deaf, dead, Infinite Injustice, as in the accursed iron belly of a Phalaris' Bull! This is and remains forever intolerable to all men whom God has made. Do we wonder at French Revolutions, Chartisms, Revolts of Three Days? The Times, if we will consider them, are really unexampled.[43]

Finally, John Ruskin's immense Victorian audience was repeatedly instructed in the vices of industrialism. He was prepared to sum up his entire message in the declaration: "Government and cooperation are in all things the Laws of Life; Anarchy and competition the Laws of Death."[44] A more explicit version runs: "It being the privilege of the fishes as it is of rats and wolves, to live by the laws of demand and supply; but the distinction of humanity, to live by those of right."[45]

A full tour through the modern critics of the competitive organization of society would be a truly exhausting trip. It would include the drama, the novel, the churches, the academies, the lesser intellectual establishments, the socialists and communists and Fabians and a swarm of other dissenters. One is reminded of Schumpeter's remark that the Japanese earthquake of 1924 had a remarkable aspect: it was not blamed on capitalism. Suddenly one realizes how impoverished our society would be in its indignation, as well as in its food, without capitalism.

It is no part of my present purpose to sketch this opposition, and still less to attempt to refute it. Many excellent replies have been penned: Southey's passage with which I began called forth the full scorn—and that is truly a vast scorn—of Macaulay:

> Mr. Southey has found out a way, he tells us, in which the effects of manufactures and agriculture may be compared. And what is this way? To stand on a hill, to look at a cottage and a factory, and to see which is the prettier. Does Mr. Southey think that the body of the English peasantry live, or ever lived, in substantial or ornamented cottages, with box-hedges, flower-gardens, beehives, and orchards? If not, what is his parallel worth? We despise those mock philosophers who think that they serve the cause of science by depreciating literature and the fine arts. But if anything could excuse their narrowness of mind, it would be such a book as this.[46]

Macaulay in fact would give Southey credit for only "two faculties which were never, we believe, vouchsafed in measure so copious to any human being—the faculty of believing without a reason, and the faculty of hating without a provocation."[47]

Later, and usually lesser, defenders of laissez-faire have proved that the critics behaved as critics usually do: inventing some abuses in the system they attacked; denouncing some of its virtues as abuses; exaggerating the real shortcomings; and being singularly blind to the difficulties of any alternative economic system, when they faced this problem at all. But these characteristics are not unique to the critics of private enterprise and may well be inherent in criticisms of any existing order.

I begin with this smattering of early critics only to suggest that important leaders of public opinion have long been opposed to a competitive economic system. There is a natural temptation to credit to them and their numerous present-day progeny the decline that has occurred in the public esteem for private enterprise and the large expansion of state control over economic life. I urge you to resist that temptation. After a preliminary look at the so-called followers of opinion, I shall return to the leaders and seek to explain their attitudes and to question their importance. If my interpretation is correct, it raises interesting questions on the future of private enterprise.

Have Attitudes Changed?: The Lower Classes

History is written by and for the educated classes. We know more about the thoughts and actions of an eighteenth-century lord than about 100,000 members of the classes which were at or near the bottom of the income and educational scales. No one can deduce, from documentary evidence, the attitudes of these lower classes toward economic philosophies, whereas the noble lord's words are enshrined in Hansard and several fat volumes of published correspondence. Hence we cannot determine from direct documentary sources what the attitudes toward laissez-faire of these lower classes have been.

Nevertheless, it is an hypothesis that is plausible to me and I hope tenable to you that these lower classes—who have increased immensely in wealth and formal education in the last several hundred years—have been strongly attracted to the economic regime of laissez-faire capitalism. One highly persuasive evidence of this is the major spontaneous migrations of modern history: the armies of Europeans that came to the United States, until barriers were created at both ends; the millions of Chinese who have sought entrance to Hong Kong, Shanghai, and other open Asian economies; the millions of Mexicans who these days defy American laws designed to keep them home. These have not been simply migrations from poorer to richer societies, although even that would carry its message, but primarily migrations of lower classes of the home populations. An open, decentralized economy is still the land of opportunity for the lower classes.

The stake of the lower classes in the system of competition is based upon the fact that a competitive productive system is remarkably indifferent to status. An employer finds two unskilled workers receiving $3.00 per hour an excellent substitute for a semiskilled worker receiving $8.00 per hour. A merchant finds ten one-dollar purchases by the poor more profitable than a seven-dollar purchase by a prosperous buyer. This merchant is much less interested in the color of a customer than in the color of his money.

If it is true that a large share of the population of modern societies (and many other societies as well) eagerly migrates to competitive economies when given the opportunity, why have these people supported the vast expansion of governmental controls over economic life in the many democratic societies in which they constitute an important part of the electorate?

I shall postulate now, and argue the case later, that the lower classes have not supported regulatory policies and socialism because they were duped or led by intellectuals with different goals. Instead, these classes have shared the general propensity to vote their own interests. Once the unskilled workers enter an open society, they will oppose further free immigration. The most poorly paid workers are aware of the adverse effect of minimum wage laws, and their representatives vote against such laws.[48] It would be feasible to devise numerous tests of this rational interpretation of lower-class political behavior: as examples, have they been supporters of heavy government expenditures on higher education, or of the pollution control programs?

Studies such as I call for will demonstrate, I believe, that the lower classes have been quite selective and parsimonious in their desired interventions in the workings of the competitive economy, simply because not many regulatory policies work to their benefit. These classes will seek and accept all the transfer payments the political system allows, but they have little to gain from regulatory policies that reduce the income of society.

But these lower classes do not dominate our political system. In the long run they have more votes in the marketplace than they have at the ballot box, despite appearances to the contrary. They do not have in full measure the necessary or useful attributes of successful political coalitions, such as common economic and social origins and interests, nor are they localized in space or cohesive in age and social background. They have access to the press or the electromagnetic spectrum only as receivers. They do not directly control the flow of information. These characteristics do not imply that they are the victims of some conspiracy or that they have no influence on political events. It does mean that the marketplace measures their preferences more finely and more promptly than the literature or the politics of the society, even if that society is as democratic as Great Britain or the United States.

This premium placed by politics on certain educational and social characteristics of the voting population is, I believe, the first of two reasons for the failure of the lower classes to play a larger role in modern regulatory policy. The second and more fundamental reason is that the lower classes are by no means a majority: the very efficiency of the competitive economic system has depleted the ranks of the poor and the ill educated! The productivity of the economy has moved the children of immigrants or poor families into the middle classes. A fair fraction of the best economists in the United States are one or two generations away from the garment trades.

When private enterprise elevates many of its lower-class supporters to the middle classes, they find a much larger agenda of desirable state action. The restrictions on entrance into skilled crafts and learned occupations will serve as an important example of the large number of profitable uses of political power that are open to the various groups in the middle classes. If Groucho Marx would not join a country club that would admit the likes of him, private enterprise has reversed the paradox and expells those who learned to play the game well.

Have Attitudes Changed?: The Intellectuals

The intellectual has been contemptuous of commercial activity for several thousand years, so it is not surprising that he has made no exception for the competitive economy. Yet the larger part of the present-day class that lives by words and ideas rather than by commodity processing owes its existence to the productiveness of modern economic systems. Only economies that are highly productive by historical standards can send their populations to schools for twelve to eighteen years, thus providing employment to a large class of educators. Only such a rich society can have a vast communications industry and pervasive social services—other large areas of employment of the intellectual classes. So it is at least a superficial puzzle why these intellectuals maintain much of the traditional hostility of their class to business enterprise—contemptuous of its motives, critical of its achievements, supportive at least of extensive regulation and often of outright socialization.

An answer that many will give is that the competitiveness of economic relationships, the emphasis on profit as a measure of achievement, the difficulties encountered by those cultural activities that do not meet the market test—are precisely the source of opposition: materialism is hostile to the ethical values cherished by the intellectual classes.

A second, and almost opposite, explanation is that these upper classes find their chief patrons and their main employment in government and its activities. Even though the growth of government relative to private economic activity is conditional on the productivity of the private economy, the self-interest of the intellectuals is in the expansion of the government economy.

I believe that this is true in the short run, and the short run is at least a generation or two. The extensive regulatory activities of the modern state are, both directly and in their influence on the private sector, the source of much of the large demand for the intellectual classes. For example, if higher education in America were private, so its costs were paid directly by students rather than so largely by public subventions, the education sector would shrink substantially, not because of increases in efficiency, although such increases would surely occur, but because for large numbers of older students, school attendance would no longer be a sensible investment of their time. The state has greatly reduced the relative cost of higher education for the individual student, although it has raised the relative cost for society. Similarly, the immense panoply of regulatory policies has generated a public employment of perhaps half a million persons, with an even larger number of people occupied in complying with or evading the policies the first group are prescribing.

In short, the intellectuals are the beneficiaries of the expansion of the economic role of government. Their support is, on this reading, available to the highest bidder, just as other resources in our society are allocated. Have not the intellectuals always been respectful of their patrons?

I am not striving for paradox or righteousness, so I would emphasize, like Adam Smith, that no insinuations are intended as to the deficient integrity of the intellectuals, which I naturally believe to be as high as the market in ideas allows. No large number of intellectuals change positions after wetting a finger and holding it in the wind; they cultivate those of their ideas which find a market. Ideas without demands are simply as hard to sell as other products without demands. If anyone in this audience wishes to become an apostle of the single tax after the scripture of Henry George, for example, I recommend that he or she acquire and cherish a wealthy, indulgent spouse.

Ideology and the Intellectuals

A self-interest theory of the support for and opposition to private enterprise will shock many people, and not simply because the theory I propose is so elementary and undeveloped (although these are admitted defects). Many and perhaps most intellectuals will assert that the opposition of intellectuals to private enterprise is based upon ethical and cultural values divorced from self-interest, and that the intellectuals' opposition has played an important leader role in forming the critical attitude of the society as a whole.

An invariably interesting scholar who urged the powerful influence of the intellectuals on social trends was Joseph Schumpeter. Schumpeter's full argument for the prospective collapse of capitalism contains an elusive metaphysical view of the need for legitimacy of a social system, and a charismatic role for its leading classes, that was, he felt, incompatible with the rational calculus of the capitalist mind. The intellectuals were playing their customary role of critics of social order:

> On the one hand, freedom of public discussion involving freedom to nibble at the foundations of capitalist society is inevitable in the long run. On the other hand, the intellectual group cannot help nibbling, because it lives on criticism and its whole position depends on criticism that stings; and criticism of persons and of current events will, in a situation in which nothing is sacrosanct, fatally issue in criticism of classes and institutions.[49]

The intellectuals are credited in particular with radicalizing the labor movement.

That intellectuals should believe that intellectuals are important in determining the course of history is not difficult to understand. The position is less easy for even an intellectual economist to understand since it sets one class of laborers aside and attributes special motives to them. On the traditional economic theory of occupational choice, intellectuals distribute themselves among occupations and among artistic, ethical, cultural, and political positions in such numbers as to maximize their incomes, where incomes include amenities such as prestige and apparent influence. On the traditional economic view, a Galbraith could not do better working for Ronald Reagan and a Friedman could not do better working for Carter or Kennedy, and I could not do better telling you that intellectuals are terribly important.[50] It is worth noticing that Schumpeter partially accepted this position in pointing out that the declining market prospects of the intellectual class were one basis for their criticism of the market.[51]

Please do not read into my low valuation of the importance of professional preaching a similarly low valuation of scientific work. Once a general relationship in economic phenomena is discovered and verified, it becomes a part of the working knowledge of everyone. A newly established scientific relationship shifts the arena of discourse and is fully adopted by all informed parties, whatever their policy stands. Whether a person likes the price system or dislikes it and prefers a form of nonprice rationing of some good, he must accept the fact of a negatively sloping demand curve and take account of its workings. The most influential economist, even in the area of public policy, is the economist who makes the most important scientific contributions.

On the self-interest theory, applied not only to intellectuals but to all of the society, we should look for all to support rationally the positions that are compatible with their long-run interests. Often these interests are subtle or remote, and often the policies that advance these interests are complex and even experimental. For example, it would require a deeper and more comprehensive analysis than has yet been made of the effects of the vast paraphernalia of recent regulation of the energy field to identify and measure the costs and benefits of these policies. But at least in principle, and to a growing degree in practice, we can determine the effects of public policies and therefore whose interests they serve.

The case is rather different with respect to the role of ideology, if that ambiguous word is appropriated to denote a set of beliefs which are not directed to an enlarged, long-run view of self-interest. If an antimarket ideology is postulated, and postulated to be independent of self-interest, then what is its origin and what is its content? Do we not face an inherently arbitrary choice if we follow this route? Antimarket values are then some humanistic instinct for personal solidarity rather than arm's-length dealings, or a search for simplicity and stability in a world where competitive technology is the sorcerer's apprentice, or a wish for a deliberately inefficient egalitarianism, or something else. Choices in this direction are surely as numerous and arbitrary as choices of ethical systems, and indeed that is what they are. Perhaps no one, and certainly no economist, has the right to disparage such nonutility-maximizing systems, but even an economist is entitled to express skepticism about the coherence and content, and above all the actual acceptance on a wide scale, of any ideology.

In the event, ideology is beginning to make fugitive appearances in the quantitative studies of the origins of public policies. Thus, if one wishes to know why some states lean to income taxes and others to sales taxes, the most popular measure of the higher values (or of intellectual confusion?) entertained by a state is the percentage of its vote cast for McGovern in 1972! At this level, ideology is only a name for a bundle of undefined notions one refuses to discuss.

The simplest way to test the role of ideology as a nonutility-maximizing goal is to ascertain whether the supporters of such an ideology incur costs in supporting it. If on average and over substantial periods of time we find (say) that the proponents of "small is beautiful" earn less than comparable talents devoted to urging the National Association of Manufacturers to new glories, I will accept the evidence. But first let us see it.

The Calculus of Morals

I arrive by the devious route you observe at the thesis that flows naturally and even irresistibly from the theory of economics. Man is eternally a utility maximizer, in his home, in his office—be it public or private—in his church, in his scientific work, in short, everywhere. He can and often does err; perhaps the calculation is too difficult, but more often his information is incomplete. He learns to correct these errors, although sometimes at heavy cost.

What we call ethics, on this approach, is a set of rules with respect to dealings with other persons, rules which in general prohibit behavior which is only myopically self-serving, or which imposes large costs on others with small gains to oneself. General observance of these rules makes not only for long-term gains to the actor but also yields some outside benefits ("externalities"), and the social approval of the ethics is a mild form of enforcement of the rules to achieve the general benefits.[52] Of course some people will gain by violating the rules. More precisely, everyone violates some rule or other occasionally, and a few people violate important rules often.

Two difficulties with enlarging and elaborating this approach to ethical codes are worth mentioning. The first is the constant temptation to define the utility of the individual in such a way that the hypothesis is tautological. That difficulty is serious because there is no accepted content to the utility function—I gave my interpretation at the end of the second lecture, and it made a person's utility depend upon the welfare of the actor, his family, plus a narrow circle of associates. Still, the difficulties in using utility theory can be exaggerated. A rational person learns from experience, so it is a contradiction of the utility-maximizing hypothesis if we observe systematically biased error in predictions: thus one cannot surreptitiously introduce the theory of mistakes. The development of a content-rich theory of utility maximizing is a never-ending task.

A second difficulty with the utility-maximizing hypothesis is that it is difficult to test, less because of its own ambiguities than because there is no accepted body of ethical beliefs which can be tested for consistency with the hypothesis. In the absence of such a well-defined set of beliefs, any ad hoc ethical value can be presented, and of course no respectable theory can cope with this degree of arbitrariness of test.

In particular, a system of ethics of individual behavior is all that one can ask a theory of individual utility-maximizing behavior to explain. Political value—values that the society compels its members to observe by recourse to political sanctions—include such popular contemporary policies as income redistribution and prohibition of the use of characteristics such as race and age and sex in certain areas of behavior (but not yet in other areas such as marriage). It requires a political theory rather than an individualistic ethical theory to account for policies and goals whose chief commendation to a substantial minority of people is that their acceptance spares them a term in jail.

With these disclaimers, I believe that it is a feasible and even an orthodox scientific problem to ascertain a set of widely and anciently accepted precepts of ethical personal behavior, and to test their concordance with utility-maximizing behavior for the preponderance of individuals. In fact Rawls's proposal of a method of constructing an inductive ethical system, which I briefly described earlier, is exactly the procedure that would show that the ethical system was based on utility-maximizing behavior. My confidence that the test would yield this result will be disputed by many people of distinction, and that argues all the more for making the test.

Conclusion

I have presented the hypothesis that we live in a world of reasonably well-informed people acting intelligently in pursuit of their self-interests. In this world leaders play only a modest role, acting much more as agents than as instructors or guides of the classes they appear to lead.

The main aspects of social development all have discoverable purposes and should run predictable courses. It is precisely the great virtue—and the great vulnerability—of a comprehensive theory of human behavior that it should account for all persistent and widespread phenomena within its wide domain.

If the hypothesis proves to be as fertile and prescient in political and social affairs as it has been in economic affairs, we can look forward to major advances in our understanding of issues as grave as the kinds of economic and political systems toward which we are evolving. Even if it does not achieve this imperial status, I am wholly confident that it will become a powerful theme guiding much work in the social sciences in the next generation. I would give much to learn what it will teach us of the prospects of my friend, the competitive economy.

Notes

1. *The Wealth of Nations*, Glasgow ed. (Oxford: Clarendon Press, 1976), I, pp. 43–44.

2. *The Coal Question* (London: Macmillan, 1865), p. 326.

3. *Wealth of Nations*, II, pp. 638–39.

4. Ibid., II, p. 641.

5. Ibid., I, p. 540.

6. David Ricardo, *Principles of Political Economy and Taxation*, P. Sraffa ed. (Cambridge: Cambridge University Press, 1951), p. 133.

7. Of which I have some doubts. Thus Smith declares that prohibiting banks from issuing small bank notes is of course a violation of natural liberty, and yet it should be undertaken for the greater good of society; see *Wealth of Nations*, I, p. 324.

8. *Principles of Political Economy* (Toronto: University of Toronto Press, 1965), I, p. 67.

9. See, however, "Smith's Travels on the Ship of State," *History of Political Economy* 3, no. 2 (Fall 1971), and "The Theory of Economic Regulation," *The Bell Journal of Economics and Management Science* 2, no. 1 (Spring 1971), as well as the underlying literature of Anthony Downs, James Buchanan, and Gordon Tullock, and the public choice field.

10. *Wealth of Nations*, II, p. 654.

11. We find complaints at window taxes as being regressive (II, p. 373) and at tithes for not being proportional to rents (II, p. 358).

12. "So essential does it appear to me, to the cause of good government, that the rights of property should be held sacred, that I would agree to deprive those of the elective franchise against whom it could justly be alleged that they considered it their own interest to invade them. But in fact it can be only amongst the most needy in the community that such an opinion can be entertained. The man of a small income must be aware how little his share would be if all the large fortunes in the kingdom were equally divided among the people. He must know that the little he would obtain by such a division could be no adequate compensation for the overturning of a principle which renders the produce of his industry secure. . . . The quantity of employment in the country must depend, not only on the quantity of capital, but upon its advantageous distribution, and, above all, on the conviction of each capitalist that he will be allowed to enjoy unmolested the fruits of his capital, his skill, and his enterprise. To take from him this conviction is at once to annihilate half the productive industry of the country. . . ." (*Observations on Parliamentary Reform*, in *Works and Correspondence*, pp. 500–501.)

13. Mill was mistaken only in believing that present values did not include unbiased estimates of future increments in rents. A similar problem lurks behind his support of progressive taxation of estates. The posthumous *Chapters on Socialism* pays

no attention to inequality (aside from that implicit in the discussion of poverty), even in discussing Blanc, Fourier, and Owen.

14. Those denied "a share of domestic pleasures" might be consoled by emigration!

15. See Francis Edgeworth, "The Pure Theory of Taxation," in *Collected Works Relating to Political Economy* (London: Macmillan, 1925), I, pp. 111–42.

16. *Wealth and Welfare* (London: Macmillan, 1912), p. 24.

17. Ibid., pp. 356–57, 358.

18. *Economics of Welfare* (London: Macmillan, 1924), p. 709.

19. For those who are more familiar with the parallelograms of Euclid than those of Owen, the latter proposed a utopia composed of communities of 500 to 2,000 people, each located in a village "arranged in the form of a large Square, or Parallelogram," with a balanced agricultural and manufacturing economy in which "a full and complete equality will prevail"; see "Constitution, Laws, and Regulations of a Community," in *A New View of Society*, 1st American ed. (New York: Bliss and White, 1825), pp. 162–63.

20. *Principles of Political Economy* (Toronto: University of Toronto Press, 1965), I, p. 207.

21. Ibid., II, pp. 956–57.

22. Ibid., II, pp. 944–45. The argument is presented fully in bk. V, ch. XI.

23. J. E. Cairnes, "Political Economy and Laissez-Faire," in *Essays in Political Economy* (London: Macmillan, 1873): "Economic science has no more connection with our present industrial system than the science of mechanics has with our present system of railways" (p. 257); W. S. Jevons, *The State in Relations to Labour* (London: Macmillan, 1882); H. Sidgwick, *Principles of Political Economy*, 3rd ed. (London: Macmillan, 1901), bk. III, ch. II; A. Marshall, "Social Possibilities of Economic Chivalry," in *Memorials of Alfred Marshall*, ed. A. C. Pigou (London: Macmillan, 1925); and J. M. Keynes, *Scope and Method of Political Economy*, 4th ed. (London: Macmillan, 1930), ch. II.

24. In Mill's view, the freedom from compulsion was the chief value justifying the presumption of laissez-faire; bk. V, ch. XI of the *Principles* is a preview of *On Liberty*.

25. (New York: Macmillan Co., 1899), pp. 4–5.

26. *Essays in Social Justice* (Cambridge: Harvard University Press, 1915), p. 201.

27. *The Economics of Welfare*, 2nd ed. (London: Macmillan, 1924), p. 754.

28. *Quarterly Journal of Economics*; reprinted in *The Ethics of Competition* (Chicago: University of Chicago Press, 1976).

29. ". . . the social order largely forms as well as gratifies the wants of its members, and the natural consequence [is] that it must be judged ethically rather by the wants which it generates . . ." (ibid., p. 51).

30. Hence, "in conditions of real life no possible social order based upon a *laissez-faire* policy can justify the familiar ethical conclusions of apologetic economics" (ibid., p. 49).

31. "The ownership of personal or material productive capacity is based upon a complex mixture of inheritance, luck, and effort, probably in that order of relative

importance" (ibid., p. 56). "The luck element is so large . . . that capacity and effort may count for nothing [in business]. And this luck element works cumulatively, as in gambling games generally" (ibid., p. 64).

32. *Mathematical Psychics*, p. 12.

33. *Principles of Economics* (1920), bk. V, ch. XIII.

34. Ibid., p. 467n.

35. See "Outline of a Decision Procedure for Ethics," *The Philosophical Review* 60 (1951): 177–97.

36. See *A Theory of Justice* (Cambridge: Harvard University Press, 1971).

37. *Principles of Economics*, 8th ed. (London: Macmillan, 1920), p. 7.

38. *Lectures on Jurisprudence* (Cambridge: Cambridge University Press, 1978), pp. 538–39.

39. The recent attention economists have paid to conservation of resources and to all varieties of pollution also represents a response to popular discussion of these matters rather than the result of autonomous professional economic research.

40. Nassau W. Senior, *Journals, Conversations and Essays Relating to Ireland* (London: Longmans Green, 1868), II, p. 271.

41. See Ronald H. Coase, "Adam Smith's View of Man," *Journal of Law and Economics* 19 (1976): 529–46.

42. *Sir Thomas More; Or Colloquies on the Progress and Prospects of Society* (London: John Murray, 1829), I, pp. 173–74.

43. *Past and Present* (Chicago: Henneberry, n.d.), p. 296.

44. *The Complete Works of John Ruskin* (New York: Thomas Crowell, n.d.).

45. *The Communism of John Ruskin* (New York: Humboldt, 1891), edited by W. P. B. Bliss, p. 52n.

46. "Southey's Colloquies on Society," in Thomas Babington Macaulay, *Critical, Historical, and Miscellaneous Essays* (New York: Mason, Baker & Pratt, 1873), II, pp. 148–49.

47. Ibid., p. 132.

48. See J. B. Kau and P. H. Rubin, "Voting on Minimum Wages: A Time-Series Analysis," *Journal of Political Economy* 86 (1978): 337–42.

49. *Capitalism, Socialism and Democracy*, 3rd ed. (New York: Harper Torchbooks, 1950), p. 151.

50. Please recall the statement that concludes the last section, that the allocation system works, usually *not* by individuals choosing merchantable ideas, but by only certain of their ideas finding markets.

51. *Capitalism, Socialism and Democracy*, pp. 152–53.

52. The expression of this social approval by an individual is itself enforced by the approval of other individuals and therefore constitutes a system of informal law. Clearly this line of argument takes us (as Michael McPherson pointed out) into political (i.e., not purely individualistic) theory.

Why Have the
Socialists Been Winning?

· *19* ·

The massive growth of governments in the twentieth century has been the most conspicuous single change in the organization of social life—a growth so large and so pervasive that it would be as difficult to deny as the existence of the Pacific Ocean. The task I have set myself here is to explore the reasons for the growth of government, on the ground that we are not likely to predict, let alone control, a movement we cannot explain.

This growth requires no explanation for a socialist: justice simply formed an irresistible merger with democracy. Of course there are numerous phenomena which require explanation even if one accepts this relaxing view; for example, nations differ widely in the degree to which they have transferred the conduct of economic life over to the state, and do the loose notions of democracy and justice help us to explain these differences?

In any event, a different explanation for the growth of the state is required for those of us who believe that the result of this growth has been a large reduction in aggregate output, quite possibly with a deterioration in the moral quality of society. The task of explanation is not only more difficult but also more important for those who oppose the growth of government. I suppose that it is conceivable that one can control a social development that one does not understand, perhaps by stopping that development through the decisive use of power. But that kind of policy is repugnant to our principles, and we do not

From *Ordo*, vol. 30, 1979. Permission to reprint courtesy of *Ordo* and Gustav Fischer Verlag.

even have a strong temptation to become unprincipled because the power is on the other side. If we are to predict and perhaps to control the role of government in the future, we need to know why it has been growing. I propose to examine the leading explanations for the present age of collectivism.

I. The Theory of Mistakes

Overwhelmingly the most popular explanation for the growth of government, among those opposed to the trend, has been that it was a mistake: a mistake in the literal sense that a misinformed populace has acted against its own interests. The mistake has presumably been induced and certainly fostered by the socialists and interventionists. The socialists have denounced the system of private enterprise and individualism with enormous vigor and persistence, presenting an indictment filled with charges that are always exaggerated and often false. The socialists have simultaneously promised vast and unrealizable benefits from the socialization of life.

It is easy enough to illustrate gross libels of private enterprise. Of the literature in this tradition, which in volume is strictly infinite relative to the reading life of a person, I choose only one example, Professor Richard Tawney, the well-known historian and one-time colleague of Professor Hayek, and only one passage from his famous book, *The Acquisitive Society*.[1]

> Because rewards are divorced from services, so that what is prized most is not riches obtained in return for labor but riches the economic origin of which, being regarded as sordid, is concealed, two results follow. The first is the creation of a class of pensioners upon industry, who levy toll upon its product, but contribute nothing to its increase, and who are not merely tolerated, but applauded and admired and protected with assiduous care, as though the secret of prosperity resided in them.... The rentier and his ways, how familiar they were in England before the war! A public school and then club life in Oxford and Cambridge, and then another club in town; London in June, when London is pleasant, the moors in August, and pheasants in October, Cannes in December and hunting in February and March; and a whole world of rising bourgeoisie eager to imitate them, sedulous to make their expensive watches keep time with this preposterous calendar!
>
> The second consequence is the degradation of those who labor, but who do not by their labor command large rewards; that is of the great majority of mankind. And this degradation follows inevitably from the refusal of men to give the purpose of industry the first place in their thought about it. When they do that, when their minds are set upon the fact that the meaning of industry is the service of man, all who labor appear to them honorable, because all who labor serve, and the distinction which separates those who

serve from those who merely spend is so crucial and fundamental as to obliterate all minor distinctions based on differences of income. But when the criterion of function is forgotten, the only criterion which remains is that of wealth, and an Acquisitive Society reverences the possession of wealth, as a Functional Society would honor, even in the person of the humblest and most laborious craftsman, the arts of creation.

These are the two fundamental themes of socialist criticism: gross inequalities of income arise under capitalism, and production is directed by profit rather than by use. The themes have been repeated by so many people so often that they have constituted a socialized form of the classical Chinese torture.

The promises of the socialists have almost always been conveniently vague; indeed, one could make a good case that socialism has seldom had any clear goal beyond the removal of capitalistic evils. One famous exception is Edward Bellamy, and I must resist the temptation to quote extensively from *Looking Backward*.[2] Still, he deserves quotation on at least two points. The first concerns the organization of labor in the good society (attained in the year 2000):

> ...we hold the period of youth sacred to education, and the period of maturity, when the physical forces begin to flag, equally sacred to ease and agreeable relaxation. The period of industrial service is twenty-four years, beginning at the close of the course of education at twenty-one and terminating at forty-five. After forty-five, while discharged from labor, the citizen still remains liable to special calls, in case of emergencies causing a sudden great increase in the demand for labor, till he reaches the age of fifty-five, but such calls are rarely, in fact almost never, made. [pp. 63–64]

Bellamy's vision of the socialist society was more accurate than most: he promised both high productivity and suppression of individual preferences, so his prophecy was at least half right. Even such limited foresight failed him in the area of politics:

> [Mr. West] But with no state legislatures, and Congress meeting only once in five years, how do you get your legislation done?"
> "We have no legislation," replied Dr. Leete, "that is, next to none. It is rarely that Congress, even when it meets, considers any new laws of consequence, and then it only has power to commend them to the following Congress, lest anything be done hastily. If you will consider a moment, Mr. West, you will see that we have nothing to make laws about. The fundamental principles on which our society is founded settle for all time the strifes and misunderstandings which in your day called for legislation." [p. 208]

This blindness to the persistence of real problems under any conceivable social system is the hallmark of the Utopian. I cannot refrain from noting finally a curious anticipation of Professor Hayek's proposal that the selection of political leaders be made by citizens over the age of forty (ibid., p. 189).

Many people, to repeat, attribute the growth of statism to the changes of opinion brought about by this kind of literature. I consider it a major complaint to make against such an explanation of a vast, persistent social movement that it rests on mistaken behavior of the public: if left in this form, the explanation is vacuous. Any behavior, even correct behavior, is consistent with a mistake having been made. Unless a theory is presented of the kinds of mistakes that will be made, there is no possible test of the mistake hypothesis. And no one, so far as I know, had offered even a mistaken theory of mistakes. If random blizzards of opinion blow societies one way and then another, there is nothing for us to do but to hope that the wind will shift, and to fear that it may increase in intensity.

The fundamental objection to the "mistake" theory, however, is that it flies in the face of both our general knowledge of society and the facts of socialization in our times. If deception by intellectuals were the motive force of social change, we would expect to observe numerous occasions on which a group of conservatives with large powers of persuasion had captured the public's fancy, and succeeded in initiating a regime of declining governmental activity. After all, which socialist philosopher has been as profound as Hayek, which socialist propagandist has been as lucidly logical as Friedman? In fact, intellectuals largely—although not wholly—respond to the demands of their times: like Detroit, they produce to demand, rather than contrive that demand. Indeed, per educated person employed, Detroit may well turn out a larger variety of products. Persistent and widespread social phenomena do not have adventitious causes.

Nor does the domestic or international pattern of support for socialization of economic life suggest that it is the uneducated or socially backward classes that provide the chief support for socialization. If the professors of America had chosen our president, it would have been McGovern from 1968 to 1976. If highly educated and even civilized peoples were less susceptible to misleading socialist arguments, we would not expect to find nations such as Britain and Sweden among the leaders in the race to expand the role of government.

II. The Bias of Political Processes

No other explanation by conservatives for the rise of socialism is remotely so popular as the deception theory I have just discussed. An alternative theory that is growing in popularity, however, is that the political process is strongly biased toward collectivism, and thus systematically misrepresents the public's true preferences. The bias theory can be viewed as a theory of rational behavior because individuals behave rationally, given the political institutions under which they live; but it can also be viewed as nonrational because the political institutions they have devised are inefficient.

The bias in the process is this: we are presented with two kinds of policies: those which greatly benefit the few and slightly injure the many, and those (including repeal of the first kind of policy) that benefit the many slightly and injure the few greatly. Hence for almost every individual policy proposal of a socialist variety, there will be a cohesive, well-financed, articulate special group to support it, and a large, poorly informed majority that, if it is informed correctly, will be weakly opposed, but often this majority will be simply unaware of the proposal.

For example, the dairy farmers about a city will seek a milk marketing order which will raise the price of milk (say) 5¢ a quart. Each of these farmers will gain perhaps $15,000 a year from the policy. Each consumer in the city will lose $10 or $20 a year. The dairy farmers will use effective lobbyists and political contributions to promote the policy. The rational consumer could not afford to spend more than an hour or two a year to become acquainted with the effects of the milk marketing order and to oppose it. No wonder that each of us vigorously supports the 15 policies that benefit us appreciably and pretty much ignore the 800 policies that individually harm us slightly.

I believe that there is much truth in this explanation. One may address certain perplexing questions to its supporters, however. Why did this kind of political machinery produce no large growth of state action before 1900 in the United States? Why has the center of governmental activity been moving from local governments to federal governments, when the bias of the machinery is surely more severe at the federal level? Thus why did we abandon the choice of U.S. senators by state legislatures in 1914, when this was a powerful support of state sovereignty? Did the public support these shifts of power by mistake?

There may be good answers to such questions—in one or two cases I believe that there are—but in any event there is a substantial amount of truth in the argument that the present policy machinery is biased toward governmental growth. It is less clear that there is any satisfactory way of dealing with the problem.

The growth of public expenditures has been so rapid in the last two decades that a slowing down and possibly a backlash would seem to be highly probable. One manifestation of that reaction is the wave of proposals to place limits on spending. This is by no means the first such wave: severe limits were put on many state governments' debts already by the 1850s, and debts and tax rates of local governments have long been regulated. I find it strange that the proponents of spending limits have not looked at this extensive experience, which—it is my impression—had little effect on the long-term trend of public expenditures.

Even if we get such limits and they resist the enormous forces for expansion of public spending, these limits will certainly not dispose of the problem of growth of government. There are literally thousands of public regulatory policies, usually involving little public spending, that have substantial effects on the vigor of economic enterprise and the distribution of income. If suitable numbers could be assigned to the income redistributions effected by these policies, I would not be surprised if in the aggregate they are of the same magnitude as direct governmental redistributions: simply consider what an extensive panoply we have of tariffs, quotas, entry and occupational controls, price regulations, conferrals of tax exemption, and the like. This avenue of income redistribution will surely grow even more rapidly if direct public expenditures are curtailed.

III. The Rational Theories

The rational theories of the growth of government explain that growth as the result of the purposeful use of public power to increase the incomes of particular groups in the society. The poor tax the rich, the farmers tax the urban consumers, the airlines levy noncompetitive prices on their passengers—and in each such case the power of the state is invoked by the particular group. On this view, the modern state is engaged in the wholesale redistribution of income, not only through direct taxes and welfare programs of expenditures but also through a large network of regulatory policies.

I pointed out that the mistake theory is not a theory at all until someone produces a theory of which mistakes will be made. The rational theories face a similar problem. Every public policy or tax or expenditure program will have beneficiaries, and it is reasonable to believe that the beneficiaries will support and the losers oppose the policy. Therefore the rational theories will have to tell us which groups will be successful in the rivalry for political power before they become useful in explaining the growth of the state. And it must be said at once that only a small amount of progress has been made in devising a theory of which groups will control the state. Nevertheless I believe that political life is rational and that the successful explanations for the growth of government lie in this direction.

I cannot hope to support this claim adequately at this time. I am tempted to say that there is not sufficient time to present the case for the rational theories, and hope that you will infer that the argument would require an hour or more. In fact a full argument may require a decade or more. Still, here are two small appetizers.

Applying the theory to the regulation of individual industries—electric power generation, airlines, trucking, television, etc., we have consistently found strong benefits for the producer groups in terms of protection from competition. Our theory predicts that strongly situated consumers will also benefit from these regulatory policies and this has been found especially in U.S. energy policies, where northeastern consumers have been vast beneficiaries of natural gas price controls. On the other hand, we have had very modest success in explaining which industries receive tariff protection.

The direct income redistribution policies have of course been of special interest, and since the appearance of Director's law the field has attracted numerous scholars. Since three of those scholars are Gary Becker, Harold Demsetz, and Sam Peltzman, we have every reason to be optimistic about the appearance of a useful explanation for the rise of heavily progressive income taxation and huge welfare programs.

The scientific problem is not to explain why the poor tax the rich: to paraphrase the Duke of Wellington, anyone who cannot understand that cannot understand anything. It is to explain why this development waited until about 1925 to begin accelerating, why it has gone much farther in Sweden than the United States, why it is proceeding more slowly in Japan than in Western Europe, and so on. The most obvious explanation for these differences is that universal suffrage is fairly modern, but the extent of the suffrage has only the loosest association with the observed facts. (For example, if breadth of suffrage were decisive, the United States should have socialized earlier than the United Kingdom.)

It appears to me that much more is to be explained by three developments: first, modern economic systems have made very aggressive levels of taxation feasible. The predominance of the corporate form, the decline of single proprietors, the proliferation of written records, make it possible to tax at rates John Stuart Mill considered wholly impossible.

Second, there has been a large increase in the concentration—to use a word from industrial organization—of the population in fewer nations. We often use a measure of concentration—the Herfindahl index—which allows us to ask: what number of nations of equal size is equivalent in (let us say) power to an observed distribution of nations by size? In 1815 the nations of Europe had only modest concentration: Russia was largest with 23 percent of Europe's population, and the distribution among nations was equivalent to eight nations of equal size. Now Russia and Poland have 46 percent of Europe's population and the index of concentration of population has risen to the equivalent of four nations of equal size. The total number of independent nations fell from 54 to 23 between 1815 and 1970. The ability of individuals to discipline overly greedy states by migrating has sharply declined.

Third, Becker and Peltzman have provided largely complementary theories of the state as an income redistributing agency. Peltzman has emphasized the demand for income redistribution. In Peltzman's theory, and probably everyone else's, the greater the income disparity between rich and poor the larger the income redistribution program of the state. His second main implication is a good deal less obvious: the more equal the incomes of the poor, and of the rich, separately, the larger will be the role of the government. Becker's theory also takes the existing redistributive policies of the state as yielding the income distribution which is desired by the members of the society. He emphasizes the influence of the costs of redistribution—costs that include deadweight losses as well as administrative costs—on the extent to which income is redistributed. Indeed the first two forces making for more government that I discussed above (ease in collecting taxes and fewer possibilities of migration) are particular reasons that the redistribution of income has become easier. (Demsetz has sought the main explanation for the rise of government in the increased specialization of modern societies.)

Truth in talking can easily be carried too far, as Frank Knight was fond of saying, but I will concede that no rational theory of the state has yet received a strong vote of confidence from empirical tests.

IV. CONCLUDING REMARKS

Suppose the rational theory of the growth of government is correct—suppose that it is soon developed to a stage where it is commended to even its critics as a useful explanation of the changing role of government. That would seem to imply that with our existing political institutions—our freely chosen political institutions—the large and growing role of government has been what the public as a whole has wanted: democratic majority rule likes what we have been doing. Do we not then face the hard choice between becoming collectivists and becoming nondemocratic in our desired political institutions?

Let me be more explicit on what becoming a collectivist would mean. It would not mean joining the appropriate majority socialist party of one's nation, and heartily endorsing the choices of the most recently elected legislators. We could still argue for a much larger role of the price system. Thus we could say that if the citizens of the United States wanted purer air or cleaner lakes or safer factories than were provided in the absence of state control, the price system is usually vastly more economical than direct regulation in achieving these goals. In such a case there is no dispute over goals, only over the costs of different methods of achieving them. I would consider this an extremely valuable function of the conservative economist even in a socialized society. Friedman's demonstration of the role of money in income fluctuations is a striking example of this kind of work.

Again, becoming a collectivist would not mean that we concurred in every program designed to help a particular group. Consider the benefits to the members of the American labor unions which are conferred by the minimum wage law. This law overprices young, untrained, inexperienced, and handicapped workers, pushing them into uncovered occupations, unemployment, or withdrawal from the labor force, and thus increases the demand for the more productive workers who constitute the membership of the unions. If we could devise a method of supplementing the union members' wages by the amount of these gains, and still preserve the employment opportunities for the unskilled workers, we would be able to increase our aggregate income.

To become collectivists, in short, would be to become market socialists— to ask us to take out a license from James Meade to practice economic reform in the United States. Whether there is a large role in the modern world for market-oriented socialists is a question I will not attempt to discuss.

The alternative is to abandon total acceptance of present-day democratic institutions. I must hasten to say that this is not to argue for totalitarianism in any form. Indeed, some alternative political systems that would insure a substantial reduction in the governmental role could be even more democratic in the sense that public policies could be closer to the desires of the individual citizens. We have been so prone to dispute the popular goals of income redistribution, however, that we have devoted little attention to more efficient methods of fulfilling existing goals.

One possible route to a reduced role of the state is to create competitive pressures on government such that any group—the well-to-do, the highly productive—can escape one government by moving to another. If the main tax, subsidy, and regulatory programs of the United States were conducted by the 50 states instead of the single Congress, there would appear states whose policies suited any group large enough to form a substantial part of that state's population. Strongly progressive taxation, highly restrictive regulations of businesses, and extensive restrictions on personal choice—would all become escapable for those who found them heavy burdens. Of course this competition would restrict the powers and resources of other states and that is why such a decentralization of political life could not be achieved by an appeal to the citizens under today's political institutions.

The second possible route toward a reduced role of government would be through the restriction of the franchise to property owners, educated classes, employed persons, or some such group. Dicey implicitly blamed the development of the modern welfare state on an unlimited electorate. Such restrictions on voting, if they were attainable, would surely change the policies of government. I am not at all clear that the narrow electorate would engage in less income redistribution through the state.

A related route would be to reduce the power of simple majorities.

346 ◆ ECONOMIC THOUGHT

Requirements of larger-than-simple majorities to pass economic legislation might reduce the exactions of smaller minorities, and of course the bicameral system had as a main purpose the blunting of majority rule. Is it not striking that the long-established trends in political structure and practice are exactly the reverse of those favorable to our policies?

It is not congenial to us to contemplate departures from simple majoritarian political systems. It is so much more pleasant to look elsewhere for the reversal of our defeats—especially to the turning of the tide of public opinion. How wonderful it will be if the public has decided on a liberal society, how wonderful if on June 6 of 1978 when the famed Proposition 13 carried in California, the reaction became a viable political force in the United States. Yet surely changes of political tastes are more convenient than probable, and I doubt that they will allow us believers in decentralized economic and political life to escape the hard question: are we a permanent minority?

If the liberal values we cherish have become minority views, I do not propose that we abandon them. Indeed my own attachment to them grows with the realization of how widely they are rejected. If in fact we seek what many do not wish, will we not be more successful if we take this into account and seek political institutions and policies that allow us to pursue our own goals?

NOTES

1. *The Acquisitive Society* (New York: 1920), pp. 34–35.
2. *Looking Backward* (Boston: Houghton Mifflin, 1890).

THE WIT OF
GEORGE J. STIGLER

◆ ◆ ◆ ◆ ◆

◆ *PART* ◆ *FIVE* ◆

THE ALARMING COST
OF MODEL CHANGES:
A CASE STUDY*

· 20 ·

Franklin Fisher, Zvi Griliches, and Carl Kaysen have shown, in an article which will command wide and respectful attention, that if consumers had been content with the 1949 automobile, they would be saving over $700 per car by 1961.[1] They properly have left open the question whether improvements such as greater speeds and automatic transmissions were worth the cost, but after all, the 1949 cars ran, and kept out the rain.[2] Perhaps the $5 billion a year of extra costs had better alternative uses—higher tuition fees, more adequate farm subsidies, a violin in every home.

   Their choice of the automobile industry was arbitrary, but reasonable; there has been much comment on overelaborate automobiles; it is a large industry; and annual model changes are a prominent feature of its behavior. Of course, every sector—even public schools and health—displays a mixture of frivolous and genuine improvements, and eventually, let us hope, estimates of the costs of product changes will be available for all. I propose here to estimate the costs for an industry in which model changes have reached an almost unbelievable pitch.

Reprinted by permission of the publishers from *The Intellectual and the Marketplace*, enlarged edition (Cambridge, Mass.: Harvard University Press). Copyright 1963 by George J. Stigler; Copyright 1984 by the Presidents and Fellows of Harvard College.

* Vulgar luxury has always been condemned by men of high taste and income. Economists have lent some support to their displeasure, and I add my mite.

The industry is publishing, and I was led to it by the comparison of editions of the same work. It is essentially correct that a man never changes, and seldom improves on, his views; certainly this is true of Ricardo (3 editions), Mill (7 editions), Marshall (8 editions), Böhm-Bawerk (3 editions), Walras (5 editions), Pigou (4 editions), Roscher (27 editions), etc. I suspect that the revision every five years of our textbooks reflects market considerations more than it expresses the march of scientific progress. The costs of this sort of minor amendment are not negligible—unlike the automobile, the older editions lose their usefulness.

But the phenomenon of change goes much deeper. Each year we publish about 11,000 books in the United States. Not *one* is in the list of 100 greatest books. Why must we have *The Rise and Fall of the Third Reich*, when *The Rise and Fall of the Dutch Republic* is a better book, and in the public domain? Is *The Tropic of Cancer* better (worse) than the works of the Marquis de Sade? What, precisely, are the respects in which Tennessee Williams surpasses Shakespeare? Samuelson (5 editions), Bach (3 editions), Harriss (4 editions) and others write our textbooks; is it abundantly clear that they are better books than *The Wealth of Nations*?

The economist cannot answer these questions. The answers rest on value judgments, which are not scientific, and the economist is a scientist. All the economist can do is report the facts. As Fisher, Griliches, and Kaysen say, we cannot tell a drunkard to stop drinking, but we can audit the bar bill. Or, to choose a metaphor without normative overtones, we cannot tell a nation to stop turning beautiful trees into waste paper, but we can weigh the ashes.

So let us assume that no new books were printed after 1900. This date is less arbitrary than 1949, I think, and in any event it yields bigger numbers. Some books of this earlier period would probably sell in only small quantities (I have in mind an item such as J. S. Mill's *An Examination of Sir William Hamilton's Philosophy, and of the Principal Philosophical Questions Discussed in His Writings*, or Sinclair's 21-volume survey of Scotland in 1791–99), although without the diversion of the new models their markets would strengthen. Some books might even disappear (I have in mind such an item as Heinrich's *Phlogiston ist die Wahrheit*). But there would be an ample selection of reading matter: the books of 1900 and before could not run or keep out the rain, but they could furnish the minds of Newton, Gauss, Beethoven, and Goethe, of Jefferson and Lincoln and Dred Scott.

The stream of savings would be immense, and it would be fed by a thousand hidden springs. Let me just cite four important components:

1. All books would be royalty-free, with savings of perhaps 10 percent on retail prices. The authors would usually have alternative products.

2. The plates of a typical book now print about 3,000 copies. This could be raised to at least 200,000 with a reduction of 98.5 percent in composition costs. Easily another 30 percent reduction in price. (This item alone exceeds the savings in the automobile study, as a percent of price.)

3. Advertising of books would fall, perhaps by 98 percent. This would cut prices another 5 or 10 percent.

4. In happy analogy to Fisher, Griliches, and Kaysen, books would get more mileage. Once a family outside Wisconsin grew up, its sturdily bound McGuffy Readers could be passed on to a second generation, and possibly a third. This would reduce costs by a factor of 2.5, making the aggregate saving perhaps 85 percent of present costs.

I shall not pause to estimate indirect savings: houses could be smaller; people would not have to change the prescription of their glasses so often; teachers would not have to think up new examination questions; etc.

When we turn to newspapers, the savings would be even greater. There is nothing new under the sun, so it would be sufficient to print a dozen volumes of news once and for all: crimes, wars, women, colonies, frontier life, emancipation, and the Irish Question, for example. In addition to a saving of, say, 98 percent on newspapers, there would be a substantial reduction in efforts by people to get into the news.

These savings are to be calculated in the billions of dollars, and the billions of hours of reader time. There would be some delay in the dissemination of new knowledge; few changes are without costs. I would beg the reader, however, to keep two facts in mind: most new knowledge is false; and the news got around in Athens.

Notes

1. "The Costs of Automobile Model Changes Since 1949," *Journal of Political Economy* (October 1962).

2. My 1950 Dodge was considerably more efficient in the latter role than in the former, however.

A CERTAIN GALBRAITH
IN AN UNCERTAIN AGE

· 21 ·

When the BBC called Professor Galbraith in 1973 to invite him to produce a series of television shows, no doubt seeking to reenact the successes of "Civilization" and "The Ascent of Man," they could not have expected the then-Harvard economist to produce any fundamentally new ideas. After all, the production of new ideas is a calling reliable in neither quantity nor quality, and even a governmental agency wishes to have something to show for several millions of dollars. That the television series, and the accompanying book, contain few ideas new even to Galbraith is therefore no occasion for surprise, let alone complaint. So a well-known preacher has returned with his customary sermon, and if it is beginning to be delivered in a somewhat garrulous fashion, that is a small sin and one customarily indulged in by people of Galbraith's (and my!) age.

It does not follow that all ancient knowledge and myths are congenial to the television tube: no one has successfully dramatized the multiplication table; nor has Greek mythology provided rich TV fare. On the whole, one would expect historical myth, indeed, to be more suitable to visual presentation than the theorems of a theoretical science. That preference of the camera may even have played a part in the BBC's selection of Galbraith, whose specialty has been nonspecialty.

From "John Kenneth Galbraith's Marathon Television Series: A Certain Galbraith in an Uncertain Age," *National Review*, May 27, 1985. Copyright by National Review, Inc., 150 East 35 Street, New York, N.Y. Reprinted with permission.

If we surveyed Galbraith's work of the last ten years or so, we should find rather complete anticipations of what I take to be the themes of the episodes of the TV series and the corresponding chapters of *The Age of Uncertainty*:

1. Adam Smith preached a narrow doctrine of self-interest, which was successfully incorporated into the harsh capitalism of the nineteenth century.

2. The resulting distribution of income was unequal in inhuman degree, and the very rich lived lives of excruciatingly vulgar ostentation.

3. A "massive dissent" in behalf of the "working classes" (what a misleading phrase, when much of the most demanding work is done by other classes, but no fault of Galbraith's) was launched against capitalism by Karl Marx, whose life is sketched and whose doctrines are hinted at.

4. Colonialism, a vast phenomenon hardly noticed by the classical economists, was a device used by capitalistic nations to stave off the contradictions of capitalism for a century to the detriment of the natives of these colonies.

5. Lenin, in a largely biographical treatment, became the leader who turned the chaos of the Russian Revolution into a structured, disciplined communist state.

6. Money, that perpetual source of joy and pain—Petty said that "it beautifies the whole, especially those who have it in plenty"—is anecdotalized into central banks, booms, and depressions. No relationship of this instrument to capitalism is proposed.

7. Keynes gave capitalism a respite when he instructed the industrial nations how to pull themselves out of a persistent depression with mass unemployment. With modifications, and assistance from Galbraith, the system was adapted to wartime and the 1970s.

8. The suicidal tendencies of the cold war period were aided and abetted by a narrow, rigid doctrinaire named John Foster Dulles and based solidly on the self-serving activities of a military-industrial complex. I shall ask the reader to guess who did not fall prey to these two decades of hysteria.

9. The Big Corporation, that self-sufficient environment-molding, consumer-molding colossus that now has a dozen national homes, is presented in the form of a parable concerning Unified Global Enterprises (mostly ITT). The corporation has become depersonalized, with the Harvard Business School performing the traditional function of a queen for these societies of social insects.

10. The excessive proportion of people to land is in most of the world the essential and stubborn source of poverty. This chapter defies generalization: it is a travelogue from Punjab, through antebellum slavery and

modern migratory workers, to Singapore (the successful "place of refuge from rural poverty"!).

11. The travelogue becomes more pronounced: we tour ancient political capital cities, medieval merchant cities, nineteenth century industrial ghettos, and reach the modern metropolis—a prosperous industrial society with traces of the earlier types. The modern city is necessarily socialistic.

12. The book closes in a mood of brooding introspection and reminiscence. The parting message appears to be that the great quality of leadership is the ability to confront the major anxiety of the age, and today that anxiety is nuclear warfare.

Before we examine more closely the content of our Age of Uncertainty, we shall briefly consider its presentation through television. The enterprise was dominated as well as initiated by the television series, and the fundamental success of the venture for most people will lie in the visual rather than the printed version. I must base my judgment on only the three episodes (one, six, ten) that were available to me, but their testimony is tolerably harmonious.

I would have dreaded Galbraith's assignment because of the extreme difficulty of presenting abstract ideas in visual form—unless one is prepared to accept a lecture, with or without a blackboard, as a visual presentation. Consider a quite fundamental theorem in price theory: that any use of resources forecloses other uses of those resources—known to some as the alternative cost theory, to others as "there is no such thing as a free lunch." Even Paul Getty had to economize on lunches, if he valued his time. Guns *or* butter. Possibly one can show a laborer leaving the ammunition plant for a job in a fertilizer plant, but this shows (too literally) only the versatility of resources, not their scarcity. Scarcity is so pervasive a phenomenon that we cannot easily photograph it. How then can we present complex ideas such as the intimate interdependence of markets in a whole variety of commodities such as meat, leather, and shoes (general equilibrium)? One picture may *describe* more vividly than a thousand words, but the ratio changes radically when the task is explanation.

In the event, my fears about the effective use of television were neither mistaken nor overcome by Galbraith: he made no observable attempt to use visual methods to illuminate ideas. The first episode, on Adam Smith and the Industrial Revolution, is (with an exception to be noted later) a disaster. A sophomoric charade is used to display the major characters (sovereign, capitalist, landlord, and workers). A set of cardboard enlargements of classical economists are placed at a table; apparently no one was made uncomfortable by the fact that John Stuart Mill, truly a prodigy, is older than his father, James. Their animation compares favorably with Galbraith's.

The later episodes—at least those I saw—make less use of such gaucheries, and are mostly travelogues in which the words of the narrator are illustrated by one of two types of scene. Often the illustration is literal: a sustained view of ripening grain when discussing food; teeming people or a long episode in the betrothal of a young Indian couple (whose conversation might have gained, and could scarcely lose, by translation) when treating population; a Mississippi sternwheeler when discussing cotton and slavery. At other times a historic place or object is shown: the handsome directors' room of the Bank of England; the farm on which Galbraith was reared; Lenin's home in Switzerland. An occasional episode is captivating: in particular I enjoyed the scene with Irving Fisher and his wife.

Galbraith is an adequate narrator, but wooden of countenance and metallic of body. His style of exposition, with its incessant use of irony and circumlocution, is better suited to the written page (from which he apparently was always reading) than to an aural medium. His lectures—"listen carefully, and I shall quickly explain central banking," or "you should and can understand Fisher's equation"—are so brief and use such unfamiliar ideas (open-market operations, velocity) that it is inconceivable that so many as one viewer in a small nation would derive instruction from them.

And now let us look at the substance.

Galbraith is concerned in this venture, and in much of his previous work, with the development and influence of intellectual ideas. He begins the book and the television series with the familiar quotation from the last paragraphs of Keynes's *General Theory* to the effect that intellectuals are much more important than vested interests in influencing the course of events, and in particular economic events. Although Galbraith accepts this as a partial truth, I would consider its truth content minor: the dominant classes (welfare and blue-collar, as well as capitalist) are not readily confused as to their interests, as Keynes claimed, by "some academic scribbler of a few years back." Fortunately, by page 90 Galbraith approvingly quotes Marx's opposite opinion. Nevertheless, to the modest extent that *The Age of Uncertainty* has a coherent theme, it is concerned with the ideas of major economists, their absurdities and their insights, and the—often nefarious—influence they are said to have exerted.

Galbraith's talents as an expositor of the ideas of other economists have received only modest exercise, and this is due, I suspect, primarily to lack of compulsion. He has not written, so far as I know, any work presenting economic analysis or measurement at a professional level of precision in several decades. If an economist becomes accustomed to casual generalization and impressionistic factual description, he develops lazy study habits and a misplaced confidence in his knowledge. This is the reason, I believe, that Galbraith, who is a man of both intelligence and efficient energy, writes about the history of economic ideas with a heavy gloss of imprecision and superficiality more appropriate to a journalist.

Consider Adam Smith, who is hardly a random sample. This man's great contribution was to explain how resources are allocated among industries and places, how the prices of goods are determined, and how the incomes of workers, landlords, and capitalists are established. The motive power of the economy, so to speak, comes from the search of buyers for low prices and of sellers for high prices. Their self-interest is disciplined, harmonized, and directed by competition. This central core of value and distribution theory, as it used to be called, has been permanently incorporated into economics. Today as in 1776 an economist considers of paramount importance the propositions that under competition resources are devoted to the uses in which they will receive the highest possible return, and that maximum product will be achieved under competition with a resource earning equal returns in all uses.

Galbraith's treatment of Smith's economics is simply irresponsible. It is observed, correctly, that Smith felt that the egregious instruction he had received at Oxford would have been greatly improved if the tutors had been compensated by the fees of freely choosing students. When Smith abandoned his £100 professorship for the £300 life annuity he received in exchange for tutoring the young Duke of Buccleuch, Galbraith says "self-interest overcame high principle." Smith thought resources should and do go where they earn the most (taking account of nonmonetary benefits and costs), and his behavior was in strict accordance with his theoretical predictions. (Galbraith later complains that Smith inconsistently accepted the Commissionership of Customs of Scotland, a "sinecure." John Rae, in the standard life of Smith, says, "Smith attended to those duties with uncommon diligence.") Galbraith does not distinguish between individual response to social institutions and the proper design of such institutions.

Galbraith overlooks the fact that self-interest must be disciplined by *competition*; in fact he explicitly identifies self-interest with the invisible hand which guides self-seeking individuals to serve the public good, when in fact it is competition (and a society based upon contract) that brings about this happy state. Self-interest without the checks of law and competition would lead often to fraud or monopolistic exploitation. To discuss Smith's theory without mention of competition is to discuss Napoleon without mention of war.

Chapters on Marx and Lenin and Keynes, and the shorter accounts of Veblen, Spencer, and others, are, by comparison with the treatments of Smith, Ricardo, and Malthus, indulgent in tone and heavily biographical in content. The change is for the better: there are a good number of amusing incidents, and the burden of doctrinal content is light enough to be borne by even a distracted and thirsty television audience.

One idea of great power in the modern world receives trifling explicit attention from Galbraith, and that idea is equality. The goal of equality was the possession of only a tiny fringe of radicals in 1800, and it is a dominant element of the ideologies of the Western world today. That is the most basic change in professional and popular thinking since Smith's time. Its prophet was not an economist—in general economists lagged in recognizing and embracing this goal—but instead a man who is never mentioned by Galbraith, Alexis de Tocqueville. Recall the powerful passage:

> The hatred that men bear to privilege increases in proportion as privileges become fewer and less considerable, so that democratic passions would seem to burn most fiercely just when they have least fuel. I have already given the reason for this phenomenon. When all conditions are unequal, no inequality is so great as to offend the eye, whereas the slightest dissimilarity is odious in the midst of general uniformity; the more complete this uniformity is, the more insupportable the sight of such a difference becomes. Hence it is natural that the love of equality should constantly increase together with equality itself, and that it should grow by what it feeds on.
>
> This never-dying, ever-kindling hatred which sets a democratic people against the smallest privileges is peculiarly favorable to the gradual concentration of all political rights in the hands of the representative of the state alone. The sovereign, being necessarily and incontestably above all the citizens, does not excite their envy, and each of them thinks that he strips his equals of the prerogative that he concedes to the crown.

Tocqueville was profoundly right: the most radical change in economic policy since his time has been the ever-widening resort to political power in order to redistribute incomes in modern Western societies. This has not been a simple case of the poor taxing the rich, although there has been that too. Rather, every well-placed and well-organized interest group in the nation— union members, farmers, trucking companies, airlines, petroleum producers, teachers, television stations, welfare recipients, veterans, tenants, home-owners, you name it—has succeeded in getting some laws that work primarily for its own particular interests. The military-industrial complex (I doubt that it can usefully be viewed as one entity) is the only such group to receive Galbraith's attention: he really is not observant.

In fact Galbraith's view of economic life is remarkably personal. Consider again the opening chapter on the classical economists and the industrial revolution. What are the telling episodes in the rise of modern industrial capitalism? They are five: (1) the production of pins, an excellent example of the division of labor, amusingly illustrated in the television episode, (2) the clearances of the Scottish highlands, (3) child labor, (4) the Irish famine, (5) the new industrial rich (which receives a whole chapter).

The first episode aside, the selection is incongruous in the extreme. In a period unprecedented in the history of mankind for the continuous, accelerating growth of output over a wide range of commodities, with the consequential rise in the standards of living (and health) of the entire population to new levels, in such a period Galbraith chooses to look primarily at phenomena wholly or largely outside the developing market system. Child labor, famine, and inequalities of income extravagantly greater than the industrial revolution produced are as old as human history. The former two were eliminated and the third substantially reduced by the end of the nineteenth century, and these changes were brought about by economic progress. Adam Smith concludes his opening chapter of *The Wealth of Nations* with a magnificent comparison:

> Compared, indeed, with the more extravagant luxury of the great, his accommodation [that of the very meanest person in a civilized country] must no doubt appear extremely simple and easy; and yet it may be true, perhaps, that the accommodation of a European prince does not always so much exceed that of an industrious and frugal peasant, as the accommodation of the latter exceeds that of many an African king, the absolute master of the lives and liberties of ten thousand naked savages.

Or consider the lengthy assault on colonialism (which includes, we are told, our Vietnam venture). Whether one denounces or defends colonialism, from the viewpoint of the development of modern economies it was a wholly minor affair. A truly fundamental development was the tide of emigration from Western Europe to the unsettled portions of the world (which Galbraith excludes from colonialism) that in a single century changed the economic face of the globe. Colonialism was negligible in its demands on resources—in 1835 India was ruled by 40,000 Englishmen—and all the world's colonial trade in Galbraith's sense was in 1910, I venture, less than that between Europe and the United States alone. The settlement of the English-speaking lands led to a major increase, not merely in world output, but also in the standard of living of both the migrants and those who stayed at home.

I would also argue, but with a diffidence inversely proportional to my modest knowledge of the subject, that traditional colonialism—the occupation of populated countries—was not a unilateral spoliation of one people by another. It would be impossible, and not merely unprofitable, for a colonial power to make extensive investments in a colony without increasing the incomes also of the native population: no one could appropriate all the rents of economic growth.

It must be irritating to Galbraith to be praised so much more enthusiastically for his writing than for the substance of his work, and although I do not wish to introduce any possible irritation into this review, I feel compelled to remark on an interesting feature of his style, which if not new at least did not seem so prominent in earlier books. This novel feature is the distribution throughout *The Age of Uncertainty* of a variety of propositions on the ways of the world. These aphoristic observations would form an excellent beginning to a compilation of the sayings of Chairman Galbraith. Consider these examples:

> 1. "A firm rule operated against [Turgot, a French economist of Smith's time]. People will always risk their complete destruction rather than surrender any material part of their advantage."
>
> 2. "It may be laid down as a broad and general rule that no one spends his life affirming the superiority of other people if he has any alternative."
>
> 3. "Three conditions are absolutely essential [for a successful revolution]. There must be determined leaders. . . . The leaders must have disciplined followers. . . . And above all, the other side must be weak. All successful revolutions are the kicking in of a rotten door."
>
> 4. ". . . the one certain thing about the efforts of some people to rule other people at a distance is that it will fail."
>
> 5. "Economists are economical, among other things, of ideas. It is still so. They make those they acquire as graduate students do for a lifetime."
>
> 6. "Personal interest always wears the disguise of public purpose, and no one is more easily persuaded of the validity or righteousness of a public cause than the person who stands personally to gain therefrom."

How well these artificial pearls display their creator—nice mixtures of what one of Galbraith's favorites, Spiro Agnew, might describe as perspicacity, paradox, and perversity. I do him an injustice, a complimentary injustice to be sure, in being annoyed by this unlearned and opinionated project: Galbraith surely means only to entertain, and many others do it less well.

STIGLER'S LAW OF DEMAND
AND SUPPLY ELASTICITIES[*]

· 22 ·

I propose the following theorem, which (I hope) is sufficiently significant in its implications and rigorous in its demonstration to deserve the title of "law":

> All demand curves are inelastic,
> and all supply curves are inelastic, too.

I have ventured to attach my name to this law because this will be its first completely explicit formulation and demonstration, although it has long lurked in the background of economic discussion. Both empirical and a priori demonstrations will be given.

EMPIRICAL DEMONSTRATION

In principle, it is impossible to establish empirically that all of the demand and supply curves that have ever existed or will someday exist are inelastic. Yet it is

Reprinted by permission of the publishers from *The Intellectual and the Marketplace*, enlarged edition, by George J. Stigler (Cambridge, Mass.: Harvard University Press). Copyright 1963 by George J. Stigler; Copyright 1984 by the President and Fellows of Harvard College.

[*] I long delayed publication of this piece for fear that too many readers would find it persuasive. Time and events have probably not affected its truth.

possible to establish a strong presumption that this is true by showing that, in a wide variety of investigations, elastic functions are conspicuous by their absence.

I begin with academic investigations, and necessarily my list of examples is insultingly incomplete, because editors' demands for brevity are also inelastic. First I shall report a few statistical findings; these deserve little weight because (aside from many technical weaknesses) almost always only short-run functions are derived.

Henry Schultz: "With the possible exception of buckwheat (first and third periods), and of rye for the third period, the demand for all the ten commodities [sugar, corn, cotton, hay, wheat, potatoes, oats, barley, rye, and buckwheat] is inelastic (i.e., $|\eta| < 1$)." [*Theory and Measurement of Demand* (Chicago: University of Chicago Press, 1938), p. 556.]

David A. Wells: "A further analysis of the experiences of the New York and Brooklyn Bridge since its construction also reveals some curious tendencies of the American people in respect to consumption and expenditures . . . In the third year, with a reduction of foot-fares to one-fifth of a cent [from one cent], the number of foot-passengers declined 440,395, or to an aggregate of 3,239,337; while the number of car-passengers (with a reduction of fare from 5 to 2½ cents) increased 10,130,957, or to 21,843,250." [*Recent Economic Changes* (New York: Appleton, 1889), pp. 386–87.]

E. H. Schoenberg: The coefficient of elasticity [of demand for cigarettes] at the means is −0.68." ["The Demand Curve for Cigarettes," *Journal of Business* 6 (January 1933): 35.]

E. J. Broster: "The elasticities of demand for tea are 0.554 with respect to price and 0.284 with respect to income." ["Elasticities of Demand for Tea and Price-Fixing Policy," *Review of Economic Studies* 6 (June 1939): 169.]

R. M. Walsh: "The elasticity of supply for cotton acreage varied from 0.1 to 0.3 at different levels of price." ["Response to Price in Production of Cotton and Cottonseed," *Journal of Farm Economics* 26 (May 1944): 372.]

Much weightier is the testimony of economists, who eschew mechanical calculation and carefully combine all the relevant information:

Alvin H. Hansen: "But most industries are confronted, at best, with a unit elasticity of demand." [*Fiscal Policy and Business Cycles* (New York: Norton, 1941), p. 326.]

A. Walters: "Demand on the copper market has always been fairly inelastic." ["The International Copper Cartel," *Southern Economic Journal* 11 (October 1944): 143.]

J. H. Jones: "If, however, we refer to the general demand [for coal] of the world as a whole, . . . it is undoubtedly true to say that it is inelastic." ["The

Present Position of the British Coal Trade," *Journal of the Royal Statistical Society* 93, pt. 1 (1930): 10.]

A. *Abrahamson:* "High whiskey prices may have some slight effect in discouraging consumption." [In W. Hamilton, ed., *Price and Price Policies* (New York: McGraw-Hill, 1938), p. 427.]

L. H. *Seltzer:* "The consumers' demand for credit is relatively insensitive to ordinary changes in interest rates." ["Is a Rise in Interest Rates Desirable or Inevitable?" *American Economic Review* 35 (December 1945): 837.]

G. J. *Stigler:* "One is struck by the narrow range of fluctuation of consumption, which certainly argues for an unusually inelastic demand [for wheat in the United Kingdom, 1890–1904]." ["Notes on the History of the Giffen Paradox," *Journal of Political Economy* 55 (April 1947): 154–55.]

J. K. *Eastman:* "The demand for tin is highly inelastic over most of the price range experienced in recent years." ["Rationalisation in the Tin Industry," *Review of Economic Studies* 4 (October 1936): 13.]

R. B. *Shuman:* "But within the usual experience range, there is no evidence that a shift of a few cents a gallon [of gasoline] has any material effect on sales." [*The Petroleum Industry* (Norman: University of Oklahoma Press, 1940), p. 144.]

W. H. *Nicholls:* "Agriculture is particularly vulnerable in [an unstable] economy, because (1) it maintains production even in the face of ruinously low prices." ["A Price Policy for Agriculture, Consistent with Economic Progress, that Will Promote Adequate and More Stable Income from Farming," *Journal of Farm Economics* 27 (November 1945): 744.]

This list of demonstrations by academic students could be continued indefinitely, but now I must turn briefly to the business community:

Steel: "The demand for steel is very inelastic." [U.S. Steel Corporation, *Temporary National Economic Committee Papers*, vol. 1, p. 169.]

Cement: "I never found that the company who made those reductions in price obtained any benefit from it whatsoever. If they reduced the price they might have gotten one particular contract,...but, in the end, they got no more business." [President Brobston of Hercules Cement, *333 U.S. Supreme Court Briefs and Records 683–740*, vol. 2 (1947), pp. 7697–698.]

Automobiles: "I do not consider that the present price level of automobiles will have any material bearing on the industry over the twelve months' period. Without question, the prices as announced at the shows were rather a shock to the automobile purchasing public... The objection to price will level itself off within a very short time." [A sales manager, *Automotive Industries*, December 4, 1937, p. 811.]

Indigo: "An increase in price by all suppliers would undoubtedly disabuse the buyers' minds of the impression now general that an indigo price reduction

is imminent and to this extent would greatly strengthen present demand."
[Mitsui Trading Company, U.S. Congress Senate Committee on Patents,
Hearings on S. 2303, 77th Cong., 2d sess., p. 2380.]

For the most comprehensive and authoritative information, however, one
must turn to the experience of men who have controlled large sectors of the
economy. Before the war was over, the Office of Price Administration had
characterized almost all salable things in the American economy, except
economists' services, in terms such as these:

"The increased use of southern pine lumber stemming from the defense
program and the accompanying expanded economic activity has caused demand to exceed supply [*sic*]. As a consequence, inflationary pressure has
caused prices to rise greatly in excess of previously existing industry levels."
[Price Schedule no. 19, November 24, 1941, p. 1.]

"As a result of the much increased demand and the temptation to specula-
tion which this has provided, prices of cattle tail hair and winter hog hair have
shown sharp increases which are not warranted by any increase in cost of
production and which can have little effect in augmenting the supply." [Price
Schedule no. 24, August 27, 1941, p. 1.]

Of course, some of these passages could be interpreted as meaning that the
demand curve had merely shifted far to the right, and was not necessarily
inelastic. But a variety of ancillary considerations oppose this interpretation.
The uses of subsidies and differential prices usually rested on inelasticity of
supply. The use of allocations, rationing, and priorities rested on inelasticities
of demand. Every price rise was "unwarranted"; but the warrant of a price rise is
to encourage supply and/or ration demand; hence, the OPA economists meant
that higher prices would fail to perform these functions. Moreover, when
pressed they will concede that price control was successful because it kept
down index numbers of prices—that is, it had no appreciable effects on output.

And finally, let us look to Great Britain where, economic events being
centrally planned, all supply and demand functions were known. Here the
evidence of ubiquitous inelasticity is silently impressive: in the economic plan
(as reported in the *Economic Survey* for 1948), no reference is made to relative
prices. For example, "In the United States we are making great efforts to
increase our exports, but any really large expansion would require a radical
change in the importing habits of that country" (p. 10). That is, lower prices
would not increase American dollar purchases. Again, in dealing with excess
peak demand for electricity, several devices are alluded to as possible solutions
(pp. 24–26), but no reference is made to raising rates, which therefore must be
ineffective. All in all, this—one may say deliberate and systematic—disregard
of prices is powerful evidence for the law.

I therefore consider the empirical evidence overwhelming. Of course elastic demands have sometimes been alleged, usually without any real evidence. But in at least two cases, evidence of a sort has been proffered:

Cranberry sauce: "Assuming income per head at the preceding year's level, the market can be expected to absorb every year a 17.5 percent increase in the quantity of cranberry sauce marketed, without a decline in price. Every percent increase in quantity *in excess of 17.5 percent* over the previous year would *depress* the price by 0.49 percent below the previous year's level." [C. D. Hyson and F. H. Sanderson, "Monopolistic Discrimination in the Cranberry Industry," *Quarterly Journal of Economics* 59 (1944–45): 348, 350.]

Domestic servants: "The price elasticity...has an even greater absolute value: −2.3. [G. J. Stigler, *Domestic Servants in the United States, 1900–40* (New York: National Bureau of Economic Research, 1947), pp. 30, 32.]

These adverse examples are not necessarily proof of the ineptitude of the investigators: they can be explained very simply as the result of Sampling Fluctuations.

A Priori Demonstration

I shall give two proofs that all demand curves are inelastic. Each covers most of the economy; the two together surely cover all industries once and most industries twice. But I do not wish to purchase elegance with uncertainty. Thereafter the elasticity of supply will be examined.

First, Alfred Marshall's proof: "The third condition [for inelastic demand] is that only a small part of the expenses of production of the commodity should consist of the price of this factor. Since the plasterer's wages are but a small part of the total expenses of building a house, a rise of even 50 percent in them would add but a very small percentage to the expenses of production of a house and would check demand but little." [Alfred Marshall, *Principles of Economics* (New York: Macmillan, 1920), p. 385.]

Now, almost every product is a small part of the expense of some other product: steel accounts for only a tenth of the cost of an automobile; transportation charges are a small part of delivered prices; the cost of a home is a small part of the cost of living. Thus, most demand curves are inelastic.[1] It may be noted that Marshall assumed for purposes of this argument that no substitution is possible among the various inputs. Who can question his right to do this?

Second, the expectation proof. When prices rise, no one will buy less of commodities, because prices are expected to rise further; and when prices fall, no one buys more, because prices are expected to fall further. The anticipation of purchases when prices rise, and the postponement of purchases when prices fall, serve to confirm and continue the expectations. (Some economists go on to say that the way to decrease quantity demanded—and increase quantity supplied—is to lower prices, but this may be making too much of a good thing.)

No one can question the general validity of this proof, but in this—its usual—form it lacks refinement and rigor. The first price change does not set off the anticipations; clearly it was also anticipated. And a seller anticipates in the case of price reductions, for example, that the first reduction would simply confirm buyers' anticipations and not help sales, so he may make the reduction in two steps to eliminate anticipation of further decreases. But, of course, the buyers can easily anticipate this. So the seller cuts the price exactly the amount they anticipated, just to get it over with; but this they did not anticipate, so business deteriorates. The seller never anticipated this result, so in panic he makes an unanticipated further price change, and at this, business naturally comes to a halt. After certain further, obvious steps, which I shall omit for brevity's sake, price eventually settles down. Sales resume—at the old rate, it is to be anticipated.

The careful reader will have noticed that supply has received little attention; this gap will now be filled. The fact is, that inelastic demands imply inelastic supplies; hence, it is sufficient to prove the existence of the former. Some economists are so inconsistent as to say that demands are inelastic but that marginal cost curves are horizontal. The following proof will show that this is ill-advised.

First, an intuitive proof. If the demand for input A is inelastic, a 10 percent decrease in its price leads to less than a 10 percent increase in the quantity taken; and similarly for other inputs. If all input prices decrease 10 percent, an even smaller increase in the quantity of A that is taken will occur, for substitution incentives disappear; and similarly for other inputs. But a fall of 10 percent in the price of each input is equivalent to a rise of (about) 11 percent in the price of product. Therefore an 11 percent rise in the price of the product leads to less than a 10 percent increase of each input, and therefore to less than a 10 percent increase of output, so supply is inelastic. This proof is deficient in that it glosses over the possibility of extreme complementarity of inputs; the deficiency will be removed mathematically.

Let us define some symbols:

$$x = \text{output},$$
$$a, b = \text{inputs},$$
$$p, p_a, p_b = \text{respective prices},$$
$$x = \phi(a, b) = \text{production function}.$$

The conditions for maximum profit are,

$$p\phi_a = p_a; \qquad p\phi_b = p_b.$$

Differentiate these equations partially with respect to p_a, and then with respect to p_b, and define the symbols:

$$\Delta = \begin{vmatrix} \phi_{aa} & \phi_{ab} \\ \phi_{ab} & \phi_{bb} \end{vmatrix},$$

$$\eta_a = \frac{\partial a p_a}{\partial p_a a},$$

$$\eta_b = \frac{\partial b p_b}{\partial p_b b},$$

$$\eta_{ab} = \frac{\partial b p_a}{\partial p_a b}.$$

Then

$$\eta_a = p_a \phi_{bb}/ap\Delta,$$
$$\eta_b = p_b \phi_{aa}/bp\Delta,$$
$$\eta_{ab} = -p_a \phi_{ab}/bp\Delta.$$

Now differentiate the maximum profit equations with respect to p, to obtain,

$$\frac{\partial a}{\partial p} = (p_b \phi_{ab} - p_a \phi_{bb})/p^2 \Delta,$$

$$\frac{\partial b}{\partial p} = (p_a \phi_{ab} - p_b \phi_{aa})/p^2 \Delta.$$

Finally, the elasticity of supply is

$$\eta_s = \frac{\partial x}{\partial p} \frac{p}{x} = \frac{p}{x} \left(\phi_a \frac{\partial a}{\partial p} + \phi_b \frac{\partial b}{\partial p} \right).$$

If one substitutes around a bit, and defines k_a as ap_a/xp, and similarly for k_b, one will reach this equation:

$$\eta_s = k_a |\eta_a| + k_b |\eta_b| - 2k_b \eta_{ab}.$$

Recall that we have shown that $|\eta_a| < 1$, $|\eta_b| < 1$. The implications are unambiguous. First, if $\eta_{ab} > 0$ (inputs are substitutes), then

$$\eta_s < 1, \text{ for } k_a|\eta_a| + k_b|\eta_b| < 1.$$

Second, if perchance $\eta_{ab} < 0$, we notice that if $\Delta > 0$, as stability of equilibrium recommends, then

$$k_a\eta_a\eta_b > k_b\eta_{ab}^2.$$

At worst, therefore,

$$\eta_s < (\sqrt{k_a|\eta_a|} + \sqrt{k_b|\eta_b|})^2$$

But the expression on the right can be assumed, with no loss of specificity, to be less than unity.

   Q.E.D.

IMPLICATIONS

The terminological implication is that demands and supplies with elasticities of zero should be called inelastic; those with elasticities numerically less than unity, elastic. Elasticity has the same range of variation as the coefficient of correlation, correctly calculated.

   The discussion of the economic implications must be reserved for another occasion, when it will be shown that there is no price system.

NOTES

   1. This proof has an august corollary. Since most or all specific costs of production are relatively small, and entrepreneurs do not bother with small costs, therefore they do not bother with costs at all. Hence they do not maximize profits. This corollary has implications for economic theory.

A Sketch of
the History of
Truth in Teaching

· 23 ·

The future is obscure, even to men of strong vision, and one would perhaps be wiser not to shoot arrows into it. For the arrows will surely hit targets that were never intended. Witness the arrow of consumerism.

It started simply enough: various people—and especially a young man named Nader—found automobiles less safe than they wished, and quite possibly than you would have wished. They demanded and in a measure obtained, if not safer cars, at least cars that were ostensibly safer. A considerable and expensive paraphernalia of devices became obligatory in new cars. These zealous patrons of the public furthermore insisted that defective products be corrected, and that damage arising in spite of the most conscientious efforts of the manufacturer should be his financial responsibility. Similar arrows were soon launched at a score of nonvehicular industries.

This quiver of truth and safety-minded arrows was thrown for a time at perfectly appropriate targets—businessmen accustomed to public abuse, who were naturally able to charge their customers for any amount of safety, frequent and successful lawsuits, and obloquy. But the arrows of reform pass through—if they hit at all—the targets at which they are aimed, and in 1973 they hit a professor. Evil day!

In that year a young man named Dascomb Henderson, a graduate of

From the *Journal of Political Economy* 81, no. 2 (March 1973). Copyright 1973 by the University of Chicago.

Harvard Business School (1969) and recently discharged as assistant treasurer of a respectable-sized corporation, sued his alma mater for imparting instruction since demonstrated to be false. This instruction—we may omit here its explicit and complex algebraic formulation—concerned the proper investment of working capital. One of Henderson's teachers at the Harvard school, a Professor Plessek, had thoroughly sold his students upon a surefire method of predicting short-term interest rate movements, based upon a predictive equation incorporating recent movements of the difference between high- and low-quality bond prices, the stock of money (Plessek had a Chicago Ph.D.), the number of "everything is under control" speeches given by governors of the Federal Reserve Board in the previous quarter, and the full-employment deficit. It was established in the trial that the equation had worked tolerably well for the period 1960–1968 (and Henderson was exposed to this evidence in Plessek's course in the spring of 1969), but the data for 1969 and 1970, once analyzed, made it abundantly clear that the equation was capable of grotesquely erroneous predictions. Assistant Treasurer Henderson, unaware of these later results, played the long-term bond market with his corporation's cash, and in the process the cash lost its surplus character. He was promptly discharged, learned of the decline of the Plessek model, and sued.

This was a new area of litigation, and Henderson's attorney deliberately pursued several lines of attack, in the hope that at least one would find favor with the court:

1. Professor Plessek had not submitted his theory to sufficient empirical tests; had he tried it for the decade of the 1950s, he would have had less confidence in it.

2. Professor Plessek did not display proper scientific caution. Henderson's class notes recorded the sentence: "I'll stake my reputation as an econometrician that this model will not [engage in intercourse with] a portfolio manager." This was corroborated with a different verb by a classmate's notes.

3. Professor Plessek should have notified his former students once the disastrous performance of his theory in 1969 and 1970 became known.

4. Harvard University was grossly negligent in retaining (and hence certifying the professional competence of) an assistant professor whose work had received humiliating professional criticism (*Journal of Business* [April 1972]). Instead he had been promoted to associate professor in 1972.

The damages asked were $500,000 for impairment of earning power and $200,000 for humiliation.

Harvard and Professor Plessek asked for dismissal of the suit, as frivolous and unfounded. Universities and teachers could not be held responsible for honest errors, or all instruction would be brought to a stop. Universities and professors could not be asked to disseminate new knowledge to previous students—this would be intolerably costly. In the lower court these defenses prevailed, and Judge MacIntosh (Harvard, LL.B. 1938) asserted that university instruction and publication were preserved from such attacks by the First Amendment, the principle of academic freedom, an absence of precedent for such a complaint, and the established unreliability of academic lectures. On appeal, however, Judge Howlson (Yale, LL.B. 1940) remanded the case for trial on the merits, and in the course of reversing Judge MacIntosh's decision, remarked: "It seems paradoxical beyond endurance to rule that a manufacturer of shampoos may not endanger a student's scalp but a premier educational institution is free to stuff his skull with nonsense."

As the reader will know, Harvard and Professor Plessek won the case on the merits, but by a thin and foreboding margin. Only the facts that (1) the Plessek question, as of 1969, looked about as good as most such equations, and (2) the plaintiff could not reasonably be expected to be informed of the failure of the equation as soon as two years after it was discovered—the lag in publication alone is this long—excused the errant professor. As for Harvard, it would have shared responsibility for the undisputed damage to the plaintiff if Plessek had been of slightly lower quality. So held the court of last resort, in a decision that professors read as carefully as a hostile book review.

The university world received the decision with what an elderly Englishman would call concern, and I would call pandemonium. Professional schools—medicine as well as business—were quick to realize its implications. Within a breathless 3 weeks, a professor in Cornell's medical school had sent an explicit retraction of his treatment of Parkinson's disease to the last 10 years' graduates of the school. This proved to be only the first of a torrent of such actions, but well before that torrent had climaxed, at least 95 suits against universities and teachers had been filed. Along with the "callbacks," as the retractions were called in honor of their automobile antecedents, the learned journals were flooded with statements of "errata" and confessions of error. A fair number of academic reputations fell suddenly and drastically.

The subsequent, explosively rapid expansion of litigation directed to error in teaching is not for this nonlegal writer to report. Many years and cases were required before a reasonably predictable set of rights and responsibilities could be established, and a man may find much to anger himself in these cases, whatever his position. That the lazy or stupid student was entitled to an exhaustive explanation for his failure in a course (*Anderson v. Regents*, 191 Cal. 426) was an intolerably expensive aberration—especially when the teacher was required to present a tape recording of the explanation. That a professor could not be held responsible for error in a field where truth and error frequently exchanged identities (*Neal v. Department of Sociology*, 419 Mich. 3), on the other hand, inevitably raised a challenge to the field to justify its existence. Rather than pursue either the main line of decisions or the aberrations, it seems preferable to look at the eventual effects of truth-in-teaching upon the universities. A conscientious observer must be cautious in his interpretation of the effect—even though the present essay is clearly exempt from challenge (*President Bowen v. Assistant Professor Holland*, 329 N.J. 1121, a tenure case)—so the following remarks are best viewed as plausible hypotheses.

In general, the new responsibility rested heavily upon those most able to bear it: those fields in which classification of given material as true or excusably false versus inexcusably false was easiest to establish with near unanimity. Theological schools were virtually exempted, and, oddly enough, also computer science. Mathematics was exempted because one could always look up the answer, and political science because one couldn't. The branch of economics dealing with how to enrich a new nation ("economic development" was the title) was actually forbidden by the courts, on the ground that no university could pay for the damage its teachers did.

In those subjects where truth-in-teaching bore most heavily—those where incorrect knowledge was costly and demonstrable, as medicine, chemistry, and tax law—the classroom became a very different place. Students were *forbidden* by most universities to take notes, which were supplied by the teacher, and the sneaky device of a tape recorder with hidden microphone was combatted vigorously, if not always successfully. Harvard's defense proved to have content: teachers were unwilling to introduce new ideas, but it can be argued that the net balance was favorable: much ancient nonsense also vanished, and courses often were completed in 2 weeks.

The learned journals underwent a remarkable transformation. Let me quote the introductory paragraph of an article on the nature of short-run price fluctuations in commodity prices (*Review of Economics and Statistics* [August 1978]):

> The present essay presents a theory, with corroborating though inadequate evidence, that there is a set of nonrandom short-run movements in the price of "wheat." (The actual commodity analyzed is secret but will be revealed to professors on written waiver of responsibility.) The present essay is concerned only with methodology. Only the crudest beginning has been made, and it would be irresponsibly rash to venture money on the hypothesis. Also, the hypothesis is virtually identical with Reslet's (1967); I contribute chiefly a more powerful statistical technique (due to S. Stigler 1973), which has its own limitations. The regressions have been calculated three times, on different computers, with similar results.[1] The author will welcome, but not be surprised at, valid criticisms of the paper.

The superscript ¹ referred to a footnote inserted by the editor of the *Review*: "The Board of Overseers of Harvard University expresses concern at the measure of nonrandomness in the residuals, which, if the author were a Harvard professor, would require a full departmental review of the manuscript." No wonder one scholar complained that there was more warning against reading his article than against smoking marijuana cigarettes!

The longer-term effects of truth-in-teaching are another story, which I shall not seek even to summarize here. The historic step was the creation in 1981 of the Federal Bureau of Academic Reading, Writing, and Research (ARWR). This body soon established licenses for participation in scholarly activities, and the license became a prima facie defense against the charge of incompetence. No university which employed an unlicensed teacher could receive federal grants, which by 1985 averaged 99.7 percent of university revenue. A fortunate by-product of this reform was the exclusion of communists, classical liberals, foreigners, and men under 36 from the licensed fields of scholarship, and of statisticians from law schools. But, to repeat, this is another story.

INDEX

Competition (*continued*)
government, 119–20; political,
120–26; spatial, 121–23; political
maximization, 126–28; and public
schools, 129–31; price cutting, 156,
158; nonprice, 169; classical theory,
266–69; freedom of trade, 266–67,
272; knowledge, 266, 270, 277, 278;
equilibrium, 267, 272–80 *passim*;
industrial, 268–69, 281–82; mathematical school, 269–74; divisibility of
commodity, 272, 273–74, 278, 279;
indefinite numbers, 272–73; and
static economy, 276; mobility of resources, 276–78, 279; collusion, 278,
279–80; homogeneity, 279; market,
281; and evolving economy, 282–83;
vitality of concept, 283–84; and Fabian socialism, 290–91, 294–95; ethical support, 313–24; marginal productivity, 315–18; ethical criticism,
324–26; attitudes of lower classes,
326–28; attitudes of intellectuals,
328–30. *See also* Concentration; Information, economics of; Market
Concentration: measurement, 168, 172,
177n.13, 186–87; evidence, 169–74;
antitrust laws, 186–92; data, 196,
198–218; and occupational licensing,
255–56; and income redistribution,
343. *See also* Competition
Conspiracy, *see* Collusion
Consumerism, 368–72
Costs: labor, 4–7; functions of firm,
15–18; and market share, 30; search,
50–51; free rider, 68; administrative,
248; legislation, 251–55; movement
of resources, 277, 279; model
changes, 349–51
Cournot, A., 270–71

Dealer market, 51–52. *See also* Informa-
tion, economics of
Decision process, political, 251–53
Democracy, and socialism, 344–46

Diminishing returns, 49
Dishonesty, 320–22, 323
Dispersion, price, 47–55, 155. *See also*
Information, economics of
Distribution, income, 10–11, 86,
90–92, 96, 296–98, 301n.36, 310–12,
343–44, 357
Divisibility of commodity, 272, 273–74.
See also Competition
Division of labor, 13–24; history, 13–15;
functions of firm, 15–18; vertical
integration, 18–21; implications,
21–23
Dominant firm, 179–83

Economics of information, *see* Informa-
tion, economics of
Economies of scale, 25–45; survivor
principle, 26–28; survivorship measures, 28–34; interindustry analyses,
34–39; intraindustry analysis, 39–42;
and market price, 51–52
Edgeworth, F., 271–73, 311, 318
Efficiency, 27, 307–10
Empirical: studies, 111–14; science,
138–39. *See also* Science, economic
Employment, and minimum wage, 7
Environmental determinism, 94,
137–39
Equality, *see* Income: distribution
Equilibrium, 267, 272–80 *passim. See
also* Competition
Ethics, 303–36; and policy advocacy,
303–13; and efficiency, 307–10; and
mistakes, 308–10; and equity,
310–13; competition, 313–33; marginal productivity, 315–18; economists', 318–322; dishonesty, 320–22,
323; self-interest, 320–21, 323–24;
lower classes, 326–28; intellectuals,
328–30; ideology, 330–32; morals,
332–33. *See also* Policy, economic
Extent of market, 13–24. *See also*
Market
External economies, 14, 146, 275, 283